LA' LAWYERS

The Language of the Law

By
LAZAR EMANUEL
J.D., Harvard Law School

Published by

emanuel®

Latin For Lawyers, 1st Edition (1999)
Emanuel Publishing Corp. • 1328 Boston Post Road • Larchmont, NY 10538

Copyright © 1999 by

LAZAR EMANUEL

ALL RIGHTS RESERVED

No part of this publication may be reproduced or transmitted in any form or by any means, electronic or mechanical, including photocopy, recording, or any information storage and retrieval system, without permission in writing from the publisher. Printed in the United States of America.

This book is not intended as a source of advice for the solution of legal matters or problems. For advice on legal matters, the reader should consult an attorney.

ISBN 1-56542-499-9

About the Author

Lazar Emanuel is a graduate of Harvard Law School. In 1950, he became a founding partner of the New York firm now known as Cowan, Liebowitz & Latman. From 1960 through 1971, he was president of Communications Industries Corp., multiple licensee of radio and television stations in the Northeast. Since 1987, he has served as Executive Vice President and General Counsel of Emanuel Publishing Corp. He has edited many of the publications in the Professor Series of study aids and in the Siegel's series of Essay and Multiple-Choice Question & Answer books. He is publisher of the New York Professional Responsibility Report, a monthly newsletter on ethics and professionalism for lawyers.

This book is dedicated to my wife Judith without whose faith, patience, support and indulgence this book would never have been started or finished, and to my assistant Theresa who corrected my many errors and encouraged me to continue and persevere.

PREFACE

I have tried in this book to do several things.

❑ To identify those words, phrases and axioms which still find their way in their original Latin into legal study and writing.

❑ To identify all words and phrases in current English used by lawyers and derived from Latin

❑ To trace the origin of the words and phrases by identifying and defining their Latin roots.

❑ To define each entry in every sense in which it has meaning for lawyers.

❑ To list in each definition appropriate references to such documents as the U.S. Constitution, the Federal Rules of Civil Procedure, the ABA Model Rules of Professional Conduct, and other documents of concern to lawyers.

My hope is that law students and lawyers will find this a useful tool for studying the origin, development and meaning of all legal words and terms which can be traced to Latin.

In my work in this book, I have been struck especially by the many different meanings which are ascribed by lawyers to some words of Latin origin. These differences reflect linguistic nuances which are important and interesting. I have tried to express these nuances simply and clearly.

I have also been struck by the enormous debt we owe to a language which is no longer spoken but which still dominates the language of lawyers.

Lazar Emanuel
Larchmont, New York
1999

A

AB [L. motion away from a fixed point]
From, away from.

AB AETERNO [L. *ab* + *aeternus* / eternal, everlasting]
From eternity; eternally.

AB ANTE [L. *ab* + *ante* / before]
In advance of; beforehand.

ABDUCT [L. *ab* + *duco, ducere* / to lead from; to lead away]
To carry a person off by force; to kidnap; to take a child from its parents or a wife from her home by force.

AB INITIO [L. *ab* + *initium* / the beginning]
From the beginning. Used generally to indicate that a document or an event — e.g., a contract, statute, deed, marriage, etc. — was effective from and relates back to its inception or creation. The term *void ab initio* establishes that an act or document never had any valid or effective existence.
See **EX POST FACTO; IN INITIO; VOID AB INITIO**

AB INITIO MUNDI [L. *ab* + *initium* + *mundi* / world]
From the beginning of the world.

AB INVITO [L. *ab* + *invitus* / against one's will; unwilling]
Against one's will.

AB IRATO [L. *ab* + *ira* / anger; angrily]
In anger, angrily.

ABJURE [L. *ab* + *iuro, iurare* / to swear]
To renounce under oath. To disclaim or reject a claim or a right, such as citizenship, in a formal way, as in a sworn document.

AB OLIM [L. *ab* + *olim* / old, formerly, in past times]
Long ago; in past times; formerly.

ABOLISH, ABOLITION [L. *abolere* / to perish; end; to destroy]
To terminate or end the effect of. To annul or cancel.

ABOLITIO LEGIS [L. *abolitio* / abolition + *lex* / covenant, law]
The repeal or annulment of a law or statute.

ABORTUS [L. *abortio, abortus* / miscarriage, untimely birth]
An aborted fetus.

ABROGATE [L. *abrogare* / to repeal (a law); to annul, terminate]
To abolish, terminate the effect of, repeal, refuse to enforce.

ABROGATIO LEGIS [L. *abrogatio* / annulment + *lex* / covenant, law]
The repeal of a statute or law.

ABSCOND [L. *abscondere* / to hide away]
To sneak or run away; to hide or conceal oneself, especially to avoid litigation or process.

ABSENTIA [L. absence]
Absence.
See **IN ABSENTIA**

ABSOLVE [L. *ab* + *solvo, solvere* / to loosen, free from]
To free of a debt or duty or of an accusation or blame. To find or resolve that an accused is innocent or that a civil defendant is not at fault and is not liable.

ABSQUE [L. without]
Without.

ABSQUE INJURIA [L. *absque* / without + *iniuria* / injury, injustice, wrong]
Without any injury or damage recognizable by the law.
See **DAMNUM ABSQUE INJURIA**

ABSQUE PROBABILI CAUSA
Without probable cause.

ABSTAIN, ABSTENTION [L. *abstinere* / to keep away from]
To refrain from acting or participating, as in a vote or decision.

ABSTRACT [L. *abstrahere* / to pull, draw away from]
Unrelated to anything objective; incorporeal, hypothetical, theoretical. A summary or synopsis. In real property law, a record of all past and existing interests and transactions with respect to a particular property, showing own-

ership, mortgages, tax liens, etc. Also used in the sense of an abridgment, as an abstract of a judgment or record on appeal.

ABUSE   [L. *abuti* / to use up, to consume]

To put to an improper use; to reduce the value of, diminish; to waste. To criticize excessively or intemperately in speech or comment. To damage or injure mentally or physically; harm, mistreat. A judge may be guilty of *abuse of discretion* (misapplication of the law through whim or caprice). *Abuse of process* is the malicious misuse of civil or criminal procedure to achieve an improper or unlawful advantage over an adversary.

ACCELERATE   [L. *accelerare* / hasten, quicken]

To cause to go faster; speed up. To move to an earlier time. An *acceleration clause* in a contract or mortgage causes the entire obligation to become due or payable immediately, upon the default of a party to pay interest or to perform any other obligation in accordance with the terms of the document.

ACCESS   [L. *accedere* / to approach, draw near]

To have freedom, permission or license to approach or communicate with another or to enter upon and/or pass through a place. The right of a landowner to proceed without obstruction to a public street or highway.

ACCESSION   [L. *accedere* / to approach, draw near]

In law, the right to anything of value produced on or from one's property, both real and personal. In real property, for example, *accession* may result from natural development; e.g., the lumber from trees or a change in the course of a stream. In personal property, *accession* may result from the owner's labor; e.g., the production of a sculpture from a piece of stone or metal.

See **ACCRETION**

ACCESSORY   [L. *accedere* / to approach, draw near]

In criminal law, a person who participates in a crime without being present when it is committed. Participation may result from such acts as planning or advising, or from obtaining or concealing a weapon, etc. An *accessory* may be *before the fact*, *after the fact*, or *during the fact* (in these contexts, the word *fact* is equivalent to the word *crime*). In most states, an accessory before the fact is now treated in the same way as the person who commits the crime.

ACCOMMODATE   [L. *ad* / towards + *commodo, commodare* / to make fit, to serve, to suit]

To please by providing with something desired or requested. To cause to agree or accept. To serve the interest of a debtor or obligor by acknowledging or accepting responsibility for a debt or obligation in the event it is not paid or satisfied by the debtor. An *accommodation endorser* is a person who, without compensation, endorses a check, note or other instrument of payment to induce the payee to accept it from a payor who would not otherwise be acceptable as a source of payment.

ACCOMPLICE   [L. *ad* / with, toward + *complere* / to fill up]

In criminal law, a person who voluntarily joins with another in the commission of a crime. The *accomplice* may be a principal, an accessory, or anyone who aids and abets in carrying out the acts constituting the crime.

ACCORD   [L. *ad* + *cor, cordis* / the heart]

To reconcile. To reach or bring into agreement. To harmonize or be consistent with. The decision of one court is said to be in *accord* with the decision of another court or with a statement by a legal authority if it agrees with or follows the reasoning of that decision or authority. Also, a formal agreement, e.g., a treaty or compact.

ACCORD AND SATISFACTION

An agreement or settlement under which a payment or a performance of less value than originally offered or agreed upon is accepted by one party in full payment of the original debt or obligation. An *accord and satisfaction* is usually reached after the parties are first in disagreement, or when one party is unable or unwilling to meet his entire obligation.

ACCRETION   [L. *accrescere* / to grow, increase]

The gradual (as distinguished from sudden) deposit or accumulation of sand or soil on one piece of property by the action of a stream or other body of water which removes it from an adjoining piece of property. Over time, the boundaries between the two parcels will be adjusted for the change. Also, sometimes, an increase in the value of shares of stock when the increase cannot readily be allocated between principal and interest.

See **ALLUVIUM; AVULSION; DERELICTION**

ACCRUE   [L. *accrescere* / to grow, increase]

To occur or happen. To mature or grow into a recognized legal right or claim. To result from development, progress or growth over a period of time. To accumulate or increase over time, as in the growth of interest or employment benefits. An *accrual* is anything which accrues or has accrued.

ACCUSARE NEMO SE DEBIT

No one is required to accuse himself.

ACCUSE, ACCUSATION   [L. *accusare; accusatio* / to accuse, accusation]
   To charge with an offense or misconduct. A formal charge of the commission of a crime or infraction, usually by indictment, information or affidavit.

A COELO USQUE AD CENTRUM
   From the sky (heavens) all the way to the center of the earth. Used originally to establish that an owner of property owned all air and mineral rights above and below the surface. These rights are now modified by the rights of aircraft and others.

A CONSILIS   [L. *consilium* / deliberation, consultation]
   Of counsel. Used to describe a lawyer who assists in the preparation or presentation of some aspect of a trial or proceeding, but is not the chief attorney; e.g., a lawyer who helps in the preparation of a brief on appeal. Also, a senior attorney who is no longer active as a member of a firm but who still occasionally participates in some matters; a retired partner in a firm.

ACRE   [L. *ager* / land]
   Used now to describe a plot of land measuring 4,840 square yards or 43,560 square feet. The shape of the plot is immaterial.

ACT   [L. *actum* / a thing done]
   A thing done; the process of doing; a voluntary deed. A formal action taken or enunciated by a legislative body.

ACTA PUBLICA   [L. *agere* / to move forward, take action + *publicus* / belonging to the people]
   A matter of concern or interest to the public.

ACTIO   [L. *ago, agere* / to take action]
   Action, activity, performance. Also, cause of action, proceeding, lawsuit. The right of a Roman citizen to enforce a right by resort to legal process.

ACTIO CIVILIS
   An action based on civil law; i.e., as distinguished from criminal law.

ACTIO CRIMINALIS
   An action to punish an offense or crime under the criminal laws.

ACTIO DAMNI INJURIA
   An action to recover damages in tort.

ACTIO DE DOLO MANO
   An action in fraud.

ACTIO FURTI
An action brought under civil law to recover a penalty from a thief of goods.

ACTIO IN PERSONAM
A civil action to enforce rights against an individual.

See **IN PERSONAM**

ACTIO IN REM
A civil action to enforce rights over an object or a piece of property.

See **IN REM**

ACTION   [L. *actio* / action]
The initiation of a suit or proceeding to enforce a right or obligation; the suit or proceeding itself.

See **EX CONTRACTU; EX DELICTO; IN PERSONAM; IN REM; QUASI IN REM**

ACTIO PERSONALIS MORITUR CUM PERSONA
A personal action dies with the person. This ancient concept is no longer recognized in our laws.

ACTIO VENDITI
A civil action to enforce a contract of sale.

ACTORI INCUMBIT ONUS PROBANDI
The plaintiff has the burden of proof.

ACTUARY   [L. *actuarius* / anything fast or easily moved; a swift-sailing ship; a shorthand writer]
A clerk. A person who is employed in mathematical calculations, especially in the calculation of life expectancy, insurance and annuity premiums, reserves and dividends.

ACTUM   [L. act]
An act, a deed, a performance.

ACTUS REUS   [L. *actus* / act + *reus* / the defendant]
A criminal act; the "guilty act" or the "deed of crime"; the objective act which defines or constitutes a crime; e.g., the killing of another is the *actus reus* of murder or manslaughter.

See **MENS REA**

AD [L. direction towards, in the direction of]
With, towards.

AD COMMUNEM LEGEM
At common law.

AD DAMNUM [L. *ad* + *damnum* / loss, damage, injury]
The amount of damages demanded in a pleading; the amount the plaintiff or claimant asserts as his damages. The *ad damnum* clause of a complaint is the formal statement of damage.

ADDENDUM [L. *addere* / to bring to, to add or join]
Something that is added; e.g., a supplement to a brief or article; an appendix.

ADDICT, ADDICTION [L. *addico, addicere* / to surrender to, give up]
To give oneself up to an obsessive habit. To commit oneself to use of a habit-forming substance. To be incapable of withdrawing from compulsive use of a harmful substance. An *addiction* is a persistent, uncontrollable commitment to the use of drugs or other products known to be harmful.

AD DIEM [L. *ad* + *diem* / day]
On a day, on a given or designated day.

ADDITUR [L. *addere* / to bring to, to add or join]
The amount by which the trial judge increases the damages awarded by the jury, usually as a condition of the court's denial of a motion for a new trial by the plaintiff. The Supreme Court has decided that *additur* is not available in federal courts because it violates the 7th Amendment to the Constitution.

ADEMPTION [L. *adimo, adimere* / to gnaw or take away, to consume]
The extinction of a legacy by acts of the testator before his death, as by destruction, consumption, sale or gift of the property constituting the legacy.
See **EXTINGUISHMENT**

AD FIN(EM) [L. *ad* + *finio, finere* / to limit, to enclose within bounds, put an end to]
To or at the end, as at the end of a cited statute or decision.

AD FINEM LITIS [L. *ad* + *finem* + *lis* / a legal controversy, a lawsuit]
At the end of the litigation.

AD GRAVAMEN [L. *ad* + *gravare* / to burden]
To the heart of the matter; to the essence of the complaint, grievance or damage.

AD GRAVE DAMNUM
   To the great damage of.

ADHESION   [L. *adhaerere* / to cling to, attach to]
   In International Law, the agreement of one nation to be bound by the terms of part or all of a treaty or agreement; e.g., a convention on copyrights. In commercial law, an *adhesion contract* is an onerous sale contract or lease prepared by one party and offered to the other party on a "take it or leave it" basis.
   See **ONEROUS**

AD HOC   [L. *ad* + *hic, haec, hoc* / this]
   For this; for this particular purpose only. Someone or something selected or designated for a special purpose, as an *ad hoc* committee; also used to describe an act done at the spur of the moment, as an *ad hoc* solution or an *ad hoc* demonstration.

AD HOMINEM   [L. *ad* + *homo* / man, a human being]
   To the person; an attack on a person's character rather than his ideas or position.
   See **ARGUMENTUM AD HOMINEM**

AD IDEM   [L. *ad* + *idem* / the same]
   To the same end or effect. Having the same idea or understanding; being on the same wave length. (e.g., the parties were never *ad idem* — the parties never had the same understanding.)

AD INFINITUM   [L. *ad* + *infinitus* / infinite, unbounded, without end]
   Without end or limit.
   See **IN INFINITUM**

AD INSTANTIAM PARTIO
   At the instance or request of a party (to the action).

AD INTERIM   [L. *ad* + *interim* / meanwhile, in the meantime]
   In the meantime; for a limited time; temporary. *Ad interim* alimony is temporary support pending the outcome of the proceeding. An *interim copyright* is a copyright for a limited time, shorter than for a conventional copyright.

ADJUDICATE   [L. *ad* + *iudicare* / to judge]
   To render judgment; to decide an issue or matter; to determine the rights and obligations of parties to an action after a hearing or trial.

ADJURATION [L. *ad + iurare* / to swear, take an oath]

A solemn oath; an entreaty; serious advice.

AD LITEM [L. *ad + litigare* / to quarrel, dispute; resort to law and the courts]

For the lawsuit or litigation in progress; used most often in *guardian ad litem*, to refer to a person appointed by a court to represent a minor or legally incompetent person in a litigation.

See **GUARDIAN AD LITEM; IN LITEM**

ADMANUENSIS [L. *ad + manus* / hand]

A person who places his hand on the bible when taking an oath.

See **AMANUENSIS**

AD MANUM

At hand.

ADMINISTER [L. *administrare* / to take charge of, manage, direct]

To perform the duties of an administrator; to supervise, direct, manage.

ADMINISTRATOR AD COLLECTUM BONA DEFUNCTI

Literally, an administrator who is appointed by the court "to gather together the goods or belongings of the decedent."

ADMINISTRATOR AD LITEM

A provisional administrator appointed by the court to act for an estate in a litigation in which the estate has an interest.

ADMINISTRATOR AD PROSEQUENDUM

An adminstrator who is appointed by the court to conduct or prosecute a specific action or law suit; e.g., to foreclose a mortgage.

ADMINISTRATOR CUM TESTAMENTO ANNEXO

Administrator with the will annexed. The name for an adminstrator appointed by the court in those instances in which the deceased failed to appoint an executor in his will, or when the executor who was named is unable or unwilling to act.

ADMINISTRATOR DE BONIS NON

An administrator who is appointed by the court to complete the administration of an estate with respect to assets which were not administered by an executor or administrator who is no longer serving.

ADMINISTRATOR DURANTE MINORE AETATE
Literally, an administrator during the existence of a minority. An administrator who is appointed "with the will annexed" to serve during the minority of an infant who is named as executor under the will.

ADMINISTRATOR PENDENTE ABSENTIA
An administrator appointed to act during the absence of a person first entitled to act as administrator.

ADMINISTRATOR PENDENT LITE
An administrator appointed by the court to act while a suit is pending regarding the validity of a will.

ADMONISH, ADMONITION   [L. *admonere* / to remind, admonish]
To express a warning or reproof. A judge may *admonish* a witness or lawyer for unacceptable conduct during the course of a trial. He may also *admonish* a jury to follow his instructions.

AD PERPETUAM
In perpetuity; forever.

AD PROPINQUIOREM CONSANGINEUM
To the person having the closest blood relationship.

AD RESPONDENDUM   [L. *ad* + *respondere* / to answer, respond]
For the purpose of eliciting a response or answer. Used in certain documents to establish that a response is required; e.g., the writ of *habeus corpus ad respondendum*.

See **HABEUS CORPUS AD RESPONDENDUM**

AD SATISFACIENDUM   [L. *ad* + *satisfactio* / amends, reparation]
In discharge or satisfaction of a debt or obligation.

AD TESTIFICANDUM   [L. *ad* + *testificari* / to give evidence, bear witness to]
Literally "for testifying". Used to describe the process by which witnesses are compelled to testify; e.g., by a *subpoena ad testificandum*.

See **SUBPOENA AD TESTIFICANDUM**

AD USUM ET COMMODIUM
For the use and benefit (of).

AD VALOREM   [L. *ad* + *valere* / to be strong]
According to value; used in taxation to describe a tax assessed according to the value of the item or property, as in property taxes or sales taxes.

ADVERSE   [L. *advertere* / to face, turn towards, address; oppose, resist]

Acting against; opposed to. Used to express the element of opposition or hostility between persons in litigation, as in *adverse party* or *adverse witness*.

ADVERSE POSSESSION

Open and notorious possession and occupation of real property under a claim or color of right; possession in hostility to the true owner. *Adverse possession* over a period of time prescribed by statute will confer title upon the possessor. The requisite period varies from state to state.

See **PRESCRIPTION; USUCAPIO**

AD VITAM   [L. *ad* + *vita* / life]

For life.

ADVOCATE   [L. *advocare* / to summon, to call to one's help]

To argue for a particular viewpoint or cause; to plead in favor of. Also, someone who pleads the cause of another, especially before a court or tribunal; an attorney.

AEQUITAS   [L. *aequus* / equal (from *aequo, aequare* / to make equal)]

Equity; good conscience.

AEQUITAS AGIT IN PERSONAM

Equity enforces its orders upon the person, not against property.

AEQUITAS SEQUITUR LEGEM

Equity follows the law; equity must first consider the law as written.

AEQUUS ET BONUS

Justice and right.

See **EQUITY**

AETAS   [L. age]

Age, a time of life.

AETAS LEGITIMA   [L. *aetas* / age + *legitimus* / lawful, legal]

Lawful age.

AFFIANT   [L. *adfirmare* / to support, state as true; to verify; to swear]

One who swears to facts in a written statement (*affidavit*) signed by him; a deponent.

AFFIDAVIT   [L. *adfirmare*]

A sworn written statement made under oath before a person authorized to administer oaths.

AFFIRMATION   [L. *adfirmare*]

In the law, a solem statement made in lieu of an affidavit by a person who cannot in good conscience submit to an oath, attesting to the facts or circumstances stated.

AFFLATUS   [L. *adflare* / to blow or breathe on, to impart]

Knowledge or inspiration derived from the Gods; divine inspiration.

A FORTIORI   [L. *a + fortis* / strong, powerful]

Proceeding from the most persuasive reasoning; in logic, the inference that something must be true if it is encompassed within another thing that is manifestly or demonstrably true and compelling; e.g., if a man is dead, then, *a fortiori*, he cannot think or speak.

See **FORTIOR**

AGENCY DEL CREDERE

Literally, an agency built on trust. Used to describe an agency in which a seller's agent is entrusted with the custody of goods or securities and the authority to deliver them to a buyer and to receive and remit payment in exchange.

See **DEL CREDERE**

AGENT, AGENCY   [L. *ago, agere* / to set in motion, to drive, to act]

Anyone who acts or performs. Anything that produces an effect or result. A person authorized to act for another. In the law, a relationship in which a principal delegates to another person the power and authority to represent and act for him in business transactions with third parties. An *express agency* is an agency created in writing or by specific oral instructions. A *general agency* is authority from the principal to perform all matters related to a particular business, such as the authority from an insurance company to an agent to bind it to policies. A *special agency* is the authority to perform only limited duties or to conduct only a single transaction for the principal. Also, a department of the executive branch of government authorized to administer the laws and regulations dealing with a particular function of government, such as communications, trade, commerce, taxation, etc. The Civil Aeronautics Board, the Civil Service Commission, the Federal Communications Commission, the National Labor Relations Board, are all agencies of the federal government.

AGGRAVATE [L. *ad* + *gravo, gravare* / to load, burden, make weighty]

To worsen or make more serious or severe. To increase the effect of. To inflame or intensify. *Aggravating circumstances* or factors are facts which suggest a more severe or serious crime or offense than that normally described. Examples: an *aggravated assault* is a criminal assault with a deadly weapon. An *aggravated robbery* may be a robbery with a deadly weapon or one committed with the use of force.

AGNATION [L. *agnascor; agnatus* / to be born after another]

Descent or relationship through the male line only. Also, to be born after an heir already exists.

See **COGNATION**

ALEATORY CONTRACT [L. *aleator* / a gambler, a person who plays dice or takes chances]

A contract under which the performance of one or both of the parties depends upon some fortuitous event.

(See Restatement of Contracts Second § 379, Comment a.)

ALIA [L. other things]

Other things.

See **INTER ALIA**

ALIAS [L. *alius* / another]

Otherwise, also known as, at another time.

ALIAS DICTUS [L. *alias* + *dicere, dictus* / to say, tell]

Otherwise named or known as; assumed or additional name; synonymous with "a/k/a" (also known as). In a case in which a person is known by more than one name, this phrase is used before the alternate names. Also, used to indicate that another or second action is required to accomplish something which was not done the first time; e.g., an *alias* summons, an *alias* subpoena, an *alias* execution, an *alias* warrant, an *alias* writ of execution.

ALIBI [L. *alius* / another, other; at another time or place]

An explanation or excuse offered to avert blame or guilt by an accused who claims that he was not present at the time or place alleged, or that other circumstances prove his innocence.

ALIEN, ALIENATE [L. *alienare; alienus* / to change the ownership or status of; strange, foreign; unrelated]

Alien: Belonging or related to another person or thing. Owing allegiance to another country; foreign, not incorporated within; a foreign-born resident who is still a citizen of a foreign country. *Alienate*: To give, sell or transfer a property right or interest.

ALIENI JURIS (ALSO ALIA JURIS) [L. *alienus* / another + *ius, iuris* / right, law]

Under the control or authority of another; e.g., a guardian or parent; unable to act for one's self (i.e., not *sui juris*).

See **SUI JURIS**

ALIMENTA [L. food]

Food, support, maintenance.

ALIMONY [L. *alimentum, alimonia* / food, sustenance]

Originally, the support of a wife by her divorced or separated husband. Now, allowances or awards for support of one spouse by the other after divorce or separation, usually by court order.

See **PALIMONY**

ALIMONY PENDENTE LITE

Temporary alimony in a matrimonial action pending the final determination by the court of the measure of support required.

ALIO INTUITU [L. *alio* + *intueor, intueri* / to look at attentively, contemplate]

To look at from another perspective or approach.

ALIOS ACTA

The acts or deeds of others.

ALIQUOT [L. *aliquis* / someone, anything; *aliquot* / some, several]

A quantity contained an exact number of times in another measure, as cents in a dollar; a number which divides into a larger number evenly. In trusts, a fixed fractional interest.

ALIUNDE [L. *aliunde* / from another source or direction]

Extrinsic, outside of. *Evidence aliunde* is extrinsic evidence of facts outside the face of a document which proves admissions, preliminary negotiations, etc., or which explains an ambiguity in the document; e.g., an ambiguity in a will.

See **EVIDENCE ALIUNDE**

ALIUNDE RULE

The rule which states that a juror's testimony will not be accepted to impeach a verdict unless there is other evidence of jury misconduct.

ALLEGATA [L. *ad* + *lego, legare* / to appoint, delegate, deputize]

An assertion requiring proof; a statement contained in a pleading; to assert a claim or cause of action.

ALLEGATA ET PROBATA

Matters alleged and matters proved. The pleadings and the evidence.

ALLEGE, ALLEGATION [L. *ad* + *legare* / to appoint, deputize]

To suggest as true. To offer a fact for consideration and determination. To set forth in a pleading. To recite the facts and circumstances upon which relief is sought. An *allegation* in a pleading is a statement which the party submitting the pleading intends to prove through the submission of evidence.

ALLISION [L. *ad* + *laedere* / to strike, hurt, injure]

Literally, the act of striking against, a collision. The collision of two vessels, one of which may be stationary, or the crush of waves against the sand.

ALLOCATUR [L. *ad* + *locare* / to place, set apart, earmark]

Formerly used to describe the allowance at the end of a trial of costs and damages, confirmed in a writ or certificate. Also, any order of a court allowing or granting a party's request or application, as in allowing a writ of certiorari.

ALLOCUTION

The words spoken by a judge to a defendant before sentencing, usually inquiring whether the defendant wishes to say anything in mitigation of sentence. Sometimes, also, the words spoken by the defendant in reply or in mitigation.

ALLODIUM

Ownership of land in fee simple, free of feudal duties or burdens, as distinguished from a *fief* or *feofdum*, which described property that carried with it the obligation to provide services for the benefit of the sovereign-owner. Except for the obligation to pay taxes and assessments and to recognize claims of eminent domain, the ownership of land in the United States may be described as *allodial*.

ALLOGRAPH [L. *alias* / another + *graphium* / a stylus]

The signature of one's name by another, as by an agent or attorney-in-fact for a principal. An autograph cannot be an *allograph*.

ALLUVIO MARIS [L. *ad* + *lavo, lavare* / to wash + *mare* / the sea]

Alluvium deposited by the sea.

ALLUVIUM (ALLUVION) [L. *ad* + *lavere* / to wash]
> The deposit of sand, clay or other sediment along or onto a bank or shore by water, as by a river, lake or ocean.
> See **ACCRETION; AVULSION; DILUVION; DERELICTION**

ALTA PRODITIO [L. *altus* / great, high + *proditio* / betrayal, treason]
> The crime of high treason; treason against the state.

ALTER EGO [L. *alter* / one of two, the other + *ego* / me, myself, I]
> The other self, a second self; the other me. Applying the *alter ego* doctrine, a court will impose personal liability on a corporate officer, even though he purported to act in a corporate capacity, if it can be shown that the transaction was really for his benefit and that the corporation did not really have an existence separate from his own; i.e., the court will pierce the corporate veil and hold the individual liable.

AMANUENSIS [L. *ad* / with, towards + *manus* / hand]
> A person who copies a document in his own hand or who transcribes a document from dictation by someone else. Also, someone who signs a document in the name of another who may be present at the time of signature.

AMBIGUITAS LATENS [L. *ambiguitas* / ambiguity + *latere* / to be concealed]
> A latent ambiguity; an ambiguity which does not appear on instant inspection but can arise later.

AMBIGUITAS PATENS [L. *ambiguitas* + *patere* / to lie open]
> A patent ambiguity; an ambiguity which is readily evident; an obvious ambiguity.

AMBIGUITY, AMBIGUOUS [L. *ambigere* / to doubt, hesitate, be uncertain]
> Capable of being understood in more than one sense; having several possible meanings.

AMBULATORIA VOLUNTAS [L. *ambulo, ambulare* / to walk + *voluntas* / wish, inclination; last will and testament]
> A man may alter or change his will at any time until he dies.

AMBULATORY [L. *ambulare* / to walk about; to proceed]
> Capable of change or modification. A will is *ambulatory*; i.e., it is subject to change until the death of the testator. A decree or order which is subject to change or modification is an *ambulatory* decree.

AMELIORATE [L. *melior* / better; to make better, to improve]

To improve the condition of; make better. In the law of property, a lessee will not be enjoined from committing waste if the result of his actions is to improve the property; i.e, if the waste is an *ameliorating waste*.

AMENABLE [L. *ad + minor, minari* / to project, to threaten or menace]

Responsible to answer for an act. Subject to be asked to account or explain. Answerable, accountable. Willing, obedient. A party who is legally subject to appear or respond to a summons or pleading is said to be *amenable to suit*.

AMEND, AMENDMENT [L. *emendare* / to free from error, correct]

To change or modify; improve, make better. Legally, an *amendment* is a change in a document to clarify its meaning or to add essential matter, as to a pleading or a statute.

AMENITY [L. *amoenus* / pleasant, delightful, pleasing]

An improvement or asset affixed to real property which has the effect of increasing the enjoyment of the property and therefore works to increase its value. A swimming pool or tennis court is an *amenity*.

A MENSA ET THORO

"From bed and board." A decree of divorce that operated more in the way of a modern separation; i.e., it did not dissolve the marriage but it did enable the parties to live apart.

See **A VINCULO MATRIMONII; ESTOVER**

AMENTIA [L. insanity, madness]

Insanity; madness, foolishness.

See **DEMENTIA**

AMICI CONSILIA CREDENDA

The advice of a friend should be respected.

AMICUS CURIAE [L. *amicus* / friend; *curia* / in ancient Rome, the meeting place of the Roman Senate]

Literally, friend of the court; applied to anyone who is not a party to the litigation but helps the court to resolve an issue or dispute. *Amicus curiae* briefs are often submitted in important cases by strangers to the litigation to argue a particular point or rule in which they have an interest.

AMORTIZE [*ad + morior* / to die]

To pay off or extinguish a debt over time, usually in fixed installments; used most often with respect to mortgages.

ANALECTS   [L. *analecta* / the term for a slave who picked up the crumbs after a meal]

Selected miscellaneous passages from a text or decision; excerpts.

ANCILLARY   [L. *ancilla* / a female servant or slave]

Someone who helps to do or achieve a goal or objective. An act or proceeding which is supplemental, subordinate or auxiliary to anothor act or proceeding but which helps to achieve the goal of that act or proceeding.

ANCILLARY ADMINISTRATION

If a decedent leaves property in a state other than the state in which his estate is being administered, the courts of the state in which the property is located will entertain and conduct an *ancillary administration* to collect and dispose of the property. The state in which the estate is being administered is called the place of principal administration.

ANCILLARY JURISDICTION

The power of a court to hear and determine issues incidental to matters falling under its primary jurisdiction. A doctrine of federal jurisdiction which permitted a federal court to decide an issue which could not otherwise have come before it, so long as it had primary or "core" jurisdiction over a case; e.g., the court could decide a claim by a party other than the plaintiff even though it might lack diversity or amount-in-controversy jurisdiction over that claim. Application of the doctrine was generally limited to claims by parties who might otherwise be deprived of the right to litigate the issue; e.g., a party with a compulsory counterclaim. *Ancillary jurisdiction* is now embodied in 28 USCA 1367, under *Supplemental Jurisdiction*.

ANCILLARY PROCEEDING

An administrative or judicial proceeding which is subordinate, but necessary, to the outcome of a primary action or proceeding; e.g., a garnishment proceeding. In bankruptcy cases, the domestic assets of a debtor who is the subject of a foreign bankruptcy proceeding may be reached in an *ancillary proceeding* brought in a federal district court by the foreign representative of the bankrupt estate.

ANCILLARY RECEIVER

The person appointed to collect and administer in one jurisdiction the assets in that jurisdiction of a debtor who is the subject of an insolvency proceeding in another jurisdiction; e.g., the appointment of a domestic receiver in a foreign bankruptcy proceeding.

ANIMO, ANIMUS   [L. *animare* / to give life to]
   The seat of feeling; the soul; will, intent, purpose, having the mind to. Used together with other words or phrases to describe particular states of mind, usually showing intent. (See the following examples.)

ANIMUS DONANDI   [L. *animus* / will, intent + *dono, donare* / to give]
   Intent to give, to make a gift.

ANIMUS FURANDI   [L. *furor, furari* / to steal]
   Intent to steal.

ANIMUS REVERTENDI   [L. *reverto, revertere* / to return, go back]
   Intent to return.

ANIMUS REVOCANDI   [L. *revoco, revocare* / to recall]
   Intent to revoke; e.g., a will.

ANIMUS TESTANDI   L. *testor, testari* / to give evidence]
   Intent to make a will.

ANNI NUBILIS   [L. *annus* / a year + *nubo, nubere* / to cover with a veil, as a bride (*nubilis* / marriageable)]
   The age at which a female becomes marriageable.

ANNO DOMINI
   In the year of the Lord. Used to indicate a date or event in the Christian era; i.e., following the birth of Christ.

ANNUITY   [L. *annus* / a year]
   The yearly payment of a fixed obligation. A yearly installment of income, usually in the form of interest from principal. The payments made by an insurance company under an *annuity contract*.

ANNUL, ANNULMENT   [L. *ad* + *nullus* / no, not, not any]
   To make void or legally unenforecable; to vacate. An *annulment* is a determination of the nullity of a marriage on account of matters in existence at the time of the marriage ceremony; e.g., a pre-existing marriage, fraud. An annulment is different from a divorce in that a divorce terminates an existing and valid marriage, whereas an annulment is in effect a determination that no marriage ever existed.

ANNUS LUCTUS   [L. *annus*/ a year + *luctus* / mourning, bereavement]
   Literally, the year of mourning. The period of mourning following the death of a spouse.

ANTE [L. before]

Before, in front of; used as a prefix in many words to indicate an action or event which precedes another. In a text, such as a judge's opinion, it is used in the same sense as *supra* to point to a prior reference in the text or to a reference in another cited text.

ANTECEDENT [L. *ante* / before + *cedere* / to go, proceed]

A preceding event or condition; earlier in point of time.

ANTECEDENT DEBT

A prior or pre-existing claim or debt. In the law of contracts, negotiable instruments and bankruptcy, an *antecedent debt* may not furnish good consideration for a new promise or instrument.

ANTEDATE

To apply to an instrument or agreement a date which is earlier than the date of its preparation or execution. Under the UCC, *antedating* a negotiable instrument does not affect its negotiability.

ANTENUPTIAL [L. *ante* + *nuptiae* / marriage, wedding]

An act, event or item affecting a marriage which occurs before the marriage itself.

ANTENUPTIAL OR PRENUPTIAL AGREEMENT

An agreement made before marriage between the prospective husband and wife, usually dealing with division of property, support, distribution of assets, effect of death, etc. Most states require that these agreements be in writing.

ANTENUPTIAL WILL

A will executed before the marriage by a party to a prospective marriage. Unless it appears on the face of the will that it was meant to survive the wedding, it may be deemed revoked by the act of marriage.

ANTI [L. against]

A prefix meaning *against*.

ANTICIPATE, ANTICIPATORY [L. *ante* / before + *capio, capere* / to take, seize]

To do or act before the agreed time. To give advance thought or consideration to. To look forward to. To foresee. To pay off a debt or obligation before the due date. To pay an installment before it is due. In patent law, to introduce an invention before another similar invention; the effect is to make the latter ineffective as an invention. An *anticipatory repudiation* in contract law is notice of refusal by one party to perform an essential term of the contract before performance is due; the notice may be written or implied. An *anticipatory breach* is the breach resulting from or manifested by an anticipatory repudiation.

ANTINOMY [L. *anti* + *nomia* / (from the Greek word *nomos*) laws]

A conflict in law. A conflict between two statutes, decisions or legal principles; a contradiction; a conflict in authorities.

APEX [L. the highest point, the peak]

The top, the highest point, the crown.

APEX RULE

A rule of mining law, codified in 30 U.S.C.A. 26, which gives to the locator of a mine on land in the public domain, all veins, lodes and ledges reaching downward from the highest point or apex of his location, whether or not the veins can be followed downward in straight vertical lines, subject to certain limitations concerning adjoining land.

A POSTERIORI [L. *ad* + *posterus* / subsequent, next, in the future]

Reaching a conclusion from known facts. A conclusion based on observed or known circumstances; reasoning backward from effect to cause.

See **A PRIORI**

APPARENT [L. *apparere* / to become visible, to appear]

Open to view, clear, visible. Evident to the senses or the mind. The word is used in many phrases by lawyers to indicate awareness of a fact or condition through the senses, as in *apparent danger, apparent easement, apparent heir*.

APPARENT AGENT

An agent with respect to whom the principal manifests or exhibits the attributes of authority to act in his behalf. This may be done through conduct, statements, silence, ratification of specific acts, etc. An *apparent agent* has apparent authority to act for his principal.

See Restatement, Agency (2d), §7, 8.

APPEAR, APPEARANCE [L. *apparere*]

To make oneself visible; to assert one's presence. In law, used to indicate the first formal entrance or participation by a party in an action or litigation; the first act of a party in court; a submission to the court's authority or jurisdiction. A *general appearance* is a submission to jurisdiction in all respects. In a *special appearance*, a party does not submit to jurisdiction but appears only to challenge some element of the proceeding; e.g., the validity of the service of process.

APPENDANT   [L. *ad + pendere* / to suspend, to weigh]

Attached to, part of; e.g., one document may be *appendant* to another. At common law, a minor right or object attached to land held in fee was said to be *appendant* to the fee.

APPROPRIATE   [L. *ad + proprius* / one's own; exclusively for oneself]

To seize exclusive possession of. To take for one's self. To put aside for a specific purpose. To make use of for one's exclusive benefit without legal right or authority. Also, the act of government in taking private property for public use, as for a park or school.

See **EMINENT DOMAIN**

A PRIORI   [L. *ad + prior* / first, former]

From what goes before; the process of deducing facts or particulars that follow logically from general principles or accepted truths. To reason that because certain facts are demonstrably true, others must follow.

See **A POSTERIORI**

A QUO (A QUA)   [L. from which]

Used to describe a court from which a case has been removed to another court. The *court a quo* is the court from which the action was removed.

ARBITRARY   [L. *arbitror, arbitrari* / to witness, see, perceive]

Action or thought not supported by any guiding rule or law. Unrestrained by rule or order. The irresponsible use of power. The phrase *arbitrary and capricious* refers to conduct which is unreasonable and unresponsive to fact and reason. The decision of a judge is *arbitrary* if it has no reasonable foundation in the record.

ARBITRATE, ARBITRATION   [L. *arbitratus* / choice, decision, direction]

The process by which a person called an arbiter or arbitrator decides a dispute between parties outside the venue of a court. The arbiter renders his decision after hearing witnesses and listening to evidence. The process is used most widely in resolving labor disputes. An *arbitration clause* is a provision in a contract in which the parties agree to resolve all disputes through *compulsory arbitration* instead of litigation.

See **INTERMEDIARY; MEDIATE**

ARBITRIUM   [L. the acts of an arbitrator]

Literally, the function of an arbitrator; the decision of an arbitrator; a decision or award in arbitration.

ARGENTARIUS [L. *argentum* / silver]

A money lender; a banker.

ARGUENDO [L. *arguo* + *arguere* / to clarify, put in a clear light]

To state a proposition for the sake of argument or to illustrate a point, without conceding it; e.g., "let us assume, *arguendo*, that Lincoln was in favor of slavery".

ARGUMENTUM AD HOMINEM

An argument directed at the character or reputation of a person, rather than the point or question at issue.

See **AD HOMINEM**

ARGUMENTUM AD INVIDIUM

An argument based on or displaying hatred or prejudice.

ARGUMENTUM AD POPULUM

An argument which is directed to the crowd.

ARGUMENTUM AD REM

An argument which is directed to the point at issue; an argument on point.

ARMA IN ARMATOS JURA SINUNT

The law allows the use of arms against those who take up arms.

ARSON [L. *ardeo* + *ardere* / to glow, burn, be on fire]

The wilful burning of a building or structure with criminal intent. The felony of destroying a building, including a building of the perpetrator, by fire or, in some states, by use of explosives.

ASPORTATION [L. *asportare* / to carry off, take away]

The removal of a person or thing from one place to another. The crime of kidnapping at common law was described as the *asportation* of a person; larceny is the *asportation* of another's property.

ASSET [L. *ad* + *satis* / enough]

An article of property. All the property, possessions and belongings of a person or entity. Any item having value. Those items shown on a balance sheet which represent property owned or earned. A *capital asset* is an item of property retained for its utility in producing products or income, not one held for resale in the regular course of business. A *current asset* is cash or anything which can be reduced to cash quickly and easily. A *tangible asset* is an asset which can be detected with the senses. An *intangible asset*, such as the good will of a business, has no physical existence, although it may have value.

ASSEVERATE [L. *ad* + *severus* / stern, rigid, strict]
   To swear to the truth of a statement or fact with solemnity and earnestness.

ASSIZE [L. *ad* + *sedere* / to sit beside, to sit together, to assist in rendering a judgment]
   Originally, the word described a group of men who came together to decide a dispute; later, it was applied to the verdict of an English jury or to a session of judges.

ASSUMPSIT [L. *ad* + *sumere* / to take; to take up, take control of]
   He undertook to perform; took on the obligation; promised. A promise by one party to another to perform or pay for something. An action at common law to recover expectation damages arising out of a breach of an express or implied contract or to recover a debt.
   See **NON ASSUMPSIT; QUANTUM VALEBANT**

ASSUMPTION [L. *adsumere; assumere* / to take up]
   The agreement of one party to take up or become responsible for the obligation of another. The grantee of premises secured by a mortgage may *assume* the underlying mortgage obligation, i.e., agree to be personally bound to its terms. The term *assumption of risks* describes a defense in an action based on negligence in which the defendant asserts that the plaintiff knew and understood the potential or risk for injury and voluntarily exposed himself to it.

ASYLUM [L. *asylum* / a sanctuary, a protected place, a place of refuge]
   An inviolate place of refuge or sanctuary. A place where a person may remain free of the risk or threat of arrest or harassment. A state or country which offers temporary residence to a foreign citizen, free of the risk of detainment. One country may grant asylum to a refugee who seeks to escape from another country, but there is no internationally recognized *right of asylum*. The right is generally controlled by treaties between nations. The U.S. will usually grant *asylum* to any applicant who satisfies the definition of "refugee".

ATTAINDER (BILL OF) [L. *ad* + *tango, tangere* / to touch]
   The practice of nullifying or extinguishing the legal and civil rights of a person convicted of treason or of a felony; attainder was the practice in England until the 19th century. A *bill of attainder* is a statute which punishes an individual or an easily ascertainable group without a trial. *Bills of Attainder* are prohibited under Article III, Section 3 of the Constitution.

ATTEST [L. *attestor, attestari* / to bear witness to, to affirm, to swear]
   To confirm as true; to verify. To affirm or authenticate by subscribing as witness. To bear witness to the truth of.

ATTESTATION CLAUSE

> The clause at the end of a will which is subscribed by the witnesses to the execution of the will and in which the witnesses affirm that the execution satisfies the formal requirements of the jurisdiction in which the will is to be probated. Also, the language at the end of a deed or other legal instrument preceding the signature of witnesses to the execution of the instrument: e.g., "in the presence of" or "in witness whereof", etc.

ATTORN   [L. *ad* + *tornare* / to turn, make round]

> Originally, to pay homage to a new lord or master. To turn over money or goods. The creation by an occupant of land of a landlord/tenant relationship by the payment of rent to the landlord; also, the acceptance of such rent by the landlord. Also, to appoint an attorney in fact.

ATTORNEY   [L. *ad* + *tornare*]

> An agent or deputy. One who is delegated or appointed to act for another. An *attorney in fact* is anyone who is given the formal power to act for another, either generally or with respect to specified matters. Also, of course, a person authorized to practice law, a lawyer, an *attorney at law*.

AUDITA QUERELA

> A common law writ which enabled a judgment debtor to petition for relief upon new facts or circumstances, or to assert a defense which was not available at trial. In jurisidictions which follow the Federal Rules of Civil Procedure, the writ has been replaced by a motion for relief from judgment.

AULA REGIS   [L. *aula* / courtyard, hallway + *rex* / king]

> The king's hall. In England, a great hall in which the king met with his officers of state. Later called the King's Bench.

AUTOPSY   [L. from Gk. *autopsia* / to see with one's own eyes]

> An examination of the body of a deceased by a trained physician or technician to determine the cause of death. Any critical examination of events or conditions in the past.

AUTOPTIC EVIDENCE

> Real or palpable evidence. Objective evidence which the jury can see, hear or touch through its own senses; e.g., a knife or gun, a forged instrument, etc.

AUXILIUM PETERE   [L. *auxilium* / help, assistance + *petere* / to ask for, beg, plead]

> To seek aid or assistance.

A VINCULO MATRIMONII

To be freed from the chains or fetters of matrimony; an absolute and final divorce.

See **A MENSA ET THORO**

AVULSION [L. *avellere* / to tear away]

The sudden or precipitate shift in the flow of a stream or other body of water resulting in a change in the affected land boundaries; the resulting displacement of land from one property owner to another. Distinguished from *accretion*, which describes the gradual deposit or movement of sand or soil from one side of a stream or body of water to the other. The distinction between the two is that the land acquired as the result of *avulsion* remains the property of the original owner, whereas land acquired through accretion does not.

See **ALLUVION** and **ACCRETION**

AXIOM [L. *axioma* / a worthy thing (from the Greek)]

An established rule or principle; an accepted truth.

BANKRUPTCY   [L. *rumpere* / break, shatter + *banca*, Italian for bank]

A system of law and courts which administers the assets of insolvent persons, partnerships and corporations with the purpose of paying debts to creditors to the extent possible and discharging the bankrupt debtor from his/its obligations. The system in the United States is adminstered by federal bankruptcy courts under the Bankruptcy Code. Also, the state of being insolvent; i.e., unable to pay one's debts as they become due.

BATTERY   [L. *battuere* / beat, knock]

In the law of torts, an offensive or harmful contact with the person of another without the consent or invitation of that person; also the apprehension of such contact. The person who intends and commits such contact is liable in damages for the *tort of battery.*

BELLIGERENT   [L. *belligerare* / to wage war]

Hostile, pugnacious. In law, the status of a nation which is at war with another nation; also, the status of an insurgent group or person attempting to take control of a nation by force.

BELLO PARTA   [L. *bello, bellare* / to wage war + *pars* / parts]

The spoils of war.

BELLUM   [L. war]

War.

BENEFICIAL   [L. *bene* / well + *facere* / to do]

To do well by. To confer a benefit or kindness. To give an advantage to. *Beneficial enjoyment* suggests the benefits of ownership without legal title, as in the case of a trust beneficiary. A *beneficial interest* is the right to enjoy the use, benefit and income of property.

BENEFICIARY   [L. See **BENEFICIAL**]

One who benefits from some act, legal interest or arrangement. Examples: the person who receives the income from a trust is the *beneficiary* of the trust; the *beneficiary* of a life insurance policy receives the proceeds on the death of the insured; a third-party *beneficiary* receives the benefit of a contract to which he is not a party.

See **BENEFICIAL**

BENEFICIUM   [L. kindness, benefit, service]

A benefit, advantage or privilege.

BENEFIT

Anything which adds to value or enjoyment. Advantage; profit; gain. An enhancement in value or rights.

See **BENEFICIAL**

BICAMERAL   [L. *bi* / two + *camera* / a large vaulted room or chamber]

A legislative body with two houses or chambers. The U.S. Congress is a *bicameral* body made up of the House of Representatives and the Senate. The British Parliament is a *bicameral* body composed of the House of Commons and the House of Lords. Most states have *bicameral legislatures*.

BIFURCATE   [L. *bi* / two + *furca* / a two prong fork]

In law, a *bifurcated trial* is a trial in two parts to determine different issues arising from the same facts. For example: a jury in a criminal case may first be asked to determine guilt or innocence and then the degree of punishment; thus, a jury in a capital case may first decide guilt or innocence and then, separately, whether the death penalty will be imposed.

BILATERAL   [L. *bi* + *latus* / side, flank]

Two-sided. Involving two parties. A *bilateral contract* is a contract between two parties involving reciprocal promises and obligations to be performed following execution of the contract. On the other hand, a *unilateral contract* involves the exchange of a promise by one party for the act of another.

See **UNILATERAL**

BILLA VERA

A true bill. The endorsement by a grand jury upon an indictment supported by sufficient evidence.

BILL OF ATTAINDER

See **ATTAINDER**

BILL QUIA TIMET

See **QUIA TIMET**

BIPARTISAN [L. *bi* + *partire* / to divide or separate; to divide in two]

Divided into two parts. In the United States, the name given to any governmental, public or quasi-public body which has as its members the representatives of two parties. Also, a legislative discussion or vote evidencing the divergent views of two parties instead of their agreement.

BONA [L. good, virtuous]

Good.

BONA [L. goods, assets, possessions]

In the original Latin, the word was used to describe both personal and real property. At common law, it was limited to personal property.

BONA CONFISCATA

Property forfeited to the sovereign.

BONA FIDE [L. *bona* + *fides* / trust, confidence, belief]

In good faith; honest; without guile or deceit; innocent.

See **FIDES; MALA FIDES**

BONA FIDE HOLDER

The holder in due course of a negotiable instrument, i.e., a holder who acquires title to the instrument in the ordinary course of business and for value without knowedge of any defect in title.

BONA FIDE PURCHASER (BFP)

A buyer who pays valuable consideration, has no notice of any outstanding rights in others to the title of his seller, and who acts in good faith.

BONA GESTURA [L. *bonus* / good + *gero, gerere* / to carry on, conduct oneself, act]

Good behavior.

BONA MOBILIA [L. *bona* + *mobilis* / moveable, easy to move]

Articles and chattels which are capable of being moved from place to place.

BONA PERITURA [L. *bona* + *perire* / to perish]

Perishable goods.

BONA VACANTIA [L *bona* + *vacare* / to be empty, void]

Literally, empty goods. Applied to goods which were not disposed of in a decedent's will and were also not covered by any provision in intestacy; assets which cannot be claimed by anyone either in intestacy or under the will. Also, any goods without an identifiable owner.

BONI ET LEGALES HOMINES
Good and lawful men. Said of men qualified to be jurors.

BONIS NON AMOVENDIS
A writ issued by the court to a sheriff directing him not to allow a judgment debtor to remove his goods from the court's jurisdiction until a writ of error could be heard.

BONOS MORES [L. *bonos* + *moralis* / morals]
Good morals. The state of being ethical and virtuous.

See **CONTRA BONOS MORES**

BONUS [L. *bonus* / good]
Compensation above what is due and expected. Money in excess of agreed-upon compensation.

BREVE [L. *brevis* / short, in time or space]
A short note. In Roman times, a writ which was issued by the ruler or a tribunal ordering an appearance, action or response by the person addressed. A brief, a writ.

BREVE DE RECTO [L. *breve* + de / of, from + *regere* / to guide, rule]
A writ as of right.

BREVIA JUDICALIA
Judicial writs.

BRIEF [L. *brevis* / a short period; short in space or time]
Short in duration. Concise. A summary of the legal arguments submitted by counsel to the court in support of a motion or on a point of law being considered by the court. A *brief* usually cites cases decided or cited by the court and by other courts relevant to the matters at issue. A brief is also any memorandum written by a law clerk or associate to guide the lawyer in charge of a matter.

BRUTUM FULMEN [L. *brutus* / immoveable, without feeling + *fulmen* / a thunderbolt]
Literally, inert thunder. An empty or ineffectual threat or charge; a judicial order or decree which cannot be enforced, as an order by a federal court directed to Congress as a body.

CADUCARY [L. *cadere* / to fall]

Property subject to escheat (escheat is the forfeiture of property to the state when there is no person to inherit, or the transfer to the state of property when the owner cannot be found or identified). In Roman Law, a caducus was a failed legacy.

See **ESCHEAT**

CALCULUS [L. a little stone, the stones used to count votes or calculate prices]

A method or system of computation or calculation, as distinguished from the calculation itself.

CALENDAR [L. *calendae* (Gr. *kalendae*) / the first day of a Roman month (from *calo, calare* / to call, summon)]

An organized list. A record of the days and months of the year. A list published by a court of the cases, proceedings and motions to be heard by it on a given day or over a period of days. A schedule of the bills and legislation to be debated and voted upon by a legislature.

CALUMNY [L. *calumnia* / a trick; a false accusation, a malicious prosecution]

Defamation; false charges. Misrepresentation of the words or reputation of another with intent to injure.

CAMERA [L. a high ceilinged chamber]

A private room adjacent to the courtroom in which a judge hears arguments and conducts conferences; also, the process by which a judge reaches a decision when court is not in session.

See **BICAMERAL; IN CAMERA; CHAMBER**

CAMERA STELLATA [L. *camera* / chamber + *stella* / star]

Star Chambers. An English court of the 15th-17th centuries characterized by secret and oppressive trials.

CANCEL [L. *cancelli* / bounds, limits]

To annul. To reduce to nothing. To destroy. To destroy the effectiveness of a document such as a will by physical obliteration. To make a negotiable instrument uncollectable by defacing it, by blocking out the amount or signature, or by marking it "paid". To terminate a contract on account of the other party's breach.

CANNABIS

A class of substances which includes marijuana and hashish; a controlled substance; i.e., a substance which is outlawed, restricted or regulated.

CANON [L. ruler or role model; a standard (from the Greek)]

A set of principles; a system of laws or regulations. Used in such phrases as *Canons of Professional Ethics* (the rules or standards which govern the conduct of the legal profession); or *Canons of Descent* (the rules regulating inheritance); or *Canons of Construction* (the principles governing the construction of language and the interpretation of written instruments.)

CANON LAW

The body or code of laws governing a church. The system of jurisprudence governing the Roman Catholic Church.

CAPACITAS RATIONALIS

Literally, the capacity or ability to reason. Used by the Romans to describe the difference between man and the animals.

CAPAX DOLI [L. *capax* / capable of + *dolus* / fraud, deceit]

Capable of committing a crime. Having sufficient competence and understanding to be responsible for a crime.

CAPIAS [L. *capere* / to take]

That you take in; you are commanded to take or seize. A type of court writ issued to compel seizure of a defendant or his property for the purpose of compelling payment of a fine or response to a particular charge.

CAPIAS AD RESPONDENDUM

A writ directed to a sheriff or court officer commanding him to place a person under civil arrest to answer for a charge against him.

CAPIAS AD SATISFACENDUM

A writ to a sheriff commanding him to place a debtor under civil arrest until the claim against him is satisfied.

CAPITA [L. *caput* / head]

    The head or entire body of a person. A person considered or counted as one; to count each person as one, as in *in capita* or *per capita*.

    See **PER CAPITA, PER STIRPES**

CAPITAL [L. *caput* / head]

    A crime for which society exacts execution and death. Punishment by execution. Also, chief in impact or importance. The seat of government. The present value of goods accumulated and held over an extended period of time, as opposed to income, which is compensation over a limited period of time. Wealth devoted to the production of income. Net worth.

CAPITALIZE [L. *caput*]

    To dedicate a portion or all of the value of a chattel, commodity or property to a permanent investment for the production of income. To convert income or investment into capital. To commit assets to a business for indefinite use and consumption in the production of income.

CAPITATION TAX [L. *caput* / head]

    A tax levied on each individual regardless of his income or the value of his property; also called a head tax or a poll tax. A *capitation tax* as a condition of the right to vote is prohibited by the 24th Amendment to the U.S. Constitution.

CAPITE [L. *caput*]

    A feudal interest in land acquired by direct grant from the sovereign.

    See **IN CAPITE**

CAPITULA, CAPITULARY [L. *capitulare* / to separate into headings or chapters]

    A code or collection of laws or ordinances.

CARCER [L. a jail or prison]

    A prison or jail; a prison cell.

    See **INCARCERATE**

CARNAL [L. *caro, carnis* / flesh, meat]

    Giving way to sensual, especially sexual, appetites. Relating to the pleasures and appetites of the flesh and body, usually in connection with sexual pleasures.

CASE [L. *casus* / a fall; an accident or occurence (from *cadere* / to fall)]

A set of circumstances or facts. Conditions requiring investigation, e.g., by the police. A suit or action in law or in equity. The *case at bar* is the action before the court at a given time. A judicial decision which enunciates a new principle of law or which is so well reasoned or written as to prompt notice by scholars and lawyers is called a *landmark case* or a *leading case*.

See **CASUS**

CAS FORTUIT [L. *cas, casus* / occasion, event + *fortuitus* / accidental, unplanned]

A fortuitous and unexpected event. An event or accident caused by a force which is unforeseen and irresistible.

CASTIGATE [L. *castigare* / to punish, chastise]

To punish, criticize, reprove. To subject to punishment.

CASUALTY [L. *casus*]

A serious or fatal injury. A person in military service who is injured or killed in battle or who is captured or missing in action. Generally, any victim of an accident. Also, the accident itself, such as a loss through fire, hurricane or earthquake.

CASUS [L. *cadere* / to fall]

A case, a set of circumstances, a condition. A set of facts requiring study or investigation. A suit or action in a court of law or equity. Anything requiring care or attention. Used by lawyers in many ways, generally to refer to a matter at issue or in litigation; e.g., *case in point, case in controversy, case of first impression*, etc.

See **CASE**

CASUS BELLI

An event of war.

CASUS MAJOR

An important event. A catastrophe. An unusual event.

CASUS OMISSUS [L. *casus* + *omittere* / to omit, leave out]

A litigation which arises because a statute has failed to cover a particular issue which must then be decided by the courts. An issue or set of circumstances which is not covered by (inadvertently omitted from) a statute and is therefore left to be interpreted and decided under common law principles by the court.

CAUSA   [L. cause, reason, contention, claim; a law suit; a dispute]

Cause, purpose, also lawsuit or case; used with other words or phrases to denote an event or precipitating cause. (See the following listings.)

See **CAUSE**

CAUSA BELLI

A precipitating cause of war or hostilities.

See **BELLIGERENT; BELLUM**

CAUSA LATET, VIS EST NOTISSIMA

The cause is unknown, but the effect is there to see.

CAUSA MORTIS

In fear, anticipation or contemplation of approaching or imminent death; e.g., a gift *causa mortis*.

See **DONATIO CAUSA MORTIS, GIFT CAUSA MORTIS**

CAUSA PROXIMA

Proximate cause; the cause which is most closely or immediately related to an event; the precipitating cause; the cause which imposes legal liability.

See **PROXIMATE (CAUSE)**

CAUSA REMOTA

A remote cause; a cause which may contribute to an event, but which combines or is influenced by other, more immediate causes.

CAUSA SINE QUA NON

Literally, not without this cause; the indispensible cause; the cause without which this event would not have occurred; the "but for" cause used in analysis of causation in negligence cases.

CAUSA TURPIS   [L. *causa* + *turpis* / deformed, morally foul, disgraceful]

Motivated by a base or evil purpose; an evil cause.

CAUSE   [L. *causa* / cause, reason, motive]

Anything that brings on an effect or result. A project or enterprise which is vigorously pursued and supported. A basis for an action at law or equity. A matter or issue requiring resolution. A *cause of action* is all the matter supporting a plaintiff's claim in an action or proceeding. Lawyers speak of *actual cause, intervening cause, proximate cause, superseding cause, probable cause, actual cause, reasonable cause, remote cause,* etc. All of these phrases use the word *cause* in its prime meaning: i.e., anything that produces a result or brings about an event.

See **CAUSA**

CAUTIO [L. caution, care]
Caution, prudence; also, security, bond, bail.

CAUTIO PRO EXPENSIS
Security for expenses.

CAVEAT [L. *cavere* / to beware of, guard against]
A warning or notice alerting the recipient to exercise caution before acting; e.g., notice to a reader to alert her to an important point in the text; to a judge to discourage him from performing certain acts or from proceeding in a litigation; or to the Patent Office by an inventor to prevent issuance of a patent to another applicant.

CAVEAT ACTOR
Let the person who will commit the act beware.

CAVEAT EMPTOR [L. *caveat* + *emptor* / buyer, purchaser]
Let the buyer beware; a warning to the purchaser that he buys at his own risk. The common law doctrine known as *caveat emptor* has been modified in favor of the consumer by statutes and decisions confirming various obligations of the seller or manufucturer, such as the warranties of fitness and merchantability.

CAVEAT VENDITOR
Let the seller beware.

CAVEAT VIATOR [L. *caveat* + *viator* / traveler]
Let the traveler beware.

CEDE [L. *cedo, cedere* / to go, proceed; to withdraw]
To yield or give. To surrender a territory or land area, usually by way of treaty. To transfer or assign.

CENSOR [L. *censor* / censor, magistrate; the Roman official responsible for the census]
In Roman times, a magistrate who was responsible for the census; also, a severe judge. An official who is delegated to examine books, movies, programs on TV or radio, etc., to determine whether they contain objectionable material or content. Also, an official assigned to examine sensitive material in time of war to eliminate messages potentially harmful to the enemy.

CENSURE [L. *censeo, censere* / to estimate, judge, form an opinion of]

A determination that some action requires criticism or condemnation. A judgment of fault. Attorneys are *censured* by disciplinary committees for violating the rules of professional responsibility. Judges are *censured* by panels of judges for violating judicial codes of conduct.

CENSUS [L. the counting or enrollment of all Roman citizens]

In Rome, the listing of citizens' names and property. The counting and enumeration of all persons within the borders of a city, state, nation or other political entity. In the United States, the first census was completed in 1790 and a new census is done every ten years.

CENTUMVIRI

The one hundred and five Roman judges who determined cases brought by commoners.

CEPI CORPUS [L. *cepi* / I have taken (*capere* / to take) + *corpus* / body]

I have taken the body. The return of a warrant for the arrest of a debtor.

CEPIT ET ASPORTAVIT

He took (it) and carried (it) away.

CERTIFICATE [L. *certificare* / to certify (*certus* / settled, decided)]

A document which attests to the proof or certainty of a set of facts or relationships. A document evidencing a right or privilege, such as attainment of an educational degree or ownership of some asset or property. A *certificate of deposit* is a document issued by a bank or financial institution evidencing its obligation to repay at maturity at a stated rate of interest an amount deposited with the bank for a stated period by an individual. A *certificate of title* is a statement to a land owner issued by a title company or registry of deeds attesting to ownership free and clear of all defects except those listed as exceptions. A *certificate of occupancy* is a document issued by a local building agency or authority establishing that a dwelling or other structure meets all construction requirements and may be used and occupied legally. A *certificate of incorporation* is the document, usually in the form of a receipt for filing fees, attesting to the legal existence of a newly formed corporation, issued by the secretary of state of one of the states.

CERTIFY [L. *certus* / settled, resolved, fixed]

To attest to the truth or authenticity of. To state as certain or fixed. To guarantee that a check is issued on good and collected funds. To assure in writing that a document or a set of records has been validly maintained. In labor law, the act of the NLRB in designating a particular labor union as the bargaining agent for a group of workers. The act of the clerk of a lower court in passing on to an appellate court for review the formal and official record of a proceeding before the court.

CERTIORARI [L. to be informed]

To confirm or make certain. A process, usually in the form of a writ, for compelling review by a superior court of the decision of an inferior court, or a review by a court of the determination of an administrative agency; a common law writ commanding an inferor court or agency in a particular case to certify and return the record to a superior court for review.

CESSANTE CAUSA, CESSANTE EFFECTUS

When the cause is removed, the effect is no longer felt.

CESSANTE RATIONE LEGIS CESSAT ET IPSE LEX

When the reasoning behind a law ends, the (reason for the) law itself ends. When a law has outlived its usefulness, it should be changed or abolished.

CESSET EXECUTIO

Stop the execution. An order staying an execution.

CESSET PROCESSUS

An order staying all proceedings in an action.

CESSIO BONORUM [L. *cessare* + *bonitas* / good things, enjoyable goods]

A procedure whereby a debtor turned all his wordly goods over to his creditors in exchange for relief from imprisonment. The precursor to the modern system of bankruptcy laws.

CESSION [L. *cedo, cedere* / to withdraw, yield]

The act of yielding and transferring an interest in property to another, as from a debtor to a creditor or from one state or country to another. The transfer of control over a land area from one country to another after sale or conquest, usually by treaty. The transfer of liability under an insurance policy from the original insurer to a reinsurer.

CESSO, CESSARE

To give in, give up, default.

CHALLENGE [L. *calumnia* / trick, artifice; also, a false charge or accusation]

To dare or invite to compete, contest or fight. To halt another and demand his identity. To dispute or call into question or account. To question the legality of, as to challenge a summons or a statute. To move to reject a juror before he is sworn. To *challenge a juror for cause* is to question his ability to hear and consider the evidence fairly and impartially. A *peremptory challenge* is the challenge of a prospective juror for any reason or no reason.

CHALLENGE PROPTER AFFECTUM

Challenge to a juror for bias or prejudice.

CHALLENGE PROPTER DELICTUM

Challenge to a juror for a crime committed by him.

CHAMBER [L. *camera* / a large, vaulted room; also a room without a roof]

An enclosed space. A meeting hall for a body of persons, especially a legislative or judicial body. A legislative body, as one of the two *chambers* making up the U.S. Congress. Also, the room adjacent to his courtroom in which a judge carries on his other judicial functions than those requiring the formality of a courtroom, e.g., a hearing or conference *in chambers*.

See **CAMERA; IN CAMERA**

CHAMPERTY [L. *campus* / a level space, part or portion of a field]

The unlawful sponsorship of litigation. Payment by a stranger or non-party to a law suit of the expenses or costs of a party, in exchange for an interest in the money recovered; *champerty* is illegal in most states.

CHARGE [L. *carrus* / a four-wheeled cart]

An obligation or duty; a commitment. To have the management or care of, as of a child. Instructions by a judge to a jury in advance of the jurors' deliberations, relating the evidence to the law. An expense. The price paid for goods or commodities or for admission to a performance. A formal accusation of the commission of an offense, crime or wrongdoing. In accounting, a debit to an account. To impose a financial burden upon.

CHARITABLE [L. *carus, caritas* / dear; affection, love]

Generous, benificent. Liberal in giving support to organizations and enterprises providing help to persons in need. A *charitable deduction* is a deduction under the Internal Revenue Code for a contribution to a charity which is qualified under the Code.

CHARITY [L. *carus* / dear, treasured]

Benevolence towards others, especially the needy and the underprivileged. An insitution dispensing care and relief of the poor. A gift to help in the care of others.

CHARTA [L. a leaf of the writing paper made from the papyrus plant; paper]

Paper, words written or inscribed on a sheet of paper.

See **MAGNA CHARTA; CHARTER**

CHARTER [L. *charta* / a leaf of the Papyrus plant. Writing paper]

A grant of power or function from an agency of government to a corporation or other entity. A written document that sets forth and defines the scope and powers of an organization such as a school or division of government. Authority to form and create a branch or chapter by a central agency such as a church or board of education. A *charter party* is the leasing of a ship by its owner to be used by the lessee for the transportation of cargo.

See **CHARTA**

CHOSE [L. *causa* / cause, reason]

Any item of personal property. A thing. A *chose in action* is any right or claim that can be reduced to recovery in a lawsuit, e.g., a debt or a claim to recover in tort for personal injuries. Also, a document creating or forming the basis for a legal claim, e.g., a contract, promissory note or check.

CIRCA [L. *circum* / in a circle]

Around, about, approximately. Used before a date to indicate a lack of precision about the date.

CIRCUIT [L. *circu(m)ire* / to go around]

The area within which a particular court has jurisdiction, derived from the practice of judges to travel around and within the boundaries of their courts. In the federal judicial system, the area over which a United States Court of Appeals has jurisdiction.

CIRCUMSTANCE [L. *circum* / round + *abstare* / to stand; to stand in a circle; to surround]

Anything that needs to be taken into account or to be considered. An event or fact that constitutes one part of a series of events or facts. A subordinate or incidental fact or circumstances. A factor to be considered in weighing the probability of an event, such as whether an accused is guilty of the crime charged. The measure of a person's status or wealth, e.g., *his circumstances before that unfortunate investment. Circumstantial evidence* is evidence of events and facts which tend to prove that the event or fact at issue has occurred even though it cannot be proved directly.

CIRCUMSTANTIAL [L. *circum* + *abstare*]

Pertinent to but not immediately impinging upon. *Circumstantial evidence* consists of facts concerning an event or transaction which permit a judge or juror to draw reasonable inferences as to the way in which the event probably occurred.

CITE, CITATION   [L. *citare* / to put into motion, summon, call upon]

To refer to, quote by way of example. To point to a case, court decision or other legal authority by reference to the source, liber and page on which it may be found. Notice to parties that a proceeding has begun, especially in probate courts. Also, a writ ordering a person to appear before a tribunal.

CIVIL   [L. *civis, civilis* / a Roman citizen; a citizen]

Concerning or relating to a political entity and/or its citizens. Matters concerning the private and public rights of citizens as distinguished from crimes and criminals. Relating to the general public and its affairs; in this sense, it is distinguished from military and religious matters or interests. Also, the body of law which developed and is now observed in countries under Roman law as distinguished from the common law of England and its former colonies. A *civil arrest* is an arrest which is not based on a criminal indictment or charge but instead on nonpayment of a debt or judgment; usually, the person arrested is released upon the posting of a bond. *Civil contempt* is a contempt imposed by the court in a civil action when a party refuses or neglects to obey a court order. *Civil disobedience* is the term applied to the action of a group of citizens in asserting or maintaining a public or political protest or in refusing to obey a court or administrative order. The *civil rights movement* of the 1960's was characterized by many instances of *civil disobedience*.

CIVILIS   [L. *civis* / a citizen of Rome]

Relating to a citizen, civic, civil; relating to public or community life. Used in *civilis actio*, a civil action. Concerning the citizens of a place.

CIVILITER MORTUUS   [L. *civiliter* / civil + *mortuus* / dead]

Dead or non-existent in the eyes of the law. In some societies, a person may be civilly dead although very much alive. This describes, for example, the status of a criminal in some countries who is deprived of his citizenship, has no voting rights, cannot sue and loses the other essential elements of existence as a person.

CIVITAS   [L. citizenship]

Community, commonwealth, citizenship in a state or civil entity; any body of people living under the same laws.

CLAIM   [L. *clamare* / to call out, shout, cry out]

The assertion of a right or obligation. A demand for payment of a debt or for the return to the person making the claim of some property interest or privilege. A right to some asset or property, as to a mine or parcel of real estate. In the law, the right to assert that an injury or wrong has occurred requiring a judicial remedy; also the assertion of that right in a formal pleading. The word is often used synonymously with the term *cause of action*. Also, the assertion by a patent applicant that his invention is novel and patentable.

CLANDESTINE [L. *celare* / to hide, conceal, keep secret]

An act or event conducted in secrecy and with intent to conceal; e.g., a clandestine marriage.

CLAUSE [L. *claudere* / to close, to shut up, to conclude]

A group of connected words containing a subject and a verb, but part of a complex sentence. In law, a section or part of a document, as a paragraph in a will or statute.

CLAUSUM

An enclosed place, a piece of land surrounded by a fence or by defined boundaries.

CLAUSUM FREGIT [L. *clausum* + *frangere* / to break]

He broke the fence or boundary line; he committed a trespass.

CLAVES CURIAE [L *clavis* / a key + *curiae* / court]

The keys to the courthouse.

CLEMENCY [L. *clemens* / mild, kind, merciful]

A lenient or sympathetic attitude. The act of moderating a sentence or other punishment; e.g., a pardon or commutation of sentence.

CODE, CODEX [L. *caudex, codex* / the trunk of a tree; wooden tablets covered with wax on which words were inscribed; a book made of such tablets]

A book; a book of accounts. The organized statement of a body of laws, regulations, principles or guidelines. A collection of laws or of regulations in a particular area of the law, such as the Bankruptcy Code, the Internal Revenue Code, etc.

CODICIL [L. *codicillus* / a small codex, a small branch; a writing tablet]

An addition to or modification of a will; a document altering or revoking provisions of an existing will. It is not a new will nor a complete revocation of the existing will, but an extension of it. Formerly a *codicil* was physically attached to the will, but now it may be contained in an independent document.

COERCION [L. *coercere* / to enclose, shut in, confine, restrain]

The threat of physical or mental force or pressure of such magnitude as to cause a reasonable person to fear death, physical violence, economic loss, or other serious risk if an act is not done by him. The act of compelling another, through of fear of consequence, to commit an act he would otherwise avoid. The defense of *coercion* may be asserted by a defendant to avoid liability under a contract.

COGITO ERGO SUM

I think, therefore I am.

COGNATE OFFENSE

A related offense. An offense which shares some of the same elements with another offense. Robbery may be said to be a *cognate offense* of larceny.

COGNATION   [L. *cognoscere* / to know through the senses; become acquainted with]

Relationship by blood. Descent from a common ancestor, male or female.

COGNIZABLE   [L. *cognosco, cognoscere* / to know, learn, understand]

Having the capacity to be known or easily ascertained or determined. In the law, the word is applied to the process by which members of a group with common characteristics (e.g., race, gender or age) are singled out for unfavorable treatment. Under the U.S. Constitution, potential jurors may not be excluded from service because they are members of a *cognizable group*. A *cognizable claim* is a claim which will be accepted by the court.

COGNOMEN   [L. *cognoscere* + *nomen* / name]

Having a common name; a surname or family name.

COGNOVIT JUDGMENT

Synonymous with the term "confession of judgment"; a judgment entered upon a written admission of liability by a debtor without the formality of a legal proceeding. The admission is generally signed and delivered in advance by a debtor who borrows or buys on credit. These judgments are considered coercive and are prohibited by statute in some states.
See **CONFESS**

COGNOVIT NOTE

A promissory note which contains a provision authorizing the attorney or agent of the holder of the note to enter judgment against the maker without advance notice in the event of default or non-payment.

COLLATE   [L. *collatum*, pp. of *conferre* / to bring or put together, to collect]

To collect a number of items and put them in some pre-determined order. To collect, compare and verify. To put a number of legal documents together in a specified order in preparation for filing or for submission to a court.

COLLATERAL (ESTOPPEL) [L. *com* / together + *lateo, latere* / to be concealed]

Parallel or side by side with and supportive of, but of secondary or subordinate standing. Relating or belonging to. Also, anything of value given to secure the payment or satisfaction of an obligation. *Collateral estoppel* is essentially the same as *res judicata* — the doctrine that a prior judgment between the same parties, or the prior judicial determination of an issue between the same parties, will operate to preclude any further consideration of that judgment or of that issue by another court.

See **RES JUDICATA**

COLLATION [L. *collatum*, pp. of *conferre*]

A collection of documents arranged in some logical sequence for study or interpretation. Also, a set of bound related documents.

COLLECTIVE [L. *collatum,* pp. of *conferre* / to put together, to collect]

A number of persons functioning as a group, such as a group of purchasers or a group of workers. Functions and activities shared by all the members of a group. *Collective bargaining* is the process under which a group of workers, usually called a labor union, organize to negotiate with the employer over hours, wages, vacations and conditions of employment. A *collective bargaining agreement* is the agreement concluded in negotiations between the union and the employer. A *collective mark* is a trademark or service mark belonging to a group, such as a trade association.

COLLOQIUM [L. *com* + *loquer, loqui* / to speak; to speak together, to engage in conversation]

In actions for slander or libel, that part of the complaint which ties the language complained of to the particular plaintiff and makes defamatory as to him matter which might otherwise be inoffensive as to others.

COLLOQUY

A discussion of serious subjects . A dialogue. A conference.

COLLUDE, COLLUSION, COLLUSIVE [L. *com* + *ludere* / to play a game; to do for amusement]

To plot together for a fraudulent, deceitful or criminal purpose. An agreement between two or more persons to obtain property, profit or advantage through unlawful means. A husband and wife may *collude* to allege and testify as to facts which will satisfy the requirements for divorce but which are not true.

COLORABLE [L. *color, coloris* / color, tint, shade]

Apparently true or real. Giving the impression of truth or validity. A *colorable right* is a right which has enough weight to be asserted in a pleading and proved to the judge or jury.

COLORE OFFICII [L. the color of office]

The appearance of authority emanating from possession of a title or office; often used to convey the sense that some action by a person in authority may appear proper but is really not, or that the person claiming to hold an office or the authority of that office does not in fact do so.

COMBUSTIO DOMORUM [L. *comburere* / to burn + *domus* / a house, a home]

The burning of a house or residence; i.e., arson.

COMITATUS [L. a retinue or following]

In England, an area governed by a sheriff; a county or shire.

COMITY [L. *comitas* / kindness, courtesy]

The practice by which one court defers to the jurisdiction of another. The decision to defer is not compelled by any rule of law but is generally based upon the sense that one court should not meddle in the determinations of another which has already taken jurisdiction of a matter or which is better able to dispose of it. *Comity* also influences an American court to honor the judgment or decree of another country. The Comity Clause of the U. S. Constitution requires each state to accord the same privileges and immunities to the citizens of other states as to its own (Article IV, Para. 2).

COMITY INTER GENTES

Comity between peoples and nations.

COMMERCE [L. *commercium* / trade, commerce (from *commercor, commercari* / to buy together)]

The exchange of ideas, thoughts and opinions. Also, the exchange of goods and commodities through all the processes relating to product growth, production, advertising, promotion, transportation, sale and purchase. All forms of business. The *Commerce Clause*, contained in Article I, Section 8 of the Constitution, is the clause which gives Congress the power to regulate commerce between the states and with foreign countries.

COMMERCIAL [L. *commercium* / trade, commerce]

Relating or pertaining to commerce in the business sense. Characterized by acceptance in the general market, rather than in the luxury market. Designed for the largest possible consumption. Concerning skills, talents and qualities useful in business. Also, a short message broadcast on radio or television, advertising or promoting a particular product or service. A *commercial bank* is a bank offering the general public the banking services of accepting deposits and permitting the use of funds on balance through withdrawals and checking accounts. *Commercial law* is the body of law dealing with and governing business transactions. The general principles of commercial law have been codified in the Uniform Commercial Code. *Commercial speech* is speech which advertises or promotes a commercial offer or transaction. Commercial speech is protected under the First Amendment, but to a lesser extent than the ordinary non-commercial expression of thoughts and ideas.

COMMISSION [L. *committo, committere* / to unite, combine; to cause to happen]

A formal written authorization to perform a stated act or to function in a particular office. Authority to act as agent for another. A government agency formed to oversee a particular administrative area or function (e.g., the Federal Communications Commission or the Civil Service Commission). A fee paid to someone for performing a given act or for consummating a transaction beneficial to the payor of the fee, such as the commission paid to a real estate broker for arranging the sale of a parcel of land.

COMMIT [L. *committere* / to unite, connect, entrust]

To bring about, do; to perpetrate, as a crime. To consign a person to a mental institution. To order the confinement of a prisoner in a jail or prison. To record for preservation (e.g., *commit to memory).*

COMMITMENT [L. *committere* / to unite, combine]

To place someone in confinement in a prison or mental institution. A promise to perform some act in the future; a term of a contract. The act of pledging oneself to an obligation or to a personal or emotional relationship. A *civil commitment* to a mental institution is the confinement of a patient by his voluntary act or by a judicial determination following a hearing.

COMMITTEE [L. *committere* / to unite; also, to entrust or charge]

A person charged with the care of another person who is not competent, such as an infant or a person who is mentally disturbed. The appointment of a committee is made by the court on application of an interested party. A group of persons chosen from a larger group and assigned or delegated to investigate and report to the larger group on some issue of interest; especially, a committee of legislators assigned to investigate specific legislative areas (in Congress, for example, the Foreign Affairs Committee or the Committee on Ways and Means). Also, any organization for the advancement of a particular social or political purpose, e.g., the Republican National Committee.

COMMITTITUR

An order providing that a defendant was to be taken into the custody of a sheriff.

COMMODITY   [L. *commodare* / to make fit, adapt, to furnish or give]

Any article or product having economic value. An agricultural or manufacturing product which is traded in commerce. Any item of personal property which can be used in barter or sale.

COMMON   [L. *communis* / shared, common, universal]

Concerning the community as a whole. Applying to the greatest number of persons. Occurring regularly. Also, in a different sense, vulgar, not in good taste, ordinary. Shared by all the members of the community, such as a common dining room or hall, or the Commons (a public park or center in a town, such as the Boston Common). *Common stock* is a class of stock issued by corporations, usually bearing the greatest risk but providing the greatest potential return. A *tenancy in common* is a tenancy in property in which two or more tenants or owners share the ownership but have no rights of survivorship. A *common easement* is an easement shared by the dominant tenant and the servient tenant, i.e., a non-exclusive easement.

COMMON LAW

The body of law developed over the centuries in England and carried to and preserved in all the American states except the State of Louisiana. A body of law based upon the gradual development of rules and principles generally adhered to and preserved, reflected and defined in the decisions of the English and American courts. The remedies provided originally by the English law courts as distinguished from the relief under principles of equity supplied by the English chancery courts.

COMMORIENTES   [L. *com* + *morior, mori* / to die]

Victims of a simultaneous death, as in a plane crash. Many states have simultaneous death statutes dealing with the disposition of the assets of *commorientes* in defined degrees of relationship.

See **SIMULTANEOUS (DEATH)**

COMMUNE BONUM   [L. *communis* / common, general + *bonus, bonum* / good, moral]

The common good, public welfare.

COMMUNE VINCULUM   [L. *communis* / common + *vinculum* / a chain]

Common ties or bonds. Consanguinity.

COMMUNIS ERROR FACIT JUS

An error which is common to all will become law. Common mistakes become the norm or the rule.

COMMUNITY   [L. *communis* / common, universal, customary, public]

Place, vicinity, neighborhood. An area with a defineable boundary fixed by regulation, or by usage, or by common characteristcs and interests. A group of people with similar characteristcs or interests. The group may be widely scattered so long as its members share elements of history, origin or circumstance together.

COMMUNITY PROPERTY

The unity of husband and wife in the common ownership of all marital assets and income (with certain exceptions), recognized by those American states (e.g., California, Louisiana) which have taken their system of marital property law from the Spanish and/or French, rather than the English common law. With the exception of gifts, bequests and legacies, all property acquired by either spouse during the marriage belongs equally to both. There are nine community property states.

COMMUTE, COMMUTATION   [L. *com* / with + *muto, mutare* / to change or exchange; to alter]

An exchange or trade of goods; a substitution of one measure of monetary exchange for another. In criminal law, the substitution of a shorter or less onerous term or punishment for another, usually by the governor of a state.

COMPACT   [L. *com* + *pactio* / agreement, covenant]

A treaty or contract. A formal agreement between or among parties, especially nations or groups of nations. The Compact Clause of the U.S. Constitution provides that no state shall enter into a compact or treaty with another state or with a foreign government.

COMPARATIVE   [L. *comparo, comparare* / to prepare, get ready; also, to put in pairs, to join together]

Measured by the degree of relationship between one thing and another. An analysis of the differences and similarities which one factor bears to another. *Comparative fault* is a doctrine in tort law under which the degree of fault of the plaintiff and of the defendant in contributing to an accident or occurrence is measured and weighed; damages are assessed accordingly. Most states have adopted this doctrine. *Comparative negligence* is essentially the same as comparative fault. In comparative negligence jurisdictions, all persons contributing to an accident are assessed in damages in accordance with the degree of their contribution. Under this doctrine, the plaintiff's contributory negligence does not preclude him from recovering some damages from someone who is more at fault.

COMPEL, COMPELLING [L. *compello, compellere* / to force to take some action; to drive to one place, as with cattle]

To apply pressure to someone to force him to take some specific action. To cause to happen. To persuade or impel. A *compelling argument* is a line of reasoning which overcomes doubt or objection. A *compelling cause* is a purpose which is difficult to resist. A *compelling state interest* is a public or civil interest which is so important as to limit individual rights or prerogatives.

COMPENSATE, COMPENSATION [L. *compenso, compensare* / to weigh together, to measure one thing against another; to balance]

To adjust for the effect of; to balance against. To counteract or neutralize. To offset a shortage, error or defect. To pay in money or property for services rendered. *Compensation* is the payment of money or property for services rendered or to adjust for a grievance or injury. Remuneration. Also, the adjustments in his physical or mental conditions which are made by a person to enable him to overcome a debilitating condition or a disabling illness or injury.

COMPENSATIO CRIMINIS [L. *compensatio* / balancing accounts + *crimen* / fault, guilt, crime]

Balancing one crime or wrong against another: "An eye for an eye and a tooth for a tooth." In an action for divorce, the defense that the plaintiff has committed acts as wrongful as those of the defendant.

COMPETENCY, COMPETENT [L. *competere* / to agree, coincide, match, equal]

Possessing the ability to observe or comply with standards deemed reasonable by the general community. Having the capacity to perform the functions or recognize the requirements of an activity. Conforming to qualifications defined as legal. The law subjects many matters to the *test of competency*. A *competent testator*, for example, must comprehend the nature and extent of his property, his relationship to the people he includes or leaves out, the meaning of a will, and simple business transactions. *Competent evidence* is evidence given by a witness who is able to understand the purpose and nature of his testimony. A *competent defendant* in a criminal trial is one who understands the nature and scope of the charges against him and has the capacity to understand and act upon the advice of his lawyer.

COMPLAIN, COMPLAINT [L. *com* / together + *plango, plangere* / to beat the breast, to lament; to bewail]

To express disapproval or hostility. To object to or about. To express unhappiness, grief or discontent. To present a grievance, as to complain about a price. To present a formal claim, accusation or charge. To submit or serve a legal complaint. The *complaint* is the initial pleading under which a plaintiff begins a lawsuit by setting forth the allegations of fact supporting and constituting his claim for relief. Also, the document attested to by a police officer alleging the commission of a crime by the defendant.

COMPLICITY [L. *complicare* / to fold together; to make involved or intricate; confuse]

Involved as a participant or co-conspirator in the commission of an unlawful act or crime.

COMPLY, COMPLIANCE [L. *compleo, complere* / to fill up; to fulfill; to complete]

To accede to a wish or command. To do as directed. To conduct oneself as required by a rule or order. *Compliance* is the act of acceding to an order, such as the order or injunction of a court.

COMPOSITION [L. *componere* / to bring or put together; to arrange, collect]

In law, an agreement between a debtor and two or more of his creditors concerning the collection of the debtor's assets and the application of those assets to payment of the creditors' claims. The agreement may include a reduction in the debts, an extension of time for payment, the surrender of certain assets of the debtor, and the release or discharge of the debtor.

COMPOS MENTIS [L. *compos* / having control of + *mens* / mind]

In control of one's mind; sane; mentally competent.

See **NON COMPOS MENTIS**

COMPOUND [L. *compono, componere* / to put or bring together; to join together]

To put together a variety of ingredients to form a new, integrated substance. To settle amicably. But also, to aggravate or make worse, as in *he compounded his error*. To agree not to prosecute a criminal offense in exchange for payment or consideration. (*Compounding a felony* was itself a felony at common law.) To compute and pay interest not only on the outstanding principal of a debt but also on the accrued interest, as contrasted with simple interest. Also, a group of buildings enclosed by a wall or fence.

COMPROMISE [L. *compromitto, compromittere* / to enter into mutual promises; to agree to arbitrate a dispute]

To adjust differences by mutual concession. To reach agreement after acknowledging and settling a variety of differing interests. Also, to make concessions which reflect in a derogatory way on the person making them, as in *he compromised his ideals.* An agreement to settle a lawsuit. A *compromise verdict* is a verdict arrived at by jurors by averaging damages or by some other arbitrary device which fails to represent the true agreement of the jurors as to liability.

COMPULSION, COMPULSORY [L. *compellere* / to force to action, compel]

A force or pressure that causes a person to act involuntarily or against his will or interest. An irresistible or coerced response. Duress; coercion. The word *compulsory* has many uses in law. A *compulsory counterclaim* is a claim which must be asserted by the defendant if it arises from the same facts or transactions as those alleged in the complaint. *Compulsory process* is the machinery used by the courts to compel the attendance of witnesses, including resort to arrest. The Constitution guarantees access to compulsory process to every accused in a criminal trial. Amendment VI.

CONCEAL [L. *com + celo, celare* / to hide, conceal]

To hide, put out of sight. To prevent discovery or disclosure of. To fail or neglect to disclose a matter which would affect, change, or modify the behavior of another, as to *conceal* a fact which would lead another party to walk away from a transaction if he knew it. To carry a dangerous weapon so as to prevent it from being seen. To prevent the discovery of stolen property.

CONCEDE, CONCESSION [L. *concedo, concedere* / to retire, withdraw; also, to yield, to give up]

To grant a right or privilege. To acknowledge as true or compelling, as to *concede* a point or an argument; to yield or surrender. A *concession* is the act of acknowledging a point in argument or negotiation. Also, the right to use the real property of another for some gainful activity, e.g., logging or mining. Also, the right to occupy and use a portion of another's real property to carry on a business, such as a *concession to sell* food at a ballpark or to distribute newspapers to homes and offices.

CONCERT, CONCERTED [L. *concerto, concertare* / to strive hard; to try together (*certus* / settled, sure, certain)]

An agreement reached after adjusting differences and grievances. Joint action to achieve a common purpose. *Concerted action* is action by two or more persons for a common end. *Concerted activity* by workers to bargain with an employer to adjust wages, hours and other terms of employment is protected under the NLRA. In criminal law, a defendant who aids and abets another to commit a crime is said to be in a *concert of action* with the other defendant.

CONCESSUM [L. *concedere* / to yield, to withdraw]

The term was used by early courts to signify that a point or argument was accepted or conceded by one party.

CONCILIATION [L. *conciliare* / to bring together, unite]

The process of adjusting or settling claims or disputes before trial to avoid the expense and pressure of litigation. Some courts require *efforts at conciliation* before trial. *Conciliation* is used in the early stages of labor disputes.

CONCLUSION, CONCLUSIVE, CONCLUSORY [L. *concludo, concludere* / to shut up, enclose, confine]

A *conclusion* is a determination arrived at by considering a number of relevant facts and issues. A final statement of a position or viewpoint. A *conclusion of fact* is a fact inferred by the trier of facts from the evidence presented. A *conclusion of law* is a determination and statement by the court of the principles of law which apply to the facts being considered by a jury, and, also, the principles upon which the court bases its judgment or decision. Resolving an issue or question permanently. Putting an end to debate or inquiry. Decisive; determinative. *Conclusory* applies to statements which have no support in evidence or fact; i.e., mere allegations.

CONCORDAT [L. *concordare* / to agree]

An agreement or covenant. A compact between two or more sovereign states dealing with problems of mutual concern. Also, the agreement between the Holy See and a sovereign temporal state.

CONCUR, CONCURRENCE [L. *concurro, concurrere* / to run together; to meet, assemble; to agree]

To reach or express agreement. To arrive at a joint decision or determination. To act together in a common cause or with a common purpose. To happen at the same time. An appellate judge *concurs* with the court's decision when he reaches the same conclusion as reported in the decision but upon a different theory or a different line of reasoning. The opinion written by a judge who concurs is called a *concurrence*.

CONCURRENT [L. *concurrere* / to run together; join, congregate]

Acting or happening together or at the same time. Parallel courses or events. *Concurrent causes* are two or more causes happening at about the same time and combining to produce a given result. *Concurrent conditions* are two or more provisions in the same contract requiring essentially simultaneous performance by the parties. *Concurrent jurisdiction* is the existence of jurisdiction to try a case in two or more courts simultaneously, e.g., a state court and a federal court. Example: in diversity cases, state and federal courts have *concurrent jurisdiction*. *Concurrent sentences* are two or more sentences in one criminal proceeding but on different counts which enable the defendant to serve both sentences over the same period of time (e.g., a defendant may be given concurrent sentences for embezzlement and tax evasion).

See **CURRENT**

CONDEMN [L. *condemnare* / to condemn]

To determine that the defendant in a criminal case is guilty. To declare an act wrong or evil. To commit the defendant in a capital case to death by execution. To declare food, or a building, or a ship as unfit and order its destruction. To appropriate property for public use.

See **EMINENT DOMAIN; APPROPRIATE**

CONDEMNATION

The process by which a governmental authority or agency takes or seizes private property for public use by the exercise of the right of eminent domain and the payment of just compensation to the owner.

See **CONFISCATE; EMINENT DOMAIN; EXPRORIATE**

CONDITION [L. *condicio* / agreement, arrangement (from *condico, condicere* / to agree with, to settle)]

A contract term or provision which renders the entire contract contingent upon the existence or occurrence of some fact or event. A term upon which performance depends. An essential ingredient in the realization of an event or objective. An act or event which may or may not occur but upon the occurrence of which the rights and/or obligations of the parties to a legal instrument depend. Conditions may be *concurrent, implied, express, precedent, subsequent or constructive*.

CONDITIONAL [L. *condicio*]

Subject to or depending upon a condition. A *conditional delivery* is a delivery not accompanied by delivery of title or ownership; ownership will be transferred only after satisfaction of a condition. A *conditional title* is a title to real estate which is subject to a condition. A *conditional sale* is a sale which becomes complete, in the sense that title passes to the buyer, only after the buyer has satisfied all conditions relating to credit and payment of the purchase price.

See **UNCONDITIONAL**

CONDOMINIUM [*com* / with + *dominium* / power, mastery, ownership, control]

Ownership of property together. A system of land ownership under which title to individual units in a multiunit project is held by individual owners, but in which each unit owner is also a tenant in common in the underlying fee and in the spaces and structures used in common by all the unit owners.

CONDONATION [L. *com* + *donare* / to give]

The act of one person in overlooking or forgiving the wrong of another. The condonation or forgiveness by one spouse of the conduct or acts of the other may constitute a defense in an action for divorce which relies on those same acts.

CONDONE [L. *condono, condonare* / to give away; to sacrifice; to overlook, forgive]

To accept a fault or transgression without retribution or punishment. To forgive a wrong or to overlook conduct which is ordinarily unacceptable. To ignore or to accept without interference or condemnation, as to *condone* violence or corruption.

CONFESS, CONFESSION [L. *confessus*, pp. of *confiteor, confiteri* / to admit, acknowledge, confess]

To tell others of some act or deed which was previously undisclosed or unconfirmed. To disclose commission of a sin or crime. To disclose one's faults or transgressions to a priest. To declare one's thoughts or attitudes. To admit as true and valid facts alleged by the other side in a litigation. A *confession* is a statement of guilt made voluntarily by an accused with respect to his alleged commission of a crime. In some jurisdictions, a confession is valid only if it deals with all the elements of the crime. A *confession of judgment* is an acknowledgment and consent by a debtor that judgment may be entered against him without further notice to him.

See **COGNOVIT JUDGMENT**

CONFIDENCE, CONFIDENTIAL [L. *confido, confidere* / to trust completely, have faith in]

Faith in one's powers and abilities; self-assurance. A sense of security arising from one's talents and the response of others. Also, a relationship of trust and intimacy. Reliance upon the qualities and integrity of another. Also, a statement made in reliance that the hearer will not disclose the statement to anyone else. A communication made with intent that it not be revealed to others. *Confidences* are communicated to lawyers, doctors, priests, reporters, etc. A *confidential communication* made to one of these persons entitles that person to assert the privilege of non-disclosure when called as a witness or otherwise asked to reveal the confidence.

CONFIRM, CONFIRMATION [L. *com* + *firmus* / firm, pp. of *firmo, firmare* / to make firm; strengthen]

To approve or ratify. To reiterate or reassert the truth or validity of a fact. To remove doubt about. To support or strengthen. To give formal endorsement or approval to, as to *confirm* a reorganization plan in bankruptcy or, the decision of a lower court by an appellate court. To vote in favor of a nomination for office. Also, to express in writing a commitment to the terms of a contract previously made orally.

CONFISCATE [L. *confiscare* / to lay upon, seize for the public treasury, deprive, confiscate]

To take or seize private property for use by the government, usually without compensation. Due process protections imbedded in the federal Constitution usually prevent acts of *non-compensatory confiscation* except in time of war and in the exercise of the police power. Recently, prosecutors have confiscated the private property of persons accused or convicted of a crime even when the property is not related to the crime itself.

See **CONDEMNATION; EMINANT DOMAIN; EXPROPRIATE**

CONFLICT [L. *conflictus*, pp. of *confligere* / to throw together; to strike or collide]

A dispute or disagreement. War or a fight or battle. Any competition, as between athletes, business competitors, ideas, political parties, etc. To be different from or antagonistic to. A *conflict of interest* is the antagonism between two relationships or two responsibilities, as, for example, the conflict between the personal interests of an elected representative and his responsibility to sound legislative principles or the conflict in a lawyer between his own interests and those of his client or between the competing interests of two different clients. A *conflict of laws* arises when the laws of two states or jurisdictions, both of which apply to the facts at issue, differ in their resolution of the issues presented.

CONFLICTUS LEGEM [L. *conflictus* / conflict + *lex, legis* / law]

A conflict between laws. *Conflict of Laws* is the legal discipline which deals with the questions raised by the competing laws of two or more relevant jurisdictions, and the principles involved in deciding and applying the appropriate laws.

CONFORM [L. *conformo, conformare* / to form, put together, assemble]

To give the same shape or form to one thing as to another. To add matter which creates a duplicate of a thing in existence. To be similar or identical to. To harmonize with. To modify or add to one document so as to make it an exact duplicate copy of the original. To comply with the terms or conditions of, as to *conform* to a contract or deed.

CONGLOMERATE [L. *com* + *glomero, glomerare* / to gather together; to roll into a ball; to form a sphere]

Consisting of many parts put together from different sources. An assemblage or mixture of things. Also, a diversified corporation or business which has acquired and controls many disparate companies and businesses which do not necessarily carry on the same activities as the parent company.

CONGRESS [L. *congressus*, pp. of *congredior, congredi* / to meet; to dispute]

To come together and meet. Also, a group or body which convenes to discuss and act upon some issue or question. A meeting or session. The body of delegates which acts as the official legislative body of a republic. The U.S. Congress is composed of two houses. The Senate, or upper house, has two senators from each state. The House of Representatives is comprised of representatives elected on the basis of population by the citizens of the fifty states.

CONJUGAL [L. *coniugare* / to join together, unite in marriage]

Concerning the relationships between husband and wife. Relating to marriage. Connubial.

CONNIVE [L. *coniveo, conivere* / to close one's eyes; to ignore]

To ignore or fail to act against an act or event which requires opposition. To wink at or be indulgent of. To cooperate secretly with or to join another in planning an illegal or immoral act, as *to connive with another* in an act of treason.

CONNUBIAL [L. *com* + *nubere* / to cover with a veil, to marry]

Of or related to marriage or the relation between husband and wife. Conjugal.

CONSANGUINITY [L. *com* + *sanguis* / blood]

Relationship through blood; having a common ancestor.

CONSCIENCE [L. *conscio, conscire* / to be conscious or mindful (of guilt)]

One's own personal sense and appreciation of right and wrong. One's appreciation of himself as a human being owing duties and responsibilities to himself and to others. A proper and reasonable sense of the balance between what is good and what is bad, of the differences between right and wrong.

When a person refuses to do something *in good conscience*, he means that he cannot violate his own sense of right and wrong.

CONSENSUS AD IDEM [L. *consensus* / agreement, consent + *ad* / with, at + *idem* / the same]

A meeting of the minds. Two minds with the same thought.

CONSENSUS FACIT LEGEM

The consent of the parties is the law of the matter. The agreement between the parties is the law between them.

CONSENT, CONSENSUAL [L. *com* + *sentio, sentire* / to feel]

To give approval to; to agree. To be in agreement with. To acquiesce in an act or event; e.g., the *consent* required of the U.S. Senate before a treaty can become effective. The *age of consent* is the age (different in each state) at which a person is deemed competent by law to give effective consent to such acts as marriage or sexual intercourse. *Informed consent* is the consent of a patient to a medical treatment or procedure after being given all the information necessary for a sound and reasonable decision, including the nature of the treatment and an assessment of the risks. An act is *consensual* when it involves two or more persons who agree to participate in the act voluntarily and without force or coercion, e.g., sexual intercourse between two *consenting* adults.

CONSEQUENTIAL [L. *consequor, consequi* / to follow, come after]

Following up; resulting from. A secondary result from a primary cause or effect. Also, significant, important. *Consequential damages* are damages caused not as the natural result of the injury suffered by the plaintiff but as the result instead of some factor or circumstance peculiar to the plaintiff, e.g., a special physical condition or economic circumstance (also called special damages).

CONSERVATOR [L. *conservare* / to keep, preserve]

A person appointed by the court to administer the affairs and protect the interests of another. *Conservators* manage the assets and property of infants and incompetents under the guidance of the court.

CONSIDERATION [L. *consideratio* / contemplation, consideration]

A necessary ingredient of an enforceable contract between two parties. Consideration exists when one party to a contract — the promisee — gives up something of value or suffers a legal detriment, and the other party — the promisor — gives his promise in exchange as part of a bargain or agreement between them. In other words, consideration requires the exchange of promises and/or detriments.

See **DETRIMENT**

CONSIGN, CONSIGNMENT [L. *consignare* / to seal or mark]

To deliver or turn over the care of. To give possession to an agent for purposes of sale or transfer. To transfer possession of goods to a customer for sale to the public without transferring title until sale and delivery by the customer to his purchaser. To deliver to a common carrier for transport to an agent or customer.

CONSILIUM [L. an assembly of advisors]

A deliberation; a deliberative body; a council. An advisory body. A convocation of persons assembled for the purpose of drafting ideas and offering advice.

CONSOLIDATE [L. *com* + *solidus*, pp. of *solido, solidare* / to make firm, strong or solid]

To bring together. To unite several components into a whole. A *consolidated school district* is a district composed of several smaller districts, united for purposes of greater economy and efficiency of management. To combine two or more corporations or businesses into one. To join and try together or to decide together two cases or lawsuits involving common questions of law and fact. In the federal courts, *consolidation of cases* is covered by Rule 42 of the Federal Rules of Civil Procedure. A *consolidated appeal* is a joint appeal by two parties having a common interest in the outcome. A *consolidated financial statement* is one which combines the balance sheets and profit and loss statements of a parent corporation and its subsidiaries. The *consolidated laws* of a state are a compilation of all its outstanding statutes indexed and arranged by subject.

CONSORTIUM [L. a partnership; having equal shares of; companionship]

The relationship between husband and wife, and the right of each to the company, support, sustenance and aid of the other. A person depriving either husband or wife of the *consortium* of the other may be subject to a lawsuit; e.g., an action for damages by one spouse to recover for injuries to the other spouse as a result of the defendant's negligence.

CONSPIRE, CONSPIRACY [L. *conspirare* / to blow or breathe together; to contrive or plan in unison]

To enter into an agreement with another for the commission of an unlawful or illegal act. To combine with others with intent to commit or facilitate the commission of a crime. Any agreement by two or more persons to commit a crime is itself the crime of conspiracy.

CONSTITUENT [L. *constituo, constituere*]

A member of a group. An office-holder speaks of the voters in his district as his *constituents*. A principal who authorizes another to act as his agent. An essential part of something; an element or component.

CONSTITUTE [L. *constituo, constituere* / to set up, place]

To designate or name to an office or function. To organize, set up or establish. To qualify as; e.g., a memorandum may *constitute* a contract. To make up or consist of, as in "New York lawyers *constitute* more than 10% of all lawyers in the United States."

CONSTITUTION [L. *constituere* / to set up, establish]

Originally, a law or ordinance. Now, a document which defines the rules under which a nation or state will be governed. A fundamental statement of principles of government, defining such matters as the branches of government, the functions of each branch, the division of responsibility between branches, the restraints and checks upon each branch, etc. The U.S. Constitution has served as the prototype for the constitutions of other countries. The United Kingdom has no formal written constitution but relies instead on the common law and a number of statutes adopted over the centuries. Smaller organizations may also be governed by constitutions specifying the number and duties of officers, directors, committees, etc.

CONSTRUCTIO LEGIS NON FACIT INJURIAM

No damage is caused by construing the law.

CONSTRUCTION [L. *construo, construere* / to heap up, build or construct]

The placement of words in a sentence. The process of building something. The meaning or interpretation placed upon the text of a legal document such as a contract or statute, especially an interpretation by a court.

CONSTRUCTIVE [L. *construo, construere* / to heap up, to build or construct]

A status or characteristic created by a legal fiction instead of one existing in fact. A right or duty arising out of a judicial interpretation of a relationship. Implied by operation of law. A *constructive bailment* is a bailment created not by voluntary act of the parties but by operation of law; it arises when someone comes into possession of the goods of another by accident or mistake, as by finding them or through a misdirected delivery. *Constructive delivery* is delivery implied from delivery of a token representing the whole; e.g., delivery of the keys to a building serves as constructive delivery of the entire building. *Constructive notice* is notice imputed and imposed by law when the law has created a system for making information available to all; under these circumstances, it is assumed that everyone has or should have that information. A prime example is the system of recording statutes to provide constructive notice to all of prior recorded land transactions. *Constructive adverse possession* is treated by the courts in the same way as *adverse possession* even though there is no physical possession by the claimant of the property involved. Instead, the court finds constructive adverse possession out of such facts as the payment of taxes by the claimant under color of right. The courts recognize and give effect to *constructive conditions, constructive contracts, constructive eviction, constructive force, constructive intent, constructive possession, constructive receipt, constructive trust*, etc.

CONSUL   [L. *consulere* / to reflect, consult]

The title given to both of the two chief magistrates of Rome. An official appointed by a sovereign government to protect the interests of its citizens and businessmen in a foreign country.

CONSULAR MARRIAGE

A marriage ceremony conducted before an American consul in a foreign jurisdiction. The marriage is valid in most states.

CONSULTATION   [L. *consultare* / to consider, weigh, ponder]

A meeting, conference or discussion between client and attorney, or between a patient and doctor, or between two doctors.

CONTEMPLATION   [L. *contemplari* / to examine, consider, contemplate]

The act of debating within one's mind whether or not to take a particular action or step. The act of anticipating or preparing for an event or act. To think about or consider. The word is used most often in the phrase *contemplation of death*. In that sense, it means the fear or apprehension of imminent death, not the general philosophical consideration of death we all engage in from time to time. For example, a person may be informed by his doctor that he has cancer and has two months to live. A transfer of property following this news would almost certainly be in *comtemplation of death*.

CONTEMPT, CONTEMNOR   [L. *contemnere* / to despise, hold in contempt]

Contempt is the wilful disregard or disobedience of the instructions or orders of a judge, a legislature or a public authority. A *contemnor* is anyone who commits or is guilty of contempt. Contempt may be punished by fines or imprisonment. A *civil contempt* is the disobedience of a court order in a civil action. Sanctions are imposed by the court to compel compliance. *Criminal contempt* is conduct by a party or an attorney in disrupting the court or prevented it from carrying on its proceedings in an orderly way; the court will impose fines and sanctions.

See **CONTUMACY**

CONTEST [L. *contestor, contestari* / to call a witness; to start an action by summoning witnesses]

To dispute or challenge. To litigate; to make the subject of a dispute or litigation. To reject a claim or demand. A competition to determine the truth or the superiority of one participant over another.

CONTIGUOUS [L. *contingere* / to touch, to have contact with]

Describes two pieces of land which have a common boundary or border or which touch at any given point.

CONTINGENT, CONTINGENCY [L. contingere]

An event which may or may not happen. A condition which may or may not be satisfied. A fortuitous event which happens without plan or anticipation. A *contingent fee agreement* is an agreement between lawyer and client under which the attorney will be compensated only if there is recovery. A *contingent beneficiary* is anyone who will succeed to a benefit only if a primary beneficiary dies before him. A *contingent liability* is a liability which can be anticipated but which will arise only if a future and uncertain event actually occurs. A guarantor is *contingently liable* for the debts of the principal debtor.

CONTINUANCE [L. *continuare* / to unite, connect]

In law, the postponement or adjournment of a hearing, trial or other proceeding to another day, usually at the request of one of the parties.

CONTRA [L. against; opposed to; on the opposite side]

Contrary to; in violation of; in defiance of; e.g., "the view of the New York court is *contra* the decision of the New Jersey court."

CONTRA BONOS MORES

Against good morals; conduct which is so bad or unacceptable as to violate general social standards.

See **BONOS MORES**

CONTRACT [L. *contrahere* / to draw together, unite, to agree or contract]

A set of enforceable promises between parties creating obligations to do or to refrain from doing specified acts. An arrangement or set of promises recognized by the law and for which the law gives a remedy in the event of breach, or the performance of which the law regards as a duty.

CONTRACTOR [L. *contrahere*]

Anyone who enters into a contract. One who agrees to provide specified services or labor in exchange for payment. Anyone who promises or undertakes to construct a building or a part of a building.

CONTRA LEGEM TERRAE
Against the law of the land.

CONTRA PACEM [L. against the public peace]
This Latin phrase was formerly used verbatim in indictments; most indictments now recite that the defendant has committed a "crime against the public peace."

CONTRA PREFERENTUM
A doctrine applied to interpretation or construction of documents which provides that ambiguities in language are to be construed against the draftsman.

CONTRIBUTE, CONTRIBUTION [L. *contribuere* / to put together with, to unite]
To give in support of. To give aid to. To pay into a common fund or give for a public purpose. To play a significant part in. In law, *to contribute* means to supply one of the causes of, to help create. For example, in the event of an accident or injury resulting from negligence, liability will be assessed against all those who *contributed* to the occurrence. *Contribution* is the term applied to the right of anyone who has satisfied a liability shared by others to ask for and receive an aliquot share from those others. In this way, one joint tort feasor is entitled to *contribution* from the other tort feasors.

CONTRIBUTORY [L. *contribuere*]
To make a contribution to. To act as a part or cause of. The act of providing funds to a common fund or enterprises such as an employee benefit plan or a group health insurance plan. Participating in or causing an end or a result. *Contributory fault* is an act by a promisor which makes performance of his promise impossible; because he is at fault, he cannot rely on the defense of impossibility. *Contributory negligence* is negligence by the plaintiff which contributes to the occurrence and/or injury complained of.

CONTROL [L. *contra* / opposite to, against + *roto, rotare* / to cause to turn]
To exercise dominion or influence over. To regulate or impose power over. To rule or dominate. To have a dominant interest in, e.g., to have a *controlling interest* in a business or corporation. A *controlled substance*, usually a drug, is a substance the sale, use and consumption of which are regulated by law.

CONTROVERSY [L. *controversia, controversus* / a dispute, especially a litigation; also, the subject of a dispute]
Opposing views. A dispute. A civil action to resolve a dispute between two parties. The U.S. Constitution delegates to the courts the power to adjudicate "cases and controversies."

CONTUMACY [L. *contumacia* / stubbornness, stubborn refusal]

The refusal of a person to obey an order or decree issued by a court. Wilful disobedience of a court order. The person who refuses to obey the order is said to be contumacious and is subject to being held in contempt.

See **CONTEMPT**

CONVENTION [L. *convenio, convenire* / to come together, to meet; to assemble]

A pact among nations resolving a dispute among them or dealing with matters of concern to all of them. Among the best known is the Geneva Convention of 1864 which dealt with the treatment of prisoners of war and of combatants who were wounded in battle. Also, any contract or agreement. Any principle or rule accepted as generally true or persuasive. Also, any assemblage of persons to consider and reach decisions on matters of common interest, e.g., the conventions of political parties to choose candidates for public office or of church groups to adopt statements of social policy.

CONVENTIO VINCIT ET DAT LEGEM

A (binding) agreement prevails and determines the law (of the case).

CONVERT, CONVERSION [L. *converto, convertere* / to turn around; move in the opposite direction]

To change a fundamental belief, as to convert from one religion to another or from one political philosophy to another. To appropriate the property of another without right. To change the physical or chemical properties of. To exchange one kind of property for another, as *to convert* the common shares of a corporation into preferred stock or bonds of the company. *Conversion* is the unlawful usurpation of control over the property of another, usually after the property has been entrusted to the converter by the owner for safekeeping. In a bailment, for example, the refusal of the bailee to return the goods to the bailor would constitute *conversion*. The defendant in an action for conversion is required to pay the full value of the property.

CONVERTIBLE [L. *convertere* / to turn around, spin around]

Capable of being exchanged for another specified asset or chattel of equivalent value. A *convertible bond or debenture* can be exchanged for common stock of the same company on the occurrence of specified conditions.

CONVEY, CONVEYANCE [L. *com* / with + *via* / road or way]

To transfer an interest in real property from one to another. Also, the document which is used to effect or execute the transfer; e.g., a deed, mortgage or assignment.

CONVICT [L. *convinco, convincere* / to convict of a crime; to prove a mistake or error]

To find someone guilty after consideration of the evidence. To determine guilt of a criminal offense. A *convict* is a person convicted, or found guilty, of a crime.

CONVICTION [L. *convincere*]

The act of determining that an accused is guilty of the acts charged. An official judicial determination of guilt in a criminal offense. Also, a compelling attitude or belief.

COORDINATE [L. *co + ordinare* / to put in order]

Of the same rank; equal to. In harmony with. Courts of the same rank or authority with equal competence to deal with a particular matter have *coordinate and concurrent jurisdiction*.

COPARCENARY [L. *co + partitio* (from *partiri* / to distribute, share) / a division or sharing]

Joint ownership, as by joint heirs.

See **PARCENARY**

CORAM

Before you personally, in your presence, openly.

CORAM NOBIS [L. *coram* / in presence of + *nobilis* / known, well-known]

Before us, in our presence. A writ which brings to the trial court's attention errors in fact, such as the existence of a valid defense, which were not disclosed earlier because of mistake, duress or fraud and which would have resulted in a different verdict or judgment if known. It differs from an appeal in that it is directed to the trial court and not an appellate court. The writ has been abolished by the Federal Rules of Civil Procedure.

See **ERROR CORAM NOBIS**

CORAM NON JUDICE [L. *coram + non + iudico, iudicare* / to judge]

A proceeding before, or determination by, a judge who has no authority or jurisdiction to deal with the matter.

CORAM VOBIS

Before you. A writ of error directed by an appellate court to the trial court instructing the court to correct an error in fact and render judgment accordingly. This writ has been abolished under the FRCP, along with the writ of *coram nobis*.

CORPORAL PUNISHMENT [L. *corpus* / body + *punior, puniri* / to punish]

Punishment inflicted upon the body of an accused or felon. *Corporal punishment* is covered under the Eighth Amendment to the U.S. Constitution, which forbids "cruel and unusual punishment." As interpreted by the Court, this language precludes most forms of corporal punishment. However, the Court has held that the death penalty does not violate this provision.

See **CRUEL**

CORPORATION [L. *corpus* / body]

An artificial legal entity formed under authority of a state charter to act and transact business in the same way as a single person and enjoying the rights and duties set forth in its charter, including the right to perpetual existence, limited liability for its owners and the right to sue and be sued. A *municipal corporation* is a political entity organized by the state under the laws governing corporations to act as an independent state agency, with the power to sue and be sued and to exercise the power of eminent domain.

CORPOREAL [L. *corpus* / the body, matter perceived by the senses]

Having a tangible form or body. Palpable to the senses. Anything possessing an objective, material existence. Distinguished from the spiritual or intangible.

See **TANGIBLE**

CORPOREAL HEREDITAMENTS [L. *corpus* + *hereditas* / inheritance]

The word *hereditaments* describes anything which can be inherited. It includes both tangible (e.g., a painting, a plot of land) and intangible (e.g., a copyright, the right to income under a trust) assets. *Corporeal hereditaments* are all tangible assets capable of inheritance. All intangible assets capable of inheritance are called *incorporeal hereditaments*.

See **INCORPOREAL HEREDITAMENTS**

CORPUS [L. body]

A body or collection of identifiable parts. An aggregation of things. In the law of wills and trusts, the collection of property and interests which constitute the principal of a trust.

CORPUS DELICTI [L. *corpus* + *delictum* / fault, crime]

Body or substance of the crime; any object proving that a crime may have been committed. A charred house and an empty gasoline can are the *corpus delicti* of arson. Objective proof that a crime has been committed. The body of the victim of a homicide. Generally, an objective showing that a crime, any crime, has been committed and that there is an identifiable victim.

CORPUS JURIS   [L. *corpus* / body + *ius, iuris* / right, law]

Body of law. Refers to a compendium of the law; *i.e.*, a series of books setting forth the civil law or canon [ecclesiastical] law or American law. One collection of American law is known as *Corpus Juris Secundum.*

CORRIGENDUM   [L. *corrigere* / to correct]

An error or omission in a printed document which is discovered only after the printing is completed; the error is usually explained and corrected on a separate sheet distributed with the document.

See **ERRATUM**

CORROBORATE   [L. *corrobare* / to strengthen, reinvigorate]

To strengthen, give support to. To confirm a fact by additional proof. To add weight or credibility. *Corroborating evidence* is additional testimony or proof tending to strengthen other evidence already given in a matter.

CORRUPT   [L. *corrumpere* / to break into pieces; destroy; spoil, damage]

Spoiled, debased, rotten. Morally depraved. Preferring wrong to right. To change from good to bad. To cause another to lose his moral values.

COUNCIL   [L. *concilium* / a coming together, a union (from *concilio, conciliare* / to bring together, unite)]

Any assembly or meeting. A legislative body elected to consult and make laws. An appointed agency or authority. A meeting of delegates representing units in a federation. An amalgamation of independent organizations with a common purpose, such as a *Labor Council* composed of individual unions.

COUNSEL   [L. *consulere* / to reflect, consider, deliberate]

To give advice after consultation and deliberation. The advice and assistance offered by a lawyer to her client after consultation with respect to any legal matter. The title given to a lawyer or attorney. The Constitution guarantees the right to "the assistance of counsel" to all criminal defendants. Amendment VI.

COURT   [L. *cohors* / an enclosure or yard, especially for cattle]

An official body for the administration of justice and the adjustment of disputes. A single unit of the justice system and of the judicial branch of state or federal government. A place or building for the dispensation of justice. A judge or judges while exercising judicial functions. A *trial court* is a court of original jurisdiction which hears witnesses and resolves disputes. The federal trial courts are known as district courts. An *appellate court* is a court which considers and rules upon allegations of error by the trial courts. A *court of last resort* is the highest appellate court in a jurisdiction. In New York, the court of last resort is the Court of Appeals.

COVENANT   [L. *convenire* / to meet, to assemble, to agree upon]

A contract. An enforceable agreement between two or more parties providing for the performance or non-performance of certain specified acts. A provision in a contract or in a legal document such as a deed or mortgage. Promises relating to conveyances of real property. For example, a *covenant of quiet enjoyment* is a promise by the grantor that no one will disturb the grantee by claiming a superior title or the right of possession. A *covenant of seisin* is a warranty to the grantee that the grantor owns the estate he is conveying.

COVER   [L. *cooperio, cooperire* / to cover, envelop, overwhelm]

To guard from attack. To protect or secure against, especially by providing compensation or indemnity for. To provide funds for, such as to *cover a check*. To conceal from sight or disclosure. To engage in business or to perform services within a designated area, as in "he covers the whole state in his delivery truck." In the law of sales, the purchase of goods by a buyer in substitution for goods which his seller has failed to deliver as agreed. Under the Uniform Commercial Code, the buyer has the option of *covering* and suing for the difference between the cost of *cover* and the original purchase price, or of seeking damages for the seller's nonperformance.

COVERTURE   [L. *cooperire* / to cover, envelop]

Under the common law, the status of a married woman, originally including the inability to own property in her own right.

CRASSA NEGLIGENTIA   [L. *crassus* / dense, thick + *negligentia* / carelessness, negligence]

Gross negligence.

CREDIBILITY, CREDIBLE   [L. *credo, credere* / to trust, rely upon, believe]

Entitled to be believed. The quality of inducing trust or belief. In law, facts or circumstances which merit belief. *Credible evidence is* evidence which appears to a reasonable person to be reliable proof, not only because it proceeds from a reliable source, but also because it conforms to general experience and is inherently plausible. A *credible witness* is one who gives *credible evidence*.

CREDIT   [L. *credo, credere* / to entrust, commit to the custody of, trust]

The balance in a person's account. The sum on deposit by a person in a bank or trust account. That sum of money which one person is willing to permit another person to owe and to pay later. Any one item, or the sum of all items, entered on the right side of the ledger in double-entry bookkeeping. To supply goods to another without demanding immediate payment therefore. To attribute or designate. Resources available in the present upon a promise of subsequent repayment, usually with interest for the use of the resources. Recognition and respect, as in the *full faith and credit* which each state must accord the laws and judicial determinations of every other state under the Constitution.

CREDITOR   [L. *creditor* / a creditor (from *credo, credere*)]

Any person to whom a debt is owed. Any person who is entitled to receive money or goods from another without further performance on his part. A *general* or *unsecured creditor* is a creditor who has no security for his debt. A *secured creditor* is a creditor with a security interest in the property or assets of the debtor.

CRIME   [L. *crimen* / an accusation or charge; fault, guilt, crime]

Any act or failure to act which is forbidden or circumscribed by law and which subjects the actor to punishment by society. Any offense defined in a statute or at common law as a harm to an individual or to society requiring punishment. All crimes share the following basic elements: a voluntary act by the perpetrator (*actus reus*); a culpable intent or state of mind (*mens rea*); a convergence of the *actus reus* and the *mens rea*; and resulting harm to someone or to society. The states have now codified almost all crimes, including those which existed at common law. A felony is generally a crime punishable by a prison sentence of one year or more, or by the death penalty. A misdemeanor is a crime which is not defined as a felony.

See **ACTUS REUS; MENS REA**

CRIMEN   [crime; the infraction or breach with which a defendant is charged]

A crime; a violation of law.

CRIMEN FALSI   [L. *crimen* + *falsus*, pp. of *fallo, fallere* / to deceive]

A crime of deceit; a crime such as forgery, perjury, counterfeiting or embezzlement, involving elements of fraud or trickery. At common law, a person convicted of such a crime was prevented from testifying as a witness in any matter.

See **FALSI CRIMEN**

CRUEL, CRUELTY   [L. *crudelis* / unfeeling, cruel (from *crudus* / bleeding, raw, harsh)]

Capable of inflicting pain or suffering upon another. Causing harm, injury or grief. The conduct of one spouse in endangering the life, health or safety of the other, or of a parent in injuring or jeopardizing the safety of a child. Mistreatment or neglect causing injury or suffering. *Cruelty* is often included as an aggravating circumstance in the definition of a crime. In most jurisdictions *cruelty* is grounds for divorce. The Constitution prohibits *cruel and unusual punishment* in the administration of justice and in the application of punishment for crimes. The definition of *cruel and unusual punishment* varies from state to state and from case to case; the Supreme Court has made it clear, however, that the death penalty does not constitute cruel and unusual punishment.

See **CORPORAL PUNISHMENT**

CULPA   [L. *culpo, culpare* / to blame, accuse]

Fault, blame, neglect, as in *culpable negligence*; i.e., negligence which goes beyond ordinary negligence; i.e., a conscious disregard of the rights or safety of others.

See **DOLUS**

CUM   [L. together with]

A preposition meaning *with, together with*.

CUM DIVIDEND

The right of a buyer of stock to receive and collect any dividend on the stock which was declared but unpaid at the time of sale.

CUM ONERE   [L. *cum + onus, oneris* / a weight, a burden]

With all the burdens. A right or privilege which comes with burdens and responsibilities.

CUM POTESTATE LEGIS   [L. *cum + potestas* / power + *lex, legis* / law, rule]

With all the power of the law.

CUM TESTAMENTO ANNEXO (C.T.A.)

Literally, with the will annexed. The designation of an administrator appointed to administer an estate when no executor has been named in a will or the executor named is unable or unwilling to serve.

CUMULATIVE   [L. *cumulare* / to heap up, fill up, load]

The addition of new material of the same kind. The result of a continuing increase in facts or circumstances. Used as an adjective to indicate that something has been added or is being added. *Cumulative dividends* are dividends which accrue over time but remain unpaid. *Cumulative sentences* are consecutive sentences for different crimes committed by the same defendant.

CURA   [L. *curare* / to care for, attend to]

Care, charge, responsibility. At civil law, the guardian of a young adult.

CURATOR [L. *cura* / care, concern]

A person responsible for the care or management of a designated person or thing. A temporary guardian or conservator appointed by the court to care for the assets or person of an incompetent or an infant. Also, a person charged with the care or administration of a library, museum or zoo.

CURE, CURATIVE [L. *curo, curare* / to care for, pay attention to; to cure]

To restore to good health. To rectify or improve. To free from harm or injury. To eliminate an error or correct a mistake, as when the decision of an appellate court *cures* an error by a lower court. Also, to restore to compliance or eliminate a defect, as when a breach under a contract is *cured* by subsequent performance. In bankruptcy, to negate a default by the debtor by restoring him to his position before the bankruptcy filing. A *curative act* is an act which eliminates a defect, failure or shortcoming, as when a party to a contract takes steps to cure a breach.

CURIA [L. A division of Roman leaders. The meeting place of the Roman Senate]

A district, ward; meeting place; court. A court of justice.

CURIA ADVISARI VULT

Literally, the court wants to look at the matter in more detail; the court wishes to take the matter under advisement. Used to indicate that a judge has reserved decision at the close of a hearing or argument. (Abbreviation: *cur. adv. vult* or *c.a.v.*)

CURIA MAGNA

The Great Court. Used to describe the English Parliament.

CURIA REGIS

The King's court.

CURRENT [L. *curro, currere* / to run, rush, hasten]

The present time. Happening or elapsing at the moment. Prevalent; existing. Also, the flow of a stream or of an electric charge. A *current asset* is either cash or another asset which can be readily converted to cash, such as bank accounts, accounts or notes receivable, saleable inventory, etc.

CURTILAGE [L. *cohors* / yard or enclosure]

The land or yard around a house, sometimes defined by a fence or other enclosure, together with those buildings thereon which are necessary for habitation and use of the house. The rules governing searches and seizures permit the police with a valid warrant to include in their search those structures and outbuildings which are within the *curtilage* of a residence.

CUSTODIAL [L. *custodia* / custody, care]

Relating to the maintenance and care of another, as in the relationship between a parent and child or a guardian and ward. Protection over. Having responsibility for the care of another. To place a person under *custodial arrest* is to incarcerate him after an arrest.

CUSTODIA LEGIS

Under custody of the law. Custody according to law. Legal custody.

CUSTODY [L. *custodia* / watching, guarding, care]

Care and charge of a thing or person. In the case of a child, the care and maintenance of the child, including control over her health and condition. *Custody* may be awarded by a court after hearing evidence about the level of current care. With respect to criminals, *custody* is the physical detention and imprisonment of an accused or of a convict. Property may be taken *in custody* by a police officer under order of a court.

CUSTOM [L. *consuescere* / to accustom, become habitual, become accustomed to]

A practice which is widely observed and tolerated in a particular place or area; accepted conduct. A practice having the force of law. A relationship recognized and enforced by the courts because of the universality of its acceptance.

CUSTOM OF MERCHANTS

The body of law governing commercial transactions which was incorporated into the common law of England. Sometimes called the law merchant.

See **LEX MERCATORIA**

DACTYLOGRAPHY [L. *dactyl* / finger + *graphium* / a stylus, a pointed instrument]

The study of fingerprints and their use in identifying each human being separately from all others.

DAMAGE, DAMAGES [L. *damnum* / loss, injury, damage]

The law makes a distinction between *damage* and *damages*. *Damage* is the loss or harm which a person suffers from the wrong of another and which is recognized as requiring reimbursement or compensation. *Damages* constitute the reimbursement or compensation itself; i.e., the money awarded by the courts to anyone who has suffered loss or injury through the acts or omissions of another.

DAMNATUS [L. *damnare* / to condemn, sentence, punish]

Illegal. Also condemned, found guilty, sentenced for a crime.

DAMNOSA HEREDITAS [L. *damnosus* / causing loss or damage, ruinous + *hereditas* / inheritance]

Anything acquired or inherited which creates more burdens than benefits; e.g., a bequest saddled with onerous debts.

See **HAEREDITAS DAMNOSA**

DAMNUM ABSQUE INJURIA [L. *damnum* / loss, damage + *absque* / without + *iniuria* / wrong, injustice]

Literally, harm or loss without wrong. The rules which distinguish between those wrongs which are legally compensible or recognized by the courts and those which are not. Some examples of harm which are not recognized by the courts: when harm results from a lawful activity or process; when the injuries fall outside a definable legal right; and when the damage is caused by an act of God.

DAMNUM FATALE [L. *damnum* + *fatalis* / concerned with destiny or fate]

Loss or injury resulting from the intervention of fate rather than from a cause within the control of human beings. The term would embrace acts of God such as lightning, earthquakes, and volcanic eruptions.

DAMNUM INFECTUM [L. *damnum* + *infectus* / unfinished, not yet done]

Damage which has not matured or occurred but which is feared or anticipated.

DAMNUM SINE INJURIA ESSE POTEST

There can be no damage without the violation of a legal right.

DARE JUDICIUM [L. *dato, dare* / to give, dispense + *iudicium* / trial, litigation, judgment]

To render judgment. To reach a decision. To decide a case.

DATUM

A thing given or done; an item of information. Also, a date. Also, the singular of data, which is always plural.

DE AEQUITATE [L. *aequo, aequare* / to make equal]

In equity.

See **AEQUITAS; EQUITY**

DE AEQUITATE ET LEGEM CONJUCTA

When equity and the law meet or converge.

DE ARBITRIATONE FACTA

An old common law writ for restraining an action which had already been submitted to arbitration.

DE BENE ESSE

Conditionally; provisionally. For whatever it's worth. Of temporary validity. Used to describe several conditional acts or documents. An *appearance de bene esse* is a conditional appearance; a *deposition de bene esse* is a deposition which is taken conditionally and which will not be used if the witness appears at the trial. *Evidence de bene esse* is evidence taken and recorded before trial to preserve it in the event the witness is later unavailable.

See **DEPOSITION DE BENE ESSE; EVIDENCE DE BENE ESSE**

DEBENTURE [L. *debeo, debere* / to owe, be bound to]

Obligations of corporations evidenced by bonds or notes and providing for fixed interest and principal payments. *Debentures* are distinguished from the capital stock or shares of the corporation. They are usually long-term and need not be secured by any specific asset. *Debenture holders* are creditors of the corporation and will receive payment before shareholders in the event of dissolution.

DEBET ET DETINET [L. *debeo, debere* / to owe + *detineo, detinere* / to hold back, detain]

He owes and detains. A common law writ to recover a debt.

See **DETINUE**

DEBITA FUNDI [L. *debere* / to owe + *fundare* / to make firm]

Debts secured by real property.

DEBITORES IN SOLIDO [L. *debere* + *solidus* / firm, solid, all-encompassing]

Joint debtors or obligors.

DE BONE MEMORIE

Possessing good memory. Of sound mind.

See **COMPOS MENTIS**

DE BONIS ASPORTATIS [L. *de* / from, of, concerning + *bonus* / goods or chattels + *asportare* / to carry away]

At common law, *trespass de bonis asportatis* was an action for the recovery of personal property.

See **TRESPASS DE BONIS ASPORTATIS**

DE BONIS DEFUNCTI

From the belongings and assets of the deceased.

DE BONIS INTESTATI

From the goods of one who is intestate.

DE BONIS NON ADMINISTRATIS [L. *de* + *bonis* + *non* + *administrare* / to administer, manage, direct]

When an administrator who has not completed his administration of an estate dies or is removed, he is replaced by an *administrator de bonis non*.

See **ADMINISTRATOR DE BONIS NON**

DE BONIS NON AMOVENDIS

A writ to prevent the removal of goods pending a court's decision on the merits.

DE BONIS PROPRIS [L. *de* + *bonis* + *propris, proprius* / one's own, belonging to oneself]

From his own goods or assets. The obligation of a fiduciary who has wasted the assets of the estate or trust with which he is charged to repay the resulting loss. To be subject to a judgment against one's own assets.

DEBT, DEBTOR [L. *debeo, debere* / to owe]

Anything owed. An obligation to pay or provide something of value. A sum of money due from one person to another, usually for money loaned or for the value of something sold. A *bad debt* is a debt which cannot be collected. At common law, an action to recover money owed was called an *action of debt*. A *debtor* is any person who owes a debt. Under the Bankruptcy Code, a person who files a petition or against whom an involuntary petition is filed is called a *debtor*.

DE CAPITE MINUTIS [L. *de* + *capite* / head + *minuere* / to make smaller]

Literally, to make the head smaller. Describes a person who has been deprived of her citizenship.

DECEIT, DECEIVE, DECEPTION [L. *decipio, decipere* / to cheat, deceive]

Deceit is a deliberate act of concealment or fraud. An action for deceit is an action in tort to recover for damages caused by the defendant's lies or concealment. To *deceive* is to lead another to believe a fact which is false. *Deception* is the act of misleading someone into believing the truth of something which is in fact false and untrue. A trick; a lie or falsehood.

DECIDE [L. *decidere,* from *de* + *caedare* / to cut down, to strike]

To reach a conclusion; to arrive at a solution or resolution. To choose a course of action. In law, a court *decides* or resolves an issue or dispute, by weighing the proof and evidence for and against.

DECISION [L. *decidere*

In law, a determination or adjudication pronounced by a court or by an administrative agency resolving the issues and matters referred to it by the parties. A statement of the findings of fact and conclusions of law reached by the court after hearing and weighing all the proof and evidence submitted to it. Decisions may be reached at various stages in a trial or proceeding, including decisions on motions, etc.

DECLARATION [L. *declarare* / to make visible or clear]

To make clear or emphatic. To announce, make public. Also, the name for the first pleading in a common law action, now commonly called the complaint. Also, the statement of incoming merchandise or goods made to customs agents by persons entering the United States.

DECLARATORY JUDGMENT

A judicial pronouncement of the rights and duties of parties who petition the court to determine and define those rights and duties without requesting any other relief (such as damages or an injunction). The court will issue a declaratory judgment if there is a controversy between the parties which can be resolved by a declaration of rights and duties. Provision for declaratory judgment in the federal courts is made in 28 U.S.C.A. 2201.

DE COMPUTO [L. *de* + *computare* / to calculate, compute]

A writ requiring the defendant to give an accounting to the plaintiff. The forerunner of the action of account or for an accounting.

DE CONCILIS CURIAE

By direction of the court.

DECREE [L. *decernere* / to decide, determine]

Originally, a determination on the merits by a court of chancery or equity. This distinguished a *decree* from a *judgment*, which was normally awarded only in courts of law. The distinction is ignored by most modern courts.

DECREE ABSOLVITOR

A decree of acquittal in a criminal matter.

DECREE NISI [L. *nisi* / if not, unless]

A provisional decree of divorce, which becomes absolute only upon the passage of a specified interval of time, usually six months. Also, a decree which becomes effective at a future date in the absence of an intervening application or order; or a provisional decree which becomes final only on the entry of a final order following a motion.

DECREE NUN PRO TUNC

An order of a court which has retroactive effect, usually as of a date specified; generally used to correct some defect in a pleading or other proceeding.

See **NUNC PRO TUNC**

DECREE PRO CONFESSO

A decree in an action in equity in favor of the plaintiff upon the defendant's default.

See **PRO CONFESSO**

DEDICATE [L. *dedicare* / to point out, indicate; to dedicate]

To commit to a particular purpose or end. To devote to. To set apart for a specific use. To donate or commit private property to public use. To surrender a copyright or patent to public use, or to release to the public material or property which is entitled to protection under a copyright or patent.

DE DIE IN DIEM

From day to day.

DEDI ET CONCESSI [L. *dare* / to give + *concessio* / a giving-up, the act of yielding]

I have given and yielded. These were the words of grant used in Roman deeds.

DE DOLO MALO [L. *de* + *dolus* / a scheme or device; fraud + *malus* / bad, evil]

From an evil or wicked scheme. Arising out of fraud or deceit.

DEDUCT, DEDUCTION [L. *deduco, deducere* / to lead away; to draw away; to take away]

To subtract from an amount; to take away part of a number. A *deduction* is any amount which can be subtracted from gross income under applicable tax laws or regulations in order to adjust or decrease the amount of tax which would otherwise be due. A *charitable deduction* is the deduction permitted for the taxpayer's contributions to a qualified charity. In computing federal income taxes, deductions are allowed for business expenses, dependents, some medical expenses, etc.

DEDUCTIBLE [L. *deduco, deducere*]

An amount allowed as a deduction in computing taxes due. Also, the clause in an insurance policy which permits an insurance carrier to subtract from its payments an amount specified in the clause.

DE FACTO [L. *de* + *facere* / to make do]

In fact; in reality; actually. Anything which exists in fact but not necessarily of right. A body, group, institution, committee, person or entity which exercises, or acts in given circumstances as though it had, the authority to perform a given act, without necessarily having such authority. A usurpation of authority. Used in conjunction with other words or phrases, as follows: *de facto authority; de facto board of directors; de facto court; de facto incumbent; de facto judge; de facto jury; de facto officer; de facto trustee; de facto segregation.* In all these cases, the sense is of authority claimed or exercised without legal right. A *de facto merger* occurs when one corporation purchases the assets of another and assumes all its debts but fails to call the transaction a merger.

See **DE JURE**

DEFALCATE [L. *de* + *falcatus* / sickle, scythe — to take another's scythe or tool]

To misappropriate funds or money in one's charge; to embezzle; to misapply trust funds.

DEFAMATION [L. *dis* + *fama* / report, rumor, reputation, public opinion]

To malign or harm the reputation of another through either libel or slander. The publication of anything which attacks or diminishes the name or reputation of another. Exposing another to public ridicule or scorn.

DEFAMATION PER QUOD

Published language or matter which is not clearly and obviously defamatory on its face but which can be shown by external proof to apply to the complainant and which were published with the intent required for either libel or slander.

See **PER QUOD**

DEFAMATION PER SE

Published language or matter which is clearly defamatory on its face.

DEFAME [L. *dis* / separate, apart + *fama* / rumor, public opinion, reputation]

To attack the reputation of. To slander or libel. To spread rumors or news about a person with intent to damage his standing or reputation.

DEFEASANCE [L. *de* + *facio, facere* / to make, do]

To undo; to make null and void. To terminate a property right as provided in a deed or other legal instrument. A term or condition in an instrument, e.g., a will or deed, which operates to terminate an interest in property.

DEFECT, DEFECTIVE [L. *deficere* / to fail, undo]

An essential lack or shortcoming. An imperfection that reduces value or utility. In law, a *defect* is a flaw that is recognized as having a negative impact on a right. The party who is responsible for the defect may be required to correct it or to compensate the aggrieved party in damages. *A defect of parties*, is the lack of all parties necessary to give a court jurisdiction over a matter. Lawyers talk of *defective pleadings, defective title, a defective record*. In all these instances, they are describing a lack of some essential requirement or detail.

DEFECTUS JURISDICTIONIS [L. *defectus* / a fault or failing + *iurisdictio* / judicial authority]

A lack or failure of jurisdiction.

DEFECTUS SANGUINIS [L. *deficere* / to fail, undo + *sanguis* / blood]

Lack of a blood relationship. Having no heirs capable of inheritance.

DEFEND, DEFENSE [L. *defendere* / to repel, fight off]

To protect against. To repel danger or an attack. To guard a place or position against an enemy. In law, to oppose a claim or action. To plead against a complaint or petition. To deny allegations or arguments by the other party. A *defense attorney* is a lawyer who regularly represents defendants in civil or criminal cases.

DEFENDANT [L. *defendere*]

The person (artificial or natural) against whom an action or proceeding is commenced and who is asked to respond. Also, a party who asks leave of the court to join in an action for the purpose of defeating the plaintiff's claim or demand.

DEFER, DEFERRED [L. *defero, deferre* / to take, lead or drive away]

To put off to a later time. To postpone or delay. *Deferred compensation* is compensation earned but not yet paid. A *deferred payment* is a payment due but withheld.

DEFICIENCY [L. *deficio, deficire* / to fail; to abandon; to be short in accomplishment or performance]

A shortage; an amount which is less than scheduled or anticipated. In tax terminology, the difference between the tax owed and the amount paid. Also, in bankruptcy or creditor's rights, the amount owing by a debtor which the creditor is unable to collect by resort to the debtor's collateral. A creditor secured by a mortgage upon real property who is unable to collect the full amount of the mortgage debt in foreclosure is entitled to recover a *deficiency judgment* for the uncollected balance. Before the IRS moves to recover a deficiency in Tax Court, it makes a *deficiency assessment* and then sends a *deficiency notice*.

DEFINE, DEFINED [L. *definio, definere* / to limit, mark, set boundaries for]

To ascertain and fix the meaning of. To set the boundaries for. The word *defined* is used to indicate that a number of interlocking and related issues have been reduced to a set of rules or standards. A *defined benefit plan*, for example, is a plan adopted by an employer which sets forth and defines the rights of employees after retirement, including a formula which governs the benefits to be paid to them upon retirement. A *defined contribution plan* fixes the amount to be contributed by the employer to a retirement plan and the formula for allocating the contributions among its employees.

DEFUNCT [L. *de* + *funerare* / to bury, inter]

Dead, no longer alive. A decedent. A non-functioning organization; e.g., a *defunct committee*.

DEI GRATIA

By the grace of God.

DEI JUDICIUM
The judgment of God.

DE INIURIA SUA PROPRIA ABSQUE TALI CAUSA
See **DE INJURIA**

DE INJURIA   [L. *de* + *iniuria* / injury, injustice, wrong]
Abbreviation for the full phrase *de iniuria sua propria absque tali causa*. This was the plea entered by a tort defendant when he was willing to admit that he had committed the injury to the plaintiff but wanted also to assert facts by way of justification, excuse or mitigation.

DE INJURIA SUA
(Resulting) from his own wrongful act.

DE JUDICIIS
Concerning judicial proceedings.

DE JURE   [L. *de* + *ius, iuris* / right, law]
By right, by justice, by force of law. Lawful; legitimate. The valid, lawful power to do or perform a given act. Contrasted with *de facto*. *De facto segregation* is segregation which exists as a matter of practice, fact and history; *de jure segration* is segregation imposed or created by a law or statute. A *de jure* corporation is a corporation created by the state after observing and fulfilling all legal requirements. A *de facto* corporation is one which conducts its business as though it had all the requisite authority but which does not in fact have it.
See **DE FACTO**

DE JURE COMMUNI
At common law.

DEL CREDERE   [L. *de* + *credere* / to trust, entrust, commit]
An agency built on trust. An agency in which a seller's agent is entrusted with custody of goods and the authority to deliver them to a buyer in exchange for payment. Also, a transaction in which one who acts as agent for another in the sale of an item guarantees the credit of the purchaser, usually for an extra sales commission. A *del credere* agent acts as surety for the benefit of his principal in transactions with third-parties.
See **AGENCY DEL CREDERE**

DELECTUS (DILECTUS) PERSONA   [L. *delectus* / a choice + *persona* / person, character (from the mask worn by actors in Roman plays)]

Choosing the person. The right of a partner in a firm or a stockholder in a close corporation to approve or reject a new partner or stockholder. The right is often reflected in restrictions on new partners or shareholders in partnership or shareholder agreements.

DELEGATE   [L. *de* + *legare* / to appoint, ordain, deputize]

To give authority to another. To appoint as one's representative or agent. Also, the person so authorized or appointed. A person designated to represent and vote the will or wish of others at a convention or caucus.

DELEGATUS NON POTEST DELEGARE

One who acts for another cannot delegate his authority to a third person. An agent cannot create the authority under which he functions without the consent of his principal, who must define the agent's duties. In an elected legislature, for example, the person holding the office of representative must cast his own vote; he cannot delegate his power to vote to anyone else.

DELIBERATE   [L. *delibero, deliberare* / to weigh, think about, consider]

To examine and consider carefully before reaching a conclusion or decision. The process by which a group or body reaches a decision on a matter or issue; the discussion and consultation which precede a decision. Also, characterized by slow and careful thought and study before taking action on a matter; having concern for the consequences of one's actions.

DELICTUM   [L. fault, offense, wrong]

A wrongful act, used both in tort law and in criminal law.

See **EX DELICTO; IN DELICTO; INPARI DELICTO**

DELINQUENCY   [L. *delinquere* / to fail, commit a crime]

A failure or neglect to do or perform something expected or required. Conduct that fails to conform to accepted behavior. A misdeed, a crime. Also, the failure to pay one's debts as they become due. Failure to perform a duty according to its terms; e.g., failure to pay a note on the due date. In the case of juveniles, conduct which violates some regulation or law or which falls outside accepted behavior.

DELIVER   [L. *de* + *liberare* / to set free]

To hand over or surrender. To take or pick up at one place and transport and turn over at another place. To accomplish or complete. To produce or act as promised. To speak or perform, as to deliver an address or recital. To convey, give or sell; place into the possession or control of.

DELIVERY [L. *de* + *liberare*]

The act of turning something over to someone else. The object delivered. In law, *delivery* of an object or of a document affecting legal rights or duties may be a manifestation of intent to transfer an interest in property, as when a donor *delivers* a gift to the donee, or a grantor *delivers* a deed to the grantee. In these cases, *delivery* evidences the intent to transfer possession or control. *Actual delivery* is the physical transfer of possession. *Constructive delivery* is transfer of property by delivery of a document or object representing the property; examples: delivery of a key from landlord to tenant to evidence transfer of control over leased property; delivery of a deed to land to represent transfer of title and control.

DEMAND [L. *de* + *mando, mandare* / to order, command, charge, entrust]

To insist upon; to claim. To summon. To require by force, legal authority or legal right. To make a formal request requiring action or response. In law, a request initiated by one party which requires response by another party. A *demand note* is a note payable by the maker or endorser upon demand of the holder. A *demand loan* is a loan payable by the borrower upon demand of the lender. A defendant in a felony trial has a constitutional right to *demand* a jury trial. One party to a contract may be required to *demand performance* by the other before claiming a default.

DEMENTIA [L. *demens* / senseless, insane]

A mental condition resulting in reduced comprehension and function, usually including loss of memory and ability to recognize abstractions.

DE MINIMIS [L. smallest, the least important]

Insignificant; minute; frivolous. In law, something so trivial the court will not act upon it, as in a *de minimis* crime.

DE MINIMUS NON CURAT LEX

The law takes no notice of insignificant things. The law will not bother with trifles.

DEMISE [L. *demittere* / to send or put down; to lower. A transfer of property by the sovereign]

The word is now used in two senses. In the first sense, it means either to transfer, convey or lease an estate in land, or the conveyance or lease itself. In the second sense, the word means death. This meaning derives from the fact that a transfer from the sovereign usually took effect at his death. In this second sense, it may refer to a person or an event, as in the *demise of communism*. As an extension of this second sense, the word is used to mean a devise or inheritance which takes effect upon death.

DE MORTE HOMINIS [L. *de* / from, coming from + *mors, mortis* / death + *homo, hominis* / man, a human being]

Of the death of a man.

DEMUR, DEMURRER [L. *de* + *moror, morari* / to linger, delay]

To object; take exception to; reject. The pleading which was interposed by a defendant to object to the complaint as a matter of law. A statement by the defendant that even if the facts pleaded are taken as true, the plaintiff is not entitled to any relief. Although the term is now used in only a number of states, the same effect is achieved by a motion addressed to the sufficiency of the complaint as failing to state a claim on which relief can be granted. *See* Fed. R. Civ P. 12(b).

DE NOVO [L. *de* + *novus* / new, young, fresh]

Renewed, revived. Once again; a second time. Trial *de novo*, a new trial; hearing *de novo*, a second hearing.

DENY, DENIAL [L. *de* + *nego, negare* / to say no to, to deny the existence of, to refuse]

To declare or state that something is not true; to refuse to acknowledge the truth of. To refuse a request or petition, as to deny a motion. A *denial* in a legal proceeding is a statement by one party that an allegation or pleading by the other side is false. A *general denial* is a denial of all the allegations in a complaint or in a particular cause of action. A *specific denial* is a denial of specified allegations of the complaint.

DE ODIO ET ATIA [L. *de* / from + *odium* / hatred + *et* / and + *malitia* / evil, cunning, malice]

Of hatred and malice.

DE PACE INFRACTA [L. *de* / from + *pax, pacis* / peace + *infringere* / to weaken, break]

Of breaking or disturbing the peace.

DEPENDENT [L. *de* + *pendere* / to hang, suspend]

Requiring aid or support. Depending on another for help or assistance. Lacking the means for self-sufficiency. In federal tax law, a *dependent* is any persons in a degree of relationship to the taxpayer which entitles the taxpaper to take a deduction from his gross income for the support of that person. A *dependent* contract is one which is conditioned upon performance of another contract.

DEPLETE, DEPLETION [L. *deplere* / to empty out; to consume]

To consume or use up. The act of using up or reducing in quantity or content. In tax law, a *depletion allowance* is a tax deduction for the consumption by a business enterprise of natural resources such as gas, oil, timber, etc.

DEPONENT [L. *de* + *ponere* / to place, put down]

One who states under oath that the facts he gives are true. A witness or affiant under oath. A person who gives testimony by deposition or affidavit. A *deposition* is a document which contains statements made and sworn to by a *deponent*.

See **DEPOSITION**

DEPORT, DEPORTATION [L. *deportare* / to carry away]

To banish or send somone out of a country. The forced removal to a foreign country by the United States of an alien who is deemed undesirable or has entered the country illegally.

DEPOSE [L. *depono, deponere* / to put down, lay down. To lay aside or deposit]

To remove from office, as to *depose* a king. To testify or aver under oath. To take and record the testimony of a witness or party other than at a trial.

DEPOSIT [L. *deponere* / to put down, deposit]

To entrust for safekeeping, as to deposit funds with a bank. Anything left or entrusted for safekeeping, as funds in an attorney's escrow account. Also, a payment on account of a larger obligation, as a *deposit* on an item purchased in a store or against the purchase price of real property.

DEPOSITARY

A person or institution receiving money or other valuable in trust or for safekeeping. A bailee.

DEPOSITION [L. *deponere* / to deposit]

A statement under oath made by a witness or party in response to questions asked either orally or in writing. Also, the document in which such questions and answers are recorded. Also, the hearing or other process during which the questions and answers are transcribed. *Depositions* are used to preserve the testimony of witnesses who may be unavailable for trial, or as part of the process of discovering the evidence of opposing parties before trial. They are usually conducted in a lawyer's office under circumstances which preserve the ability of the parties to submit any objection for decision by the court.

See **DEPONENT**

DEPOSITION DE BENE ESSE

A deposition by a witness who cannot attend at a trial and which is read in substitution for his testimony.

See **DE BENE ESSE**

DEPOSITORY

The place or building in which an institutional depositary is housed or conducts business; e.g., a bank, insurance company, credit union or trust company.

DE PRAESENTI

For the present.

DEPRAVED [L. *de* + *pravus* / deformed, vicious, rotten]

Evil, corrupt. In criminal law, a *depraved* mind is one which exhibits a fundamental lack of morality or an indifference to the lives or safety of others.

DEPRECIATION [L. *de* + *pretium* / value, price]

A reduction or loss in value. The process in accounting by which the cost of a capital asset is allocated over its estimated life. The annual deduction permitted on tax returns for that portion of the capital value of an asset charged to that tax year. An estimation of the loss in value of an asset over a period of time, attributable to wear and tear or decay.

DEPRIVATION [L. *de* + *privare* / to strip, deprive of]

A taking away, seizure or confiscation of the property, rights or privileges of a person. The Fourteenth Amendment of the Constitution — the due process amendment — guarantees to each citizen freedom from the deprivation of his private property by the federal or state governments without just compensation.

DE QUO JURE

By what right?

DE RECTO [L. *de* + *rego, regere,* / to guide, direct (*rectus* / straight, right)]

A writ of right granted to a petitioner to restore his rights to property.

DERELICTION [L. *derelinquere* / to forsake, neglect, abandon]

A failure or neglect of duty. The abandonment or neglect of property. Also, land created by the gradual withdrawal of waters, such as a new beach created by the withdrawal of the ocean.

See **ACCRETION; AVULSION; DILUVION**

DERIVATIVE [L. *derivo, derivare* / to turn into another channel, change the course of]

Anything which owes its existence to another thing from which it came. A thing which emanates from another. A *derivative action* is an action brought by the stockholders of a corporation to enforce a right which the corporation itself ought to enforce but which it neglects or abandons. *Derivative evidence* is evidence which cannot be introduced at trial because the evidence from which it is drawn is itself tainted.

DEROGATE, DEROGATION [L. *derogo, derogare* / to modify or repeal; to diminish, detract from]

To lessen or take away from. To remove authority or power from, as from an official or executive.

DESCEND, DESCENT [L. *descendere* / to come down, climb down]

To pass down from one generation to another. To be transferred from a decedent to his heirs under the terms of his will or by intestacy. Hereditary succession. The passage of title to property from a *decedent* to his successors.

DESCRIPTION [L. *describere* / to transcribe; to describe or represent]

Expressing the nature or character of an object or thing in words or by diagram. In law, the legend setting forth the boundaries and dimension of a parcel of land and usually contained in a deed, mortgage or other title instrument. Also, in patent law, the explanation of an invention in a patent application.

DESCRIPTIVE MARK

A trademark which is merely descriptive of the goods or services it identifies. A *descriptive mark* will be registered only if it can be shown that the mark has attained secondary meaning, i.e., the mark is recognized not only in its primary descriptive sense but also as indicating the source of the product or service it describes. For example, if the word "speedy" were used as a trademark for a car, it would be merely descriptive unless it acquired a secondary meaning by becoming associated in the public's mind with a particular make of car. If it were used as the trademark for a line of toys, it would not be considered descriptive.

DESECRATION [L. *de* + *sacrare* / to dedicate to a god, to make holy]

To violate the integrity or sanctity of. The wanton destruction of a holy or venerated place or thing; e.g., the national flag. The wilful disturbance of a cemetery or of any burial place. Many states have statutes making *desecration* of venerated objects a crime. *See* Model Penal Code §250.9.

DESERT, DESERTION [L. *deserere* / to sever connection with; to leave or abandon; to forsake]

To abandon or forsake a relationship or a commitment. To leave a spouse without consent or justification and without the intent to return. To terminate the care or custody of one's child or dependent. To abandon one's military post or duty without authorization and with the intent not to return.

DETAIN [L. *de + teneo, tenere* / to hold back; to restrain or stop]

To impede the movement of; to restrain. To hold in custody. To deprive a person of his freedom.

DETAINER [L. *de + tenere* / to hold]

A writ authorizing a penal officer to continue to hold a prisoner. Also, the detention of a person without his consent. Also, the act of keeping an object from the rightful owner.

DE TEMPUS EN TEMPUS

From time to time.

DETENTION [L. *de + tenere*]

The act of restraining the free movement of another. To hold someone on a charge of crime. To take custody of a defendant or prisoner.

DETER, DETERRENCE [L. *deterreo, deterrere* / to frighten, discourage, restrict]

To frighten into inaction. To prevent from acting. To discourage or inhibit criminal activity for fear of punishment or reprisal. To discourage military attack through the buildup of military power.

DETERMINABLE [L. *de + termino, terminare* / to limit; to set the limits of]

Capable of being fixed, determined or decided. Also, subject to being terminated upon the occurrence of a contingency. Some interests in land are considered *determinable*. Example: A, the owner of Greenacre, conveys title to "the Nantucket Library, for only so long as Nantucket uses Greenacre for its library." The Library has a *fee simple determinable*. If the library ceases to use Greenacre as its site, title will revert to A.

DETERMINATE [L. *determinare*]

Having fixed limits or boundaries; limited in time or space. In criminal law, a *determinate sentence* is a custodial sentence with a fixed term.

DETINUE [L. *de + tenere* / to hold back]

A common-law action for the recovery of personal property which is detained wrongfully, even though possession may originally have been obtained lawfully. The defendant could either return the goods or pay their full value, plus damages for the detention.

See **DEBET ET DETINET; NON DETINET; REPLEVIN**

DETRIMENT [L. *de* + *terere* / to rub against, to wear away]

Harm, injury, disadvantage. A forebearance, loss or assumption of duty or responsibility given in exchange for or in support of a promise or act by another party. One party's *detriment* may form the consideration for an enforceable contract.

See **CONSIDERATION**

DEUS

A god or deity. God.

DEVASAVIT [L. *dividere* / to divide]

He divided or separated into parts; he devised.

DEVASAVIT VEL NON [L. Did he devise or didn't he?]

An inquiry by a court of law under direction of a probate court into the validity of a purported will or provision of a will.

DEVASTAVIT [L. *dis* / apart, separated from + *vestire* / to dress, to clothe — to unclothe, to denude]

The failure of a personal representative to administer an estate as required. Waste. A writ to impose personal liability upon an administrator or executor who has been guilty of mismanagement or misapplication of assets.

DE VERBO IN VERBUM [L. *verbum* / word]

Word for word.

DEVISE [L. *divido, dividere* / to divide]

To give or convey property by will. Formerly, a devise referred only to testamentary gifts of real property. The Uniform Probate Code uses the term to describe any gift by will.

DEVOLVE, DEVOLUTION [L. *de* + *volvo, volvere* / to turn around, twist, roll]

To pass from one person to another. To be subject to transfer or succession. To fall upon or be forced on, as in, "In case of the Removal of the President from Office...the Same shall *devolve* on the Vice President..." (Article II, U.S. Constitution).

DICTUM [L. *dictare* / to say again, repeat]

The formal statement or announcement of a rule or principle. An authoritative declaration. Also, a statement made incidentally or in passing. A conclusion, line of reasoning or observation of a judge in an opinion which is not central to, or the grounds for, his decision. Because it is not necessary to his decision, it is not binding in subsequent cases.

See **IPSE DIXIT**; **OBITER DICTA**

DIES, DIEI

A day, an anniversary, a designated day.

DIES AD QUEM

The date to which; the last day.

DIES A QUO

The date from which; the beginning date.

DIES DATUS

A given date; a day certain.

DIES JURIDICUS

A day on which a court may lawfully sit and adjudicate.

DIES NON JURIDICUS [L. *dies* / days + *non* / not + *iurisdictio* / the administration of justice]

A day on which the courts are closed. Sometimes, a day on which the only judicial business transacted is by a judge in chambers.

DIFFERENTIA [L. *differre* / to spread in several directions, scatter, be different, differ]

A feature or characteristic which distinguishes one thing from another. A characteristic trait that separates one class or species from another. Used by scientists and lawyers to classify data. The plural is *differentiae*.

DIGEST [L. *digero, digerere, digestum* / separate; arrange]

A summary or condensation of written material drawn from different sources. In law, a compendium of legal rules, principles or decisions arranged for ease in reference.

DILATORY [L. *differre* / to scatter, defer, delay (pp. *dilatum*)]

Tending to cause delays; to procastinate. In the law, a *dilatory* plea or motion is one which delays a trial or determination of the issues in an action. Any tactic employed by a party or his attorney solely for the purpose of delay.

DILITIONES IN LEGE SONT ODIOSAE

Delays are hateful to the law. The law dislikes delays.

DILIGENCE [L. *diligentia* / carefulness, accuracy (from *diligere* / to choose, to prize)]

Dedication to duty as defined in a contract or other relationship recognized and enforced by the law. Care; attentiveness. *Due diligence* is the care expected of a reasonable person under the prevailing circumstances; reasonable efforts. The term is used most often to describe the standard of professional care expected of business executives, lawyers and accountants in the examination and evaluation of risks in a proposed business transaction. Also, the process followed by a law firm or accounting firm in examining and reporting on the integrity of the information and data supplied by the other side in a proposed acquisition or other business transaction.

DILUTION [L. *diluere* / to wash away, dissolve]

A lessening or diminution. In corporate law, the action of a corporation in reducing the unit value of its shares by issuing new shares of the same class at a lower price than those outstanding, or in reducing the voting power of outstanding shares. In trademark law, the doctrine which protects a strong trademark against use of the mark by another, even though that use may be noncompetitive.

DILUVION [L. *diluere* / to wash away]

Soil and other matter washed away from the edge of a body of water over time or through a storm or flood.

See **ACCRETION; ALLUVIUM; DERELICTION**

DIMINUTION [L. *de* + *minuere* / to chop up, cut into pieces, make smaller]

A lessening or decrease in number or value. A record which is inaccurate or incomplete when it is sent from a lower court to an appellate court. *Diminution in value* is a measure of damages computed by subtracting the value of a property or right after a damage or loss has occurred to it from its value before the loss.

DIRECT [L. *dirigo, dirigere* / to arrange, direct]

Stemming without hindrance from a source. Running in a straight line from start to finish without deviation, or from person to person without interruption (as from parent to offspring). Unaffected by an intervening agency or interruption. A *direct examination* is the first examination of a witness at trial by the party who calls him.

DIRECTOR [L. *dirigere* / to arrange, direct]

A person who manages or directs. An administrative officer elected or appointed to manage some or all the affairs of a corporation or company. A person elected by the shareholders of a corporation to serve on the board of directors, a group entrusted with overall control and supervision of the corporation's affairs. A *director* has a fiduciary duty to the shareholders. The board of directors appoints and dismisses corporate officers, declares and pays dividends, and oversees the general affairs of the corporation.

DISABILITY [L. *dis* / apart, the opposite of + *habilitas* / aptitude]

Physical or mental impairment. Incapacity to pursue an occupation or employment. The civil rights of individuals with disabilities are protected under the Americans with Disabilities Act, which guarantees them equal opportunity in public accommodations, employment, transportation, government services and telecommunications. A *disability* may be partial or total, or temporary or permanent. Also, a lack of legal capacity to do or perform some act, as in the case of a minor or a person who is mentally incompetent.

DISAFFIRM [L. *dis* + *adfirmare* / to strengthen, make firm; to prove]

To cancel, rescind or repudiate. To refuse to be bound by. A minor may *disaffirm a contract* made by him.

DISCHARGE [L. *dis* + *carrus* / a four-wheeled vehicle]

To relieve of a burden. To release from an obligation, debt or duty. To get rid of a debt by payment, the rendition of services or a release. To cause an instrument to become unenforceable. To release a prisoner from custody or confinement. To terminate the employment of a worker. To satisfy a requirement or comply with a demand or duty. In bankruptcy law, to release a debtor from the obligation to pay some or all of his debts. To release a jury from further service or deliberation.

DISCIPLINE [L. *disciplina* / instruction, teaching (*discipulus* / pupil)]

Controlled conduct. Good behavior. The maintenance of order; observance of rules. A field of study. Training or instruction intended to encourage high moral standards. The American Bar Association and other associations of attorneys, as well as the courts and governmental agencies, have enunciated rules for the *discipline* of attorneys who fail to observe defined standards of professional conduct.

DISCLAIM, DISCLAIMER [L. *dis* + *clamo, clamare* / to call, cry out]

To issue a *disclaimer*. To refuse or give up a claim or interest in property. A *disclaimer* is the rejection or disavowal of a right or interest, as of an estate in land; also, a rejection or denial of responsibility for an act; also, words or conduct limiting or negating a seller's warranty in the sale of goods.

DISCLOSE, DISCLOSURE [L. *dis* / separately, apart + *claudere* / to shut, close]

To make known, reveal, expose. In patent law, the *disclosure* is the statement of specifications of the invention, describing its subject matter and its method of operation. In securities law, *disclosure* is the guiding principle under which persons or firms who deal with the public sale or distribution of securites are expected to provide sufficient information to enable the public to make informed decisions about the securities. In general commercial law, *disclosure* is the duty to inform the consumer of sufficient facts to enable him to determine whether he wishes to undertake or proceed with a transaction. See Truth in Lending Act, 15 U.S.C.A. §1601 *et seq.*

DISCONTINUANCE [L. *dis* + *continuare* / to connect, unite, continue]

The voluntary termination of a law suit or proceeding by one party, usually by notice to the court and to the adversary party. At common law, the failure of a party to pursue his action, resulting in dismissal against him.

DISCOUNT [L. *dis* + *computare* / to count, calculate]

Any reduction from gross value to achieve a lower value. An allowance from an obligation or from the price of a commodity. The collection of interest in advance. The difference between the value of an obligation at maturity; i.e., its face value, and its current market value. An allowance reducing an obligation for payment in advance.

DISCOVERY [L. *dis* + *cooperire* / to cover completely, envelop]

The recognition of hidden or previously unrevealed facts and circumstances. In law, all the tools available to a litigant to determine and learn facts and evidence available only to the adversary and upon which the adversary intends to rely at trial. The adversary must make available documents, books and records in his possession. The tools of *discovery* include written interrogatories, depositions, the production of documents, physical and mental examinations, examination of physical evidence, and requests for admissions.

DISCRETION, DISCRETIONARY [L. *discernere*, (pp. *discretum*) / to sever, separate]

The power to make choices between options and alternatives. The power of a jury, judge or public official to reach decisions between options defined by principles and rules of fairness, reason and law. A *discretionary act* is an act resulting from the exercise of free choice between reasonable and lawful alternatives. When an official acts beyond the limits of choice set for his job or office, he is said to *abuse* his *discretion*. A *discretionary trust* is a trust which permits the trustee to exercise her choices in the allocation and distribution of principal and interest.

DISCRIMINATE, DISCRIMINATION [L. *discrimino, discriminare* / to separate, break apart, divide]

To recognize a difference or distinction between two things. To exercise [sound] judgment. To prefer one thing to another; to treat two things or two persons differently without cause or justification. To impose a difference in treatment of persons on a basis prohibited by law, such as race, sex, color, religion, disability or national origin. Federal law prohibits *discrimination* in employment, voting rights, housing, public education and access to public facilities.

DISHONOR [L. *dis* + *honoro, honorare* / to honor, dignify]

Lack of respect; shame, rejection. To refuse or neglect to pay a bill, check or note upon presentment. An instrument may be *dishonored* by nonacceptance (i.e., it is duly presented and acceptance is refused or cannot be obtained) or by nonpayment (i.e., it is duly presented for payment but payment is refused). *See* U.C.C. § 3-507(1).

DISMISS, DISMISSAL [L. *dis* / apart + *mittere* / to send, let go]

To send away or remove from office or employment; to discharge from employment. To bring about or order the termination of an action or pleading, as when a judge *dismisses* an action or complaint or a party moves for *dismissal*. The Federal Rules of Civil Procedure distinguish between *involuntary dismissals* (which have *res judicata* effect) and *voluntary dismissals* by the plaintiff (which do not).

DISPOSE, DISPOSABLE [L. *dispono, disponere* / to put in different places; to distribute; to put in order]

To transfer to the control or possession of another. To make a decision about, as to *dispose* of a problem or a matter. To deal with. *Disposable income* is the income available to a taxpayer after the payment of his taxes. The money available to a person for his own support and benefit.

DISPOSITION [L. *disponere*]

A ruling or decision of a court or judge which resolves an issue or determines the rights of the parties. The final determination of a matter or a motion. In a criminal trial, the sentence imposed by the court upon the defendant.

DISPUTE [L. *disputare* / to debate or discuss (from *dis* + *puto, putare* / to think, estimate, clear up)]

A contest between opposing claims or interests. The underlying basis for litigation. A difference in views or opinions. To meet a demand or assertion with contrary claims or demands. To fight over.

DISSENT [L. *dis* + *sentire* / to feel, experience]

A difference of opinion. To withhold agreement or consent. The view or opinion of a judge on a multi-judge court who does not agree with the view or opinion of the majority. The judge who disagrees can express his views in a *dissenting opinion*.

DISSIPATE [L. *dissipare* (or *dissupare*) / to scatter, disperse, spread around]

To waste assets. To spend foolishly and wastefully. To misuse funds entrusted to one's care. To pursue pleasure excessively.

DISSOLVE, DISSOLUTION [L. *dis* + *solvere* / to loosen, untie]

To undo, break up, disperse. The act of breaking up or terminating a relationship. The *dissolution* of a corporation is the termination of its legal existence either by voluntary act of its stockholders or through an act of the state. The *dissolution* of a partnership occurs upon the separation of one partner from the partnership. The *dissolution* of a marriage occurs upon divorce.

DISTINGUISH [L. *distinguere* / to separate, divide up; to distinguish]

To see the difference between two things. To point out or identify. To separate into kinds or classes. In an opinion or analysis, to explain the difference in reasoning, approach or conclusion between two cases or decisions. To justify a ruling or decision which seems at variance with another decisions by reconciling the differences in fact or reasoning.

DISTRIBUTE [L. *distribuere* / to divide, distribute]

To move goods or products in the stream of commerce. To purchase goods from a manufacturer for resale to a retailer. To allot or spread out. To give out or dispense. To serve as warehouseman and/or wholesaler.

DISTURB [L. *disturbare* / to drive out; to frustrate; to disturb; to uproot]

To cause confusion or disorder. To uproot or upset the peace and tranquility of. To interfere with or interrupt.

DIVERSITY [L. *divertere* / to turn in another direction, turn away from]

The condition of being different or distinct. *Diversity jurisdiction* is required by the federal courts before actions which do not turn on constitutional or federal questions can be brought before them. This means that an action based on *diversity of citizenship* can be brought only if no party on one side of the action comes from the same state as any party on the other side of the action. In all diversity cases, the amount in controversy must exceed an amount fixed by Congress from time to time.

DIVERT [L. *divertere* / to turn around; to turn in opposite directions; to differ]

To move from one course to another; to change the course or path of. To change the direction or purpose of. To distract. To misuse funds or assets intended for one purpose and apply them to another. Also, to entertain or give pleasure to.

DIVEST [L. *dis* + *vestio, vestire* / to dress, clothe]

To deprive a person of property or possessions. To remove the clothing or garments of. To strip away.

DIVESTITURE [L. *di(s)* + *vestis* / dress, cloth]

To unclothe, to denude. The act of disposing of assets, such as stock or property, in response to an order by an agency or court in an anti-trust action. The order requiring such a disposition. Also, the voluntary act of a corporation or business in selling off a part of its business or assets.

DIVESTMENT [L. *di(s)vestire* / to unclothe, denude]

The termination or cutting off of an interest in property before its anticipated or scheduled end. An interest in property which has *vested* (become absolute or perfected), may be *subject to divestment* under stated conditions.

DIVIDEND [L. *dividere* / to separate into parts]

A part or share in an asset which is divided and distributed among several recipients. A gain or profit. The distribution of pro-rata portions of current earnings or of earned surplus to shareholders of a corporation. A *dividend* may be paid in cash or by the issuance of stock. Also, a payment made to general creditors in a bankruptcy proceeding.

See **EX DIVIDEND**

DOCUMENT [L. *doceo, docere* / to teach, instruct]

noun: A writing or instrument containing data or information or recording a transaction or event, e.g., a contract or deed. Any item having physical form which may be used as evidence. Under the best evidence rule, a *document* is the physical embodiment of any information relevant to the trier of fact, e.g., a letter or medical report. An official paper establishing a right or privilege, e.g., a driver's license, passport or Army discharge. *verb:* To record in writing; to create a record of. To prove by reference to data or other supportive information. To issue, or furnish with, a document.

DOGMA [L. a philosophical doctrine (from the Greek)]

Codes or formal statements of rules and beliefs. A recitation of established principles. The official pronouncements of a church or ecclesiastical authority.

DOLI CAPAX [L. *dolus* / fraud, deceit, guile + *capax* / capable of, fit for]

The capacity to distinguish between right and wrong. This capacity must be present in a criminal defendant before he may be convicted of a crime.

DOLI INCAPAX

Incapable of distiguishing right from wrong. An infant or insane person is said to be *doli incapax* because he cannot be expected to distinguish right from wrong.

DOLUS

An intentional or wilful wrong; a harm committed with malice. Also, a fraud or deceit.

See **CULPA**

DOMESTIC [L. *domesticus* / belonging to the house or family (*domus* / house)]

Belonging or relating to a particular place; e.g., a country, state, etc. Each state has corporations which are *domestic* to it; i.e., they were organized in that state. *Domestic jurisdiction* is the power of a court to exercise control over persons, property and acts within its boundaries.

DOMICILE [L. *domicilium* / a dwelling or place of residence]

The law distinguishes between a mere residence and a *domicile*. A *domicile* is a person's legal home; i.e., the place he acknowledges as his principal place and to which he always intends to return. A person may have only one *domicile*. This concept is important because it is used to determine citizenship and jurisdiction.

See **RESIDE; HABITANCY**

DOMICILIARY [L. *domus, domicilium* / a house or home; a dwelling]

Relating to a person's place of residence. A resident of a particular place, as in "he is a *domiciliary* of Great Britain". The administration of a decedent's estate in the state or country of his final residence is called *domiciliary administration*.

DOMINION [L. *dominium* / rule, power, ownership]

In law, the ownership, posssession and control of an object. A nation has *dominion* over its territory and possessions. A person has *dominion* over his property and possessions.

DOMINIUM PLENUM

Full and complete authority.

DOMINUS PRO TEMPORE [L. *dominus* / lord, master; head of the household + *pro tempore* / for the time, temporarily]

A temporary owner.

See **PRO TEMPORE**

DOMITAE NATURAE [L. *domitare* / to tame, subdue + *natura* / birth, nature]

Domestic animals; creatures which have the disposition to become tame and gentle and which can be tamed by man.

See **FERAE NATURAE**

DONATE, DONATION [L. *dono, donare* / to give as a present; to present]

To make a gift of. To give to a public institution or charity. *Donated stock* is stock turned over to a corporation by a stockholder without payment or reimbursement.

DONATIO [L. *dono, donare* / to give, make a gift of, donate]

That which is given; a gift. A donation.

DONATIO CAUSA MORTIS

A donor's gift of property in expectation or fear of imminent death. If the death does not occur, the gift is not effective.

See **CAUSA MORTIS; GIFT CAUSA MORTIS**

DONATIO INTER VIVOS

A gift of property from one living person to another living person. An ordinary gift.

DONATIO NON PRAESUMITUR

A gift is not presumed to have been made. The legal presumption is against construing a transfer of property as a gift.

DORMANT [L. *dormio, dormire* / to sleep]

Inactive, suspended, asleep. Held in abeyance. A *dormant claim* is one which cannot be enforced; e.g., because it is barred by the statute of limitations. A *dormant judgment* is one which can no longer be pursued because of the lapse of time or the death of a party. A *dormant partner* is a partner whose participation as partner is not disclosed and who takes no active role in management.

DOWER [L. *dotare* / to give a dowry; to endow]

The life estate of a widow in the land owned by her husband at his death. In some states, the life estate has been expanded into fee ownership. In many states, *dower* has been abolished and replaced by the widow's statutory elective share.

DRACONIAN [L. *draco* / a snake or dragon (from the Greek *Draco*, referring to an Athenian who imposed a severe code of laws upon the populace)]

A cruel or severe law, ruling or decision. Any edict, order, judgment or law which is unreasonably or excessively harsh or severe.

DUAL [L. *duo* / two]

Consisting of two parts. Divided into two components. The *dual capacity doctrine* enables an employee to recover from his employer for injuries sustained under the general principles of tort law instead of under workers' compensation, if the injuries are unrelated to his employment. *Dual citizenship* is conferred upon an individual when the laws of two countries recognize him as a citizen. A citizen of the United States is permitted to establish dual citizenship in another country. All citizens of the United States are citizens of the nation and also of the state in which they reside. One consequence of this dual federal-state citizenship is that both the federal government and the state may prosecute a criminal defendant without invoking double jeopardy, so long as the crime committed violates the laws of both. This is known as the *dual sovereignty doctrine*.

DUCES TECUM [L. *ducere* / to bring or take (with one) + *tu, te* / you + *cum* / with]

Literally, bring with you. The name for a subpoena or writ which requires a party or witness to produce and bring with him documents, papers, records or other evidence relevant to a case, trial or controversy.

See **SUBPEONA DUCES TECUM**

DUE DILIGENCE
See **DILIGENCE**

DUE PROCESS
See **PROCEDURAL DUE PROCESS; SUBSTANTIVE DUE PROCESS**

DUODECEMVIRALE JUDICIUM [L. *duo* / two + *decem* / ten + *vir* / man + *iudicium* / trial; the inquiry and judgment of twelve men]

Trial by a jury of twelve men.

DUPLICITY [L. *duplico, duplicare* / to double or divide]

Contradictions in thought, action or communication. Deception in words or action. Double-dealing. Also, the joinder of inconsistent claims or allegations in a single pleading or count.

DURABLE [L. *duro, durare* / to last, continue, survive]

Capable of long-life without deterioration. *Durables* or *durable goods* are consumer goods that can be used over long periods without significant repair, e.g., motor vehicles and appliances. A *durable power* is a power of attorney which survives the principal's incapacity or disability and enables the attorney to continue acting for the principal even after his incapacity ends.

DURANTE MINORE AETATE [L. *durante* / during + *minore* / smaller + *aetas* / age]

During the age of minority.

DURANTE VIDUITATE [L. *durante* + *viduus* / bereaved, widowed + *aetas* / age]

During the time of widowhood; while a widow.

DURANTE VITA

During a person's lifetime.

DURESS [L. *duro, durari* / to make hard (*duritia* / harshness, severity, oppression)]

Coercion by the use of force or the threat of force. Apparent but unwilling consent induced by compulsion or restraint. Fraud which induces another to act without volition. The defendant in a criminal action may assert *duress* as a defense, if the pressure upon him to commit or join in a crime induced a reasonable apprehension of death or serious bodily injury.

EADEM AUCTORITATE
By the same authority.

EADEM EST RATIO, EADEM EST LEX
(If) the reason is the same, the law is the same.

E CONSENSU PATRIS
By the father's consent.

EDICT   [L. *edicere* / to declare, pronounce]
A proclamation or order having the force of law. In Roman Law, an order to appear before a judge.

EDICTUM PERPETUUM   [L. *edicere* + *perpetuus* / continuous, uninterrupted]
An edict with indefinite or perpetual existence.

EFFECT, EFFECTIVE   [L. *efficio, efficere* (pp. *effectum*) / to produce, effect, make]
To cause or bring about. To create or make real. To place in operation. Also, the result of action by an agent or cause. Also, personal property or goods. *Effective:* The point at which a cause or action creates its impact or comes into play, e.g., the statute became *effective* on…Also, capable of producing a desired result; e.g., a criminal defendant is entitled to *effective* assistance of counsel.

EFFECTS   [L. *efficere* / to do, produce, make]
One's possessions or belongings. Usually in the phrase *personal effects*. Amendment IV to the Constitution guarantees the right of the people to be secure in their persons, houses, papers, and *effects*.

EFFECTUS SEQUITUR CAUSAM
The effect follows the cause. The cause produces the effect.

EFFLUENT [L. *effluere* / to flow out]

Waste matter discharged into a stream or other body of water; more generally, any waste matter or pollutant; e.g., smoke, industrial waste, sewage discharged into the environment.

EFFLUVIUM [L. *effluere*]

An offensive odor. A by-product released as waste.

EFFLUX [L. *effluere*]

An expiration or end. The passage or expiration of time.

EFFLUXION OF TIME [L. *effluere*]

The orderly passage of time, undisturbed by human intervention or a sudden, unanticipated event. With the effluxion of time, leases terminate, contracts end, statutes expire, etc.

EFFUSIO SANGUINIS [L. *effusio* / a pouring forth + *sanguis* / blood]

The flow or shedding of blood; bloodshed.

EGO [L. I. the first person pronoun]

The pronoun I.

See **ALTER EGO**

EGRESS [L. *egredior, egredi* (pp. *egressus*)/ to go out, step out]

The act of departing or going out. The means which permit someone to leave a place. An exit. The tort of false imprisonment occurs when one person intentionally confines another without means of escape or egress.

EJECTMENT [L. *eicio, eiciere* / to throw out, cast out]

At common law, an action to remove another from land to which he was not entitled. The plaintiff had to show not only that he was entitled to possession but that the defendant was in wrongful possession. Actions for the recovery of land are now defined by statute in most states and are given different names; e.g., summary proceedings, action for eviction, etc.

EJECTUM [L. *eicere* / to cast out]

Objects cast up by action of the sea. Flotsam and jetsam.

EJUSDEM GENERIS [L. *eiusdem* / of the same, belonging to the same kind + *genus, generis* / class]

A rule of construction which states that words of general application following a listing or enumeration of specific components of a class of things shall be interpreted as including only other components of the same class as those specifically listed; e.g., in a statute prohibiting the possession of "handguns, rifles, shotguns, pistols and other weapons," the words "other weapons" might not be construed as including knives and swords.

See **NOSITUR A SOCIIS**

ELECT [L. *eligo, eligere* / to pick out, choose]

To choose among candidates or alternatives. To select by vote to fill an office or position. The act of a spouse in selecting his or her statutory share in lieu of the provision made in the will of the deceased spouse.

ELECTION [L. *eligere* (pp., *electus*)]

The process by which candidates for office appeal to the voters to be selected among a group of candidates and the voters select one or several among the candidates. The process of voting by ballot for one's candidate for office. The right or power to make a choice among options. The right of a party to a dispute to choose among several remedies (i.e., to exercise an *election of remedies*).

ELECTIVE SHARE [L. *electus*]

The statutory share which a spouse may claim when inadequate provision is made in the will of the deceased spouse. Almost all states have *elective share* statutes, usually permitting the spouse to elect to take one-third of the estate.

ELECTORATE [L. *eligo, eligere* (pp. *electus*) / to pick out, choose]

All those persons entitled to vote in a given election. Eligibility to vote is usually defined along geographical lines. Example: the *electorate* in an election for a member of the House of Representatives consists of all eligible voters in the congressional district; the *electorate* in an election for U.S. Senate is all the eligible voters in the entire state.

ELEEMOSYNARY [L. *eleemosyna* / alms]

Relating to or concerned with charity. An *eleemosynary* corporation or organization is an entity created for charitable purposes.

ELEMENT [L. *elementum* / the initial components; first things or principles]

The most rudimentary essential component of a thing. The letters of the alphabet. The basic principles of any science. Originally, any of the four substances — water, fire, air and earth — which were thought to comprise the universe. Now, the elements are those chemical units identified by science as basic constituents of all matter. In criminal law, one of the components defining a particular crime; the prosecution must prove all the elements of a crime beyond a reasonable doubt.

ELOGIUM [L. a maxim or proverb. An epitaph]

A will or testament; a clause in a will. Also, the inscription on a gravestone.

ELOIGN [L. *ex* / out of + *longus* / long]

To take far away; remove to a distant place. To take beyond the reach or jurisdiction of a court. To remove personal property to avoid a lien.

EMANCIPATE [L. *emancipare* / to release a son from his father's control]

The surrender, usually by his or her parents, of the care and custody of a child. The surrender may be partial or complete. As a result of the surrender, the child is freed from control and becomes an independent agent. *Emancipation* generally occurs when the child reaches maturity (the age of 18 in most jurisdictions), but may occur at other times by agreement or conduct. Also, to free from restraint, control or bondage. The release of individuals from slavery or servitude, as in the case of Lincoln's Emancipation Proclamation.

EMENDATIO [L. *emendare* / to free from error, correct]

An amendment or revision; a correction. Also, compensation for a person's injuries.

EMERGENCY [L. *emergo, emergere* / to cause to rise up. To get clear of an impediment; to free oneself]

An unexpected or unforeseen event or circumstance requiring immediate attention and action. An urgent need for assistance, e.g., a *medical emergency*, or a fire, earthquake, flood or tornado. The *emergency doctrine* is a principle of tort law which absolves a person who acts reasonably in an emergency from liability for any injury or damages he may cause by his actions. Also, a police officer confronted by an *emergency* is entitled to respond to protect life or prevent injury without waiting for a search warrant.

EMERITUS [L. *emereo* / to deserve; to earn compensation; to serve]

An honorary title conferred on one who has served out a term in a professional position and is permitted to retain as a privilege the last title or rank held by him; e.g., professor *emeritus*.

EMIGRATE [L. *emigrare* / to move from one place to another]

To leave one place, especially a country, and go to another. To go out of one country and into another.

See **IMMIGRATE**

EMINENT DOMAIN [L. *eminere* / to stand out + *dominare* / to rule, dominate]

The right or power of government to take the private property of its citizens for a public purpose upon the payment of just compensation. The principles governing *eminent domain* are inscribed in the Fifth Amendment to the Constitution, which states " . . . nor shall private property be taken for public use, without just compensation."

See **CONDEMNATION; CONFISCATE; EXPROPRIATE**

EMISSARY   [L. *emitto, emittere* / to send forth, dispatch, to let loose, free]

A messenger or agent. A representative. A person designated to perform a diplomatic or political assignment.

EMOLUMENT   [L. *emolumentum* / the result of effort; reward]

The compensation resulting from services in a position or office; salaries, fees, perquisites. Article 1, Section 9, cl. 8 of the U.S. Constitution is known as the *Emolument Clause* because it provides that no official of the U.S. shall accept any title or gift from a foreign country unless approved by Congress.

EMPIRICAL   [L. *empiricus* / an untrained physician who learned by experience alone]

Depending on experience or observation alone without an accompanying or underlying system or theory. Data gathered through observation or trial.

EMPLOY, EMPLOYEE   [L. *implico, implicare* / to enfold, entangle, involve]

To *employ* is to hire another to perform particular work or services, usually for wages or salary, although the word also has the general sense of utilizing any of the services of another, including executive and professional services. The word *employee*, however, generally refers to persons who work for wages or salary and are under the direct control and supervision of the employer. In this sense, employees are generally called servants and are distinguished from independent contractors, who perform their services without direct control by the person who hires them. An employer is vicariously liable for the torts of his employees, but not for the torts of the independent contractors he engages.

EMPLOYMENT   [L. *implico, implicare*]

The act of utilizing the services of another for pay. The act of being hired or retained to perform labor or services.

EMPTOR   [L. *emptitare* / to buy]

A buyer or purchaser.

See **CAVEAT EMPTOR**

ENABLE   [L. *in + habilis* / easily managed, handy (from *habere* / to have, be able)]

To make possible; to cause. To give power to.

ENABLING ACT

Legislation which removes some legal disability; e.g., a limitation on the rights of immigrants. A statute which grants new powers to the government or to individuals.

ENABLING CLAUSE

That section of a statute which gives executive authorities or agencies the power to put its provisions into effect and to enforce them.

ENDORSE, ENDORSEMENT [L. *in* + *dorsum* / the back of men or animals. A mountain ridge]

To write on the back of. To sign one's name as payee or endorser on the back of a check or note. To transfer or negotiate an instrument to another by inscribing one's name on the back of the instrument. To support or announce approval of a candidate for office or a public issue. To approve openly or publicly. An *endorsement* is the act of signing one's name to the back of an instrument in order to facilitate its transfer or negotiation to another. Also, an *endorsement* is a supplemental rider or attachment to an insurance policy altering or modifying its terms.

ENDOW, ENDOWMENT [L. *in* + *doto, dotare* / to provide with a dowry; give; endow]

To make a gift of money or assets for the support and maintenance of an individual or of an institution, such as a library or school. To provide with a source of income and support. To possess a gift or talent, as he is *endowed* with great intelligence. An *endowment* is a fund organized for the support of a public institution; also, the income from such a fund. An *endowment policy* is a life insurance policy the proceeds of which are payable to the beneficiary at the end of a stipulated term, providing the assured is still living at the end of the term. Also, in insurance law, a type of term life insurance policy that combines insurance and investment. If the insured outlives the term, the policy's value is paid to him. If he dies before the end of the term, the proceeds are paid to his beneficiary.

ENJOIN [L. *in* + *iugare* / to bind together, connect]

To issue a judicial order directing the person addressed to do or refrain from doing a specified act. To require or prohibit by judicial order (i.e., through an *injunction*). To forbid.

See **INJUNCTION**

ENTIRE, ENTIRETY [L. *in* + *tango, tangere* / to touch, move]

Complete, whole, intact. Without distortions or indentations. Homogeneous, pure. An *entirety* is a complete self-contained unit. Also, an indivisible interest in real estate. Example: A *tenancy by the entirety* in a husband and wife is a joint tenancy which gives each of them an undivided interest in property, subject to the right of survivorship.

See **JOINT TENANCY**

ENTITLE, ENTITLEMENT   [L. *in* + *titulus* / label, title]

To *entitle* is to give a legal right, title or claim to someone or to furnish someone with the basis for a claim or right. *An entitlement* is a right conferred by government upon a defined class of individuals, or a government program which provides those rights. One example of an entitlement is the federal social security program which confers benefits upon older citizens. Entitlements are property interests which may not be abridged without due process.

EODEM DELICTO   [L. *eodem* / the same place or person + *delictum* / fault, crime]

Equally guilty of the crime or offense. Said of co-conspirators in the same crime.

EO INSTANTI   [L. *eo* / to that point (in space or time) + *instare, instans* / to stand with, follow closely upon]

At that very moment. Instantly. Immediately.

EO INTUITU   [L. *eo* + *in* + *tueri* / to look at, contemplate]

With that very intent.

EO NOMINE   [L. *eo* + *nomen* / name]

In that name or by that designation or mark. In law and commerce, the name given to a commodity in the marketplace, generally a product name which is in common use and therefore well known.

E PLURIBUS UNUM   [L. *ex* / out of + *multus, plus, plurimus* / many + *unus* / one]

From many, one. From many people or states, one entity. The official motto of the United States of America — out of many, one nation.

EQUAL, EQUALITY   [L. *aequalis* / level, same, equal (*aequo, aequare* / to make equal or level)]

Entitled to the same consideration or treatment as others. Similar in all essential qualities. Similar in characteristics to other members of a group or class. *Equality* is the state or condition of being equal. All Americans are guaranteed equality before the law and equality in employment, regardless of race, color, religion, national origin, sex or disability.

EQUITABLE [L. *aequare*]

Applying the principles of justness, fairness and right. Rights enforceable in the courts of equity. Examples: an *equitable* action; an *equitable* defense; an *equable* distribution; *equitable* estoppel; *equitable* lien; *equitable* relief.

See **EQUITY**

EQUITABLE SUBORDINATION
See **SUBORDINATION**

EQUITAS SEQUITUR LEGEM [L. *aequare* / to make equal or fair + *sequor, sequi* / to follow + *lex* / law]

Equity follows the law. The general sense that equity, or justice tempered with fairness, should be applied to mitigate the harsh effects often resulting from applying the letter of the law.

EQUITY [L. *aeqare* / to make equal]

The system of law and jurisprudence originating in the chancery courts of England which was created and designed to apply a sense of fairness to the more stringent common law. If frustrated in the courts of law, a litigant could seek relief in the equity courts. Today, equitable and legal issues are tried in the same courts but the concept of "doing equity" still survives as an essential element of American jurisprudence.

EQUIVALENTS [L. *aequare* + *valere* / to be strong]

Two things which are equal in value or effect. Corresponding to or identical with. In patent law, *equivalents* are two devices which may be different in name, form, shape or design but which perform the same function or work. The *equivalents doctrine* protects an earlier patented device by declaring that a later device infringes upon it.

ERGO

Therefore; consequently; hence; because.

ERRATUM [L. *erratus* / a wandering about or straying]

An error. The correction for an error in a printed document, usually printed separately.

See **CORRIGENDUM**

ERROR [L. *erro, errare* / to wander about, roam, stray; to be mistaken]

A mistake or oversight. A departure or deviation from a standard which defines what is right and acceptable. A miscalculation or blunder. In litigation, *error* is a mistake made by a lower-court judge in ruling on a motion, admitting evidence, or conducting the proceeding before him. *Judicial errors* may be raised on appeal, but, usually, only if the party raising them has made timely objection during the trial.

ERROR CORAM NOBIS

The basis for the writ which initiated an inquiry by the trial court into errors of fact which might have resulted in a different verdict if known at the time of decision.

See **CORAM NOBIS**

ESCHEAT [Thought to be from the L. *ex* / out of + *cadere* / to fall]

The reversion of property to the state when there is no person legally competent to own it, e.g., upon the disappearance or death of the person legally entitled to the property. The transfer to the state of property which is unclaimed by the owner or his agents; e.g., a bank account or a stock certificate or dividend.

ESQUIRE [L. *scutum* / a shield made of wood and covered with hides]

Formerly, a member of the English gentry ranking just below a knight. A term expressing courtesy or respect, used after a person's name. A term of address used in the United States to acknowledge that a person is licensed as a lawyer, e.g., John Smith, Esq.

ESSENTIALIA NEGOTII

Those things which are essential to a business transaction.

ESTABLISH [L. *stabilio, stabilire* / to make firm or stable]

To institute or put in place, as to establish rights under a statute. To bring into existence or give effect to. To make firm or stable. To give form or substance to, as to *establish* a new business. To make clear and definite, as to establish the truth of a fact.

ESTOPPEL [L. *stupere* / to stand still, to halt]

A bar or waiver. A restraint or impediment imposed by the law; the prevention of further action or claim by a party. In real estate law, an *estoppel certificate* is a sworn statement by a party to the transaction as to some important fact; e.g., the principal amount of a mortage. The statement is binding upon him for all purposes thereafter. *Promissory estoppel* prevents a party who has made a promise upon which another party has relied, from repudiating that promise.

ESTOVER [L. *aestus* / heat, boiling. Thought to be from *est opus* or *opus est* / there is work to be done]

The right of a tenant to take as much wood from the land as he needed for his fuel and fences. Also, an allowance made from an estate to support a benefi-

ciary's need for food and clothing. Also, the allowance (alimony) given to a woman by her husband after a divorce *a mensa et thoro*.
See **A MENSA ET THORO**

ESTUARY [L. *aestus* / boiling, seething]
The place at which a stream or river flows into the sea and meets the seatide; the enlarged mouth of such a stream.

ET AL [L. abbreviation for *et alius* / and another, and of *et alii* / and others]
Used following the first name in the caption of a case to indicate that other parties are involved and to avoid the listing of these other names.

ET CETERA (ETC.) [L. *et* / and + *ceterus* / the other, the rest]
And so forth; and more of the same. And others of the same kind.

ETHICS [L. and Greek *ethice* / moral philosophy]
A system or code defining the proper and improper conduct of a society or a professional or commercial group or activity. A codification of what is perceived as good and moral and what is seen as bad, immoral or unacceptable; e.g., the canons of legal and judicial ethics adopted by the American Bar Association and other associations of lawyers.

ET NON
And not. Used to make negative a phrase or name which follows.

ET SEQUITUR (ET SEQ.) [L. *et* + *sequor, sequi* / to follow]
And the following; and as follows. Used to indicate that notes or pages of a text follow sequentially after a specified number or that one element of a list follows another.

ET UXOR (ET UX.) [L. *et* + *uxor* / wife, spouse]
And his wife. Used in conveyances and deeds to indicate that husband and wife are joining in the conveyance to or from them.

EVADE, EVASIVE [L. *evadere* / to go forth, go out]
To elude. To escape or slip away. To be elusive; to avoid responding. To avoid through neglect or artifice. To fail to pay.

EVICT, EVICTION [L. *evinco, evincere* / to overwhelm, conquer, subdue]
To recover possession of property through legal process or intervention. To remove or dispossess a tenant.

EVIDENCE [L. *evidens, evidentis* / visible, clear, plain (fr. *ex* / out of + *video, videre* / to see]

Anything that furnishes proof or tends to prove. The transcribed record of testimony submitted during a trial for consideration and deliberation by jury and/or judge. *Circumstantial evidence* is evidence of events or circumstances from which the trier can draw a reasonable inference that other events or circumstances occurred. *Direct evidence* is the antithesis of circumstantial evidence; it is evidence which, if believed, establishes a fact as manifestly true; example; the testimony of a direct eye witness or of a participant in the event. *Competent evidence* is evidence that is admissible because it is relevant and material to an issue requiring proof. *Hearsay evidence* is any statement made out of court and not under oath. Hearsay is not admissible unless it falls within one of several exceptions. *Parol evidence* is evidence outside the four corners of a writing, offered as evidence of oral agreements modifying or interpreting the writing.

EVIDENCE ALIUNDE

Extrensic evidence of facts outside the face of a document to prove admissions or to explain or clarify an ambiguity.

See **ALIUNDE**

EVIDENCE DE BENE ESSE

Evidence taken and recorded before trial to preserve it in the event the witness is later unavailable.

See **DE BENE ESSE**

EVICTUM PERPETUUM

Perpetual eviction; permanent ouster from possession.

EX

From, out of, according to. Also, former, without.

EX AEQUO ET BONO

From what is fair and good. In equity and good conscience.

EXAMINE, EXAMINATION [L. *examino, examinare* / to weigh, consider, examine]

The act of inquiring or questioning. To conduct an inquiry into the knowledge and achievements of students in a particular course or curriculum. The act of asking questions of witnesses during a trial or court proceeding to compel answers by the other side and develop proof. *Direct examination* is the first examination of a witness conducted by the attorney who calls him as a witness. *Cross examination* is the examination of a witness who has testified on direct, to test his veracity and knowledge of the facts.

EX ANIMO [L. *ex* + *animo* / the soul, the heart, the spirit]

From one's mind or conscience.

EX ARBITRALE JUDICUS

At the will of the judge.

EX ASSENSU CURIAE

With the consent of the court.

EX ASSENSU SUO

With his own consent.

EX CAPITE DOLI [L. *ex* + *capite* / head + *dolus* / device, artifice]

On the grounds of deceit.

EX CAPITE FRAUDIS

On the grounds of fraud.

EX CATHEDRA

From the chair (formerly used to describe a chair occupied by the pope); from the source of authority.

EX CAUSA METUS

On account of fear.

EXCEPTIO PROBAT REGULAM

The exception proves the rule.

EXCESS, EXCESSIVE [L. *excedo, excedere* (pp. *excessum*) / to go out, to go away; to leave; to exceed]

More than is required or wanted. The amount by which one measure is greater than another. Beyond or greater than acceptable standards; intemperate. The law is intolerant of acts or conduct which are deemed excessive, i.e., beyond reasonable or accepted bounds. Amendment VIII to the U.S. Constitution provides, "Excessive bail shall not be required..." A verdict which is deemed excessive may be reduced through the device of remittitur or by ordering a new trial.

See **REMITTITUR**

EXCISE, EXCISE TAX [L. *ex* + *caedo, caedere* / to cut, cut down, strike]

A tax on the manufacture, sale or consumption of some product or commodity, as on the sale of gasoline or tobacco. A tax or levy assessed as a license fee, e.g., for a taxi medallion. Article I, Section 8 of the U.S. Constitution gives Congress the power to "lay and collect Taxes, Duties, Imposts and Excises..."

EXCLUDE [L. *ex* + *claudo, claudere* / to close, shut down. To conclude or bring to an end. To hide]

To keep out or bar from. To prevent access to. To remove from a position or office. To eliminate a risk from the coverage of an insurance policy.

EXCLUSIONARY RULE

A rule of evidence in criminal trials which provides for the exclusion of evidence which was obtained illegally, i.e., in violation of the Constitution, e.g., as the result of an unreasonable search and seizure. The rule is based upon the Fourth and Fifth Amendments to the U.S. Constitution. The rule prevents the introduction of the evidence by the prosecution as direct proof, but does not preclude its use for impeachment purposes.

EXCLUSIVE [L. *ex* + *claudere* / to close]

Limiting the possession, ownership or enjoyment of a right or asset to one or several persons without participation by others. Belonging to a person or persons alone. Barring or shutting out all others. In law, the word describes a number of relationships which are limited in their scope to a restricted group or purpose. Examples: *exclusive* agency; *exclusive* contract; *exclusive* jurisdiction; *exclusive* possession; *exclusive* use.

EX COLORE [L. *ex* + *color* / color; outward show, external appearance]

Under color of. Under the pretense of.

EX COMITATE [L. *ex* + *comitas* / courtesy, kindness]

Out of comity or courtesy. In recognition of sound public policy or social harmony.

EX CONTRACTU [L. *ex* + *contrahere, contractus* / drawn together, narrow]

Arising out of contract; a cause of action arising under the terms of an agreement. An action for breach of a promise in a contract is an action *ex contractu*. But an action for breach of a duty imposed by a contract may be an action ex delicto.

See **EX DELICTO**

EXCULPATE [L. *ex* + *culpa* / blame, fault]

To clear of blame or guilt, to exonerate or vindicate.

EXCULPATORY CLAUSE

A clause in a document such as a contract or lease which relieves a party from liability for his wrongful act; e.g., his negligence in performing his duties. These clauses are common in leases drawn by a landlord, in trust instruments or in any instance in which one party has a stronger bargaining position than the other.

EX CURIA   [L. *ex* + *curia* / the meeting place of the Roman Senate]

Out of court; in a place away from the court.

EXCUSE, EXCUSABLE   [L. *excuso, excusare* / to excuse a person; to exempt from blame]

To free, exempt or release from a duty. Examples: he was *excused* from service on the jury; she was *excused* from attending class. Also, to forgive or accept. To justify. In the law, an *excusable act* is one which would ordinarily be regarded as illegal or criminal except for exigent circumstances. These circumstances are regarded as sufficient justification to release the perpetrator from punishment or liability. An *excusable homicide* is the killing of a human being either in self-defense or as the result of an unavoidable accident. *Excusable neglect* is the failure to comply with a duty or condition when the failure is caused by circumstances beyond the party's own control, e.g., in an accident or by intervening force.

EX DEBITO   [L. *ex* + *debere* / to owe]

Arising out of a debt or obligation. An obligation which may be enforced by the obligee as a matter of right.

See **EX GRATIA**

EX DELICTO   [L. *ex* + *delictum* / fault, crime]

Arising out of a wrong; a cause of action in tort or based upon a wrongful act. A cause of action for breach of a duty arising under a contract can be *ex delicto*, in contrast with an action for breach of a contractual promise, which will be *ex contractu*. (*Ex delicto* is used interchangeably with *ex maleficio*.)

See **DELICTUM; EX CONTRACTU; EX MALEFICIO**

EX DELICTO TRUST

A trust created for an unlawful purpose; e.g., a trust created to frustrate the claims of the settlor's creditors.

EX DIVIDEND

Literally, without a dividend. A stock or security which is purchased or traded without a right by the purchaser to claim a dividend which was declared prior to the trade. On trades *ex dividend*, the seller retains the right to the declared dividend.

See **DIVIDEND; EX WARRANTS**

EX DOLO MALO   [L. *ex* + *dolus* / device, act + *malus* / bad, evil]

Growing out of a bad deed or act. The consequences of conduct arising from fraud or deceit.

EX DOLO MALO NON ORITUR ACTIO

No action can arise from or be based on a bad deed or on deceit. The principle which directs a court not to consider an action based on an illegal or immoral act.

See **EX TURPI CAUSA NON ORITUR ACTIO**

EXECUTION   [L. *exsequi* / to follow to the grave; to pursue till the end]

The act of carrying out or performing a task or duty. The act of putting someone to death. Also, the process by which a judgment or other declaration of a legal right is enforced. The act of a sheriff or other court officer in collecting a judgment debt.

EXECUTIVE   [L. *ex* + *sequor, sequi, secutus* / to follow to the end; to keep up; to carry out or execute]

A person who has administrative or managerial duties. Having administrative duties. In the American constitutional system, that branch of government charged with carrying out and enforcing the law; one of the three branches of government (along with the judicial and legislative branches). An *executive agreement* is an enforceable treaty-like agreement between the U.S. and a foreign state which is authorized by the President without approval by the Senate. An *executive pardon* is a pardon issued to a prisoner by the President or by the governor of a state. An *executive session* is a meeting of a committee or board which is closed to all but its members.

EXECUTOR   [L. *ex* + *sequi* / to follow till the end]

The person named by a testator to carry out the purposes specified in his will and to manage and dispose of his property in accordance with his testamentary instructions.

EXECUTORY   [L. *ex* + *sequi*]

Waiting to be executed or carry out. To be done or completed in the future. Having future effect or impact. An *executory contract* is one in which the parties promise to perform some act in the future. An *executory use* is a use which will come into existence at some future time, as in the case of a springing use.

EXEMPLI GRATIA (E.G.) [L. *exemplum* / a sample, example + *gratia* / a favor, kindness]

For example, used generally in the abbreviated form; e.g., Example: "We stock a variety of books; e.g., mysteries, travel books, biographies, etc."

EXEMPT [L. *exemptus*, from *eximo, eximire* / to take out, take away. To remove from a list]

To free someone from performing a duty which is generally expected of others in his group or class. Example: he was *exempted* from military services because he was needed more as an entertainer of troops than as a soldier. To discharge or release from liability. To exclude an asset from liability for the payment of taxes. To exclude certain items of income from liability for income taxes; some income may be *exempt* from federal taxation but not from taxation by a state. An *exempt organization* is an organization which is not liable for the payment of taxes. Some of the property or income of a debtor or a petitioner in bankruptcy may be exempt from levy, attachment or sale.

EXEMPTION [L. *eximere* / to take out, take away]

Release or immunity from a general obligation, such as the obligation to serve in the military or on a jury. Freedom of a debtor from the claims of creditors or from judicial process. Property not included in a bankruptcy proceeding or in the computation of net income for tax purposes. A privilege granted by the Constitution or by statute conferring immunity from a stated consequence, such as *exemption* from arrest in a civil case. *Exemption laws* are state laws which exclude certain property of a debtor from attachment or judgment by creditors.

EX FACIE [L. *ex* + *facies* / shape, form, figure]

(Clear) on its face. Clearly, without doubt or question. Those elements which are clear from the face of a document.

EX FACTO [L. *ex* + *factum* / an accomplished fact, a deed or fact (from *facere* / to make or do)]

As a result of the act. As a consequence of the act or fact.

See **FACTO**

EX FACTO JUS ORITUR

The law is born of fact.

EX FICTIONE JURIS

Through a legal fiction.

EX GRATIA [L. *ex* + *gratia* / pleasantness, kindness, thankfulness. Willingly]

Out of a sense of fairness. An action done as a favor, not because it was required, due or owed. A decision made not in recognition of right but out of a sense of fairness and justice.

See **EX DEBITO**

EXHAUST, EXHAUSTION (OF REMEDIES) [L. *exhaurio, exhaurire* / to take out or remove; to use up, drain dry, empty out. To impoverish]

To consume or use up. To cause extreme fatigue to. To remove a valuable or essential ingredient or component of. The doctrine of *exhaustion of remedies* requires that a party first proceed through all available administrative remedies before seeking the assistance of the courts. The doctrine also requires that a party exhaust all his remedies in the state courts before turning to the federal courts for relief. One result of the doctrine is that the federal courts will not issue a writ of habeas corpus until a criminal defendant has exhausted all available remedies in the state courts. The doctrine derives from the principles of comity.

See **COMITY**

EXHIBIT [L. *exhibitus*, from *exhibeo, exhibere* / to produce in court; to show, display]

A document or other matter produced in court for use as evidence. An attachment to a brief, report or memorandum, labelled and identified for reference. A display for examination by the public. Also, to offer as evidence in a litigation or proceeding. To present officially or in legal form. To evidence a quality, state or characteristic, as *to exhibit fear*.

EXIGENT, EXIGENCY [L. *exigo, exigere* / to drive out; to force out. To demand or compel]

A circumstance or condition requiring immediate attention or action. A matter requiring resolution; an emergency.

EXIGENT CIRCUMSTANCES

In criminal law, circumstances justifying a police search without a warrant. These circumstances may include the imminent destruction of evidence by the suspect, a threat of harm or injury to persons, and searches in "hot pursuit" of a suspect.

EXIGI FACIAS [L. (That you) cause to be done]

A writ commanding the sheriff to demand delivery and surrender of the defendant.

EXILE [L. *eicere* / to throw out, eject, banish]

To force from one's home or country. To banish or expel from one's own country.

EX IMPROVISO

(Done) without forethought or preparation. Suddenly, spontaneously.

EX JURE NATURALE

From the law of nature. The natural law.

EX JUSTA CAUSA

Out of or originating from a just and legal cause.

EX LEGE [L. *ex* + *lex, legis* / a fixed group of words. A contract. A law. The law generally]

(Proceeding) from the law, as a matter of law.

EX MALA CAUSA NON ORITUR ACTIO

No cause of action can arise from a bad act or cause. The court will not enforce an evil act.

EX MALEFICIO [L. *ex* + *malus* / bad or evil + *facere* / to make or do]

Growing out of wrongdoing. An act done illegally, wrongfully or tortiously. Malfeasance.

See **EX DELICTO**

EX MALEFICIO NON ORITUR CONTRACTUS

A contract cannot arise from wrong or evil. The court will not enforce an illegal contract.

EX MALITIA [L. *ex* + *malitia* / wickednness, cunning, malice]

(Done) with malice; maliciously.

EX MALITIA PRAECOGNITA [L. *ex* + *malitia* + *prae* / before + *cognoscere* / to know, think]

With malice aforethought. Conceived out of malice.

See **EX PRAECOGNITA MALITIA**

EX MERITO JUSTITIAE [L. *ex* + *meritare* / to earn + *iustitia* / justice, fairness]

In the interest of justice. For the sake of justice.

EX MERO MOTU [L. *ex* + *merus* / complete + *motus* / motion]
Of his own doing; voluntarily; without being asked. On motion of the court without application by either party.

EX MORA [L. *ex* + *mora* / delay]
Because of the delay. By reason of delay.

EX MORE [L. *ex* + *mos, moris* / will, mood. Also custom, usage]
According to custom or usage.

EX NECESSITATE LEGIS
(Done or ordered) out of legal necessity.

EX NIHILO NIHIL FIT [L. *ex* + *nihil, nihilum, nihilo* / nothing + *facere* / to act, do]
The result of nothing is nothing.

EX NUDO PACTO NON ORITUR ACTIO [L. *ex* + *nudus* / naked + *pactum* / agreement + *non* / not + *oriri* / to rise, occur + *actio* / action]
No action will grow out of a naked promise; i.e., a promise for which there is no consideration.

EX OFFICIO [L. *ex* + *officium* / service, duty, function, office]
From the office, by virtue of the office; powers necessarily held or implied by virtue of an office or title. Powers which need not be specified but which may be exercised nevertheless because they are necessary to the administration of the office by the officeholder.

EX OFFICIO MEMBER
One who is entitled to be a member of a board, committee or other body by virtue of his possession of another designated office and who does not require further appointment.

EX OFFICIO SERVICES
Services which are imposed on a public officer by virtue of his office.

EXONERATE [L. *exonerare* / to unload, unburden]
To remove an obligation or hardship. To relieve of guilt or burden. To absolve of a charge.

EX PACTO ILLICITO NON ORITUR ACTIO
No action can be taken under an unlawful agreement.

EX PARTE

By or on the application of one party only; applied to proceedings which are initiated by or for the benefit of one party without notice to the other; e.g., an *ex parte* proceeding. An *ex parte* injunction is an order issued by the court upon the application of one party without notice to the other. Other proceedings which may occur *ex parte*: *ex parte* divorce; *ex parte* hearing; *ex parte* license revocation.

EX PARTE MATERNA

From the side of the mother. Proceeding from the mother; the maternal line.

EX PARTE PATERNA

From the side of the father. Proceeding from the father; the paternal line.

EXPATRIATION   [L. *ex* + *patria* / fatherland]

To renounce the citizenship of one country and elect the citizenship of another. To terminate one's civil and political rights in one country and resume them in another.

EXPECTANCY   [L. *exspecto, exspectare* / to look for, wait for; anticipate]

Anything anticipated in the future. A person's *life expectancy* is the number of years he may expect to live based upon statistical tables. An interest in property which may or may not mature in the future and which may not be possessed or enjoyed in the present.

EXPECTATION   [L. *exspectare* / to await, anticipate]

Anything awaited or anticipated. *Expectation damages* are damages awarded to a party in an action for breach of contract measured by the benefit he would have received if the contract had been performed according to its terms.

EXPENSAE CIRCA FUNUS   [L. *expensus* / anything paid out + *circa* / at the time of + *funus* / a funeral]

Expenses connected with burial. Funeral expenses.

EXPENSE   [L. *expensus*, from *expendo, expendere* / to weigh out, pay out, pay for]

Anything spent to secure a benefit or a thing of value. An outlay of money or effort in exchange for a benefit. A *business expense* is one in connection with the operation of a business or commercial enterprise, as opposed to a *personal expense*, i.e., an expense in the furtherance of one's personal affairs. A *capital expense* is a current business outlay or investment in exchange for a long-term business benefit.

EXPERT [L. *expertus*, fr. *experior, experiri* / to try, prove; put to the test. To know through trial or experience]

A person with special skill or knowledge in a particular field or area of experience or knowledge, entitling him to form and express an opinion on matters in dispute. An *expert witness* is a witness who is qualified as an *expert* and who has knowledge of a particular subject not ordinarily possessed by the average person. An expert witness is allowed to give his opinion and to assist the court and jury in understanding and determining a complex and technical subject.

EX POST FACTO

After the fact. After the thing has been done. The phrase applies to any law that criminalizes an act that was innocent when committed; any law that makes a crime greater or more serious than when it was committed; or any rule of evidence which adversely affects a criminal defendant's rights as they existed prior to the rule. Article I, Section 9 of the U.S. Constitution precludes the passage of such a law or rule by any state or by the federal government. The provision has been construed to apply only to crimes, not to civil rights.

See **AB INITIO; FACTO**

EX PRAECOGNITA MALITIA

With malice aforethought.

See **EX MALITIA PRAECOGNITA**

EXPRESS [L. *expressus,* from *exprimo, exprimere* / to force out, to describe, to say in words]

Clearly and explicitly stated. Exact, precise. Not left to inference or implication. An *express agency* is an agency created in clear language, either in writing or verbally. An *express condition* is a condition in a contract in plain and simple language.

EXPRESSIO FALSI [L. *exprimere* / to represent, portray, express + *fallere, falsus* / to deceive]

A false statement; a lie.

EXPRESSIO UNIUS EST EXCLUSIO ALTERIUS

The statement of one thing or fact suggests the exclusion of all others. The expression of one thing in a statute or document will be interpreted to mean that another thing which is not specifically mentioned will be excluded; e.g., a statute which is applicable to "doctors, nurses, nurses aids, and other hospital employees" will be construed as excluding the employees of nursing homes.

EXPRESSUM FACIT CESSARE TACITUM
>A thing expressed takes priority over a thing implied. A law which is plainly and clearly written must be followed as written.

EXPROPRIATE   [L. *ex* + *proprius* / one's own; peculiar to one's self; personal]
>Originally, the surrender of a claim to property. Now, to deprive one of his property or possessions. Also, to condemn private property for public use.
>See **CONDEMNATION; CONFISCATE; EMINENT DOMAIN**

EX PROPRIO MOTU   [L. *ex* + *proprio* / one's own + *motu* / motion, movement]
>Of his own decision; of his own accord.

EX PROPRIO VIGORE   [L. *ex* + *proprio* + *vigor* / force, energy]
>By its own force or strength. Without restraint. Automatically.

EX PROVISIONE MARITI (OR VIRI)   [L. *ex* + *proviso*, from *providere* / to look forward, to provide + *maritus* / relating to marriage; husband; (or *vir* / man, husband)]
>By provision of the husband, as provided by a husband.

EXPULSON   [L. *ex* + *pellere* / to strike back, to beat back]
>An enforced removal from memberhip or participation. The act of removing a member from a body or organization, e.g., expulsion of a member from a legislature or professional society, or a student from a school. Also, an eviction or forcible removal from premises.

EXPUNGE   [L. *ex* + *pungere* / to stab or puncture]
>To blot out, erase, destroy; e.g., to wipe data from a criminal record, as from the record of a juvenile defendant.

EX RELATIONE (EX REL.)   [L. *ex* + *referre, relatum* / to carry back, to report, to bring before]
>Upon relation or report. Refers to actions or proceedings brought by attorneys general or by other government entities or agencies which are based upon the information or the inititiative of a private individual or group with an interest in the outcome. The phrase is made part of the title of the action; e.g., "United States *ex rel.* Ames v. Barton".

EX STATU   [L. *ex* + *statuere* / to stand up, put in place, establish]
>By virtue of the statute. According to the statute.

EX TEMPORE [L. *ex* + *tempus, temporis* / a division, a section, as of time or space; time]

Measured or controlled by the passage or lapse of time. For the time being; temporarily. Also, on the spur of the moment; as the occasion demands.

EXTENDI FACIAS [L. *extendere* / to extend, expand + *facere* / to make, do]

You shall cause to be extended. A writ requiring the sheriff to seize the lands of a debtor, to appraise them, and to apply the value in satisfaction of the claims of a creditor.

See **FACIAS, FIERI FACIAS**

EX TERRITORIAL

See **EXTRA TERRITORAL**

EXTERUS NON HABET TERRA

A foreigner or alien cannot hold land.

EX TESTAMENTO [L. *ex* + *testari* / to bear witness, give evidence]

By the will. According to the will or testament.

EXTINGUISH [L. *ex* + *stinguere* / to wipe out or annihilate]

To terminate or cancel. To discharge. To make void, as a debt or commitment.

EXTINGUISHMENT [L. *extinguere*]

The termination of a right, power, duty or obligation or of an interest in property or contract. Used in *extinguishment of a debt* (as by payment or through bankruptcy); *extinguishment of a legacy* (as through ademption); or *extinguishment of a lien* (discharge or cancellation of a lien by court order or operation of law).

See **ADEMPTION**

EXTORT, EXTORTION [L. *ex* + *torqueo, torquere* / to twist, wind around, wrench; to torment, plague]

To take by force. To remove money or property from a person by the use or threat of force or the exercise or threat of excessive or unlawful authority. To compel or coerce by overpowering a person's free will or ability to resist, as to *extort a confession*. The crime of *extortion* (called *blackmail* in some states) is the taking of property by a threat of future harm.

EXTRADITE, EXTRADITION [L. *extra* / outside, beyond + *traditio* / a giving up or surrender (fr. *trado, tradere* / to hand over, give up, surrender)]

To surrender a prisoner to another jurisdiction or country. The act of one country or state in surrendering to another country or state a person accused or convicted of crime in the latter, to permit his trial or punishment. *Extradition* is usually controlled by a treaty between nations. Article IV, Section 2 of the U.S. Constitution requires each state to deliver up to another state from which he has fled, any person charged with treason, felony, or other crime. (See THE UNIFORM CRIMINAL EXTRADITION ACT adopted by many states of the United States.)

EXTRA JUDICIUM   [L. *extra* +*iudicium* / trial or legal investigation]

Out of Court; out of the proper legal channels; without a court's intervention; extrajudicial.

EXTRA JUS   [L. *extra* + *ius* / right, law]

Beyond or outside the law. Not within the scope of the law. More than the law demands.

EXTRA LEGEM   [L. *extra* + *lex, legis* / contract, rule, law]

Outside the law. Beyond the protection of the law.

EXTRA LEGEM POSITUS

Placed outside the law. Subjected to civil death. As punishment for treason or other high crime, a defendant was deprived of such rights as the right to serve as witness, the right to sue, the right to vote, and the other rights of citizenship.

EXTRA LEGEM POSITUS EST CIVILITER MORTUUS

A person outlawed for his crimes is civilly dead.

EXTRAMURAL   [L. *extra* + *muralis* / the wall around a city]

Outside the proper scope. Activities outside the regular scope or function of an organization. In the case of a municipal corporation, powers exercised outside of corporate limits or boundaries. In the case of a school, student activities outside of the classroom.

EXTRATERRITORIAL   [L. *extra* + *territorium* / the area included in or belonging to a town]

Outside the boundaries of a state or country. *Extraterritoriality* is the privilege extended to ministers or representatives of a foreign country to be free or immune from the effect or consequences of the domestic laws of the country they are assigned to. The exercise of this privilege often brings the foreign representative into conflict with local police authorities.

EXTRATERRITORIAL JURISDICTION

The power of a court to extend its reach or jurisdiction beyond the limits of the state or country in which it sits; e.g., through the use of long-arm statutes.

EXTRA VIAM [L. *extra* + *via* / road, highway, way]
Outside the road. Off the regular and usual path.

EXTRA VIAM RIGHTS
The right of a traveler to pass over the lands of an abutting owner without being charged in trespass when a road or highway is impassable. The right of the owner of an easement to pass over servient property when the servient owner has obstructed the easement.
See **SERVIENT**

EXTRA VIRES [L. *extra* + *vis, vires* / force, strength, power]
Beyond the power of.
See **ULTRA VIRES**

EXTREME CRUELTY [L. *exter, exterior, extremus* / on the outer edge, extreme + *crudelis* / unfeeling, cruel]
In family law, violence or the threats of violence by one spouse upon another. Acts of one spouse calculated to destroy the health or peace of mind of the other. Recognized in most jurisdictions as grounds for divorce.

EXTREMIS [L. *exter, exterior, extremus* / outward, at the outer limits of, at the end]
A situation or circumstance of extreme concern or seriousness, such as illness or injury. Used to describe imminent death.
See **IN EXTREMIS**

EXTREMIS PROBATIS, PRAESUMUNTER MEDIA
If the extremes at either end of a problem are solved, all things or issues between the extremes are also deemed solved.

EXTRINSIC [L. *exter* / from without, foreign + *sequor, sequi* / to follow]
Originating from an outside source. *Extrinsic evidence* is evidence which is not apparent from the face of a document, but is derived from external sources, e.g., through testimony of the parties. An *extrinsic ambiguity* is an ambiguity or question which is not apparent on the face of the document but is created by some collateral fact or circumstance external to the document.
See **INTEGRATED CONTRACT; INTRINSIC**

EX TURPI CAUSA [L. *ex* + *turpis* / unsightly, deformed, foul, base, disgraceful + *causa* / a case, an action]
A claim or action based on the defendant's violation of a law forbidding some conduct or act.

EX TURPI CAUSA NON ORITUR ACTIO

No disgraceful, foul, immoral, or obscene matter can be the basis of an action. This principle is often cited by courts which refuse to consider claims based upon fraud or illegality.

See **EX DOLO MALO NON ORITUR ACTIO**

EX WARRANTS

The sale or conveyance of a security without the warrants which are associated with it or which are a part of it. The seller retains the warrants.

See **EX DIVIDEND**

FABRICATE   [L. *fabricare* / to form, make, forge]

To make or construct. To assemble parts into a finished whole. Also, to falsify; to create "facts" for the purpose of deception. To construct a story or report out of lies and distortions. In the law of evidence, a *fabricated fact* is a "fact" without any foundation in truth.

FACIAS   [L. *facio, facere* / to make or do]

(The thing) you have done. (What) you have done. (What) you caused to happen.

See **EXTENDI FACIAS; FIERI FACIAS; LEVARI FACIAS; SCIRE FACIAS; VENIRE FACIAS**

FACINUS QUOS INQUINAT AEQUAT

Villainy and crime pollute all things equally. Crime infects all that it touches.

FACIO UT DES

I do as you give. An agreement by the parties to exchange work or services for money.

FACIO UT FACIAS

I do that you may also do. An agreement by the parties to exchange performance for performance.

FACT   [L. *factum, factus,* pp., *facio, facere* / to make, do]

Objective reality. Capable of verification through the senses. Any event or condition whose existence or occurrence has been or can be confirmed. In any trial or legal proceeding, the principal objective is to analyze the proof submitted by both sides to find the facts. In a jury trial, this is the function of the jury. In a non-jury trial, the judge performs this function.

FACTA SUNT POTENTIORI VERBIS

Deeds are more powerful than words.

FACTIO TESTAMENTI   [L. *facere* / to make, do + *testamentum* / last will or testament]

The making or execution of a will. Also, the capacity to make a will.

FACTO [L. *facere* / to make, do]
> In fact. As the result of a deed, accomplishment or exploit.
> See **DE FACTO, EX FACTO, EX POST FACTO, IPSO FACTO**

FACTO ET ANIMO
> In fact and with intent.

FACTOR [L. *facere* / to make, do]
> Originally, an agent employed by a principal to sell goods or commodities for the principal's account. The agent usually dealt in his own name and often took possession of the goods pending the sale. The agent was paid by a commision known as a *factorage*. Also, now, a firm which advances money to a business in exchange for an assignment of the business' accounts receivable. The factor may be given authority to process and collect the receivables. A *factor's lien* is a general lien held by a factor on goods of the principal which come into his possession, to secure the payment of his fees or commissions.

FACTOTUM [L. *facere* / to do + *totus, totum* / the whole, entire, all]
> One who does all. A general servant or agent with many duties. A person having many duties or responsibilities.

FACTUM [L. *facere*]
> That which is done. A deed, act, exploit or accomplishment. An integral fact which is essential to the resolution of a problem or question. An act which is integral to a legal issue or definition. *Fraud in the factum* is a deception which induces a party to perform an act or to execute a document.

FACTUM PROBANDUM [L. *factum* + *probare* / to approve, recommend, show, prove]
> The fact to be proved. The phrase is used especially in the law of evidence.

FACTUM PROBANS
> A fact which acts as proof. A fact which has probative value or which tends to prove the existence of another fact.

FAIL [L. *fallo, fallere* / to deceive; to be mistaken]
> To cease to function. To breakdown. To be unsuccessful. To suffer a total business loss or reversal; to become bankrupt. To achieve a score on an exam or test lower than the passing grade. To fall below an acceptable standard or measure.

FALSA DEMONSTRATIO [L. *fallo, fallere* / to lead astray, deceive + *demonstrare* / to indicate, point out]
> A false or deceptive statement or description.

FALSARE CURIAM [L. *fallere* / to deceive + *curia* / meeting house, court]
To deceive the court.

FALSE, FALSIFY [L. *fallo, fallere* / to deceive]
Not truthful or reliable. Not genuine or authentic; counterfeit. Deceptive; misleading. To *falsify* is to counterfeit or forge; to convert something which is true into something which is untrue and misleading; to make a statement or document untruthful through mutilation, alteration or substitution.

FALSE ARREST
The physical restraint of an individual without his consent and without lawful authority. An arrest made by any person, including a police officer, without legal authority. *False arrest* is both a tort and a crime.

FALSE IMPRISONMENT
The intentional or negligent physical restraint of a person without his consent and without lawful authority. The restraint may occur anywhere and may be accomplished not only by imposing physical barriers but by the threat of force or assertion of authority. "A person commits a misdemeanor if he knowingly restrains another unlawfully so as to interfere substantially with his liberty." Model Penal Code §212.3

FALSE LIGHT
A tort consisting of an offensive or objectionable portrayal of a person, usually by publication in a newspaper or journal. The portrayal need not be defamatory but must appear to a reasonable person to be an unwarranted invasion of a person's privacy. This tort is not recognized in all jurisdictions.

FALSE PRETENSES
A crime consisting of the false representation of a material past or present fact, made with knowledge that the representation is false and with intent to defraud, which causes the person to whom it is made to convey an interest in property. The crime is recognized in all jurisdictions.

FALSI CRIMEN [L. *fallere* + *crimen* / an accusation or charge; fault, guilt or crime]
A violation or crime characterized by fraud, deception and concealment. Examples: forgery, false pretenses, false weights.
See **CRIMEN FALSI**

FALSUS [L. *fallere* / to deceive]
Wrong, mistaken, misled. Also false, deceitful.

FALSUS IN UNO, FALSUS IN OMNIBUS

One who is false in one thing will be false in all things. In the law of evidence, if a witness has lied about one matter, the jury may disregard his testimony about other matters unless they are proven by testimony other than his own.

FAMA   [L. talk, report, rumor, public opinion, reputation]

Good name or reputation. A person's standing. The public's opinion of a person.

FAMILIA   [L. a household of slaves; a household. A family or group]

A group of persons of common ancestry. A number of individuals living together and usually headed by one or two members.

FAMILY   [L. *familia* / a household, a family estate; a group of related persons]

A group of persons living together under one roof. A group of persons united by ties of blood and marriage. Persons having a common ancestry. Traditionally, a husband and wife and their children, either natural or by adoption. Now, any group living together in a social unit equivalent to the traditional family. Also, any group of related things, e.g., languages, plants, animals. *Family Law* is an area of the law dealing with marriage, marital relations, divorce, paternity, custody, support and adoption.

FAMOSUS LIBELLUS   [L. *famosus* / widely spoken of, notorious, infamous + *liber, libellus* / a little book]

A letter, advertisement or writing which is publicly circulated or becomes widely known, generally having derogatory or defamatory content. In law, a libelous writing; a libel.

FAULT   [L. *fallere* / to deceive, disappoint]

A lack or deficiency; a weakness. A mistake or omission. In law, a mistake in judgment. The breach of a legal duty or responsibility. Negligence. A failure of prudence or reasonable care.

FEALTY   [L. *fides, fideles, fidelitas* / faithfulness, loyalty, trust, faith]

The obligation or allegance of a vassal or tenant to the lord of the manor. Intense devotion or loyalty.

FEDERAL   [L. *foedus* / a league; a compact or agreement; from *fido, fidere* / to believe or confide in]

Arising from a compact or treaty. A compact among individual political entities which retain control over many of the aspects and functions of government but surrender sovereignty and central authority to a common government known as a federation. The central government in a union of states or other territorial divisions. The government of the United States, as distinguished from the government of any one of the American states. Central governmental authority. The courts created by Congress to decide *federal* law questions and disputes between the states and between citizens of different states are called the *federal courts*.

FELO DE SE [L. *feles* / a thief + *de se* / of himself]

One who is or does evil to himself. One who destroys himself; self-destruction. A suicide. Attempted suicide is a felony in many jurisdictions.

FELON [L. *feles* / a thief or villain]

One who has committed a crime defined as a felony.

FELONICE CEPIT [L. *feles* / a thief + *capere, cepi* / to take, seize]

He took it (away) feloniously.

FELONIOUS [L. *feles* / a thief, villain]

Relating to or having the quality of a felony. An act forbidden by law. Intent to commit a serious crime.

FELONY

A serious crime usually punishable by imprisonment for more than one year and sometimes by death, distinguished from the lesser crimes known as misdemeanors. Examples of felonies: homicide, robbery, burglary, rape. Most states and the federal code have extensive provisions defining felonies and dividing them into various classes.

See **MODEL PENAL CODE**

FENERATION [L. *faenerari* / to lend at interest]

To lend with interest. The interest or income from a loan. Also, to lend at an excessive rate of interest. Usury.

FERAE NATURAE [L. *ferus* / wild + *natura, naturae* / nature, in the nature of things, by its nature]

The wild beasts of nature. Animals which are not generally tamed by man, distinguished from domesticated animals.

See **DOMITAE NATURAE**

FERIAE [L. feasts]

Holidays or festivals in ancient Rome.

FETICIDE [L. *fetus* / offspring brood; an unborn child + *caedere* / to cut down, kill]

Destruction of a fetus, as by abortion. A criminal abortion.

FETUS [L. pregnant, fertile]

Fruitful, fertile; child-bearing. An unborn offspring or child. A developing human being beginning three months following conception.

FIAT [L. *facere (fieri)* / to make or do]

Let it be done. An official order, a command, a decree. The order of a judge or executive directing that some act be performed. An order by an authorative source requiring that something be done.

FIAT JUSTITIA

Let justice be done.

FIAT UT PETITUR [L. *facere* + *ut* / how, as + *petere* / to ask for, beseech]

Do what he asks. Let it be done according to his petition.

FICTIO

An assumption; a deception. A fiction.

FICTIO CEDIT VERATI [L. *fictio* + *cedere* / to withdraw + *veritas* / truth]

Fiction gives way before truth.

FICTIO JURIS NON EST UBI VERITAS

A legal fiction will not prevail over the truth.

FIDEI COMMISSUM [L. *fides* / trust, confidence, reliance + *commissum*, pp., *committere* / to unite, connect, combine]

Under the Civil Law, a bequest to a party with instructions to convey title to a third party or to utilize the property for a particular purpose.

FIDELIS

True, steadfast, loyal. Capable of being trusted or relied on (as in *semper fidelis,* always faithful, the motto of the U.S. Marines).

FIDELITY [L. *fidelis* / faithful]

The quality of being loyal or faithful. Allegiance; loyalty. A *fidelity bond* is an insurer's indemnity to the insured against the dishonesty, defalcation, breach of trust or negligence of an employee or agent holding a position of trust. The policy or bond issued by the insurer is called *fidelity guaranty insurance.*

FIDES

Trust, confidence, reliance (related to **FIDELIS,** *supra)* used in *bona fide,* in good faith; *mala fides,* in bad faith.

See **BONA FIDE; MALA FIDES**

FIDUCIARY [L. *fiducia* / confidence, trust, reliance (from *fidere,* to trust or rely on)]

A relationship founded on trust and reliance. Also, a person placed in a position of trust or responsibility to others, as the trustee of a trust. A person having the duty to act in good faith and with integrity towards others. An adjective used to define documents or relationships which depend on trust or obligation; e.g., *fiduciary bond, fiduciary capacity*, etc.

FIERI [L. past form of verb *facere* / to make or do]

Made or done.

FIERI FACIAS

To cause it to be done or made. A common law writ of execution enabling a creditor to enforce the collection of a claim that has gone to final judgment, issued to and carried out by the sheriff.

See **EXTENDI FACIAS; LEVARI FACIAS**

FIERI FACIAS DE BONIS TESTATORIS

A writ of execution directed against the executor of an estate levying upon the goods of the testator to satisfy the testator's debts.

FIERI FECI

I have caused to be done. The statement of the sheriff or court officer to the effect that he has satisfied his obligation to execute upon property of the debtor; usually by writing the word "satisfied" across the writ of execution.

FILIATION [L. *filius* / a son]

The relationship between father and son. A judicial finding of paternity.

FILIATION PROCEEDING

A judicial proceeding to establish paternity of, and to impose a consequential duty to support, a child.

FILIUS NULLUS [L. *filius* / son, child + *nullus* / no, none, not any]

The child of no one. The common law designation for an illegitimate child.

FINE [L. *finis* / boundary, border, limit; end]

A sum of money exacted from a defendant as punishment for a crime. A civil penalty imposed for infractions or violations of regulations or rules. A forfeiture or penalty sometimes paid by the losing party in a civil litigation.

FIRM [L. *firmus* / strong, stout, durable]

Strong or unmovable. Securely fastened. Inflexible. Unchanging, constant. A commercial enterprise having a separate existence and with an identifiable name or title. A partnership recognized as a legal entity separate from its members, as a *law firm*.The name or title utilized by a business or professional partnership.

FIRM OFFER

An irrevocable offer in writing by a merchant to buy or sell an item or commodity for a stated period of time or for a reasonable period of time, not to exceed three months. The offer need not recite or be accompanied by consideration. UCC §2-205.

FISCAL   [L. *fiscus* / a basket or container, a money bag; also, the emperor's treasury; money]

Pertaining to matters of money and finances, as in *fiscal period* or *fiscal policy*. A *fiscal period* is any period of twelve consecutive months chosen by a corporation or business as its accounting and reporting period. Also, relating to public financing or taxation or the public debt.

FIXTURE   [L. *figere* / to fix, fasten, affix]

Anything which is originally personal property but which is physically attached to real property and becomes a permanent part of the realty; e.g., a furnace, store counters, etc. Generally, fixtures installed by a tenant become a part of the building and cannot be removed by the tenant upon termination of his occupancy.

See **RES IMMOBILES**

FLAGRANS CRIMEN   [L. *flagrare* / to burn, glow, blaze + *crimen* / fault, crime]

In the course of committing a crime. While a crime is committed.

FLAGRANTE DELICTO   [L. *flagrare* / to burn, glow + *delictum* / fault, crime]

In the very act of committing a crime or misdeed; also, to be discovered in an illicit sex act.

See **IN FLAGRANTE DELICTO**

FORCE   [L. *fortis* / strong, powerful, brave, energetic]

Power, strength or energy. A source of motion or change, as in the force of the wind, or the *force of public opinion*. A group of persons organized for collective action, as a *military force*, the *labor force*, a *police force*, etc. An *intervening force* is any action or event which follows an initial act of negligence and which contributes to the injury caused the victim of the negligence. An *irresistible force* is any action which cannot be thwarted or resisted, e.g., an unpredictable event which prevents performance of a contract term.

Deadly force is force intended by the user to cause either death or the risk of death.

FORCE MAJESTURE   [L. *fortis* / strong + *maiestas* / greatness, majesty; the Roman gods]

An act of God such as lightning, earthquakes, floods, etc., which operates to prevent or delay the performance of a contract or of a duty or obligation. Synonymous with the more common term *force majeure* (from the French).

See **VIS MAJOR**

FORCE MAJEURE

In insurance law, a superior or irresistible force, an act of God. In contract law, an event which is beyond the control of the parties and which excuses performance.

FORCIBLE (ENTRY)

Carried out by force or the threat of force. *Forcible entry* at common law was the seizure of another's property by the use of force or violence or by any means creating fear of violence. In many states, the term is used to describe any wilful entry upon another's property without his consent. Model Penal Code §221 defines the misdemeanor of Criminal Trespass as any unprivileged entry at night onto any building or occupied structure; if the entry is during the day, it is defined as a petty misdemeanor.

FORECLOSE   [L. *foras, foris* / outside, out of doors + *claudo, claudere* / to close, shut]

To shut out, prevent, cut off. To conduct a judicial proceeding which extinguishes all rights of a mortgagor to a parcel of real property, including his equity of redemption. In a foreclosure, the court orders a sale, the proceeds of which are applied first to the costs of the proceeding and then to liquidation of the mortgage. Under Article 9 of the UCC, a creditor with a security interest in personal property may *foreclose* and extinguish the rights of his debtor by judicial action and sale.

FOREIGN   [L. *foras, foris* / out of doors, outside, without]

Situated outside or beyond the boundaries of a state or country. Belonging to another state or country. Distinguished by characteristics different from those at hand. Strange, unknown. Not native or natural to. A *foreign corporation* is a corporation organized in another state. A *foreign decree* is a judgment or order of a court in another state.

FORENSIC [L. *forensis* / relating to the market or forum; relating to the legal proceedings of the Roman forum]

Relating to, used in or useful for the courts and for judicial determinations. The application of scientific knowledge to law and legal issues. *Forensic medicine,* for example is the discipline which relates all of medicine to the needs and purposes of the law. The medical data which are submitted to and considered by the courts in civil and criminal actions. Used also in *forensic engineering, forensic linguisrics,* etc.

See **FORUM**

FORFEIT, FORFEITURE [L. *foris* / outside + *facio, facere* / to make, do]

To give up or lose as the result of some error or offense. To pay an unwilling price for. To lose a right or privilege in consequence of some action or failure to act, as for a breach of contract or a failure to appear in court. To become liable for the payment of a sum of money or the loss of property after a criminal act. Several federal statutes provide for the *forfeiture* of assets as a penalty for commission of a crime. Also, the divestiture of assets without compensation. A judicial act resulting in the deprivation of a party's property, as the *forfeiture* of bail (resulting from the bail bondsman's failure to secure the court appearance of a defendant).

FORMA PAUPERIS
See **IN FORMA PAUPERIS**

FORO SECULARI [L. *forum* / an open place, a market place, a place of public business + *saeculum* / a generation, the current period, these times]

A secular or civil, as opposed to ecclesiastical, court.

FORTIOR [L. *fortis* / strong]

Stronger, more powerful. Used to describe evidence which is persuasive enough to shift the burden of proof from one party in the litigation to the other.

See **A FORTIORI**

FORTIOR EST CUSTODIA LEGIS QUAM HOMINIS

The law is a more forceful custodian (of rights) than man.

FORTUITOUS [L. *fortuitus* / accidental, casual, occurring by chance]

An event or act which happens accidentally and without human planning or intervention. An unavoidable event. The law of insurance deals with reimbursement and compensation for *fortuitous events.*

FORUM [L. The center of a community; the market place; later, a place where legal relief or remedy could be sought]

A courthouse; the court; a tribunal. The place where justice is dispensed. Also, a public meeting place; a place for the exchange of discussion and ideas.

FORUM ACTUS

The court controlling or having jurisdiction over the place where the event or act at issue took place.

FORUM CONSCIENTIAE

A court with conscience or a sense of right and fairness. A court of equity.

FORUM CONTRACTUS

The court controlling the place where a contract was made.

FORUM CONVENIENS

That court which is most appropriate for resolution of a dispute or issue.

FORUM DOMICILII

The court which presides or has jurisdiction over a party's place of residence.

FORUM DOMICILII ACTORIS

The court having jurisdiction over the plaintiff's place of residence.

FORUM DOMICILII REI

The court having jurisdiction over the defendant's place of residence.

FORUM LITIS MOTAE

The court in which the action is brought.

FORUM NON CONVENIENS

An inconvenient forum or court. The doctrine which enables a court to decline to hear a case even though it has jurisdiction, if in the court's judgment there is no compelling substantive reason for the case to be brought there and there is another court which would be more convenient or fairer to the parties. The principle which authorizes and enables a court to reject a litigation if in the court's judgment another court would be more appropriate.

See **INCONVENIENT FORUM**

FORUM REI GESTAE

The jurisdiction in which the act at issue was done.

FORUM REI SITAE

The jurisdiction in which the subject matter of the law suit is located.

FORUM SELECTION

The process by which the affected parties agree, usually in a clause of their contract or agreement, to select and designate in advance the jurisdiction in which any subsequent dispute between them will be heard and resolved. The agreement will generally be respected by the courts.

FORUM SHOPPING

The deliberate effort of one party to an action to select a particular court or jurisdiction because he anticipates more favorable treatment in that court than in other courts which have simultaneous jurisdiction.

FOUNDATION   [L. *fundo, fundare* / to lay the foundation of; to found. To strengthen, make firm]

A primary support for the construction or creation of something else, as a building or a culture. An underlying basis for the development of ideas or principles. An organization or fund established for charitable, educational or benevolent purposes and supported by contributions from others. *Foundations* have been established to support museums, schools, charities, cultural events, exhibits, etc. To *lay the foundation* in a trial is to ask preliminary questions to connect evidence which will be offered later on the issues requiring proof.

FOUNDER   [L. *fundo, fundare* / to found, make firm]

One who begins or establishes. We speak of the members of the Constitutional Convention of 1787 as our *Founding Fathers. Founders* begin or establish schools, colleges, corporations, etc.

FRATER CONSANGUINEUS   [L. *frater* / brother + *consanguineus* / related by blood]

A brother born of the same father but a different mother; a half brother on the father's side.

FRATERNAL   [L. *frater* / a brother]

Of or pertaining to the relationship of brothers. Of or pertaining to a group with similar interests. A *fraternal society* is one created by its members with a common purpose and for the common benefit of its members; e.g., to provide charity, health insurance, death benefits, etc.

FRATERNIZE   [L. *frater* / brother]

To be friendly with. To mingle with as with brothers. In military law, association or cooperation with the enemy in violation of military orders.

FRATRICIDE [L. *frater* / brother + *caudere* / to cut down, kill]

The killing of one sibling by another.

FRAUD, FRAUDULENT [L. *fraus* / deceit, deception; a crime or offense (from *fraudare* / to cheat, deceive)]

The distortion or misstatement of truth with intent to deprive another of his property or to induce him to give up a legal right. Any act calculated to deceive or mislead. The false representation of a material fact, either by words or conduct or by concealment, with intent to cause injury or loss to another. *Fraud* gives rise to an action in tort or to criminal prosecution. A contract *induced by fraud* may be canceled by the party subjected to the fraud.

FRAUDEM FACERE LEX

To commit a fraud on the law.

FRAUD IN THE FACTUM

A misrepresentation or misstatement which induces another to sign or executive an instrument without knowing the true character or nature of the instrument. An example of *fraud in the factum*: one person puts a check in front of another with intent to deceive him and the second person signs it thinking it's a promissory note payable a year from date instead of a check requiring immediate payment.

FRAUS ET JUS NUNQUAM COHABITAT

Fraud and justice can never reside together.

FRAUS LEGIS

A fraud upon the law.

FRAUS MERITER FRAUDEM [L. *fraus* / fraud + *merere* / to deserve]

One fraud deserves another fraud. One fraud leads to another.

FRIVOLOUS [L. *frivolus* / trifling, worthless]

Lacking in seriousness. Asserted without genuine purpose or in bad faith. Intended to confuse or delay. Palpably false or without merit. A document such as a pleading, an appeal, or a brief which contains spurious and empty matter or arguments is *frivolous*. Frivolous documents or frivolous steps in litigation are frowned upon by the courts and by the rules of professional responsibility and can result in penalties and sanctions against the lawyers who introduce them.

FRUCTUS CIVILES   [L. *fructus* / proceeds, produce, fruit + *civilis* / relating to a citizen; civic, civil]

The fruits of society's labor or production. The compensation due one as wages for his labor or in interest on his money.

FRUCTUS INDUSTRIALES   [L. *fructus* / proceeds + *industria* / industry, purpose]

The fruits of labor, diligence or industry. Annual crops harvested through the labor and effort of man.

FRUCTUS LEGIS   [L. the fruits of the law]

Anything which is produced by intervention of the law; e.g., an indictment, an injunction, an execution. NOTE: The English word *fruit* is itself applied in many legal contexts. Example: *fruit of the tree doctrine* — the doctrine which states that one may not assign the income of his labor and efforts to another to avoid taxation. Also, *fruit of the poisonous tree doctrine* — a doctrine which provides that evidence obtained by unlawful means in violation of the 4th Amendment, such as by an illegal search, may not be admitted at trial. Also, the *fruits of a crime* — applied in the law of evidence to objects acquired in the commission of a crime.

FRUCTUS NATURALES   [L. *fructus* + *naturalis* / natural, not artifical]

The fruits of nature itself; things which develop or are produced in nature, without the help or intervention of man; e.g., timber, metals, flowers, pearls, the trees of the forest, grasses, etc.

FRUSTRA EST POTENTIA QUAE NUMQUAM VENIT IN ACTUM

If power is never exercised, it is wasted and becomes worthless.

FRUSTRA PROBITUR QUOD PROBATUM NON RELEVAT

It's useless to prove something which is not relevant. It's a waste of the court's time to offer evidence or arguments which are not relevant to the issues.

FRUSTRATE, FRUSTRATION   [L. *frustro, frustrare* / to disappoint, deceive]

To thwart or make impossible or difficult. To prevent or impede. To make ineffectual, as to frustrate the purposes of a law. The term *frustration of purpose* is used in contract law to define a supervening event which completely defeats the purpose for which one of the parties entered into the contract and which entitles that party to avoid the contract. The event must have been unforeseeable at the making of the contract and must deprive the party of all benefit under the contract.

FUGITIVE [L. *fugio, fugere* / to flee]

A person who runs away to avoid arrest, prosecution or imprisonment. In immigration law, a foreign citizen who flees to the United States and who qualifies as a *fugitive from political persecution* is given special status and treatment.

FUNCTION [L. *functio* / a performance; the act of performing (from *fungor, fungi* / to perform, do]

Official position or occupation. The duties performed in a particular job. The acts or operations which define a specific occupation or mechanism.

FUNCTIONARY [L. *fungor, fungi* / to perform, execute]

An official or employee of a government or governmental authority; a public official.

FUNCTUS OFFICIO [L. *functus* / deed, performance + *officere* / to act against, impede, hinder]

An act done or completed. An official whose authority has ended or an organization which ceases to function or a thing or document which has no further purpose.

FUND [L. *fundus* / ground; the base for everything]

A sum of money dedicated for use in a specific way or for a specific purpose. Also, an organization set up to administer a particular group of assets. A *mutual fund* is a fund contributed by investors which invests in the stocks or bonds of other companies or in the securities of a defined class of companies or institutions. *To fund* is to invest capital for earnings or interest or to make provision in advance for the discharge of a debt.

FUNDAMENTAL [L. *fundare* / to lay the foundation of; to make firm; to support]

Of central importance. Forming the support for; basic. Used in the term *fundamental law* (the constitution or basic legal framework governing a nation or state, whether codified or developed over time by judicial decisions and interpretation). *Fundamental rights* are those individual rights supported by or based upon the provisions of the Constitution; e.g., freedom of speech and religion, the right to travel, etc.

FUNDI PUBLICI [L. *fundus* / soil, land, a farm + *publicus* / belonging to the people]

Public lands. Lands belonging to the state.

FUNGIBLE [L. *fungor, fungi* / to perform]

The quality of being so identical to other objects of the same general nature and description as to be indistiguishable from them; e.g., grains of sand, peas in a pod, etc. Originally applied to such objects as grain or gravel to permit ease of performance in satisying an obligation to deliver similar goods, it is now also applied to shares of stock of one company of the same class and value.

See **IN SPECIE**

FURANDI ANIMUS [L. *furari* / to steal + *animus* / the soul, heart, center of feeling; the mind]

With intent to steal.

FURIOSI NULLA VOLUNTAS EST

A madman has no free will.

FUROR BREVIS [L. *furor* / madness, insanity + *brevis* / short, sudden]

Sudden anger.

FURTUM MANIFESTUM [L. *furtum* / theft, robbery + *manifestus* / palpable, evident]

Open and notorious theft. To be caught in a theft.

FURTUM OBLATUM

The crime of selling stolen property. To receive stolen property.

FUTURE [L. *futurus* / future participle of *sum, esse* / to be or exist]

Coming after the present moment. Time that has yet to come. *Future damages* are damages awarded to a plaintiff to anticipate the effect upon him in the future of personal injuries incurred by him. A *futures contract* is a contract traded on a commodities exchange providing for delivery of a commodity at a specified future date at a fixed price. The subject of *Future Interests* is the study of interests in real and personal property which will be possessed or enjoyed in the future and not at present.

GENEALOGY [L. *generare* / to beget, bring to life]

A record or account of a family, tracing relationships from the earliest born to the present. The study of family trees and histories.

GENDER, GENDER DISCRIMINATION [L. *genus* / kind; birth, descent, origin; race, family]

The sex of a living organism. The traits and characteristics of one sex. *Gender discrimination* is discrimination against a person because of his or her sex.

GENERAL [L. *generalis* / belonging to a kind or class; in general]

Encompassing many common elements or components. Including all the members of a class or group. Defining those qualities which are enjoyed in common by a class or group. Widely spread. Of universal application.

GENERAL AGENT

In the law of agency, a *general agent* is one who is authorized to conduct a series of transactions in the *continuing* service of his principal.

GENERAL APPEARANCE

In trial practice, a *general appearance* is one in which a party submits himself to the jurisdiction of the court and consents that the court may determine all issues in a litigation in which that party is involved. A waiver of all jurisdictional defects relating to service of process.

GENERAL ASSIGNMENT

A conveyance under common law, or by statute, by a debtor to a designated trustee of all the debtor's assets and property for pro-rata allocation and distribution among his creditors. The conveyance is deemed an act of bankruptcy.

GENERAL CREDITOR

A creditor whose obligation is not secured by a mortgage, pledge, judgment lien or other security. An unsecured creditor.

GENERALIBUS SPECIALIA DEROGANT

Special words or ideas subtract from the meaning or power of general words or ideas.

GENERAL PARTNER

Every partner in a general partnership — i.e., any partnership which is not a limited partnership — is a general partner. In a *general partnership*, each partner is fully liable for all partnership debts regardless of the amount of his capital contribution. In a limited partnership, a *general partner* is a partner who conducts the partnership business and who assumes personal liability for all the obligations of the partnership. The limited partners of a limited partnership do not participate in management and are liable for partnership debts only to the extent of their capital contributions.

GENERAL POWER OF APPOINTMENT

A power which permits the holder of the power to appoint anyone he choses, including himself.

GENERATION   [L. *generare* / to give birth to, produce]

A measurement of the succession of human lives which assigns a different designation at each level of descent; e.g., my father's generation, the current generation, the post-war generation, etc. One level of lives in the succession of human history. Also, the successive degrees in computing the order of descent in the law of Wills. The average length of time between the birth of a parent and the birth of his first child.

GENERIC   [L. *generare*]

Characteristic or representative of an entire class. In trademark law, a *generic mark* is one which has such common and widespread use that it cannot be protected as a trademark. The *generic name* of a drug or prescription is the original scientific name assigned to it, as opposed to the brand name given to it by a pharmaceutical company.

GENTRIFICATION   [L. *gens* / a group of people with common ancestors linked by a common surname]

The process by which a neighborhood of poorer people and rundown dwellings is converted into an upscale middle class or more affluent neighborhood by the influx of new residents and the renovation of existing housing.

GENUINE   [L. *genuinus* (from *gigno, gignere* / to give birth to) / natural, inherent]

Real, authentic. Free from contamination or adulteration. True; not false or counterfeit. As applied to documents, instruments or creative works such as paintings or literature, the word means that they can be verified as true originals, not forgeries or counterfeits. A *genuine issue of fact* — one which raises doubt — precludes summary judgment in an action.

GESTATION [L. *gestare* / to carry or bear]

To carry in the uterus during pregnacy; the period from conception to birth. The creation or birth of ideas and thoughts.

GESTIO (GESTUM) [L. *gestire* / to exult, celebrate]

An act, transaction or performance.

GIFT CAUSA MORTIS

A gift of personal property in anticipation of death. An *inter vivos* gift by a donor in expectation of death. An effective *gift causa mortis* must satisfy the following conditions: a gift to take effect on the death of the donor; the imminent death of the donor; death in fact from the anticipated cause of death without intervening recovery; delivery of the gift itself to the donee.

See **CAUSA MORTIS; DONATIO CAUSA MORTIS**

GIFT INTER VIVOS

An absolute and unconditional gift of personal property between donor and donee during the life of both. A voluntary transfer of personal property without consideration during life. In the case of assets capable of delivery, delivery must be completed. In the case of assets not capable of delivery, the donor must surrender all control of the asset to the donee.

See **INTER VIVOS**

GOOD SAMARITAN [L. *samaritanus* (from the Greek) / a resident of Samaria]

A person who helps others in distress. In law, the *Good Samaritan Doctrine* provides a degree of protection for those who go voluntarily to the help of others who are hurt or in danger. The *good samaritan* is not liable for his actions unless he has proceeded recklessly or unless his actions have aggravated the risk or injury. The doctrine is codified to some extent in the laws of most states. Note, however, that there is no recognized duty or responsibility to go to the aid of others.

GOVERN [L. *gubernare* / to steer (a ship), direct, govern]

To control or direct. To exercise sovereignty over. To possess and utilize the power to control the affairs and activities of constituent members. To determine policy for and regulate the functions of the body politic.

GOVERNMENT [L. *guberno, gubernare* / to steer; to lead to safety; to govern]

The organization of society into a central authority to manage and control common affairs and activities. The process of controlling society. The concentration of public power and responsibilty the hands of a few to control the general public. The class of persons who are designated or who function to manage the affairs of the entire populace. Government in the United States functions at two levels — the federal level and the state level. At the federal level, it is divided into the executive, judicial and legislative branches.

GOVERNMENTAL IMMUNITY
  See **IMMUNITY; SOVEREIGN IMMUNITY**

GRACE [L. *gratia* / agreeableness, charm, attraction; beloved]

A special favor or privilege. A reprieve or exemption from performance of a duty. Indulgence or forgiveness. A *grace period* is a stated period of days during which a duty or responsibility is suspended without penalty, e.g., a period of time in a loan agreement during which default will not be invoked although the date for payment has passed.

GRATIS [L. *gratia (gratus)* / pleasing, free, without compensation]

For nothing; given or performed without expectation or receipt of compensation or consideration.

GRATIS DICTUM [L. *gratia* + *dico, dicere* / to say, speak]

A statement which is made freely and without compulsion or obligation. A statement made without purpose or without expectation that it will be relied on.

GRATUITOUS [L. *gratia, gratuitus* / spontaneous, unprovoked, free]

Anything not paid for or expected. Given or conveyed without legal consideration; e.g., a *gratuitous promise*. A *gratuitous guest* is one who is extended an amenity or service without paying for it; e.g., a non-paying passenger in a car.

GRATUITY [L. *gratuitus*]

A gift or present. Anything given without consideration or obligation. A voluntary reward. A tip.

GRAVAMEN [L. *gravis* / weighty, important]

The essential part of a statement or thought. The material parts of a grievance, pleading, complaint, cause of action or indictment.

GRIEVANCE [L. *gravare* / to burden, to weigh upon]

A cause for complaint. A complaint about an injustice or wrong. The formal expression of a complaint. In labor law, a statement by an employee, or by his union representantive, alleging violations of employment terms or conditions by the employer and initiating a procedure for resolving the complaint. Also, a complaint by an employer for relief under the grievance machinery set up under a collective bargaining agreement with a union. Each state has machinery for the resolution of *grievances against lawyers*, usually in the form of *grievance committees* which hear complaints and refer their decisions to the courts when discipline is required.

GUARDIAN AD LITEM

A special guardian appointed by the court during the course of a litigation to protect the interests of an infant or mentally incompetent person involved in the litigation. The authority of the *guardian ad litem* is confined to the litigation for which he is appointed.

See **AD LITEM**

HABEAS CORPORA JURATORUM [L. *habere* / to have, hold + *corpus* / body + *iurator* / a person under oath, a juror]

A writ commanding the sheriff to round up the jurors for a trial panel and to have them available on the day of trial.

HABEAS CORPUS

Literally, you have the body. The name introducing a number of *writs* which directed a custodian to bring a party before the court. There are several forms of the writ. The most important is *habeus corpus ad subjiciendum*, a direction to the custodian of a prisoner to bring him before the court issuing the writ. Others are *habeus corpus ad prosequendum; habeus corpus ad respondendum* and *habeus corpus ad testificandum*.(See definitions following.)

HABEAS CORPUS AD PROSEQUENDUM

A writ requiring the removal of a prisoner to the proper jurisdiction; e.g., the place in which the alleged crime was committed, or to another court which has before it another complaint against him on a separate offense.

HABEAS CORPUS AD RESPONDENDUM

An order requiring the removal of a prisoner from an inferior court to a higher court which wishes to try a complaint against him. Also, in civil cases, a writ to compel production of a defendant in another jurisdiction to enable him to be sued there.

HABEAS CORPUS AD SUBJICIENDUM

A cornerstone of Anglo-Saxon jurisprudence, this *writ* initiates a judicial determination of the legality of an individual's custody or detention; the writ is called the *great writ* because of its importance in securing a judicial review of the proceedings which led to a prisoner's detention. In criminal law, it is an order to bring a prisoner before the court to enable the court to review the circumstances surrounding his confinement. The writ may be issued by a federal court to review whether the defendant in a state court criminal trial has been accorded due process. Access to the writ is guaranteed by Article I, Section 9 of the Constitution. In civil matters, the writ enables the court to review custody or deportation proceedings.

HABEAS CORPUS AD TESTIFICANDUM

A writ requiring production of a prisoner before the court to enable him to give testimony.

HABENDUM (CLAUSE) [L. *habere* / to have, hold]

That portion of a deed or conveyance usually following a description of the property and following the words *to have and to hold*, which defines and limits the interest or estate being granted; e.g., a life estate, a joint tenancy, etc.

HABENDUM ET TENENDUM

To have and to hold.

HABERE FACIAS POSSESSIONEM [L. *habere* / to have, hold + *facere* / to make, do + *possidere, possessio* / to take possession, possession]

A writ enabling a judgment creditor in an action for ejectment to obtain possession of his property. A writ directing the sheriff to give possession of property to the plaintiff after an action to determine title.

HABERE FACIAS SEISANUM

A writ directing the sheriff after an action over title to real property to put a successful plantiff in actual possession.

HABERE FACIAS VISUM

A writ directing the sheriff to inspect property subject to a dispute.

HABITABLE, HABITABILITY [L. *habito, habitare* / to inhabit, dwell, reside in]

Capable of being lived in. Ready for human habitation. The condition of premises which enables people to live in them free of disturbances to health and safety. Under the *warranty of habitability*, which attaches to every new unit of housing, the owner warrants to his buyer that he has complied with all zoning and building requirements and that the housing unit is free of defects and ready for occupancy. The warranty is also imposed by statute in most states against any landlord who rents a dwelling unit to a tenant.

HABITANCY [L. *habitare*]

A fixed home or residence regarded by the occupant as the place to which he intends to return after absence. A permanent dwelling.

See **DOMICILE**

HABITUAL   [L. *habitare* / to dwell or inhabit]

An act or acts performed on a regular basis. In the nature of a compulsion. Frequent and recurring. Constant, repetitive.

HABITUAL CRIMINAL

One who commits successive crimes. Most states impose increasingly severe penalties for successive crimes. The most recent manifestation of this treatment is "three strikes-you're out" legislation, which imposes life sentences on criminals who have committed three successive felonies. The concept of fitting the punishment to the number of crimes committed is also contained in the federal sentencing guidelines.

HAEC VERBA   [L. *hic, haec, hoc* / this + *verbum* / word]

In these very words.

See **IN HAEC VERBA**

HAEREDES PROXIMI

Nearest or next of kin. The children or direct descendants of a decedent.

HAEREDITAS

An inheritance.

HAEREDITAS DAMNOSA   [L. *haereditas* + *damnosus* / harmful, ruinous]

A regrettable or burdensome inheritance, one which carries more burdens than value; e.g., an inheritance which makes the beneficiary liable for the debts of the testator.

See **DAMNOSA HEREDITAS**

HAEREDITAS PATERNA

A paternal inheritance. An inheritance which passes from father to child.

HAERES NATUS   [L. *haerus (heres)* / an heir + *nascor, natus* / born of]

The natural heir of someone; entitled to inherit by descent.

HEIR   [L. *haeres, heres*]

One who succeeds to the interest in real or personal property of an intestate decedent. Under modern statutes, anyone who takes an interest in the real property left by a decedent who leaves no will. More broadly, anyone who inherits any form of property from a decedent.

HEREDITAMENT   [L. *hereditas* / inheritance]

Anything which is capable of being inherited by one person from another, both real and personal. A *corporeal hereditament* is anything tangible; e.g., land, furniture, jewelry, personal effects. An *incorporeal hereditament* is anything intangible; e.g., a right to or an interest in property, a debt receivable, etc.

See **CORPOREAL HEREDITAMENT; INCORPOREAL HEREDITAMENT**

HEREDITARY [L. *hereditas* / inheritance]

Traits and characteristics which are transmitted genetically from parent to child. Transmitted or received by inheritance, i.e., from a person having a blood relation to the recipient. Originally, the receipt of property by an heir upon the death of an ancestor under the rules of inheritance; now, also, the devise of property to an heir by will.

HEREDITY [L. *hereditas*]

The qualities and characteristics transmitted from one generation to another; the transference of accumulated qualities from parents to child through the genes of the parents.

HIATUS [L. *hiare* / to yawn, to gape, to be open]

An interruption or gap in time or continuity. A period of inaction between two events or acts.

HIERARCHY [L. (from the Greek) a ruler or leader; a person in authority]

A ranking of persons in an identifiable group (a political entity, a church, a corporation) in accordance with some measure of relative authority, importance or value, i.e., degree of authority, position, ability, etc.

HIIS TESTIBUS CLAUSE

The attestation clause of a will. The clause at the end of a will signed by the witnesses who attest that they have signed before each other and with the other requisite formalities.

HOLOGRAPH [L. *holographus* (from the Greek) / to write)]

A document, usually a deed or will, entirely in the handwriting of the person creating the document (the grantor or testator). Generally, the document must be dated and signed by the maker but need not be witnessed.

HOLOGRAPHIC WILL

A will which meets the requirements of a holograph. It must be in the handwriting of the testator and should be dated and signed by him. *Holographic wills* are recognized in most states, but not all. The Uniform Probate Code recognizes the validity of holographic wills.

HOMAGE   [L. *homo* / a human being, a man]

A feudal ceremony by which one man acknowledged himself to be the vassal or servant of his lord. A heroic act performed in the service of the lord, usually in exchange for a grant of land. Praise, tribute, an expression of high regard.

HOMICIDE   [L. *homo* / human being, man + *caedere* / to cut down, to kill]

The killing of one human being by another. The word is used in its generic sense and is applied both to criminal killings and non-criminal killings. A criminal killing may be murder, manslaughter or the result of criminal negligence. Examples of non-criminal killings: the execution of a criminal after sentence, a killing in self-defense, the killing by a police officer of a suspect who is forcefully resisting arrest.

HOMICIDE SE DEFENDENDO

A killing carried out in self defense.

HOMICIDIUM IN RIXO   [L. *homocaedere* / the killing of a human being + *in rixo* / in a fight or quarrel (from *rixor, rixam* / to engage in a brawl)]

A homicide committed in the course of a fight or brawl.

HOMINUM CAUSA JUS CONSTITUTUM EST

The law is designed to benefit mankind.

HOMO LIBER   [L. *homo* / a man + *liber* / free]

A free man. Only free men were eligible to serve as jurors.

HONOR   [L. *honorare* / to honor, pay tribute to, adorn]

In the law, the word has several distinct meanings. It is used as a form of courteous address to judges and public officials of high rank; e.g, the Mayor of New York. In the law of negotiable instruments, it means the acceptance or payment of a note, check or bill of exchange according to its terms. To *dishonor* a negotiable instrument is to refuse or fail to pay it upon maturity or according to its terms.

HONORARIUM   [L. *honorarius* / done as an act of honor or respect]

A fee or benefit paid to someone who performs a service for which payment is not legally required or the value of which cannot legally be fixed. A service for which payment is not usually expected. A voluntary payment for a performance; e.g., a speech, under circumstances in which payment is not usually expected and cannot be demanded. Members of Congress cannot freely accept *honoraria*.

HOSPITIA CURIAE   [L. *hospitium* / a guest house or inn + *curia* / the meeting place of the Roman senate; a court or courthouse]

The inns of court. In London, an association of lawyers with common or adjacent quarters designed to further collegiality in the practice of law and to offer instruction to students of the law.

HOSTAGE   [L. *hostis* / a stranger, an enemy, a public foe]

A person seized by another to secure or enforce compliance with a demand; e.g., the detention of a victim by a kidnapper to secure payment of ransom. In time of war or conflict, the seizure and detention of individuals by one party to the conflict in order to exact conditions and terms from the other.

HOSTES HUMANI GENERIS

Enemies of the human race. Enemies of the people.

HOSTILE   [L. *hostis* / an enemy or foe]

Marked by an attitude which is antagonistic and unfriendly. The acts and attitudes of an enemy. In the law, the word is applied both to the possession of real property and the acquisition and control of corporations. *Hostile possession* is possession of real property adverse to all other interests, including the record owner's. A *hostile takeover* is the usurpation of control of a corporation or business in opposition to existing management.

See **ADVERSE POSSESSION**

HOSTILE WITNESS

A witness who shows such antagonism on direct examination to the party by whom he is called as witness as to warrant his treatment as an adverse witness. This means that he is regarded as a witness called by the opposing party and may be cross-examined and asked leading questions by the party who originally called him.

HUMANITARIAN (DOCTRINE)   [L. *homo, humanis* / relating to human beings]

Promoting the welfare and improving the condition of others. Considerate, sympathetic. Motivated by a desire to help others and society in general. The *humaniarian doctrine* — a doctrine followed only in a few states — holds that a person who has the last chance to avoid an accident or an injury to others has an affirmative duty to do so; if he does not fulfill the duty, he relieves the other party of responsibility for any negligence which may have contributed to the accident.

HYBRID [L. *hybrida* / born of parents of different kinds or species]

The offspring of two parents having different genes or physical characteristics, or of different biological species or genera. An animal or plant possessing the genes or other basic characteristics of two parents different from each other. A combination of different cultures or sources. A *hybrid security* is a security which combines the elements of a debenture or bond and of common stock, i.e., it is composed both of debt and of equity. A *hybrid defense* in a criminal trial is a defense conducted in part by the defendant pro se and in part by his attorney.

HYPOTHECATE [L. hypothecare / (from the Greek) to pledge]

To pledge property as security for the payment of a debt or the performance of an obligation. Usually, this is accomplished by written agreement and a filing under the Uniform Commercial Code, without surrender of the property itself or the transfer of title to the property. However, on default, the secured party is entitled to sell the property to enforce collection.

HYPOTHESIS [L. (from the Greek) less than a full dissertation]

An assumption made for the purpose of argument. A conjecture. Anything not proved but offered as fact for the purpose of persuasion. In law, a theory offered by one party to convince the trier of fact that an event probably occurred in a certain way.

HYPOTHETICAL QUESTION

At trial, a question put to an expert witness which assumes a given set of facts favorable to the party asking the question and which asks for the opinion of the expert with respect to those facts. The facts contained in the questions are usually some or all of the facts adduced from testimony or from other proof submitted at the trial.

IBID. OR IB. [L. abb. of *ibidem* / in the same place, at that place]
Used to mean "on the same page" or "in the same book."

IBI JUS, IBI REMEDIUM
Where law exists, a remedy (also) exists.

ID. [L. abb. of *idem* / the same]
Identical to something previously mentioned. Used to tell the reader that a fuller reference to a name, title, citation or other element of the text has been made previously in the same text.

ID CERTUM EST QUOD CERTUM REDDI POTEST
If language can be made certain, we will make it certain. If an ambiguity can be resolved by proof, the court will hear the proof and resolve the ambiguity.

IDEM PER IDEM
The same for the same. Like for like.

IDEM SONANS [L. *idem* / the same + *sonare* / to sound, make a noise]
Sounding the same; having the same sound. Applied to two names that are spelled differently but pronounced alike; e.g., Allan and Allen or John and Jon. Usually, the misspelling of a name in a pleading or other document is not material so long as the proper identification can be made from other sources.

IDENTATE NOMINIS
The name for a judicial writ which provided for the release of an innocent prisoner who had the same name as the real culprit.

IDENTITY [L. *identidem (idem et idem)* / over and over, again and again]
Those elements which distinguish one person from another. Also, sameness in general characteristics or qualities. The process of describing a person so as to distinguish him from all others.

ID EST (abb. *i.e.*) [L. *idem (id.)* + *esse* / to be]
That is, or that is to say. In its abbreviated form, i.e., it is used to expand upon, explain or clarify a point in speech or writing.

IGNORAMUS   [L. *ignorare* / to be unaware of, not to know]

Literally we do not know. Formerly used by lawyers in the sense of, "we choose not to know." In this sense, the word was subscribed by a grand jury on a bill of indictment if the jury chose not to indict after hearing the evidence. Nowadays, the jury writes "no bill" or "not found" instead. Also, an ignorant person, a fool.

IGNORANTIA JURIS NEMINEM EXCUSAT

Ignorance of the law excuses no one.

IGNORANTIA LEGIS EST LATA CULPA

It is an act of negligence to be ignorant of the law.

IGNORANTIA LEGIS NON EXCUSAT

Ignorance of the law is not an excuse. A breach of the law will not be excused or waived simply because the defendant did not think he was breaking the law or did not know that his act was illegal.

ILLEGAL   [L. *in* / without, not + *lex, legis, legalis* / legal]

Not recognized or authorized by law, regulation or rule. An act falling outside the limits imposed by law.

ILLICIT   [L. *in* / not + *licere, licitus* / allowed, permitted]

Not permitted, unlawful. Prohibited by custom or law.

ILLUSORY   [L. *in* + *ludere* / to play, mimic, mock; also, to deceive, delude]

Deceptive, not real, having no substance, fallacious.

ILLUSORY CONTRACT

A document which contains language of commitment and obligation, but which does not actually obligate at least one of the parties to do anything. The language may be couched in promissory terms but performance is really at the option of the promisor and the promisee cannot enforce the promise e.g., because it is too vague or impossible to perform.

ILLUSORY TENANT

In real estate law, a tenant who is set up as the landlord's *alter ego* to enable the tenant to enter into a sublease which would be illegal or invalid if made as a major lease by the landlord in his own name; e.g., a lease which would violate rent control laws if made by the landlord but not by a tenant.

ILLUSORY TRUST

A trust in language, construction and form, but one in which, on analysis, the settlor retains so much control over the trust property that it is clear he did not really intend to surrender any of his rights to the trustee.

IMMATERIAL [L. *in* / not + *materia* / matter]

Not composed of matter; insubstantial; non-existent. Irrelevant, unessential, of no consequence. *Immaterial evidence* is evidence without probative value. Upon motion by counsel, it will be excluded by the court.

IMMIGRATE [L. *in* + *migrare* / to move from one place to another]

To come into a country from another country of which one is a citizen, for the purpose of establishing a new and permanent residence.

See **EMIGRATE**

IMMINENT [L. *imminere* / to project or hang over; to theaten]

Ready to happen or take place; impending. Hanging over one's head; threatening.

IMMINENT DANGER

The condition confronting a person who cannot reasonably escape fom a threat to his life or safety except through his own actions or devices; a threat which puts a reasonable person to his own immediate defenses; a condition used to justify a homicide or other act of defense.

IMMINENT DEATH

Impending or approaching death; to be on one's death bed. A condition which is recognized by the law as legitimating *gifts causa mortis*.

See **CAUSA MORTIS; DONATIO CAUSA MORTIS; GIFT CAUSA MORTIS**

IMMOBILIA SITUM SEQUUNTUR

Immoveable things follow the law of their location.

IMMUNITY [L. *in* + *munus* / office, duty, function]

Literally, free from a duty, as a duty to pay taxes. Protected from; not susceptible to; having resistance to. A special status conferred upon some and not available to others. A right or freedom, or an exemption from a duty, not generally enjoyed by others. (Examples: *executive immunity, absolute immunity, immunity from prosecution, interspousal immunity, judicial immunity*, etc.)

IMMUNITY FROM PROSECUTION

The process by which a witness is promised by the authorities that he will not be prosecuted if he gives testimony regarding the commission of a crime.

Immunity is often offered to witnesses in anticipation of their assertion of the Fifth Amendment privilege against self-incrimination. There are two types of immunity. In *transactional immunity*, the witness is protected from any prosecution growing out of the events or transactions about which he testifies. In *use immunity*, he is protected only against prosecution based upon the facts contained in his own testimony; he can still be prosecuted and convicted of complicity in the transaction based upon facts and evidence not contained in his own testimony but offered by others.

See **TRANSACTIONAL IMMUNITY**

IMMUNITY (GOVERNMENTAL IMMUNITY; SOVEREIGN IMMUNITY)

The right of a governmental entity to be free from liability for torts committed by its employees or agents except in cases in which it has consented to be sued. Most states have passed statutes renouncing immunity in some circumstances.

IMMUNITY (SPOUSAL)

Under the common law, the right of one spouse to be free of tort liability to the other. Some states still adhere to this doctrine, but many have abolished or limited it, especially in cases arising from negligence in the operation of motor vehicles.

IMPAIR [L. *in* / not + *malus* (bad), *peior* / worse]

To make worse. To damage or injure. To weaken or lessen in quality or value. The capital of a company is *impaired* when its net value is less than the capital originally invested. Article I, Section 10 of the Constitution prohibits any state from passing any "Law *Impairing* the Obligation of Contracts."

IMPARTIAL [L. *in* / not + *partio, partire* / to divide, share, distribute]

Acting without preference or bias towards either side in a dispute. Disinterested; fair and equitable. Judges, arbitrators and juries are expected to be *impartial*. The Sixth Amendment to the Constitution guarantees the accused in a criminal prosecution the right to a speedy and public trial by an *impartial* jury.

IMPEACH [L. *in* + *pedica* / (from *ped* / foot), a fetter or restraint]

To bring an accusation against; to charge with the commission of a crime or misdemeanor, especially a public officer. To begin the process of removing a public official from office under the applicable constitutional or statutory provisions; e.g., a judge or the President of the United States. Only the House of Representatives has the constitutional power to bring articles of impeachment against the President. In 1998-99 the House brought articles of impeachment against President William Jefferson Clinton. In the law of evidence, to *impeach a witness* is to call his veracity into question by showing prior inconsistent statements or contradictory facts or by challenging his character or reputation. To *impeach a verdict* is to challenge the integrity of a verdict for alleged improprieties by the jury.

IMPEDIMENT   [L. *in* + *ped* (see **IMPEACH**)]

A bar or hindrance; an obstacle. A disqualification or disability preventing entry into a legal relationship or the execution of a binding contract; e.g., infancy or insanity, or, in the case of marriage, the relationship between first cousins.

IMPERFECT   [L. *in* / not + *perficio, perficere, perfectus* / to complete, finish, achieve]

Defective or incomplete in some element required by the law, e.g., an *imperfect obligation*, an *imperfect title*, an *imperfect right*. Unenforceable because lacking in some essential.

IMPERITIA CULPAE ADNUMERATUR

Ignorance or lack of skill may constitute negligence.

IMPERSONATE   [L. *in* / not + *persona* / a role or part; also, a mask worn by the actors in a Greek or Roman play]

To represent oneself falsely as possessing a public office or a license required for the performance of a skill or profession, e.g., to *impersonate* a police officer or a doctor. Also, to pretend to be someone else; to play the role of another person.

IMPLICATE   [L. *implicare* / to involve, entangle]

To involve in an act or event. To accuse someone of participation in an act, as in an accident or the commission of a crime. A suggestion or conclusion drawn from a set of circumstances.

IMPLICIT   [L. *implico, implicare* / to enfold, entangle, involve]

Contained within something but not fully revealed, as "your anger is *implicit* in that statement." Potential. Existing but unexpressed.

IMPLY, IMPLIED   [L. *implicare* / to unfold, entangle]

To express indirectly, as through deeds, conduct and manner, rather than explicitly or directly. In law, to suggest the intentions of the parties to a transaction when the parties have themselves failed or neglected to define them expressly but have manifested them through their conduct. Examples: *implied agency, implied consent, implied contract, implied easement, implied lien, implied malice, implied notice, implied power, implied waiver. implied warranty.*

IMPOSSIBILITY   [L. *in* + *possum, posse, potui* / to be able]

Not capable of fulfillment. In the law, *impossibility* applies generally to the performance of contracts or the discharge of duties. If a commitment is impossible of performance by its very nature or because of some supervening natural occurrence or event, rather than because of the inability of the obligor to perform, then the performance is excused.

IMPOSSIBILIUM NULLA OBLIGATIO EST

There can be no obligation to perform the impossible.

IMPOSTER   [L. *imponere* / to place, lay upon, put on]

One who pretends to be another, usually with intent to deceive or defraud. Anyone who poses as another to obtain the benefits of the person he pretends to be. A check drawn to an *imposter* may be indorsed and negotiated by anyone. UCC § 3-405(1)(a).

IMPOTENTIA EXCUSAT LEGEM

The law must defer when an act becomes impossible.

IMPRESS   [L. *imprimere* / to press into or upon]

The process by which a court imposes a constructive trust for equitable reasons, as when a party performs services for a testator in reliance on the testator's promise to include him in his will and the testator fails to do so. Also, to force into public service, as in military conscription.

IMPRIMATUR   [L. *imprimere* / to press into, engrave]

Literally, let it be printed. A licence granted by a government permitting the publication of a particular book. Formerly, an *imprimatur* was required in England before a book could be published. Many countries still require official approval before publication. Any attempt to require an *imprimatur* would violate the U.S. Constitution. The word now is also used to mean a mark or stamp of approval.

IMPROPER   [L. *in* / not + *proprius* / exclusive to oneself, peculiar, special; also proper, correct]

Unsuitable or unfit. In violation of. Not in accord with general attitudes or principles.

IMPROVEMENT   [L. *in* + *probare* / to make good, approve]

A change or addition, usually to real property, which enhances its utility or value. The term requires the use of labor and capital in new or modified construction, as opposed to expenditures for repairs and maintenance. Anything attached or appurtenant to land may be *an improvement*; e.g., buildings, outbuildings, roads, utilities, sidewalks, roofs, etc. In patent law, an *improvement patent* is an addition or modification to an existing invention; the improvement must contain a complete and operative art or instrument not affecting the essential character of the original patent but enabling it to produce its intended results more economically or efficiently.

IMPUNITY   [L. *in* + *poena* / punishment, penalty]

Exemption or freedom from punishment. Without responsibility. Free of risk.

IMPURIS MANIBUS NEMO ACCEDAT CURIAM

No one is permitted to approach the court with unclean hands.

IMPUTE   [L. *in* + *putare* / to clear, settle, consider, believe]

To charge a person with responsibility or liability for the act of another, because of the relationship between the two or the need to protect the interests of innocent third parties.

IMPUTED KNOWLEDGE

Knowledge charged to a party either because he had the duty and the means of acquiring the knowledge or because a reasonable person would have acquired the knowledge. Under some circumstances, the knowledge of an agent will be imputed to his principal.

IMPUTED NEGLIGENCE

The attribution or charge to one person of the negligence or lack of care of another. For example, the negligence of an employee or agent within the scope of his authority or employment is imputed to his employer or principal.

IN ABSENTIA

In absence; in his/her absence; in the absence of.

INADVERTENCE, INADVERTENT   [L. *in* / not + *adverto, advertere, adversus* / to turn one's attention to, turn towards]

Resulting from inattention or carelessness. Unfocused. Careless. Failing to pay prudent attention to, as to the progress of a matter or trial. Under the Federal Rules of Civil Procedure, a party may move to set aside a judgment or order for "mistake, *inadvertence*, surprise or excusable neglect." FRCP, Rule 60(b).

INADVERTENT DISCOVERY

An unexpected find or discovery. In the conduct of a search pursuant to a valid search warrant, police may seize items not specifically listed in the warrant if the items are in plain view, even if the discovery of the items is not *inadvertent* but, rather, anticipated by the police.

INALIENABLE [L. *in* / not + *alienus* / belonging to another, foreign to]
Incapable of being sold or transferred from one person to another, as in the case of a navigable river or a public park, bridge or highway. Also, an individual right which cannot be seized or usurped by public authority and can be surrendered only by the individual possessing it, such as the *inalienable rights* conferred upon all Americans by the Bill of Rights (the first ten Amendments to the Constitution).

IN ARBITRIO JUDICIS
In the discretion of the court. As the court may decide.

IN ARCTA ET SALVA CUSTODIA
In safe custody.

IN ARTICULO MORTIS
At the point of death.

IN CAMERA [L. *in* + *camera* / a vault or vaulted room]
In a judge's chambers, as distiguished from the public courtroom. The room can be either the judge's office or a room off the courtroom. Proceedings held in a room from which the public is excluded. Sometimes means actions taken by a judge in private when court is not in session. Occasionally, a judge will examine a sensitive document *in camera* before deciding whether to admit it into evidence.

INCAPACITY, INCAPACITATE [L. *in* / not + *capio, capere* / to take, seize; take possession of]
The inability to exercise the legal rights available to others because of some condition which suggests a lack of maturity or ability, as in the case of a minor or a person who is mentally ill. Also, the inability of a worker or employee to discharge the duties of his job because of illness or injury. The period in which an employee is incapable of performing the usual tasks required of his job. To *incapacitate* is to determine that someone may not legally act for himself; also, to bring about the inability of a person to perform the duties of his job or employment.

IN CAPITA [L. *in* + *caput* / the head]
By the head; inheritance *in capita* occurs when all persons entitled to take, take in equal shares. Also, a challenge directed to an individual juror as opposed to a challenge to the entire panel. A challenge to the entire panel is a *challenge to the array*.

IN CAPITE

    A feudal land interest or tenement held directly from the king.

    See **CAPITE**

INCARCERATE [L. *in* + *carcer, carcerare* / prison, jail]

    To imprison or place in confinement.

IN CASU CONSIMILI

    In a similar case.

INCENDI CRIMEN [L. *incendere* / to set afire, to burn + *crimen* / accusation, crime]

    The crime of arson.

INCEST [L. *in* / not + *castus* / chaste, pure, morally pure]

    Sexual intercourse or cohabitation between two persons so closely related to each other as to make marriage between them illegal; also, the crime of participating in such intercourse.

INCHOATE [L. *inchoare* / to begin work on]

    Partly or incompletely done or formed. Something not yet completed or finished. In criminal law, an *inchoate offense* is one in which the initial steps leading to another crime have been commenced but in which execution of that other crime is not yet complete. The offenses of attempt, solicitation, or conspiracy to commit a crime may all be described as inchoate offenses (see Model Penal Code).

INCHOATE DOWER [INCHOATE RIGHT OF DOWER]

    The contingent life interest which a wife has in her husband's lands prior to his death and which ripens and becomes effective only if she survives him. Her *inchoate right* could not be defeated by a transfer of title to others by the husband. The right of dower has now been eliminated in all but a handful of states.

INCHOATE INSTRUMENT

    An instrument which has been executed and delivered by one party to another and is therefore effective as between the two parties and their assigns, but which requires recording or registration before it is effective against third persons without notice.

INCHOATE INTEREST

    An interest in real property which ripens only upon the happening of a later condition or event and which is subject to being barred, divested, extinguished or terminated upon failure of that condition or event.

INCHOATE PATENT RIGHT

The right of a patent applicant to be protected in his invention pending action by the Patent Office upon his application. The right matures or ripens upon granting of the patent.

INCIDENT [L. *incido, incidere* (from *cadere* / to fall) / to fall in or on; to have an encounter with]

A distinct happening or event. A subordinate or resulting part of a larger action or effect, as in "the discovery of drugs within the premises was incident to the *search* for the weapon." In connection with life insurance policies, an *incident of ownership* is one of several rights available to an assured.

INCIDENTAL

Attached to or deriving from something which is paramount and primary. Appurtenant to a main purpose or effect. A third party who derives an unintended benefit from a contract between two other parties is deemed an *incidental beneficiary* of the contract. Under the Uniform Commercial Code, a party who recovers for breach of contract may obtain *incidental damages* to cover expenses such as the handling of goods, e.g., the cost of inspection, transportation, etc.

INCITE [L. *in* + *citare* / to set into motion, excite, start up]

To instigate or abet. To lead or influence others to take some action, as to *incite* to riot. To foment, stir up. To solicit the commission of a crime.

INCLUSIO UNIUS EST EXCLUSIO ALTERIUS

To include one thing is to exclude another.

INCOGNITO [L. *in* + *cognosco, cognoscere* / to know]

To hide one's identity. To act or travel without revealing one's true identity.

INCOLAS DOMICILIUM FACIT [L. *incolas* / residence + *domicilium* / dwelling, domicile + *facere* / to make, do]

Residence creates domicile.

IN COMMENDUM [L. *in* + *commendare* / to entrust to the care of]

In trust.

IN COMMUNI [L. *communis* / things shared, public]

In common.

INCOMMUNICADO [L. *in* + *communicare* / to share, divide, inform]

To be without the means of commmunicating with others; to be held in custody or restraint and deprived of contact with anyone except one's captors.

INCOMPETENT [L. *in* / not + *competo, competere* / to be equal to, to match; to be capable]

Not qualified to undertake or exercise a legal right or to perform a legal obligation, as in the case of minors. Also, not capable of performing a job or office by virtue of physical, mental or moral shortcomings. *Incompetent evidence* is evidence which does not satisfy the rules of evidence and is therefore inadmissible.

See **COMPETENCY**

IN CONSIMILI CASU, CONSIMILI DEBET ESSE REMEDIUM

Similar cases require similar remedies.

INCONVENIENT FORUM

A court which is inappropriate for the conduct of a particular proceeding or trial, e.g., because it is too distant from the place where the action arose or from the homes of the parties, or because it is not the court which can best enforce the judgment. The court may dismiss the action and direct the parties to secure a better venue.

See **FORUM NON CONVENIENS**

INCORPORATE [L. *in* / in + *corpus* / body, substance]

To form a corporation, a legal entity recognized by the state and having the attributes of perpetual life and limited investor liability. To bring a document within the terms of another by specific reference (*incorporation by reference*). To include within; to give substance to; to unite in one body.

IN CORPORE [L. *in* + *corpus* / body, substance]

In body; in substance.

INCORPOREAL [L. *in* + *corpus*]

Having no body. Not existing in a tangible sense. Without physical form.

INCORPOREAL HEREDITAMENT

A chose in action which is capable of being inherited. Anything inheritable which has no tangible form. An inheritable right which arises from an interest in property but which is not itself visible or concrete; e.g., the rents owing from real property.

See **CORPOREAL HEREDITAMENT; HEREDITAMENT**

INCORRIGIBLE [L. *in* + *corrigo, corrigere* / to set right, put straight]

Incapable of being correct or reformed. Unmanageable. Delinquent. As applied to juvenile offenders, not controllable by parent or guardian.

INCRIMINATE [L. *in* + *criminor, criminari* / to bring a charge, to accuse]

To accuse of a crime or to acknowledge commission of a crime. To offer or give proof of the commission of a crime.

IN CUJUS REI TESTIMONIUM

In witness whereof. At the foot of a document, the words initiating the acknowledgment of execution by the parties.

See **IN TESTIMONIUM**

INCULPATE, INCULPATORY [L. *in* / in + *culpo, culpare* / blame, find fault with, accuse]

To blame or accuse of a crime. In the law of evidence, *inculpatory evidence* is evidence which tends to prove guilt or to incriminate.

INCUMBENT [L. *in* + *cumbere (cubare)* / to lie down, to go to bed]

The present holder of an office or title. One who is legally delegated to discharge the duties of a particular office.

INCUR [L. *in* + *curro, currere* / to run or rush]

To be the recipient or victim of, as to incur the wrath of another. To become liable for or subject to. To bring upon oneself, as to incur expenses or liabilities.

IN CURIA

In court.

IN CUSTODIA LEGIS [L. *in* + *custodia* / care, custody + *lex, legis* / law]

Under the control of the law. Used when property is held or attached by a court officer, e.g., a sheriff, pending the outcome of an action or proceeding.

IN CUSTODY

A person accused of crime is *in custody* when the police either restrain his movements or advise him that he is not free to go. At that point, he is entitled to his *Miranda* rights.

INDEBITATUS ASSUMPSIT [L. being indebted, he undertook]

To undertake a debt; to agree to become indebted. At common law, this was the name given to the action by a creditor to collect a debt which the debtor had agreed, but failed, to pay.

See **NUMQUAM INDEBITATUS**

INDEFEASIBLE [L. *in* + *de* + *facere* / to make or do]

Not capable of being undone or nullified. A right which cannot be voided or taken away; e.g., an irrevocable interest in property or an estate.

IN DELICTO   [L. *in* + *delictum* / fault, crime]

At fault, guilty.

See **DELICTUM; IN PARI DELICTO**

INDEMNIFY   [L. *in* + *damnum* / harm or damage]

To protect against loss or damage. To save harmless from injury or financial loss. To reimburse someone for a loss he has already suffered. Insurance, for example, is a form of contract under which the insurer *indemnifies* or reimburses the insured for loss or damage.

INDEMNITY   [L. *in* + *damnum*]

An agreement or undertaking under which one party commits to make another party whole upon the occurrence of a loss or injury. An agreement under which one party undertakes to pay the liability imposed upon another for his negligence or fault. An insurance contract providing reimbursement for loss or damage of the insured. Also, the reimbursement or compensation paid under such a contract.

INDENTURE   [L. *in* + *dent* / tooth; to bite into; to make a dent in]

An official document executed in two or more copies. A contract under which one person agrees to perform services for another over a period of years. An agreement between a corporate issuer of securities and its investors, describing the terms of a bond or debenture and, often, the assets which will secure the debt. The agreement is administered by an *indenture trustee*. Also, a mortgage, lien or other security instrument creating a secured claim against a debtor in bankruptcy.

INDENTURE TRUSTEE

A representative named in a *trust indenture to* hold title to the security under a bond or debenture and to represent and protect the interests of the bond or debenture holders.

IN DESCENDU

By descent.

INDEX   [L. *indicare* / to make known, show]

That part of a book or manuscript which summarizes and refers by categories arranged alphabetically to the contents of the book in order to give access to specific pages and sections. A list of items contained in a written document referring to the page or section where each item may be found. A set of mathematical references, usually keyed to a group of basic standards, used to calculate changes and adjustments; e.g., an index of stock funds.

INDEX ANIMI SERMO

Discourse and discussion are an index of the mind.

INDICIUM, INDICIA

Indications; signs or circumstances which tend to suggest that a fact or relationship may exist, but which are not in and of themselves sufficient to establish the existence of that fact or relationship. *Indicia of partnerhip* are circumstances which would suggest that someone is a partner in a firm. *Indicia of title* are documents which suggest ownership but do not confirm it; e.g., the carbon copy of a bill of sale. An owner of property who allows another to display or use the *indicia of ownership* may enable that person to convey good title to a third party without notice. Circumstantial evidence may be described as *indicia* from which a fact or happening may be inferred or from which a reasonable conclusion may be drawn.

INDICT   [L. *indico, indicare* / to make known, betray, inform against]

To charge with the commission of a crime, usually in a formal document known as *an indictment* or a *true bill*. An indictment is generally issued by a grand jury after the presentation of evidence by a prosecutor. An accusation of crime.

IN DIEM

On a given day. For a day.

INDIGENT   [L. *(egere), indigere* / to need, to lack, to be destitute]

A person who lacks the means to obtain life's necessaties without help from others. A person without food or lodging.

INDIGENT DEFENDANT

A defendant accused of a crime who is unable to pay for the services of an attorney. Under the terms of the Sixth and Fourteenth Amendments to the U.S. Constitution, he may apply for and be given a court-appointed attorney without cost to him. The court will also waive his costs and fees on appeal.

See **IN FORMA PAUPERIS; PRO BONO PUBLICO**

INDISPENSABLE   [L. *in* + *dispensare* / to measure, weigh out, distribute]

Absolutely necessary; essential; a thing or person who cannot be done without. An *indispensable party* is a party whose interest is essential to a full and complete determination of all claims arising in a proceeding or litigation. Under the Federal Rules of Civil Procedure, Rule 19(a), if an indispensable party cannot be joined, the action must be dismissed.

INDORSE

See **ENDORSE**

IN DUBIO [L. *in* + *dubitare* / to doubt, be uncertain]

When in doubt. In a doubtful case.

IN DUBIO, PRO LEGE FORI

In case of doubt, the law of the forum will govern.

IN DUBIO, SEQUENDUM QUOD TUTIUS EST

When in doubt, follow the safest course.

INDUCE, INDUCEMENT [L. *in* / in + *duco, ducere* / to draw from or away; to lead into]

Anything which motivates someone to take a specific course of action. Consideration for entering into a contract or other legal relationship. Also, facts which explain, or support, the principal allegation of a cause of action, as in liable or slander. Also, to entice or lead another into action. USCA § 271 labels as an infringer anyone who "actively *induces* infringement of a patent."

IN DUPLUM [L. *in* + *duplus* / twice as much]

In twice the amount or quantity.

IN EADEM CAUSA

In the same action, case or cause. For the same purpose. In the same condition or state.

IN EMULATIONEM VICINI [L. *in* + *aemulus* / jealous of, envious + *vicinus* / nearby, neighboring, neighbor]

Envy or hatred of one's neighbor.

IN ESSE [L. alive, in being]

In being; in existence. Contrasted with *in posse*, which means in the future, not yet in existence. A child is *in posse* before birth, *in esse* after birth.

See **IN POSSE**

INEVITABLE [L. *in* / not + *evito, evitare* / to avoid, shun]

A thing or event which cannot be avoided. An act produced by a force which cannot be controlled by human intervention or effort. An effect produced by natural causes, as a flood or earthquake. An *inevitable accident* is one caused by other circumstances than the negligence of a human being. In criminal law, an *inevitable discovery* is the discovery during an unlawful search or arrest of evidence which would have been found in any event if the search or arrest had been lawful; the evidence is admissible as an exception to the exclusionary rule.

IN EXTENSO

Fully, at full length. A text, such as a judicial opinion, which is recited or reproduced *in extenso* is reproduced in its entirety or verbatim.

IN EXTREMIS [L. *in* + *exter, exterior, extremus* / at the outer limits, at the edge]

In extremity; in extreme circumstances; at or close to the end. Imminent death; especially, in anticipation of death. A dying declaration is a disposition or statement *in extremis*. The dying declaration of the victim is admissible as evidence in a trial for homicide. The term is also used to describe any extreme or urgent circumstance.

See **IN LECTO MORTALI**

IN FACIE CURIAE

Facing the court. Before the court.

IN FACTO

In fact. As a matter of fact.

INFAMIA, INFAMIS

Ill fame. Dishonor, disgrace. In bad repute, disgraced.

INFAMIA FACTI

Dishonor or disrepute following alleged commission of a crime but before a judicial determination of guilt or complicity.

INFAMIA JURIS

Infamy in law. The dishonor or disrepute which attaches to a defendant after conviction for a crime.

INFAMOUS [L. *in* / not + *fama* / rumor, report, reputation]

Having an unfavorable or shameful reputation. Known for qualities which are considered disgraceful or socially unacceptable. Guilty of a crime of infamy. A person imprisoned for a crime.

INFAMY [L. *in* + *fama* / fame, report, rumor, public opinion]

An evil reputation resulting from the commission of a reprehensible act, such as a felony or treason. At common law, an infamous criminal could not serve as witness. The word "infamy" became a national byword when President Roosevelt called December 7, 1941, the date on which the Japanese bombed Pearl Harbor, "....A date which will live in infamy...."

INFANCY [L. *infans* / speechless; without the gift of speech; a little child]

The state of being a minor, i.e., under the age at which a person is deemed to have the legal capacity to act for himself.

INFANTICIDE [L. *infans* + *caedo, caedere* / to strike; to kill]

The killing of a child after its birth.

INFER, INFERENCE [L. *in* + *ferre* / to carry, take away]

To draw a conclusion from a set of facts or beliefs. To deduce a fact or finding from other facts presented as proof. A process of reasoning by which a conclusion may be drawn from facts which are known or proven. In the law of evidence, a proposition or conclusion supported by the facts presented to the trier.

IN FIERI [L. *in* + *facere* / to make, do]

In progress or process, in the process of being made or done; incomplete, inchoate. A trial is *in fieri* until the verdict is in and judgment is entered.

IN FLAGRANTE DELICTO

In the very act of committing a crime or misdeed. Also, to be discovered in an illicit sex act.

See **FLAGRANTE DELICTO**

INFLAMMATORY [L. *in* + *flammo, flammare* / to burn; to set fire to]

Tending to excite or inflame. Inducing anger, violence or disorder.

INFORMANT [L. *informo, informare* / to mold or give shape to; to have an idea]

A person who supplies information to another, especially information which comes from a confidential source and is not meant to be disclosed. One who informs the police of the criminal behavior of another, especially for money or other concessions.

See **INFORMER**

IN FORMA PAUPERIS

In the form or manner of a pauper. Impoverished, indigent. The right of a pauper to apply for and receive the court's permission to bring an action without being responsible for costs or fees. Also, the right of an indigent criminal defendant to court-appointed counsel.

See **INDIGENT DEFENDANT; PRO BONO PUBLICO**

INFORMATION [L. *informo, informare*]

Data or knowledge. The dissemination of news or reports. In law, an *information* is an accusation of the commission of crime issued against an individual by a public official authorized by law to issue it, e.g., a state or county prosecutor. An *information* functions in the same way as a grand jury's indictment and requires appearance and response by the accused. Some states require a grand jury indictment; others permit the issuance of informations.

INFORMATIONAL PICKETING

A form of concerted activity by labor unions designed to inform the general public that a particular employer does not have a contract with the picketing union and/or does not employ members of the union. Informational picketing is permitted under the National Labor Relations Act.

INFORMATION AND BELIEF

A term used by lawyers in connection with pleadings and affidavits to indicate that the person sponsoring the pleading or the affidavit has no personal or firsthand knowledge of the statements made, but nevertheless believes, in good faith, that the statements are true.

INFORMER [L. *informare* / to give shape to, to fashion]

Anyone who secretly supplies information to the authorities of the commission of a crime or infraction by another. Informers may receive compensation for their information. A person who supplies information to the police in the regular course of an investigation is not an informer.

See **INFORMANT**

IN FORO [l. *in* + *forum* / a square or marketplace; a public place; a court]

In a court, forum or tribunal; in a courtroom.

IN FORO LEGIS

In a court of law.

INFRA [L. Underneath, below, following]

Used in a text, *infra* refers to items, facts, terms or citations, which come after the point or place of reference. Contrasted with *supra*, which refers to items, facts, terms or citations which come before or precede the point or place of reference.

See **SUPRA**

INFRA AETATEM

Before or under the age. Under age.

INFRACTION [L. *infringo, infringere* / to break; to impair]

Any violation or breach, as of a duty or contract, or a law or regulation. The violation of a statute or regulation punishable only by a fine.

INFRA DIGNITATEM CURIAE

Beneath the dignity of the court.

INFRA JURISDICTIONEM

Within the jurisdiction.

IN FRAUDEM CREDITORUM [L. *in* + *fraudo, fraudere* / to cheat or deceive + *creditor* / a creditor]

In fraud of creditors.

IN FRAUDEM LEGIS [L. *in* + *fraudo* / to cheat + *lex, legis* / law or rule]

(To commit a) fraud upon the law.

INFRINGEMENT [L. *in* + *frangere* / to break, to shatter]

To break in upon, to trespass. To encroach upon the property or rights of another. The unauthorized usurpation or violation of another's property right or interest. In the law of Intellectual Property, the unauthorized use of a copyright, patent or trademark.

IN FUTURO

Later, in the future. Contrasted with *in praesenti*, at present, at this moment.

See **IN PRAESENTI**

IN GENERE [L. in kind; of the same class or species]

Describes a thing which is similar in quantity and quality to something else, but not exactly the same. Two laws are *in genere* if they deal with the same subject but are not identical.

INGRESS [L. *ingredior, ingredi, ingressus* / to step into, enter]

The act of entering into a place or area. Also, the legal right to do so.

INGRESSUS ET EGRESSUS

To enter and to exit. The right to enter upon land of another, to travel through it and to exit from it.

IN HAC (HAEC) PARTE

On this side. In behalf of this matter, person or thing.

IN HAEC VERBA

In these words. In these very words. In these same words.

INHERENT DEFECT

A latent defect. A defect which is present within a product or property but which is not visible or discernible to the user or occupant upon ordinary and reasonable inspection or use.

See **LATENT**

INHERIT   [L. *inhaerere* / to cling to, hold onto]

To take or receive property from a decedent by the process of descent and distribution. To take upon the death of another in accordance with the rules governing intestacy or, in accordance with his will or testament. Also, to come into possession of or feel the effect of.

INHERITANCE   [L. *haeres* / an heir; *haereditas* / an inheritance]

The acquisition of title to real or personal property under a will or under the laws of intestacy. Succession to property upon the death of another. An *inheritance tax* is a tax imposed by the state upon the acquisition of property by an heir or legatee, measured by the value of the property.

IN HOC

In this; respecting this thing.

IN HUNC MODUM

In this way or manner.

IN INFINITUM

Without end; to the end; indefinitely. A continuous succession of things or events.

See **AD INFINITUM**

IN INITIO

At the very beginning. The opening phases of a lawsuit are said to be *in initio litis*.

See and distinguish **AB INITIO**

IN INVITUM   [L. *in* + *invitus, invitum* / unwilling]

Against the will, or without the consent, of another party.

INIQUUM EST ALIQUEM REI SUI ESSE JUDICEM

It's wrong for anyone to judge his own complaint or cause.

INITIALIA TESTIMONII

The preliminary interview of a witness.

INITIATIVE [L. *initio, initiare* / to initiate or begin]

The first steps towards a goal or result. The quality of enterprise or energy which introduces new ideas and actions. A political process in some states which enables a stipulated number of voters to compel a public referendum or a vote by the legislature. The power of the general electorate to propose legislation or constitutional changes. There is no provision for initiatives under the Constitution but several states do permit them.

INIURIA, INJURIA [L. a wrong or injury; a wrongful act]

An act which deprives another of his rights or possessions. An attack upon a legal right. Harm to a person's body or property. The law recognizes a wrongful injury by awarding damages for it and for its consequences.

IN JUDICIO

Before a judge. Facing the judge. In court.

IN JUDICIO NON CREDITUR NISI JURATIS

The court will believe only those who are sworn.

INJUNCTION [L. *iniungere* / to join, fasten to; to inflict upon]

A remedy afforded by courts of equity to protect a plaintiff from irreparable injury to his property or rights when they are threatened by acts or impending acts of the defendant. The remedy consists of an order or command of the court directing the defendant to refrain or desist from committing or from continuing the act complained of or to undo the effects of an act already committed.

See **ENJOIN**

INJUNCTION PENDENTE LITE

A temporary injunction issued by the court upon application of the plaintiff at the outset of a law suit restraining the defendant from some action complained of until the final disposition and order of the court.

IN JURE

In the law; in accordance with the law; legally.

IN JURE PROPRIO

In a person's own right.

INJURIA ABSQUE DAMNO

A wrong or insult without compensable damage. The law compensates anyone who has been hurt or injured through the negligence or tort of another by the award of damages. If no damage has been sustained, the law will not entertain an action even if a wrong has been committed. In some instances, however, the law will allow nominal or punitive damages.

INJURIA ATQUE DAMNUM

The violation of a legal right which results in a loss or harm for which damages are awarded.

INJURIA NON EXCUSAT INJURIAM   [L. an injury does not excuse an injury]

One wrong does not justify another.

INJURY, INJURIOUS   [L. *iniuria* / injury, wrong]

Any act which causes loss or harm to another. Any violation of duty which one person has to another. Any act which the law recognizes as requiring redress or compensation to its victim. The invasion of a legal right or interest belonging to another.

IN JUS VOCARE   [L. *in* + *ius, iuris* / right, law + *voco, vocare* / to call, summon]

By summoning someone into court.

IN LECTO MORTALI   [L. *in* + *lectus* / couch, bed + *mortalis* / mortal, subject to death]

On one's death bed.

See **IN EXTREMIS**

IN LIMINE   [L. *in* + *limen* / threshold, home, dwelling]

At the very beginning or threshold. A *motion in limine* is a pretrial motion which seeks to prevent opposing counsel from referring to evidence which may be irrelevant or prejudicial until the court has had an opportunity to rule on the evidence at the proper juncture in the trial.

IN LITEM

During the course of a litigation.

See **AD LITEM**

IN LOCO   [L. *in* + *locus* / place]

In that place; in place of; instead of.

IN LOCO PARENTIS

In place of a parent. One who has assumed parental status and discharged parental duties, usually temporary in character, over a ward, without the formality of a decree of adoption or other permanent placement. Sometimes applied to an administrative body or educational institution (e.g., a college) which assumes the temporary care and custody of minors.

IN MORTUA MANO [L. *in* + *mortuus* / death + *manus* / hand]
In the hands or arms of death.

IN MEDIA RES [L. *in* + *medius* / the middle + *res* / a thing or object]
In the middle of things. At the heart of the matter.

INNOCENCE, INNOCENT [L. *in* / not + *noceo, nocere* / to hurt, injure, harm]
An absence of guilt or sin. Freedom from legal fault. A determination by a judge or jury of non-guilt in the commission of a crime. Relief from charge or accusation. Ignorance of facts requiring inquiry or investigation by a prudent person. An *innocent purchaser* is one who buys in good faith and without knowledge of facts which would lead a reasonable person to suspect the seller's title or right to sell. An *innocent spouse* is a husband or wife who is relieved of tax liability for income not reported by his or her spouse, because of his or her ignorance of any facts relating to the income.

IN NOMINE DEI
In the name of God.

INNUENDO [L. *innuere* / to make a sign or signal to; to hint]
An oblique allusion; a hint; a suggestion; an insinuation. Usually a deragotory reference to character or reputation. In actions for slander or libel, that part of the complaint which explains the meaning of the defamatory language and shows its application to the plaintiff. It is the plaintiff's burden to show how words which might ordinarily be construed innocently have a defamatory meaning when applied to him. Also, a parenthetical explanation inserted into the main text of a legal document.

IN NULLIS BONIS
The goods or possessions of no one; unclaimed property.

IN OMNIBUS
In all things; in all respects. In all the world.

INOPERATIVE [L. *in* / not + *operor, operari* / to work or labor]
Ineffective; without consequence. Without force or impact. Inapplicable. An entire statute or will may be inoperative, i.e., without effect.

INOPS CONSILII [L. *inops* / without, in need of + *consulere* / to seek the advice of, consult]
Without the benefit of counsel. In need of counsel.

IN PARI CAUSA [L. *in* + *par* / equal, a match for + *causa* / cause, reason]

Equally responsible. In equal fault or guilt. Equally culpable, guilty, wrong, or criminal. At common law, a party who was *in pari causa* with another party could not sue the other party with regard to the acts in which he had participated.

IN PARI DELICTO [L. *in* + *par* / equal + *delictum* / fault, crime; in equal fault]

Equally culpable or guilty. The general rule is that illegal transactions or contracts are not legally enforceable by anyone. But when parties to an illegal agreement are not *in pari delicto*, i.e., are not equally at fault, the agreement may be enforceable in equity by the less guilty party. A party may, for example, have participated in the illegal agreement only because he was compelled to do so under fraud or duress. In tort law, the party most responsible for the wrong may be liable for all the damages without contribution by others who may be less responsible.

See **A PARTICEPS CRIMINIS; DELICTUM; IN DELICTO; PAR DELICTUM**

IN PARI JURI

In equal right. With equal rights.

IN PARI MATERIA

On a similar or intertwined subject matter. A rule of statutory construction which provides that all relevant legislation, whether sections of one statute or parts of several statutes, dealing with a particular subject or directed to a common purpose, should be read and interpreted together to determine the legislative intent. The rule may be applied also in the interpretation of instruments and contracts.

IN PARI PASSU [L. *in* + *par* / equal + *passim* / here and there, far and wide, indiscriminately]

On an equal footing. Requiring equal treatment.

IN PERPETUAM (IN PERPETUITY) [L. *in* + *perpetuare* / to continue; to maintain unbroken]

To last or exist forever; interminable. A gift or transfer *in perpetuity* is a gift or transfer that is meant to last forever. In the law of real property, a *perpetuity* is a limitation or condition which prevents or suspends the transfer of title to property for a period longer than a life or lives in being plus twenty-one years. The Rule Against Perpetuities is designed to prohibit such conditions or limitations.

See **PERPETUITY**

IN PERPETUAM REI MEMORIAM [L. to preserve recollection of the matter]

A deposition taken before trial, to record the recollection of a witness who may not be available at the trial.

IN PERSONAM [L. into or against the person]

Relief or recovery against a person, not against his property. Pleadings or actions *in personam* require jurisdiction over the person of the defendant, usually acquired either by personal service or by substituted service. The decisions of equity courts are generally *in personam* in that they order the defendant himself either to do or to refrain from doing some act.

See **IN REM; QUASI IN REM.**

IN PLENA VITA [L. *in* + *plenus* / full + *vita* / life]

In the fullness of life. Civilly and physically alive.

IN PLENO LUMINE [L. in full light]

In the light of day.

IN POENAM [L. *in* + *poena* / loss, hardship, penalty]

By way of punishment or penalty.

IN POSSE [L. *in* + *possum, posse* / to be able to]

To be possible in the future. Potential.

See **IN ESSE; POSSE**

IN POTESTATE PARENTIS

To be under the control of a parent.

IN PRAESENTI

At the present time. In the present. Effective at once.

See **IN FUTURO**

IN PRAESENTIA ET AUDITU ALIORUM

In the presence and hearing of others.

IN PRIMIS [L. *in* + *prior, primus* / the former, the first]

At the very beginning. At first; at the outset.

IN PROPRIA PERSONA [L. *in* + *proprius* / one's own + *persona* / mask, role, part]

Sometimes shortened to *in pro per* or *pro per*. For one's self; acting for himself. A litigant who appears in court for his own account and without counsel. Originally, a litigant was required to appear personally before the court to plead lack of jurisdiction. A lawyer, as officer of the court, could not challenge its jurisdiction and was deemed to have accepted the jurisdiction when he appeared.

See **PROPRIA PERSONA; PRO SE**

IN QUANTUM MERUIT

An equitable doctrine supporting a plaintiff's right to recover for "as much as he deserved." For a more extended discussion:

See **QUANTUM MERUIT**

INQUEST   [L. *inquiro, inquirere* / to investigate, inquire into, search for]

An official investigation by a body (e.g., a jury) appointed by the court to determine the facts surrounding an event. The investigation by a coroner's jury into the circumstances of a suspicious death. The word is also used to describe the jury itself.

INQUIRY   [L. *in* + *quaero, quaerere* / to seek or search (*inquiro, inquirere*)]

A search for facts or information. A formal investigation by a commission or a legislative or prosecutorial committee of a matter of public interest, often with the power to compel testimony and disclosure. Under common law, a writ to determine plaintiff's damages after default by a defendant.

INQUISITION   [L. *inquirere* / to seek or search for; *inquisitio* / a searching for]

A judicial determination, usually based upon the findings of a jury. An inquest. Formerly, the inquiry into heresy by the Catholic Church and by the rulers of Spain and Portugal.

INQUISITIO POST MORTEM

An inquiry, investigation or inquest after death.

See **POST MORTEM**

IN RE

In the matter of, concerning, in the affair of. Used in the title of a legal proceeding or action which is not inherently adversarial but which requires the determination of some right or matter or an interest in property; e.g., *In re Estate of Murphy*. Also used more generally, as in the heading of a letter or memorandum, to indicate the subject matter dealt with by the writer.

IN REM   [L. *in* + *res* / a thing, fact or object]

Concerning a thing or item of property, rather than a person. An action in which the plaintiff seeks recovery against or affecting property or things. The judgment in an action *in rem* determines the rights of all parties claiming an interest in the property involved. (Examples of actions *in rem*: action to partition real estate; action to foreclose a mortgage; attachment.)

See **ACTIO IN REM; IN PERSONAM; QUASI IN REM**

IN REM JURISDICTION

The power of a court to seize or exercise control over a thing or item of property pending determination of the rights of all parties concerning the property.

IN REM SUUM

Concerning his own things or his own affairs. His own business.

IN RIXA   [L. *in* + *rixor, rixa* / to quarrel, a quarrel]

During a fight or quarrel.

See **HOMICIDIUM IN RIXO**

INSANITY   [L *in* / not + *sanus* / sound, healthy (from *sano, sanare* / to heal)]

Incapacity or inability to enter into enforceable legal relationships. A mental defect which makes a person unable to understand the nature of his actions or to distinguish right from wrong. The Model Penal Code recognizes insanity as a defense to crime. Under the Code, a defendant is insane if "he lacks substantial capacity either to appreciate the criminality (wrongfulness) of his conduct or to conform his conduct to the requirements of law." § 4.01.

INSCRIBE   [L. *in* + *scribo, scribere* / to engrave or write]

To write upon. To place one's signature upon. To create a permanent written record. To enter a name upon a public record.

IN SCRINIO JUDICIS   [L. *in* + *scrinium* / a case for papers or books + *iudex, iudicis* / judge]

Among the judge's own papers. Notes and papers used by a judge during a trial but not forming a part of the official record.

INSCRIPTION   [L. *in* + *scribere* / to engrave, to write upon metal or stone with a sharp instrument; to write]

Anything that is written or engraved. For example, a mortgage is *inscribed* or "recorded" in a public record, usually in a Book of Mortgages.

INSECURITY CLAUSE

A clause in a contract or other instrument which permits a party who becomes concerned about the other party's performance to require either immediate payment or performance or the deposit of sufficient collateral to protect against future loss or damage.

IN SITU   [L. *in* + *situs* / place, position]

In its place or location. In its original place; in its proper position. Used to describe the location of a parcel of property.

INSOLVENCY   [L. *in* + *solvo, solvere* / to free, release, loosen]

To be fettered by debt; to be unable to pay one's debts. To have more debts than assets. In bankruptcy law, to be incapable of meeting one's financial obligations as they become due. This is a stricter test than the test of measuring one's net assets by subtracting his liabilities from his assets.

IN SPECIE   [L. *in* + *specere* / to look at, behold]

Of that very kind. Specifically. A decree or order *in specie* is a decree or order requiring specific performance. An object is *in specie* when it exists as a distinct unit of a class or group. Also, money or coin. To pay *in specie* is to pay in silver or gold or other coin, not in paper money.

See **FUNGIBLE**

INSPECT, INSPECTION   [L. *in* + *specto, spectare* / to look at, study, watch]

To look at carefully and critically; to examine in detail. An examination of goods or property by a public agent authorized to inquire into compliance with laws or regulations, as the inspection of property by a building inspector to determine conformity with building and zoning requirements or the examination of imports by a customs agent. A buyer's examination of goods prior to acceptance or payment. UCC § 2-513(1). Under the rules of discovery, *inspection* refers to the examination by one party of the papers, documents and other evidence of the opposing party.

INSTANTER   [L. *insto, instare* / to stand on, to pursue. Also, to persist, insist on]

Immediately, forthwith. An act which must be done expeditiously, often within twenty-four hours. A judge may order a pleading to be filed *instanter*, or an appellate court may order or permit a brief or memorandum to be filed *instanter*.

IN STATU QUO   [L. in the present position]

In an existing situation or condition. In contract law, a party may be required to place the other party in the position he was in before the execution of the contract, i.e., *in statu quo ante*. A party seeking rescission of a contract must first place the other party to the contract *in statu quo*.

See **STATUS QUO**

IN STIRPES [L. *in* + *stirpes* / the main stem and roots of a tree; source, origin]

In intestacy, a decedent's heirs take by right of representation from an ancestor who can be identified. Distribution of an intestate estate *in* or *per stirpes* occurs when the living heirs are not all of the same generation. In that case, the estate is first divided according to generation and then among the members of each generation. Distribution *in* or *per stirpes* is distinguished from distribution *per capita*, which provides for distribution among all eligible takers equally, regardless of the levels of generations involved.

See **PER CAPITA; PER STIRPES**

INSTITUTE [L. *instituo, instituere* / to set up, put in place; establish]

To put in motion or begin. To start, as to *institute* an action or suit. To install in a position or office. A collection of laws or principles. Also, an organization devoted to educational functions or purposes.

IN STRICTO JURE

In strict law. By the letter of the law.

INSTRUCT [L. *instruo, instruere* / to build; to train, teach]

To impart knowledge to. To teach or educate. The act of a judge in advising a jury concerning the rules of law controlling the evidence and its deliberations. To explain an applicable rule of law to a jury. At the close of evidence, the parties to a trial may submit written *requests for instructions* to the judge.

INSTRUMENT [L. *instrumentum* / equipment, tool, from *instruo, instruere* / to build]

The means for producing or furthering an act or objective. A legal document, such as a deed, mortgage, insurance policy, etc., fixing rights and obligations. A *negotiable instrument* is a transferable note, check or draft containing an unconditional promise to pay a specified sum to the holder of the instrument or to his order, or to bearer, upon demand or at a definite time.

INSULAR [L. *insula* / island]

Relating to or characteristic of an island. Isolated, narrow-minded.

INSULAR COURTS

Federal courts created to deal with matters arising on or concerning the island possessions of the United States; e.g., the Virgin Islands.

IN SUMMA [L. *in* + *superus, superior, summus* / at the highest level; greatest]

In sum. On the whole.

INSURGENT [L. *in* + *surgo, surgere* / to rise up]

Rising up against civil or political authority. One who rebels against established authority. A person who challenges the laws of a country or state, sometimes with force.

INTANGIBLE [L. *in* + *tangere* / to touch]

Incapable of being touched or felt. Incorporeal. Without form or substance. A right, asset or property which has no physical being but which may be evidenced by a receipt or document. A chose in action. A right, such as a copyright, patent or trademark, which may be described, valued or measured but which has no physical existence.

See **TANGIBLE**

INTEGRATE [L. *integrare* / to make whole, to form, to make part of a larger unit]

To blend a part into a larger whole. To make part of a unit. To end the separation or isolation of one group or race from the general population and to incorporate the group or race into the general society.

INTEGRATED CONTRACT (OR WRITING)

A document intended by the parties to be complete within itself, without further amplification or amendment. The final and complete recital of matters agreed upon. Evidence extrinsic to the document, such as parol evidence, is inadmissible.

See **EXTRINSIC**

INTENT [L. *intendo, intendere* / to stretch in one direction; to strain; anxious, taut; leaning towards]

Purpose. The mental state of volition necessary for the commission of a specific act. A plan to execute a specific act. As used in the law of torts, intent is the conscious decision to commit an act or to bring about a result which will hurt or injure another. In criminal law, intent is a necessary ingredient of some crimes and must be proved by the prosecutor beyond a reasonable doubt. In the crime of aggravated assault, for example, the prosecutor must prove the *intent to kill* as well as the commission of a battery.

INTER

Between, among. Amidst. During.

See **INTRA**

INTER ALIA   [L. among other things]

Used when quoting only a portion of a statute or regulation, or a part of a judge's opinion, or a document or writing; e.g., "the statute provides *inter alia...*"

INTER ALIOS

Among or between others (other persons).

INTER ARMA SILENT LEGES

In time of war, law falls silent.

INTERCEPT   [L. *inter* / among + *capio, capere* / to take or seize]

To stop an action after it has begun. To seize an object which has been launched or released, as to *intercept* a plane or a missile. To eavesdrop upon or divert a communication directed to another recipient, as to intercept a telephone call. It is a violation of federal law to intercept any "wire, oral, or electronic communication." USCA § 2511.

INTER CONJUGES   [L. *inter* + *coniungo, coniungere* / to join together]

Between husband and wife. Matters relating to a marriage.

INTERDICT   [L. *inter* + *dicere* / to point out, to indicate, to say]

To forbid or prohibit. A decree or order asserting a prohibition. A decree of censure by the Catholic Church withdrawing the sacraments and the right of Christian burial.

INTEREST   [L *inter* / between, among + *sum, esse* / to be]

The right to own, possess or share in something. A right or privilege recognized and protected by the law. Interests are of all types and all degrees. A *beneficial interest* is the right to enjoy the use and benefit of property. A *controlling interest* is the ownership of sufficient stock in a corporation to control decision-making. A *future interest* is an interest which will come into existence only at some future time or upon the happening of some event in the future. An *insurable interest* is such an interest in a person or in property as to guarantee that the holder of the interest would prefer the continued existence of the person or property insured to recovery under an insurance policy. The *public interest* consists of all those things which the general public needs to secure its welfare. *Interest* is also a charge for the borrowing of money, usually computed at a percentage of the amount loaned. The income earned from the investment of capital.

INTERFERENCE   [L. *inter* / between among + *ferio, ferire* / to strike or hit]

The act of entering into or influencing the affairs and concerns of others. To meddle, disturb or infringe upon. In patent law, *an interference* is a proceeding conducted by the Board of Patent Appeals to determine conflicting claims among competing patent applicants. The tort of *interference with business or contractual relationships* occurs when a party intentionally interferes with the right of another party to an existing contract, causing a financial loss to that party.

INTERIM [L. in the meantime, for the time being]

An act or condition which is short-term or temporary and which comes before a more permanent act, e.g., *interim financing; interim order; interim appointment; interim statement* etc.

INTERLOCUTORY [L. *inter* + *loquor, loqui* / to speak or converse]

A finding, decision or decree which occurs during the course of a litigation and which is necessary for the resolution of an intervening issue but which does not resolve the entire matter or represent a final determination of the rights of the parties. The word is used in such phrases as *interlocutory appeal; interlocutory decision; interlocutory divorce; interlocutory order,* etc.

INTERMEDIARY [L. *inter* / between, among + *medius* / middle, midpoint]

One who acts to negotiate or resolve a matter or dispute between two parties. Anyone who acts as agent for two parties simultaneously. A broker, arbitrator or mediator.

See **ARBITRATION**

INTERMEDIATE (SCRUTINY) [L. *inter* / between + *medius* / middle]

The midpoint. In the middle between two poles or extremes. *Intermediate scrutiny* is judicial scrutiny of a statute affecting questions under the equal protection clause of the Constitution which is more critical and severe than the rational basis test, but less severe than strict scutiny. An *intermediate court* is a court which ranks below the highest appellate court of a jurisdiction.

See **STRICT SCRUTINY**

INTERNAL [L. *internus* / inward; directed within]

Existing within confines or borders. Within the limits of an organized structure. Domestic, not foreign. An *internal audit* is an examination into the financial records and affairs of a company conducted by its own personnel, not by independent accountants or auditors.

INTER PARES [L. *inter* + *par* / equal, by similar]

Among peers; among persons of equal rank. Among equals.

INTER PARTES   [L. *inter* + *pars* / side, party]

An instrument or document in which two parties join for a common purpose, such as a deed or contract.

INTER PRAESENTES

Among those who are present.

INTERPRET   [L. *interpres* / a negotiator or mediator; also, a messenger (from *inter* / within + *pretium* / value or worth)]

To explain or give the meaning of. To construe; to clarify the meaning or intent of. To review the terms of a statute or Constitutional provision and to derive and explain to others the meaning intended by their draftsmen. In its opinions, the Supreme Court often interprets the provisions of the U.S. Constitution for other courts and for the general public. At different points in our history, the Court has given varying interpretations of the same clause.

INTERROGATE   [L. *inter* + *rogo, rogare* / to ask, inquire, question]

To question systematically. To examine or propound questions to a witness or prospective witness. Questioning by the police of a suspect in a crime.

INTERROGATORIES

A pretrial device in which the attorneys for one side frame and propound written questions to be answered by principals and witnesses for the other side. Interrogatories are part of the modern pretrial discovery process. *Interrogatories* are subscribed under oath and may be offered to the jury as evidence.

IN TERROREM   [L. *in* + *terror* / fear, fright]

In apprehension, fright or fear. A clause or provision, usually in a lease, deed or will which is intended by the maker of the instrument to induce or coerce someone into not taking some action, as not to contest a will provision. For example, a testator may provide that a gift will be forfeit if the recipient contests the will. In most jurisdictions, provisions of this kind are unenforceable as against public policy. They are always unenforceable if the action they try to force or induce is illegal or impossible.

INTER SE [INTER SESE]   [L. among or between themselves]

A matter which concerns only the parties involved and no one else; e.g., the relationship between the trustee under a trust instrument and the designated beneficiaries.

INTER SE LIABILITY

The liability of two or more parties to each other in a legal relationship that concerns only them. For example, the liability of one partner to another with respect to the allocation of partnership debts would represent an *inter se liability*.

INTERVENE, INTERVENTION   [L. *inter* + *venio, venire* / to come]

To come between. To interfere with. To insert oneself. The steps which enable a third party not originally a party to the action to enter the action in order to support the claim of an existing party or to assert a new claim of his own. The process of intervention is controlled in the federal courts by the Federal Rules of Civil Procedure, and in each state by its own rules and statutes. A third party may intervene as a matter of right or after approval in the discretion of the court.

INTERVENING CAUSE

An independent act or occurrence which follows and contributes to the loss or injury caused to the plaintiff by defendant's negligence. If the act could reasonably have been foreseen by the defendant, he will be liable to the plaintiff for the intervening cause as well as for his own negligence.

INTER VIRUM ET UXORUM   [L. *vir* / man, husband + *uxor* /wife]

Between husband and wife.

INTER VIVOS   [L. *inter* + *vivo, vivere* / to live, be alive]

Between or among the living. A transaction between one living person and another, hence a transaction intended to be consummated during life, as opposed to a transaction *causa mortis*, or one in comptemplation of, or intended to take effect upon, death. The term is used to describe a variety of transactions, all during the life of the initiating party; e.g., an *inter vivos* gift, an *inter vivos* transfer, or an *inter vivos* trust.

See **CAUSA MORTIS**

INTESTABLE   L. *in* + *testari* / to bear witness or make a will + *habilis* / able]

Not competent to make a will, as in the case of a minor or a deranged or insane person. Also, incapable of being a witness.

INTESTACY   [L. *in* + *testor, testari* / to give evidence; to bear witness. Also, to make a will]

The act of dying without a will or with a will which is determined to be invalid. In an *intestacy*, the disposition of assets is determined in each jurisdiction under the laws governing intestate succession.

INTESTATE   [L. *in* + *testare* / to make a will]

To die without a valid will; also the person who dies without a will. In cases of intestacy, the disposition of the intestate's property is determined in each state under the laws defining intestate descent.

IN TESTIMONIUM [L. *in* + *testimonium* / witness, evidence, testimony]

An affirmation or declaration under oath; used now to mean "in witness or evidence thereof." The phrase *In Witness Whereof* is still used by legal draftsmen to introduce that part of a document which precedes the place of execution or signature.

See **IN CUJUS REI TESTIMONIUM**

INTIMIDATE [L. *in* + *timeo, timere* / to be afraid of, to dread]

To compel action through threats or fear of harm or reprisal. To take from another through coercion or extortion.

IN TOTO [L. in entirety; in total]

A repayment *in toto* is repayment in full.

INTOXICATE [L. *in* + *toxicum* / poison used for arrows; poison]

To place under the influence of a drug or liquor. To cause a person's physical and mental control and acuity to be diminished by the use of drugs or liquor. To excite or arouse.

INTRA [L. within, inside, near]

Within. Used as part of another word to convey the notion of occurring within, as in *intragalactic* (within a single galaxy); *intracranial* (within the skull); or *intramural* (within the student body).

See **INTER**

INTRALIMINAL [L. *intra* + *limen* / threshold or entrance]

Used in mining law to define the right of a miner to take deposits of ore within the area defined by the outer bounderies of his claim and then extending downward from the surface of the land as far as he can reach.

INTRA LUCTUS TEMPUS [L. *intra* + *luctus* / mourning, bereavement + *tempus* / time]

Within the period of mourning.

IN TRANSITU [L. *in* + *transigere, transitus* / to pass through or over]

On the way; in transit. The movement of an item or article from one place to another. In the law of sales, that period between the moment at which goods are delivered to a common carrier and the moment they are delivered to the buyer.

INTRA VIRES [L. *intra* + *vis, vires* / force, power, strength]

Within one's strength or power. An act or deed which is within the power or authority of the person committing it; e.g., the act of presiding at a meeting is *intra vires* for the president or chairman of a corporation; the sale of its goods is *intra vires* for a corporation engaged in manufacturing.

See **EXTRA VIRES: ULTRA VIRES**

INTRINSIC [L. *intrinsecus* / inwards, inwardly (from *inter* + *sequor, sequi* / to follow)]

Emanating from within a unit or body. Belonging to the very essence of a thing. Originating and occurring entirely within. *Intrinsic evidence* is proof contained entirely within a writing or document. *Intrinsic fraud* is deception by a party during the trial of a matter, e.g., perjury, the introduction of false documents, or the wilful failure to introduce relevant testimony. *Intrinsic value* is inherent value without influence by outside factors.

See **EXTRINSIC**

INTRUDE, INTRUSION, INTRUSIVE [L. *in* / in + *trudo, trudere* / to push or press; to thrust in; to force]

To thrust oneself upon another without invitation or permission. To enter upon the property of another without license or permission. To encroach upon a privilege or right. An *intrusion* is the act of wrongfully entering upon or seizing the property of another. At common law, intrusion included the usurpation of a freehold estate before the rightful owner could take possession. A trespass. An act is *intrusive* when it is committed without consent or permission of those affected.

INTUITI MATRIMONII [L. *intueri, intuitus* / to look at, contemplate + *matrimonium* / matrimony]

In contemplation of marriage.

INTUITI MORTUS [L. *intuere* + *mors, mortis* / death]

In contemplation of death.

IN UTERO (MATRIS) [L. *in* + *uterus* / the womb (*mater, matris* / mother)]

In the uterus of the mother. The condition of an embryo before birth. An unborn child.

IN VACUO [L. *in* + *vacuare* / to empty, make void]

Void, empty, in a vacuum.

INVADE [L. *in* + *vado, vadere* / to go, rush]

To enter with intent to conquer or occupy. To encroach or infringe upon. To assault or attack. Also, to reach into and spend a fund of money for a purpose not intended or authorized, as to *invade* the principal of a trust fund in a medical emergency.

INVALID [L. *in* / not + *validus* / strong, powerful, effective]

Without force or effect. Illegal. Ineffective. Lacking in authority. Also, a person who is sick or physically impaired.

INVALIDATE [L. *in* + *validus* / strong, effective]

To cause to become ineffective or without force. To nullify or make illegal.

INVASION OF PRIVACY [L. *invado* / to enter, attack + *privatus* / private, a private citizen]

In the law of torts, the term *invasion of privacy* encompasses four distinct torts, all of which intrude upon a person's right to privacy: 1) misappropriation of a person's identity, e.g., by using his name or photo for financial gain without his permission; 2) intrusion upon his seclusion, e.g., by using a wiretap to record his conversations; 3) publicizing the details of his private life; and 4) putting him in a false light by publishing information about him that would be considered offensive by a reasonable person.

INVENT [L. *invenio, invenire* / to come upon, encounter, find, discover; *inventio* / an invention]

To devise or create through independent investigation and thought. To discover something new and not previously utilized. To originate through the process of research and study. To introduce a new device, process or machine.

INVENTORY [L. *invenire* / to find]

Any list of assets or items having a common characteristic or common ownership, as the assets of an individual or a business. A schedule showing all the property of an identifiable entity. Also, goods on hand and available for sale or distribution by a business. *Inventory* may be valued at cost or at market; it may also be valued under FIFO (items first received are assumed to be the first sold) or LIFO (items last received are assumed to be sold first).

INVENTORY SEARCH

A search conducted by the police without a warrant following seizure of an item such as a motor vehicle to determine and list all its components and contents; the purpose is to forestall loss of property and resulting claims against the police.

INVEST [L. *in* + *vestio, vestire* / to dress, cloth]

To commit funds or resources to a business or enterprise for the purpose of producing gain and income. To devote a particular asset to a specific purpose for future gain or profit. To purchase a security or place money in an interest-bearing fund or account. Also, to place someone in a position of honor or authority, or to give him the symbols of office or authority.

INVESTIGATE [L. *in* + *vestigium* / foot-print, trace, mark (from *vestigare* / to track or trace)]

To inquire into. To subject to close study, examination or scrutiny. To examine and survey all the facts and circumstances surrounding a crime in order to identify the perpetrator and to establish probable cause.

INVESTITURE [L. *in* + *vestio, vestire* / to dress, cloth]

The act of conferring the symbols of office; also, the act of installing in an office or position. The act of ratifying a decision or commitment. The act of clothing someone in the adornments of office.

IN VINCULIS [L. *in* + *vinculum* / a band, chain, restraint]

To be restrained or in chains. To be in physical custody. To be under undue influence, pressure or duress. Also, the condition of a person who is oppressed by circumstances or events beyond his control, or one who is forced to accept terms or conditions imposed upon him by pressures he cannot defy or escape.

See **A VINCULO MATRIMONII**

IN VITA [L. in + vita / life]

In life. While living or alive.

INVITO BENEFICIUM NON DATUR

A benefit will not be conferred upon an unwilling recipient. No one can be forced to accept a gift or benefit.

INVITO DEBITORE

Against the will of the debtor.

INVITO DOMINI

Against the will of the owner.

INVITEE [L. *invito, invitare* / to invite; to summon]

A person who is invited onto land or premises of another to conduct business with the owner or lessee (*a business invitee*), and/or who is invited for any purpose for which the public as a whole is invited (*a public invitee*). The person in control of the land or premises has an affirmative duty to the invitee to use reasonable care to protect his safety.

IN VITRO [L. *vitrum* / glass]

Used in the term *in vitro fertilization*, i.e., laboratory insemination and maintenance of the resulting embryo in a vitreous solution.

INVOCATION [L. *in* + *voco, vocare* / to call, summon]
　The act of beseeching help or support, as a prayer for help at the beginning of a religious service. The act of implementing or enforcing a legal claim or right, as the *invocation* of the provisions of a treaty or of a contract.

INVOKE [L. *in* + *voco, vocare* / to call, summon]
　To call upon for help or support. To petition or appeal to. To cite as authority for a decision. To put into legal effect or urge the observance of, as to *invoke* a statute or a Constitutional provision. To place in operation, as to invoke economic sanctions.

INVOLUNTARY [L. *in* / not + *voluntarius* / voluntary, of free will]
　Action or effect forced upon an individual against his will. Done or committed without choice or desire. An *involuntary confession* is a confession which is coerced or induced through fear or fraud. *Involuntary manslaughter* is an unintended killing resulting from wanton and reckless conduct by the defendant or an unreasonable disregard for the probable consequences of his conduct. An *involuntary bankruptcy* is a proceeding in the bankruptcy court initiated not by a voluntary petition of the debtor but by a petition of his creditors.

IPSE DIXIT [L. *ipse* / I, myself, he, himself + *dicere* / to say, speak]
　Literally, he himself said it; he was the source. A statement without any authority or precedent except the statement itself. A bald, unproved statement. Sometimes used in place of *dictum*.
　See **DICTUM**

IPSISSIMIS VERBIS [L. *ipse* / that very thing + *verbum* / a word]
　In those very words. In those exact words.

IPSO FACTO [L. *ipse* / self + *factum* / fact]
　By that very fact itself; in and of itself; the inevitable result. The end of a marriage results *ipso facto* from a decree of divorce.
　See **FACTO**

IPSO FACTO CLAUSE
　A clause in a contract invoking the remedies of a party upon the bankruptcy or insolvency of the other party, such as the right to accelerate performance or to cancel the contract. *Ipso facto clauses* are invalid under the Bankruptcy Code because they inhibit the performance of duties by the trustee in bankruptcy.

IPSO JURE [L. *ipse* + *ius, iuris* / law, right]
From the law itself; merely because of the law.

IRA FUROR BREVIS EST [L. *ira* / wrath, anger + *furor* / madness + *brevis* / short (in time) + *esse* / to be]
Anger is a kind of brief insanity. Anger is a form of insanity.

IRA MOTUS [L. *ira* / anger + *moto, motare, motus* / motion, emotion]
Moved by anger. Responding to or acting in anger.

IRRATIONAL [L. *in* / not + *ratio* (calculation), *rationalis* (reasonable, rational)]
Not possessing reason or understanding. Without mental clarity. Lacking the power to reason or understand. Manifesting ignorance of facts necessary for a sound decision. Arbitrary.

IRREPARABLE [L. *in* / not + *reparo, reparare* / to restore, renew, repair]
Incapable of repair. Impossible to make whole or undo. A party threatened with *irreparable injury* to his property or to a vital interest may invoke the remedy of a preliminary injunction. For these purposes, *irreparable injury* means any harm which cannot be adequately compensated in money.

IRRESISTIBLE [L. *in* / not + *resisto, resistere* / to stand again; to oppose, resist, withstand]
Impossible to avoid or resist. Inescapable. An *irresistible force* is an unforeseeable event external to the provisions of a contract which cannot be avoided and which prevents a party from performing his obligations under the contract. An *irresistible impulse* is an urge which overcomes all reason and which is produced under mental disease or defect; in some jurisdictions, *irresistible urge* is a basis for an insanity plea in a criminal action.

IRREVERSIBLE [L. *in* / not + *reverto, revertere* / to turn back]
Incapable of being reversed or undone. A course of action or a decision may be *irreversible*.

IRREVOCABLE [L. *in* + *revocare* / to call back, to recall]
Incapable of being changed or reversed. Not capable of being reversed or pulled back by one party. An *irrevocable offer* is an offer which cannot be revoked. An *irrevocable letter of credit* is a commitment to pay which remains outstanding until it is utilized by the beneficiary.

ISSUE [L. *exeo, exire* / to go out, go away]
To put forth or distribute, as a statement or a document. To proclaim, as a declaration. To put into circulation, as currency. The first delivery of a secu-

rity or document to the person entitled to possession. To deliver a pleading to the party named, or a security to an investor. Also, a point of fact or law advanced or offered by one party and disputed by the other, requiring resolution by the court. In jury trials, *issues of fact* are decided by the jury; *issues of law* by the judge. Any relevant question requiring determination. Also, all persons descended from a common ancestor. Offspring, lineal descendants.

ITA LEX SCRIPTA EST

The law is so written.

ITEM, ITEMIZE [L. *ita* / thus, in this way]

One of several things included in a list or series. One component of an account or schedule. An object of attention or study. Any thing or matter under consideration. To *itemize* is to record or list the individual ingredients of a group of related things, as to list all expenses.

IUS COGENS [L. *ius, iuris* / law, right + *cogere* / to bring together, to collect]

Literally, the collective law. The name given in International Law to the body of rules or laws followed by the international community. All states are expected to observe these rules. For example, a treaty which provided for genocide or slavery would conflct with *jus cogens* and would not be recognized by the other nations.

See **JUS COGENS**

IUS COMMUNE

See **JUS COMMUNE**

Author's note: In ancient Rome, the letter **i** served at the beginning of words for the vowel sound **i** plus the consonants **y** and **j**. Later, the consonant **j** was substituted for the initial letter **i**. We list here under **j** those Latin words or phrases which, in their modern English form, begin with the letter **j**. In many cases, the same words or phrases appear under the initial letter **i** as well.

JACTATION, JACTITATION [L. *iactare* / to throw, to cast about, swing the body]

A boastful public statement which is usually false; e.g., a false claim of marriage; a false or slanderous claim of title. Also, violent movements of the body.

J.D.

See **JURIS DOCTOR**

JOINT TENANCY [L. *iungere* / to join, *unite* + *tenere* / to hold]

A property interest under which two or more parties hold individual but equal and indivisible title to the same property, with right of survivorship.

See **JUS ACCRESCENDI; TENANT**

J.N.O.V. (JUDGMENT NON OBSTANTE VEREDICTO)

Judgment notwithstanding the verdict. A judgment by the court for one party after, and despite the fact that, the jury has entered a verdict for the other party. Rule 50 of the Federal Rules of Civil Procedure has replaced the J.N.O.V. with the Judgment as a Matter of Law in Actions Tried by Jury.

JUDEX [L. *iudico, iudicare* / to judge]

In Roman law, a private person appointed to hear and resolve a dispute between citizens; a mediator or arbitrator. A judge.

JUDEX AD QUEM (JUDGE AD QUEM) [L. *iudex* / judge + *ad* / to, towards + *quem* / whom]

The judge to whom. The judge to whom a case has been referred by the assignment judge or by an appellate court.

JUDEX A QUO (JUDGE A QUO)
 The judge from whom. The judge from whose court a case has been removed or reassigned.

JUDEX DELEGATUS [L. *judex* + *delegare* / to transfer, assign]
 A judge who has been specially assigned to hear a case.

JUDEX EST LEX LOQUENS [L. *judex* + *esse* / to be + *lex, legis* / law + *loqui* / to speak]
 A judge speaks for the law. Judges act as spokesman for the law.

JUDEX PRO TEM (JUDGE PRO TEM)
 An acting judge. A substitute judge.
 See **PRO TEMPORE**

JUDGE [L. *iudico, iudicare* / to decide, to judge; also, to be a judge (*iudex* / a judge)]
 To form an opinion about after study and deliberation. To render a binding decision in a trial or proceeding after hearing evidence and determining the applicable law. To preside over a court or tribunal. To select between alternatives. Also, the person who presides over a court, interprets the law and renders judgments. A public official elected by popular vote or appointed by the executive to hear and decide disputes.

JUDGMENT [L. *iudicium* / a trial or investigation, from *iudico, iudicare* / to judge]
 The formal decision of a court after hearing all evidence and applying the applicable rules of law. The binding determination of a court at the conclusion of the litigation. The final decision, decree or sentence of a court after trial.

JUDGMENT BY COGNOVIT ACTIONEM
 A judgment rendered against a defendant who acknowledges his liability after he is served with process.

JUDGMENT BY CONFESSION RELICTA VERIFICATIONE
 Judgment rendered against a defendant who withdraws all his defenses and confesses judgment before trial.

JUDGMENT DEBITUM SINE BREVE (JUDGMENT D. S. B.)
 A confession of judgment.

JUDGMENT DE BONIS INTESTATI

A judgment affecting the estate or property of a person who dies intestate. A judgment rendered against the administrator of an estate.

JUDGMENT DE BONIS TESTATORIS

A judgment affecting the property of a person who dies with a valid will. A judgment rendered against the executor of an estate.

JUDGMENT IN PERSONAM

See **IN PERSONAM**

JUDGMENT IN REM

See **IN REM.**

JUDGMENT IN RETRAXIT   [L. *retraho, retrahere* / to draw back; because he has drawn back or withdrawn]

A voluntary renunciation of his action by the plaintiff in open court and the resulting dismissal of the action by the court. Also, a statement by the parties in open court that they have settled the action and that the court may remove the case from its calendar.

JUDGMENT NIHIL DIXIT (OR NIL DIXIT)   [L. *nihil, nil* / nothing + *dico, dicere* / to say, speak]

Literally, judgment because he says nothing. The judgment entered for a plaintiff when the defendant has failed to answer the complaint, or has withdrawn his answer; in effect, a judgment by default.

JUDGMENT NON OBSTANTE VEREDICTO

See **J.N.O.V.**

JUDGMENT NON PROSEQUITUR (NON PROS)

Judgment because "he is not pursuing his action." Judgment entered for the defendant because the plaintiff has failed to comply with one or another rule or requirement for maintaining an action; e.g., his failure to serve a complaint or a bill of particulars. An involuntary dismissal.

See **NON PROSEQUITUR**

JUDGMENT NON SUNT INFORMATI

Judgment entered after the defendant's attorney acknowledges that he knows of no defense to plaintiff's allegations.

JUDGMENT NUNC PRO TUNC

Literally, judgment now for then. A judgment which is given retroactive effect as of a specified date past. A judicial method for correcting a record which contains an error by entering a corrected judgment as of the date of the original judgment, in effect, cancelling the original judgment.

See **NUNC PRO TUNC**

JUDGMENT OF CASSETUR BILLA

The decree of a court of equity finding a complaint without merit and ordering a dismissal.

JUDGMENT OF NIL CAPIAT

A judgment that the plaintiff shall recover nothing. A judgment entered after issue has been joined in the pleadings but before trial.

JUDGMENT OF NOLLE PROSEQUI (NOL PROS)

Judgment because "I do not wish to continue." Judgment entered after the plaintiff in a civil action, or, more commonly, the prosecutor in a criminal action, announces that he does not wish to continue the action against the defendant. A voluntary dismissal.

See **NOLLE PROSEQUI**

JUDGMENT PRO CONFESSO

A judgment taken after confession.

JUDGMENT-PROOF

Describes a debtor against whom judgment has been entered but who is without assets or is bankrupt or insolvent, or whose assets are beyond the jurisdiction of the court or exempt from execution by statute.

JUDGEMENT QUOD COMPUTET

A judgment ordering the defendant to account to the plaintiff in connection with a transaction between them.

JUDGMENT QUOD EAT INDE QUIETUS   [L. that he go in peace]

A judgment of acquittal after a criminal trial.

JUDGMENT QUOD PARTITIO FIAT

A judgment ordering the partition of real property.

JUDGMENT QUOD RECUPERET

That he may recover. A judgment in favor of the plaintiff on the merits.

JUDICATURE   [L. *iudicare* / to judge]

The act of judging. The system for administering justice, including the system of courts, judges and other court officials. The courts.

JUDICIAL [L. *iudico, iudicare* / to judge; *iudex* / a judge]

Concerning the process of judging, the administration of the courts, the entry and enforcement of judgments, and the judiciary. Under the American Constitutional system, that branch of government charged with responsibility for trying all litigation, for resolving disputes, and for interpreting and applying the law. The system of federal courts is controlled by Article III of the Constitution. Also, any act or document issued by a judge, as a judicial order or writ.

JUDICIAL NOTICE

Acceptance and recognition by a court of a fact which is so universally accepted as to require no evidentiary proof. A court may take *judicial notice*, for example, of the fact that New York has a larger population than Chicago.

JUDICIARY

That branch of government which is empowered to administer the courts and to interpret and apply the laws. All the judges of a particular jurisdiction. All judges everywhere. The system of courts operating in any jurisdiction.

JUDICIUM

A trial or inquiry. A judicial proceeding. An investigation. Also, judicial authority. A judgment or decision.

JUDICIUM CAPITALE [L. *judicium* / + *capitalis* / of or relating to the head]

A judgment that the defendant suffer execution. A sentence of death.

JUDICIUM DEI [L. *judicium* / judgment + *Deus, Dei* / God]

The judgment of God. In Rome, the judgment which followed a trial by ordeal of fire and water.

JUDICIUM PARIUM [L. *judicium* + *par, paris* / equal]

The judgment of his peers.

JUNIOR [L. *iuvenis* / young; *iuvenor, iuvenari* / to act like a youth]

Of less advanced age; younger. Lower in rank or position; inferior or subordinate. A *junior lien* is a lien that has a lower priority than another lien, which is called the senior lien. A *junior mortgage* is a mortgage which by its terms is inferior to another mortgage or which was recorded subsequently to another. The latter is called the senior or prior mortgage.

JURA [L. *ius, iuris, iura* / right, law; pertaining to law]

Rights, laws. Concerning the laws. Founded in law. All those elements of a society covered by rules of law as distinguished from moral rules.

JURA AD PERSONAM [L. *ius, iuris* / right, privilege, law + *ad* / towards + *persona* / mask, person]

Rights against the person (as distinguished from property).

See **IN PERSONAM**

JURA AD REM

Rights against property (as distinguished from the person).

See **IN REM**

JURAL [L. *ius, iuris*]

Of or pertaining to the law and legal matters. Pertaining to rights and obligations. Elements which are based or founded in law; e.g., a *jural society* is an organized state or community operating under law; a *jural matter* is an issue arising under the law.

JURAMENTUM CORPORALIS [L. *iuro, iurare* / to take an oath + *corpus, corporalis* / relating to the body; corporeal]

An oath confirmed by some act. An oath evidenced by more than words; e.g., an oath taken with hand on the bible.

JURA NATURAE SUNT IMMUTABILIA

The laws of nature never change.

JURA PERSONARUM

The rights of persons and individuals. Inalienable rights.

JURA PUBLICA

Those rights which belong to all the people and not to the state. Examples: the right of access to streams and the ocean.

JURA RERUM [L. *iura* + *res, rei* / thing, object]

Rights over things. The rights of a person to the objects he owns or possesses.

JURAT [L. *iurare* / to swear; *iuratum est* / it has been sworn]

Certification by an officer authorized to administer oaths that a writing has been sworn to before him. The text appearing at the end of an affidavit showing the date and place of execution and the name and signature of the person before whom the affidavit was sworn.

JURATION

The act of taking an oath. The administration of an oath by an officer who is authorized to take oaths.

JURATORES SUNT JUDICESFACTI
Jurors are the judges of fact.

JURE
In right, in law. As a matter of law.

JURE BELLI [L. *ius, iuris* + *bellum* / war]
The rights and privileges conferred by war.

JURE DIVINI [L. *divinus* / relating to a deity]
By divine right.

JURE GENTIUM [L. *ius, iuris* + *gens, gentis* / a clan, a people, all people]
By the law of nations. According to International Law.
See **JUS GENTIUM**

JURE MARITI [L. *maritus* / relating to marriage; a husband]
In accordance with the rights of a husband.

JURE NATURAE
By the laws of nature.

JURE PROPINQUITATIS [L. *propinquis* / hear]
In accordance with the rights conferred by close relationship.

JURE UXORIS [L. *ius, iuris* + *uxor* / wife]
In accordance with the rights of a wife.

JURIS, JUS PRIVATI
The private rights and property of each person. Those individual rights which are not invested with any public interest.

JURIS CONSULTUS [L. *ius, iuris* + *consultare, consultor* / one who gives legal advice]
One who is learned in the law. A counsellor.

JURISDICTION [L. *iuris* + *dictio* / the act of speaking or orating]
The right, power and authority of a court or of an administrative agency to hear and determine a class of cases, as conferred either by the federal or state constitution or by a governing statute. Also, the power of a court to exercise control over specific parties or matters in a particular litigation. The power of a court to decide a matter in controversy and to adjudicate and define the rights of the parties. The *jurisdiction* of a court is defined both geographically and substantively.

JURISDICTIONAL AMOUNT

That amount which must be asserted by the plaintiff in a particular litigation to invest the court with power to consider and try the litigation. The jurisdiction of a court is often limited by the amount in controversy. Small claims courts, for example, may not try cases in which the amount in controversy is greater than a few thousand dollars. In the federal system, litigation between citizens of different states (diversity jurisdiction) requires an amount in controversy greater than a stipulated minimum (currently in excess of $75,000). 28 USCA § 1332.

JURISDICTIONAL STRIKE

A strike called by a union against the employer to protect the right of its members to perform a particular job or function, in opposition to another union which claims the same right for its members.

JURISDICTION IN PERSONAM

That power which a court must have over the person of an individual to enable it to issue a judgment affecting his personal rights or liabilities, i.e., a *judgment in personam.*

See **IN PERSONAM**

JURISDICTION IN REM

That power which a court must have over an object, thing or asset to enable it to issue a judgment affecting the rights of all parties to possession or ownership of that object.

JURIS DOCTOR (J.D.)

Degree awarded to graduates by most American law schools upon completion of formal legal studies. Before the 1960's, the degree awarded was the LL.B. (Bachelor of Laws).

JURIS ET DE JURE

Of law and of right. Legal presumptions which are deemed conclusive and irrefutable.

JURISPRUDENCE [L. *ius, iuris* / right, law + *prudentia* / knowledge, wisdom, knowledge of a subject]

The study of the law and its processes. The science or philosophy behind law as a process. A system of laws. Also, study of a particular area of the law. The history of court decisions.

JURIST [L. *ius, iuris* / right, law]

A scholar learned in the law. A judge.

JUROR [L. *iuro, iurare* / to swear, take an oath]

A member of a sitting jury. Also, anyone summoned to serve on a jury but not yet empaneled.

JURY [L. *iuro, iurare* / to swear, take an oath]

A group of citizens summoned and selected to decide the facts at issue in a litigation. A group of persons sworn to hear a body of evidence and to render a decision based upon the evidence. The *jury* in the usual civil or criminal trial is called a *common jury*. A *grand jury* is a jury of citizens sworn to inquire into the commission of a crime, to hear and consider the evidence, and to issue an indictment if it is satisfied that the defendant should be tried. A *blue ribbon jury* is a jury selected from persons who are specially qualified to consider a particular complaint or controversy. Criminal defendants are guaranteed a trial by jury under the Constitution. Juries vary in size from state to state, but may not be less than six. Juries consider and determine issues of fact; judges interpret, determine and apply the law.

JUS ACCRESCENDI

The right of survivorship which vests title in the surviving tenant in a joint tenancy.

See **JOINT TENANCY**

JUS AD REM

The right of an individual to the control or possession of a particular object or thing.

JUS COGENS

Any principle of law which is recognized by the entire international community as essential to the preservation of human values and is therefore observed by all governments except outlawed governments. Examples of practices which violate *jus cogens*: genocide, slavery.

See **IUS COGENS**

JUS COMMUNE [L. *ius* / law + *communis* / common, universal]

The common law. The common law of England, the United States, Canada and all the other countries acquiring their systems of laws from the English.

See **LEX COMMUNIS; JUS SCRIPTUM**

JUS GENTIUM [L. *ius, iuris* / right or law + *gens, gentis* / a clan or family; the people]

The law of all nations. International law. A body of law recognized by all nations.

See **JURE GENTIUM**

JUS LEGITIMUM [L. *ius* + *legitimus* / lawful, legal, according to law]

A right recognized by law. A right which must be recognized and protected and for violation of which the courts will afford a remedy.

JUS NATURALE

The laws or rules imposed on all beings by the circumstances and forces of nature. The law as it exists before the intervention of men. The basic rules of existence and survival which can be perceived and observed by all mankind.

See **LEX NATURALE**

JUS PUBLICUM [L. *ius* + *publicus* / belonging to the people, public]

A right enjoyed by all citizens equally. A right which cannot be infringed by the state or by any one individual.

JUS SANGUINIS [L. *ius* + *sanguis* / blood]

The right of an individual to succeed to the citizenship of his parents. In some countries, citizenship derives from the mother; in others, from the father; in others, from both or either. Also, all the rights deriving from common origin or descent. The right to be protected by the laws of the place in which one is born.

JUS SCRIPTUM [L. *ius* + *scribo, scribere* / to engrave or write]

The written law. The laws enacted by the controlling legislature; e.g. Congress or Parliament. In English jurispridence, the written law is distinguished from the common law, which is the law growing out of custom and usage and the decisions of judges in disputed matters.

See **JUS COMMUNE**

JUS SOLI [L. *ius, iuris* / right, law + *solum* / the lowest point; the soil or earth]

A rule of law which provides that a person's citizenship is determined by the place of his birth. Amendment XIV to the U.S. Constitution provides that all persons born in the U.S. are citizens of the U.S.

JUST COMPENSATION

A doctrine which requires fair and proper compensation to a property owner whose property is taken by eminent domain. The amount of compensation is usually the fair market value of the property. The doctrine of *just compensation* is imbedded in Amendment V of the U.S. Constitution.

JUS TERTII [L. *ius* + *tertius* / third]

The legal rights of a third party. In cases involving two parties with conflicting claims to possession of a parcel of real property, both parties may be precluded from relying on *jus tertii*, i.e., the rights of a third party.

JUSTICE [L. *iustus* / just, equitable, fair]

The Administration of Law and the courts. The fair, impartial and equitable resolution of disputes between parties. Administration of the courts and of particular litigation in an even-handed and just way. Also, a judge, especially a judge of a federal or state appellate court.

JUSTICIABLE

A controversy appropriate for determination by a court. An issue ready for trial or disposition by a court or tribunal. A controversy arising from a set of facts which can be reasonably disposed of in a trial. A real and substantial legal question which is ripe for decision, as distinguished from a question which is hypothetical, moot or abstract.

JUSTIFIABLE

An act which would otherwise be legally unaccepable but which is made acceptable or excusable by circumstances. In a *justifiable homicide*, for example, a killing is excused by circumstances of self-defense, public necessity, unavoidable intervention by a police officer to prevent commission of a crime, etc.

JUSTIFY [L. *iustus* / justice, what is right]

To show or explain the reasons or motivation for an act. To prove that some act is fair and reasonable. To swear an oath regarding ownership of property or to qualify as a surety, e.g., to establish compliance with the requirements for bail.

JUSTITIA NEMINI NEGANDA EST [L. *iustitia* / justice, fairness + *nemo, nemini* / no one + *negare* / to deny, say no + *sum, esse* / to be]

Justice must never be denied to anyone. No one should be denied access to justice.

JUS UTENDI

The right to use one's property or tools.

JUVENILE [L. *iuventus* / youth, the prime of life]

In Roman days, the term was used to describe anyone between the ages of 20 and 45. Today, it is applied to persons who are not yet adults; the age of maturity may differ from jurisdiction to jurisdiction. It is also often used to describe conduct by the young, as in *juvenile delinquent, juvenile offender* or *juvenile court*.

Author's note: The letter **k** was a part of the Latin alphabet but was rarely used to introduce a word. The letter **c** came to be used instead. Only a few words need be listed.

KALENDAE   [L. *calo, calare* / to call, summons]

The first day of each month of the Roman calendar. Interest on debts was due on this day, giving rise to the phrase *tristes kalendae* (sad days). The origin of our word *calendar.*

KLEPTOMANIA   [L. *clepo, clepere* (from the Greek) / to steal]

A morbid but irresistible impulse or propensity to steal. A mental disease characterized by the inability to refrain from or to resist theft. Because the *kleptomaniac* has no ability to control his actions, the condition is deemed a defense to the crime of larceny in some jurisdictions.

LABOR   [L. *laboro, laborare* / to work, toil, strive]

The application of human effort and activity to the production of goods and services. As generally used, labor is work for compensation as opposed to investment of time or money for profit. The work can be manual or mental or involve the use of tools or machinery.

LABOR CONTRACT

The agreement between an employer and his employees which deals with the terms of employment and with working practices and conditions, including wages, hours, vacations, fringe benefits and grievances.

LABOR DISPUTE

A controversy, dispute or disagreement between an employer and his employees, usually dealing with the terms and conditions of employment, or concerning the right of the workers to organize in a labor union.

LABOR UNION

An organization of workers of a common employer to secure through group action the most favorable conditions and terms of employment; e.g., higher wages, shorter hours, better working conditions, fringe benefits, etc.

LACHES   [L. *laxare* / to loosen, extend, enlarge]

Failure or neglect to assert a right or privilege in a timely way, resulting in prejudice or injury to others. The concept of *laches* is an equitable concept designed to protect against those who fail to assert their rights over an unreasonably long period of time. The person guilty of *laches* is estopped from asserting his legal rights because his delay has worked to the disadvantage of other parties.

LAPSE   [L. *lapsus* / a downward movement, a fall; an error]

The loss of a legal right or privilege by virtue of the failure to exercise it within a requisite period of time, or because of the failure of a condition or contingency. An insurance policy *lapses* if the premium is not paid by the requisite date. A testamentary gift *lapses* if the legatee dies before the testator, in the absence of a statute to the contrary.

See **LAPSE STATUTES**

LAPSE STATUTES

Statutes intended to correct the consequence of a lapsed legacy or device. In the absence of a *lapse statute*, a legacy or devise fails if the legatee or devisee dies before the testator, and the property passes by intestacy. Under a lapse statute, the legacy or devise passes to the issue of the deceased legatee or devisee instead of in intestacy.

See **LAPSE**

LAPSUS CALAMI   [L. *lapsus* / a failure or error + *calamus* / a reed, a Roman writing instrument made of a reed]

A lapse or mistake of the pen. The use in an opinion or agreement of the wrong word which conveys a possible, although incorrect or inappropriate, meaning.

LAPSUS LINGUAE   [L. *lapsus* + *lingua* / tongue]

A slip of the tongue. A statement which contains words the speaker never intended to say.

LARCENOUS   [L. *latrocinium* / military service; robbery; piracy (*latro* / a mercenary; a robber)]

Concerning the crime of larceny. Having the disposition to commit larceny. Planning, intending or committing larceny.

LARCENY   [L. *latrocinium* / service as a mercenary soldier, highway robber or pirate]

In the law, a felonious crime consisting of the actual or constructive taking of another's property against his will with intent to deprive the owner permanently of its possession and use. Under modern statutes, the term *larceny* includes the common law crimes of embezzlement, obtaining property under false pretenses, and larceny.

LASCIVIOUS   [L. *lascivio, lascivire* / to play or frolic, but also to run riot, to indulge in wanton conduct; *lascivus* / wanton, licentious]

Indecent, obscene, lewd. Indulging in or encouraging indecent sexual behavior. Tending to exite, especially sexually, and to deprave.

See **LICENTIOUS**

LATA CULPA   [L. *latere* / to hide, be concealed + *culpa* / fault, blame]

A hidden fault or neglect. In the law, gross or extreme negligence or neglect; used especially to describe negligence by a bailee.

LATENT [L. *latere* / to be hidden or concealed]

Dormant, hidden from view or recognition; not immediately apparent. Not disclosed by inspection. A *latent defect* in a deed or will is one which is not immediately apparent but which reveals itself at some date or event following execution.

See **INHERENT DEFECT**

LATENT AMBIGUITY

An ambiguity which cannot be discovered by reading the language of an instrument but is discovered only when the language is applied to some external fact. Thus, a gift to Harry Brown becomes ambiguous and indeterminate without further proof, when we discover that there are two Harry Browns who are both relatives of the donor.

See **PATENT AMBIGUITY**

LATITAT ET DISCURRIT

He hides and wanders about. A fugitive who escapes and avoids arrest.

LATORI PRAESENTIUM [L. *lator* / the bearer or the proposer + *praesentia* / presence, for the present]

To the bearer of these presents.

LAUDAMENTUM PARIUM SUORUM

The praise (or lack of it) of his peers. The determination of his peers. The verdict of a jury.

LAUDATOR [L. *laudo, laudare* / to praise, extol, commend]

One who offers praises. A character witness. An adviser.

LAUDUM [L. *laudare* / to praise; to deliver a funeral eulogy]

The sentence of a court or of arbitrators. A sentence of doom. A judgment.

LAW MERCHANT

See **LEX MERCATORIA**

LEGACY [L. *lego, legare, legatus* / to leave in a will, bequeath; to ordain, appoint, deputize]

A gift under a will, usually of money or personal property. A testamentary gift. The person who receives the gift is known as a *legatee*. The person who disposes of property in his will is known as a *legator*. Originally, a gift of personalty was called a *legacy*, and a gift of real estate, a *bequest*, but the distinction between the two is no longer made.

LEGAL [L. *legalis* / legal, from *lex, legis* / the law; a rule or law]
Concerning the law. Authorized by a law or rule. Created or established by a statute or regulation. Arising under principles of the English common law as opposed to the principles of the English courts of equity. Relating to the profession and practice of law by lawyers. Concerning the study of law, as in the programs of continuing legal education required of practicing lawyers in most states.

LEGAL FICTION
A fact assumed by the court regardless of its truth to enable it to reach a decision on the law. Contrived facts which may or may not be accurate but which are cited and utilized by the court in reaching its conclusions on the law.

LEGALIBUS [L. *legare* / to leave as a legacy; ordain, appoint]
Any chattel or item of personal property which can be disposed of by will.

LEGALIZE
To make legal. To give lawful status to an act or condition which does not conform to the laws. To validate an existing circumstance of questionable legal status.

LEGATEE [L. *legare* / to leave in a will]
Any person who receives a gift of personal property under a will.

LEGATION [L. *legare* / to ordain, appoint; also, to leave in a will]
A person or persons sent by one country to another to act as its official representatives; a diplomatic mission. Also, the official residence of the head of the mission.

LEGEM ENIM CONTRACTUS DAT
The law of a contract is determined by the provisions of the contract.

LEGEM FACERE [L. *lex, legem* / law, laws + *facere* / to make, do]
To enact a law. To swear on oath.

LEGES HUMANAE NASCUNTUR, VIVUNT ET MORIUNTUR
The laws made by humans are born, live and then die.

LEGES SCRIPTAE [L. *leges* + *scribo, scribere* / to write]
The written law. Statutory law, as opposed to judge-made or common law.
See **JUS COMMUNE; JUS SCRIPTUM**

LEGISLATE [L. *lex, legis* / law, rule; *lego, legare* / to appoint, ordain, bequeath]

To perform the functions of a body authorized to consider, debate and adopt laws to govern the general public. To exercise the power to make and promulgate rules and regulations having the force of law. To enact enforceable laws by the process of debate and exchange among representatives of the people, as opposed to law made by courts and judges.

LEGISLATIVE IMMUNITY

Describes two immunities enjoyed by members of the U.S. Congress. The first is the privilege from arrest during their attendance at sessions of Congress, except for "Treason, Felony and Breach of the Peace." The second is their privilege "not [to] be questioned in any other place"... "for any Speech or Debate in either House." Art. 1, § 6, cl. 1. The latter privilege guarantees their freedom to speak openly and without challenge on the floor, in committee, in their ballots, and in their writings and reports.

LEGISLATURE [L. *lex (lego)* / the law + *lator* / a bearer or proposer of laws]

A duly constituted body having the power to make laws for the body politic. An elected or designated body with the authority to make laws for a governmental unit such as a state or nation. Congress is the bicameral legislature of the United States. The United States has a tripartite system of government of which the Congress is one part. The judiciary and the executive branch form the other two parts.

LEGITIMA POTESTAS [L. *legitimus* / lawful + *potestas* / power, control]

Lawful power.

LEGITIMATE (VERB) [L. *legitimus* / legal, lawful, legitimate]

To make lawful; to give legal status to. To give a child born out of wedlock the same rights and standing as a child born to a couple who are lawfully married.

LENITY [L. *lenio, lenire* / to make mild, to relieve or alleviate, as of pain; to make more lenient]

Leniency, clemency. The *lenity rule* provides that if there is ambiguity in a statute or rule defining punishment for a crime, the ambiguity should be resolved in favor of the more lenient interpretation.

LETHAL [L. *letalis* / deadly, fatal]

Capable of causing death. Any device or instrument which can be used to cause death is a *lethal weapon*.

LETTERS AD COLLIGENDUM BONA DEFUNCTI

An order instructing a person to gather and preserve the goods and possessions of a deceased. These instructions did not of themselves make the designee the executor or administrator of the deceased's estate.

LETTERS AVOCATORY   [L. *advoco, advocare* / to call up, to summon]

An order instructing a person to return to his home country from another country with which his country is at war.

LETTERS ROGATORY   [L. *rogo, rogare* / to ask, entreat]

The request of a court in one country to a court in another country asking the latter to force a witness to answer interrogatories or to produce a document.

LEVARI FACIAS   [L. *levare* / to raise or pick up + *facere* / to make or do]

A type of common law writ of execution issued to the sheriff enabling a judgment creditor to seize both the debtor's assets and the profits from his land.
See **FACIAS; FIERI FACIAS**

LEVERAGE   [L. *levare* / to raise, lift up]

The relationship between the amount invested or committed to the capital of a business and the amount borrowed from outside sources; the greater the amount of borrowing relative to capital, the greater the leverage. A *leveraged buyout* refers to the acquisition of a company essentially by the use of borrowings secured by the assets of the acquired company.

LEVY   [L. *levare* / to lift up]

To impose or collect a fine or assessment. To require payment by exercising legal authority. Also, to conscript for service in the military. To wage war. To seize property under an order or writ of a court.

LEX   [L. A law, a statute, a collection of laws]

In the broad sense, *lex* is synonymous with *jus*. However, more precisely, *jus* conveys a sense of law based on ethical or moral right, while *lex* is more simply a statement of law in its pragmatic applications.

LEX ACTUS   [L. *lex* / law + *actus* / the act of doing or moving something]

The place in which something is done; the place where the action takes place; e.g., in a tort action, the place where the accident happens. In cases involving conflicts of laws, the *lex actus* may be controlling in resolving the issues.

LEX AEQUITATE GAUDET   [L. *lex* + *aequitas* / equity, fairness, evenness + *gaudere* / to be glad, to rejoice]

The law rejoices when it imparts equity.

LEX AMISSA [L. *lex* + *amitto, amittere* / to send away, deport, let go]
>To be banished or outlawed. To be declared civilly dead.

LEX COMMISSORIA
>The Roman law under which a pledge securing a debt was forfeited upon the failure of a debtor to pay his debts in accordance with their terms.

LEX COMMUNIS [L. *lex* + *communis* / common, general]
>The common law. The historical development of law through custom and usage and through the decisions of the courts in England and in the other English-speaking countries, including the United States. Case-derived law and the law of custom and usage, as opposed to the law contained in constitutions and statutes.
>
>See **JUS COMMUNE; JUS SCRIPTUM**

LEX CONTRACTUS [L. *lex* + *contrahere* / to draw together, unite, narrow]
>The law of the contract. The law which governs the contract, which can be the law of the place where the contract was executed, or of the place where the contract is to be performed, or of the place intended or designated by the parties in their agreement.

LEX DILATIONES SEMPER EXHORRET
>The law dislikes all delays.

LEX FORI [L. *lex* + *forum, fori* / market-place, public square, courthouse, court]
>The law of the court or forum; the law of the jurisdiction in which an action is commenced or is pending. The *lex fori* will control all procedural and substantive matters required for decision except in those instances in which some principle of conflicts resolution requires the court to look at the law of another jurisdiction.
>
>See **LEX CONTRACTUS; LEX LOCI CONTRACTUS**

LEX LOCI [L. *lex* + *locus, loci* / place, location]
>The law of the place. Generally followed by a word or phrase which specifies the place which is intended; e.g., *lex loci contractus*. If no word is added, the assumption is that *lex loci* means *lex loci contractus*.

LEX LOCI ACTUS
>The law of the place in which he acted.

LEX LOCI COMMISSI
>The place where the act was committed.

LEX LOCI CONTRACTUS

Literally, the place in which a contract is made. In cases involving conflicts of laws, the *lex loci contractus* generally controls issues of substance and the *lex fori* controls issues of procedure.

See **LEX CONTRACTUS; LEX FORI**

LEX LOCI DELICTI   [L. *lex* + *locus* + *delictum* / fault, crime]

The place of the wrong. The place where the crime or the tort took place. Also, the place of the last of a series of acts resulting in a tort or crime. In resolving conflicts in substative laws controlling torts, the court would look to the *lex loci delicti* or the *lex delicti*.

LEX LOCI DOMICILII   [L. *lex* + *locus* + *domicilium* / dwelling, residence]

The law of the place of domicile, i.e., a person's principal and permanent legal home or residence.

LEX LOCI REI SITAE (LEX SITUS)

The law of the place in which the thing is situated. The law of the site of the subject matter, usually with reference to real property.

LEX MERCATORIA (LEX MERCHANT)   {L. *lex* + *mercator* / merchant, wholesaler, shopkeeper]

The law of merchants. Now called the Law Merchant, a code or record of international precedents, principles and practices which became recognized by merchants in most trading countries and was enforced in a system of courts outside the regular legal system. Many of the elements of the code were taken into English common law and into our own commercial codes and practices.

See **MERCANTILE LAW**

LEX NATURALE

The laws of nature.

See **JUS NATURALE**

LEX NEMINI FACIT INJURIAM

The law never causes injury to anyone.

LEX NIL FACIT FRUSTRA

The law does not function in vain.

LEX NON COGIT AD IMPOSSIBILIA

The law never compels the impossible.

LEX NON CURAT DE MINIMIS

The law does not trouble itself with unimportant matters.

LEX NON SCRIPTA   [L. *lex + non + scribo, scribere* / to engrave, draw lines, write]

The law which is not written. The unwritten law. Non-statutory law; the law derived from the decisions and opinions of judges and from the customs and usages of society. The common law.

See **LEX COMMUNIS**

LEX PATRIAE   [L. *lex + patrius* / relating to the father, fatherland, native]

The law of one's own country.

LEX POSTERIOR DEROGAT PRIORI

A later law repeals the prior one.

LEX PUNIT MENDACIUM   [L. *lex + pumio, punire* / to punish, avenge + *mendax, mendacium* / lying, lie]

The law punishes lies and liars.

LEX REPROBAT MORAM   [L. *mora* / delay]

The law dislikes delay.

LEX SCRIPTA   [L. *lex + scribo, scribere* / to engrave, write]

The written law. Statutory or codified law, as opposed to judge-made law.

See **LEX NON SCRIPTA**

LEX SEMPER DABIT REMEDIUM   [L. *lex + semper* / always + *dare* / to give + *remedium* / remedy, cure]

The law always supplies a remedy.

LEX SUCCURIT IGNORANTI ET MINORIBUS

The law helps those who do not know or understand and also those who are underage.

LEX TERRAE   [L. *lex + terra* / the earth, land]

The law of the land.

LIABILITY   [L. *ligare* / to bind, tie together + *habilis* / capable of]

A word used broadly in the law to describe any duty, obligation or responsibility, civil or criminal. A debt; a burden; an obligation to perform. In business law, all the debts of and claims against a business. Liabilites are divided into *current liabilities, deferred liabilities, contingent liabilities*, etc.

LIABILITY IN SOLIDO

Joint and several liability. The liability imposed upon joint obligors to a contract or upon joint tortfeasors, i.e., persons who have joined in causing harm to the plaintiff through their negligence. Enables the plaintiff to sue and collect in full from either or both the defendants; but plaintiff is not entitled to recover more from both together than the total of her actual damages. Some states have enacted legislation adjusting the liability among joint tort feasors who are not responsible equally for the injuries to the plaintiff.

LIABILITY INSURANCE

A contract of insurance under which the insurer agrees to defend and indemnify the insured in a stated sum against claims for injury or loss to others caused by the non-criminal acts of the insured. As part of its contract, the insurer usually selects the attorney who will defend against the third party's claims. *Liability insurance* does not cover losses by the insured himself; but standard auto policies provide both liability insurance and coverage for property damage to the vehicle of the insured.

LIABLE   [L. *ligare* / to bind, tie together]

Obligated in law or equity. Answerable for. Obliged to respond or pay after commission of a wrong or the assumption of a debt. Responsible for a contingency or risk which is likely to occur, or for damages or a penalty.

LIBEL   [L. *libellus* / a little book, a short declaration or memorandum]

A defamatory statement expressed in writing, printing, pictures, art, or signs. Any statement that injures the reputation of another. Any accusation or attribution in writing or art which holds a person up to ridicule or exposes him to public contempt, shame or ridicule.

LIBELLANT/ LIBELLEE

The *libellant* is the plaintiff in an action for libel. Also, the plaintiff in a divorce proceeding. The *libellee* is the defendant in either proceeding.

LIBEL PER QUOD

An ambiguous or imprecise statement which requires proof to render it defamatory or injurious to the reputation of another. A statement may not be libellous on its face but may be shown to damage the reputation of a person by virtue of the special circumstances or conditions under which it is uttered. A statement may be so ambiguous as to be capable of two interpretations, one libellous and the other not; only testimony and proof will establish whether a libel has occurred.

LIBEL PER SE

A statement is libellous *per se* if the words used are so clearly defamatory that injury to an individual can be presumed as a matter of law. In the case of *libel per se*, the plaintiff need not prove damage to his person or property. The words used are so obviously harmful to his reputation that injury or damage to him is presumed.

LIBER   [L. *liber* / free, independent, without restraint]

Free; at liberty. The root for the words *liberal* and *liberty*.

LIBERATE   [L. *libero, liberare* / to set free, liberate]

To set free. To release from restraint or custody. To remove from control or dominion, as of one country or people by another.

LIBER ET LEGALIS HOMO

A free and lawful man.

See **HOMO LIBER**

LIBERTAS OMNIBUS REBUS FAVORABILIOR EST

Liberty is favored above all other things.

LIBERTY   [L. *liber* / free; *libertas* / freedom]

Freedom from restraint or control by others in the pursuit of one's lawful activities. Enjoyment equally with all others of the rights and privileges accorded to a democratic society, free from all governmental restraints except those required for the safety and welfare of its citizens. Freedom from physical or mental restraint. Possessing all the rights guaranteed to American citizens under the U.S. Constitution, especially as expressed in the Bill of Rights and Fourteenth and Fifteenth Amendments.

LICENSE   [L. *licet, licere* / it is allowed or permitted]

A special right not enjoyed by everyone, usually after application to and approval by some governmental body, as a driver's license, a marriage license, a liquor license. Other examples: a license to practice law or medicine. Also, authorization by a person or business having a proprietary right, such as a patent or trademark, to another, permitting the use of that right in commerce.

LICENTIOUS   [L. *licentia* / excessive freedom; the abuse of freedom, untrained]

Excessive and arbitrary use of one's rights and privileges; ignoring the rights of others. Disregarding sexual and moral restraints. Uninhibited. Lewd; lascivious.

See **LASCIVIOUS**

LICET CEPIT NON ASPORTAVIT

He took it, but he did not carry it away.

LICIT [L. *licet, licere* / to be allowed; it is allowed or permitted]

Conforming to law. Lawful, proper.

LIEN [L. *ligamen* / a string, tie, covering, bandage]

A charge upon the property or assets of one person to secure to another the payment of a debt or obligation. An interest conferred by the law upon one person in the property of another. The right to retain or take possession of the property of another to satisfy a debt, obligation or judgment. A security interest in the property of another, created by mortgage or assignment, or by court order or judgment.

LIMINE

See **IN LIMINE**

LIMITATION [L. *limes, limitus* / a path, especially a path forming a boundary; a boundary line or limit]

A restriction or limit. A restraint; a condition imposed by the law. Any statement in a legal document, e.g., a will or contract, limiting the duration of a period of ownership or otherwise restricting the rights or obligations of the parties. Also, a period of time imposed by law after which a particular type of action or proceeding may no longer be commenced. The statutes limiting these periods of time are called *statutes of limitations*. In a will or deed, words limiting the duration of an estate are called *words of limitation*.

See **STATUTE OF LIMITATIONS**

LIMITED [L. *limes, limitus* / a boundary line or limit]

Restricted in scope, time or degree. Confined within prescribed bounds. Following the title of a business enterprise, the word (usually abbreviated as "Ltd.") indicates that the business is a corporation. A *limited guaranty* is a guaranty confined to a particular transaction or liability. *Limited liability* is the liability enjoyed by limited partners, i.e., liability restricted to the partners' original investment. A *limited partnership* is a partnership with general and limited partners; the general partners manage the business and are generally liable for its debts; the limited partners have limited liability. A *limited power of appointment* is a power which the donee may exercise only in favor of others than himself. Some courts have only *limited jurisdiction*, i.e., they are authorized to deal only with a particular class of cases; e.g., the bankruptcy courts, small claims' courts, probate courts, juvenile courts.

LINEAGE [L. *lineo, linare* / to draw a line, to make straight]

Descent in a direct line from a common predecessor. A group of persons who are descendants of a common ancestor.

LINEAL [L. *linea* / a string, a straight line]

A direct line of descent, as the line from father to son. Direct descent. Descent in a line from one generation directly to the next: grandfather, son, grandson, great-grandson, etc. Distinguished from *collateral descent*.

LIQUID [L. *liquare* / to make liquid, liquify]

Having the properties of a water-like substance. The condition of a business which has sufficient cash — and/or other assets quickly and easily convertible to cash — to enable it to meet its obligations as they mature. *Liquid assets* are either cash or other assets quickly convertible to cash.

LIQUIDATE [L. *liquare* / to liquify]

To pay or settle an obligation in full. To convert a debtor's assets to cash, and, if necessary, to identify his creditors and other persons with rights to the cash, and then to distribute the cash as the legal rights of all interested parties may determine.

LIQUIDITY [L. *liquare*]

The measurement of the health of a business by reference to its ability to reduce its assets to cash — the greater and faster the ability, the more liquid the business.

LIS

A legal controversy; a law suit or action. Also, the subject of a law suit.

LIS ALIBI PENDENS [L. *lis* + *alibi* / elsewhere, in another place + *pendo, pendere* / to hang down, be suspended, to exist in time]

There is an action in another place; there's another action pending. If there is an action pending in another jurisdiction between the same parties on the same issues, the court will refuse to entertain another action. Notice of the pending action may be raised by a party in his pleadings.

LIS PENDENS [L. *lis* / a lawsuit + *pendere* / to be in progress]

Notice that an action is pending. A statement to all that a court has before it a suit or action affecting the named parties, or a parcel of land, in which the court is being asked to determine or resolve a dispute set forth and described in the pleadings. The purpose of the statement is to give notice of the action to all and to bind purchasers or encumbrancers of any property involved in the action to the court's decision. A notice of *lis pendens* or notice of pendency is a document filed in a public record office which has the effect of advising the world, including purchasers and encumbrancers, that title to a property or asset is in litigation and that they will be bound by the terms of the court's judgment.

LITE PENDENTE [L. *lis, litis* / a legal controversy + *pendere* / to be suspended]

Pending the outcome of the litigation or suit. Matters the resolution of which depends on the outcome of a lawsuit (e.g., title to property whose ownership is in dispute) are *lite pendente*. The alternative form *pendente lite* is more commonly used.

See **PENDENTE LITE**

LITERAE PATENTES [L. *littera, litera* / any letter of the alphabet; also a letter or communication + *pateo, patere* / to lie open]

Open letters. Letters Patent.

LITERAE SCRIPTAE MANENT

The written word lasts forever.

LITIGATE [L. *litigare* / to resort to the law; to quarrel or dispute]

To initiate or carry on a lawsuit or other judicial controversy; to seek judicial relief. To sue or be sued.

LITIGIOUS [L. *litigare*]

To have a propensity or eagerness to bring or engage in law suits. To be fond of resorting to the courts. Also, a matter or issue contested in a law suit.

LITIS AESTIMATIO [L. *lis, litis* / a lawsuit + *aestimare* / to appraise, estimate, assign value to]

The measure of damages in a law suit.

LITTORAL [L. *litoralis* / of or connected to the shore]

The area between the low — and high — water mark of land abutting waters such as lakes, seas and oceans. Also, rights affecting the use of properties along or on such land.

LOCAL [L. *locus* / place, neighborhood, region]

Limited in space or location. Relating to a particular and limited place. Confined to a relatively small and definable area. Characteristic of a particular place. *Local law* is the law of a particular place or state without reference to the law of any other place or state; the study of the interrelationship of one local law with another is called the study of conflicts of law. Also, in labor law, a local is a union organization limited to a particular area or a particular group of companies; local unions are consolidated into national unions, which are in turn joined into international unions.

LOCATIO CUSTODIAE   [L. *locatio* / a contract for letting and hiring, a lease + *custodia* / custody, care]

Services performed for hire on an object delivered under a bailment.

LOCATIO OPERIS   [L. *locatio* / a lease or bailment + *opera* / work, services]

The obligation to supply the materials and to perform the services on an object delivered for repair or renovation, as by a tailor to mend a dress or suit.

LOCATIO REI

Any hiring of a thing or chattel.

LOCO CITATO   [L. *locus* / place, neighborhood + *citare* / to put in motion]

At the place cited or described. Abb. *loc. cit.*

LOCO PARENTIS

See **IN LOCO PARENTIS**

LOCUM TENENS   [L. *locus* + *tenere* / to have or hold]

The position of an assistant or deputy who serves in the place of his superior when the latter is no longer able or eligible to serve, until the deputy is replaced by the person entitled to hold the office permanently. An interim deputy or substitute.

LOCUS

The place. In law, the place where a thing or matter at issue has been done or taken place.

LOCUS CONTRACTUS   [L. *locus* + *contrahere* / to draw together, collect]

The place where the contract was made. The place of execution of a contract, or the place at which some act of the parties rendered a contract effective and in force.

LOCUS CONTRACTUS REGIT ACTUM

The place where the contract was made controls the act.

LOCUS CRIMINIS   [L. *locus* + *crimen* / accusation, charge, crime]

The location of a crime. The place where the crime was committed.

LOCUS DELICTI   [L. *locus* + *delictum* / fault, delinquency]

The place where the wrong or offense occurred or was committed. Although used sometimes interchangeably with *locus criminis* — *locus delicti* is broader in meaning and includes civil torts as well as crimes.

LOCUS IN QUO
> Literally, the place in which or where. In pleadings, designates the place where an action occurred or an offense was committed.

LOCUS PAENITENTIAE [L. *locus* + *paenitere* / to repent, be sorry]
> The moment of regret or repentance. The point at which a person is still able to change his mind before it is too late to avoid liability, as before committing a wrongful act or crime.

LOCUS REI SITAE [L. *locus* + *res* / thing, object + *situs* / place, position]
> The place where the thing is located. The location of the property at issue.

LOCUS SIGILLI (L. S.) [L. *locus* + *sigilla* / small ornaments or figures; engraving cut into a ring]
> The place for affixing a signature or seal; usually abbreviated "L.S." Originally, a formal seal was used to indicate that a document had been executed. In current use, a party's signature is generally sufficient, but the designation "L.S." survives to indicate the place of execution.

LOCUS STANDI
> The place where one stands. A litigant's standing in court. The right to appear and be heard before a body such as a court, a legislature, a committee, etc.

LONGA POSSESSIO JUS PARIT
> Continuous possession ripens into right.

LUCID [L. *lux* / light, daylight]
> In complete command of one's faculties; sane, rational; clear, intelligible. Used in *lucid interval* to indicate a period during which a person who may be generally insane or deprived of mental capacity, has sufficient temporary capacity and clarity of mind to act in a legally binding or consequentual way, e.g., so as to execute a valid will or enter into a binding agreement.

LUCRATIVE [L. *lucror, lucrari* / to gain or profit; to win]
> Affording gain or profit. Free of cost, charge or consideration.

LUCRI CAUSA [L. *lucrari* / to gain or profit + *causa* / reason for, motivation, purpose]
> Intent to profit or gain from a wrongful act; an element of the crime of larceny.

LUCTOSA HEREDITAS [L. *luctus* / causing sorrow or mourning + *hereditas* / inheritance]

A regretful or sorrowful inheritance, as an inheritance from a child by a parent or from one friend or lover by another.

LUNATIC [L. *luna* / moon]

A deranged person; a term formerly used to describe the mental condition which constituted legal incapacity. The word developed from the early notion that mood and sanity fluctuated with the phases of the moon.

LUXURY TAX [L. *luxuria* / exuberant growth; excess, extravagance + *tango, tangere* / to touch]

An excise tax upon the sale or use of products which are not considered necessary for human support or maintenance, e.g., a tax on liquor, jewelry or cigarettes.

MACHINATION   [L. *machinor, machinari* / to contrive, invent, devise]
A scheme or contrivance intended for some fraudulent or dishonest purpose.

MAGISTER   [L. *magis* / more than]
Master, chief, head, director. Also, a learned person, teacher, schoolmaster.

MAGISTER CANCELLARIAE
A master in chancery.

MAGISTRATE   [L. *magister* / chief, superintendent]
A public quasi-judicial official whose functions are usually strictly defined. In the judicial system, an inferior judicial officer, generally at a local level, authorized to hear petty offenses and misdemeanors. A police judge or justice of the peace. In the federal courts, an officer appointed by the judges of the district courts to hear pretrial matters.

MAGNA CARTA [MAGNA CHARTA]
Called the "great charter", to which King John gave his assent in 1215. It is considered the fundamental guarantee of rights and privileges under English law. It guaranteed that every citizen would be assured the enjoyment of life, liberty and happiness and that he would be judged for any alleged misdeeds only by a jury of his peers. These essential principles are now embodied in the U.S. Constitution.

MAGNA CULPA   [L. *magnus* / large, great + *culpa* / fault, blame]
Great fault; gross negligence.

MAINTENANCE   [L. *manus* / hand + *teneo, tenere* / to hold, have a grip on]
In matrimonial law, the obligation of one party to provide for and support another, as a parent his child, or a husband his wife. Also, financial support given by an outsider who has no interest in a law suit, to a party to the suit, to enable him or her to continue the law suit; this support is unlawful. To meddle in the disputes or conflicts of others; especially, to give financial support for the purpose of stirring up litigation.

MAINTENANCE CURIALIS [L. *manus* + *tenere* + *curia* / the senate building in Rome; a central place; a courthouse]

To commit maintenance in direct support of a litigation before the courts. To meddle in, encourage or finance the conduct of a litigation in progress.

See **MAINTENANCE**

MAJOR [L. *magnus, maior, maximus* / great, large]

Greater in rank or importance. Greater in quality or quantity. Important, consequential. Also, a person of full legal age; a person who has reached the age at which he is considered competent to manage his own affairs. A *major dispute* under the Railway Labor Act is a dispute relating to formation of a collective bargaining unit or the negotiation and execution of a collective bargaining agreement.

MAJORITARIAN [L. *maior* / great, large]

A person who believes in majoritarianism, the principle that all decisions affecting a group should be made by a majority of the group.

MAJORITY [L. *magnus, maior* / great, greater]

The age at which a person becomes fully responsible for his own acts and becomes entitled to the rights of adulthood; e.g., the right to vote, the right to contract. The age of emancipation. Also, a number greater than half of a group of constituent numbers, as a majority of voters or a majority of Congress. A *majority opinion* is the opinion of more than half of the judges hearing a matter and represents the official opinion of the court.

MALA [L. *malus, peior, pessimus* / bad, evil]

Bad, evil, wicked; improper.

MALA FIDES [L. *mala* + *fides* / trust, reliance, faith]

Bad faith, in bad faith. With evil intent. The opposite of *bona fides*.

See **BONA FIDES; FIDES**

MALA IN SE

See **MALUM IN SE**

MALA MENS [L. *mala* / bad, evil + *mens* / mind, reason, intellect]

An evil mind. A mind motivated by bad intentions.

MALA PRAXIS

Professional malpractice. Lack of skill in the practice of a profession. Usually, but not always, applied to medical practitioners and their associates, the term denotes neglect or lack of reasonable skill in treatment or advice to a patient or client.

MALA PROHIBITA
See **MALUM PROHIBITUM**

MALEFACTOR   [L. *malus* + *facere* / to make or do]
An evil-doer. One who commits a crime or offense against the law.

MALEFICIUM   [L. *male* / badly + *facere* / to make, do]
A wrongdoing, an evil deed. A crime or misdeed. Unprovoked mischief.

MALFEASANCE   [L. *male* + *facere*]
An act or deed which is unlawful or improper. An act forbidden by law. An excess assumption of authority by a public official in the performance of the duties and function permitted by his office. The unlawful performance of an act by a public official who is not authorized or entitled to perform the act at all.
See **MISFEASANCE; NONFEASANCE**

MALICE (AFORETHOUGHT)   [L. *malitia* / meanness, wickedness, spitefulness]
As used in the law, the word has a wide variety of applications, all tending to describe a state of mind which permits the intentional commission of wrongful acts without legal excuse or justification. The state of mind necessary for dangerous acts in deliberate disregard of the safety of others. The term *malice aforethought* describes a criminal act which was intended or planned. The word has application in the law of bankruptcy, libel and slander, etc.
See **PREMEDITATE**

MALICIOUS PROSECUTION
The commencement or maintenance of a criminal proceeding without adequate foundation in proof, with the intent to cause injury to another; the misuse of his office by a prosecutor who brings unwarranted charges against a defendant. Also, the misuse of the civil courts by instituting and maintaining an unjustified action against another with intent to cause damage or injury to him or his property.

MALITIA PRAECOGNITA   [L. *malitia* / malice + *prae* / before, in front of + *congnoscere* / to know, learn]
An act prompted by malice. Malice conceived and then acted on. Malice aforethought. An action committed with evil intent and knowledge of the consequences.

MALO ANIMO [L *malo* / bad, evil + *animus* / the conscious mind, the spirit, the source of feeling]

With an evil mind. With a bad purpose. Motivated by malice.

MALUM IN SE

Evil in itself; naturally evil. Acts or deeds which are evil or immoral in and of themselves; acts which offend the human conscience, whether or not specifically forbidden by statute or regulation. A wrong judged by all to be evil in its very essence. The unjustified killing of another is an act recognized by all societies as *malum in se*.

MALUM NON PRAESUMITUR

Evil is not presumed.

MALUM PROHIBITUM [L. *malus, malum* / bad, evil + *prohibere* / to check, restrain, forbid]

Wrong because prohibited or made unlawful by statute or rule. An act which may not be criminal in and of itself but which is made criminal by legislation.
See **MALUM IN SE**

MANDAMUS [L. *mando, mandare* / to order, command]

An extraordinary writ or order issued from one court to another court, or to a public official, or to a corporation or person, compelling performance of a ministerial act that the law recognizes as an absolute duty. The writ is used to correct abuses of judicial and administrative power and to compel action.

MANDATE [L. *mandare* / to command]

An order or command. An order issued by one court to an inferior court or to a public official requiring the performance or discontinuance of some act or deed. The order of an appellate court to a lower court advising it of the court's decision. Also, the authority to act for another, similar to a power of an attorney. Also, loosely, the scope of authority of an elected official as inferred from the public's response to his platform or campaign rhetoric; e.g., "The President has a mandate to lobby for increased taxes."

MANDATORY [L. *mandare* / to command]

Requiring performance, obedience or compliance. Describes a statutory provision, or a professional rule or code, which must be followed to the letter, as opposed to a provision or rule which is discretionary or permissive. *Mandatory provisions* utilize the words "shall" or "must". *Non-mandatory (precatory) provisions* use such terms as "should" or "would."
See **PRECATORY**

MANIFEST [L. *manifestus* / caught out, found, detected]

Clearly, plainly. Readily perceived and understood. Obvious. Self-evident. Also, to show or display, as to *manifest an interest* or to *manifest an intent*. Also, a ship's list of passengers or cargo. A mistrial will be declared in a criminal trial under the doctrine of *manifest necessity* when it becomes impossible for the court to proceed to a fair and equitable verdict. Circumstances invoking *manifest necessity* include the illness of an essential witness, the death of counsel, an irremediable error in the indictment, etc. In these circumstances, the defendant may be retried and may not invoke the defense of double jeopardy in the new trial.

MANIFESTO [L. *manifestus* / found, detected]

A written or published statement explaining the acts of the author or issuer. A statement of policy by an organization, society or political party; e.g., the Communist Manifesto. A formal declaration issued by a state or sovereign announcing an important act or policy; e.g., a declaration of war.

MANIPULATE [L. *manipulus* / a small bundle or handful]

To control. To cause to deviate or change. In securities law, to control artificially the price of securities by a series of purchases and sales designed to create an unwarranted sense of market action; the purpose is to raise or depress the price of a security for quick gain. The practice is prohibited under the Securities Exchange Act.

MANUAL [L. *manus* / hand; *manualis* / fitted to the hand]

Related to the hand. Work or activity done by hand without the aid of machines. Also, a small book easily held in the hand, usually describing some mechanical process or offering instruction on some technique or process.

MANUCAPTIO [L. *manus* + *capere* / to seize, take hold of; to control]

Formerly, a writ issued to a sheriff directing him to seize and hold a prisoner until sufficient surety was deposited with the sheriff.

MANU FORTI [L. *manus* + *fortis* / strong, powerful]

With force and violence. A forcible entry on the real property of another.

MANUMISSION [L. *manus* + *mittere* / to send, to let go, release]

The voluntary release or emancipation of a slave by his master.

MANUSCRIPT [L. *manus* + *scribere* / to write, inscribe by hand]

A document which is either hand- or type-written (also, now, one which is produced on a word-processor), but before printing or publication. Also, the original version of a writing submitted for publication.

MANUS MORTUA [L. *manus* + *mors, mortis* / death]

Literally, a dead hand. At common law, the phrase was reduced to the word *mortmain* and was used to describe the transfer of real property to the church or to a corporation, thereby making the land inalienable.

MARE CLAUSUM [L. *mare* / the sea + *claudere* / to close]

A closed sea. A body of water that is within the jurisdiction and control of one nation.

MARE LIBERUM [L. *mare* + *liber* / free]

A navigable body of water that is open to the ships of all nations.

MARINE INSURANCE

A contract of insurance under which the insurer agrees to indemnify the insured's vessel and/or cargo in a stated amount against losses at sea.

MARITAGIUM [L. *maritus* / of or related to marriage]

The rights conferred by marriage. Land given as part of the marriage agreement; dower in land.

MARITAL [L. *maritus* / related to marriage]

Describes anything growing out of or related to marriage or the state of being married. A *marital deduction* is an income tax deduction available only to married couples.

MARITIME [L. *maritimus* (from *mare*) / belonging to the sea]

Relating to or describing any activity concerning navigable waters such as the sea, large lakes, rivers, etc. Navigation or commerce on these waters.

MARITIME LAW

The law governing all matters relating to commerce on navigable waters, including matters relating to seamen, harbors, ships, etc.

MARITUS

Of or relating to marriage. Also, a husband; a married man.

See **NUPTIAL**

MARKET [L. *mercor, mercari* / to carry on trade; buy and sell]

A place designated by a municipality for the display of merchants' wares and for the carrying on of trade. Also, any place in which people trade goods for other goods or for money. An organized facility for trade in commodities or securities, as a stock exchange. A retail establishment.

MARKETABILITY   [L. *mercatus* / trade, commerce; buying and selling]

Fitness for trade or sale. A measure of the ability of a particular item or object to be sold in the open market. *Marketable title* is ownership which is free from encumbrances or from reasonable doubt as to its validity, i.e., title which will support an action by the seller for specific performance of a contract to buy.

MARKET VALUE

The price established for any article or commodity in the ordinary course of business. The price which a willing buyer will pay to a willing seller. The price fixed by reference to indices of comparable sales over a period of time, as in the case of real estate.

MARTIAL LAW   [L. *Mars* / the Roman god of war]

The imposition of governmental controls over the public during times of emergency, war or catastrophe. The exercise of arbitrary governmental powers by a military junta or commander or by military authorities over civilians and civil authority. A system of decrees issued by a military commander in time of war imposed on an occupied foreign territory; also, steps taken to control unruly mobs or to maintain public safety. Also, the cessation of civil law and authority.

MASTER   [L. *magister* / master, chief, head]

In the law, this word has many uses and meanings. In the law of Agency, a principal who employs a servant or employee to perform work or services for him under his control and direction. A person appointed by a state or federal judge to perform a specified judicial function, such as the taking of testimony. A *master agreement* is an agreement between a labor union and one employer in a particular industry which is intended to act as a model for all contracts in that industry. A *master deed* is a deed drafted by the sponsor of a condominium which is used in the conveyance of title to individual condominium units. The *master of a ship* is the captain and chief officer of a vessel under maritime law. A *master plan* is the overall plan of a governmental entity for the development of land and construction within its borders, including laws covering zoning, housing, industry, schools and parks. A *master in chancery* is a court officer appointed to carry out the functions of the equity court.

MATER FAMILIAS   [L. *mater* / mother + *familia* / a household]

The mother of a family. The feminine head of a household. A widowed mother.

MATERIAL [L. *materia* / the items or contents of which a thing is composed; subject matter]

As an adjective, the word describes matters of great consequence. A *material allegation* is a statement in a pleading which is essential to the action and to the relief sought. A *material breach* is a breach of contract sufficient to support a claim for damages or for injunctive relief. A material misrepresentation is an essential element of fraud. It is a representation which induces the other party to enter into a transaction to his detriment.

MATRICIDE [L. *mater* + *caedo, caedere* / to strike down, beat]

The murder of a mother by her child or children.

MATRIMONIA DEBENT ESSE LIBERA

Marriages should be free of restraints. In Rome, voluntary divorces were recognized and allowed.

MATRIMONIUM [L. marriage, matromony]

Literally, a marriage conforming to the requirements of Roman law. Also, property given or descending as a result of a marriage.

MATTER [L. *materia* / matter, material, substance]

The subject of a discussion or a dispute; the item at issue. The issues involved in a litigation. Cases in litigation are sometimes referred to as *"Matter of..."* or *"In the Matter of..."* Also, those facts which require determination in a law suit. A *matter in controversy* is an issue to be resolved during the trial or hearing. A *matter of fact* is an issue of fact to be resolved by the jury. A *matter of law* is an issue of law to be resolved by the judge. A *matter of record* is any documentation of the proceedings before a court or tribunal or of the filing of an instrument with the proper public office.

MATURE [L. *maturo, maturare* / to ripen; to rush]

To come to fruition. To vest or ripen. To become due or payable, as in "the obligation will mature on..." To come into existence, as in "her pension rights will mature on..."

MATURITY [L. *maturo, maturare* / to make ripe, ripen]

At the stage of full growth and development. The point in time when a legal obligation becomes due or is fixed. For example, the *maturity date* of a note or mortgage is the date upon which the last installment of principal is due and payable.

MAXIM [L. *maximus* / superlative of *magnus* / large]

A basic or general truth. A statement expressing a concept accepted by all. A principle tested and accepted over time.

MEDIATE [L. *medius* / middle, midpoint, to be in the middle]

To intercede between two conflicting parties to enable them to reach agreement or reconcile their differences. To hear both sides of a dispute and offer an acceptable compromise. The function is carried out by a *mediator*, who can suggest compromises but cannot impose a decision. In this, he is different from an arbitrator, whose decision is final.

See **ARBITRATE**

MELIORATION [L. *melior* / better, the comparative form of *bonus* / good]

The process of improving a property or object. In equity, the doctrine which allows the court to compensate an occupant who has made improvements to real property.

MEMENTO MORI [L. *memini, meminisse* / to remember, recall + *mors, mortis* / death.

Anything that reminds us of our mortality; a sign of death.

MEMORANDUM [L. *memoro, memorare* / to call to mind, tell, relate]

A note or reminder. An informal note setting down the terms of a decision or agreement. A written summary of a transaction that is meant to serve as a guide for the draftsman of the formal contract or instrument.

MEMORANDUM CLAUSE

A clause in a marine insurance policy limiting the liability of the insurer with respect to certain risks, e.g., a loss to unusually perishable goods.

MEMORANDUM DECISION

A short statement by the court usually in a single paragraph, announcing its decision on a motion or at the end of the trial, without opinion.

MENACE [L. *minitor, minitare* / to threaten]

A threat or a display of intent to harm or injure. A fear of force or bodily harm. To act in a threatening way. Also, a person who is deemed a threat to public safety or who threatens others.

MENS

Mind, understanding, intellect, judgment.

MENSA ET THORO [L. *mensa* / a table + *thoro* / bed, resting place]

From bed and board. A divorce.

See **A MENSA ET THORO**

MENS LEGIS [L. *mens* / mind + *lex, legis* / law]

The mind or spirit of the law. The purpose of the law.

MENS REA   [L. *mens* / mind + *reus* / a litigant, defendant, a person accused]

A guilty mind; a criminal or wrongful purpose. An essential element of most crimes. The mental state accompanying or inducing an unlawful act.

MENS TESTORIS IN TESTAMENTIS SPECTANDA EST

In interpreting wills, we should look at the intention of the testator.

MENTIRI EST CONTRA MENTEM IRE

To lie is to ignore one's better thoughts or judgment.

MENTAL   [L. *mens, mentis* / the mind, intellect, reason]

Relating to the mind, especially the human mind. Those aspects of a person's health or condition which reflect the quality and state of his mind, as opposed to his physical state. *Mental anguish* is aggravated mental suffering which the law recognizes as a basis for increased damages in a tort action or in defining a crime. *Mental cruelty* — the torment of one spouse by another — is recognized in most states as a ground for divorce.

MERCANTILE   [L *mercor, mercari* / to trade, buy and sell]

Having to do with trade and commerce. All matters relating to the buying and selling of merchandise and goods.

MERCANTILE LAW

The codification of rules, laws and statutes controlling commerce. It is virtually synonymous with commercial law. Most commerce in the U.S. is now controlled by the Uniform Commercial Code.

See **LEX MERCATORIA**

MERCHANT   [L. *mercator* / merchant, trader, shopkeeper (from *mercor, mercari* / to carry on trade)]

Any person who trades in goods, but especially a person who trades in a particular class or category of goods and has a specialized knowledge concerning those goods. Also, any person who buys goods at wholesale prices and offers them for resale at retail. Also, the operator of a retail business.

MERCHANTABLE   [L. *mercor, mercari* / to trade, engage in commerce; to buy and sell]

Describes goods which are fit to be used in the manner intended and which conform to the facts or statements contained on the label. The term implies that the goods conform to ordinary standards of care and that they have a grade, quality and value equal to similar goods sold under similar circumstances. (See Uniform Commercial Code, § 2-314.)

MERGER   [L. *mergere* / to dip, to plunge into a liquid, to immerse]

To cause to combine. The incorporation of one thing into another. In contract law, the absorption of one contract into another. In corporate law, the amalgamation of two corporations, only one of which survives. In criminal law, the absorption of a lesser offense into a more serious offense which involves essentially the same elements. In property law, the swallowing of a lesser estate by a larger one; e.g., a leasehold *merges into* a fee simple.

MERIT   [L. *mereo, merere* / to deserve, earn]

Deserving recognition or reward. To be worthy of recompense. In a legal sense, the intrinsic value of a party's case or argument. The *merits* of a case are the essential issues to be determined. Also, the *merit system* is the system utilized by federal and state governments to insure that civil service employees are hired and earn advancement on the basis of ability only.

MERITORIOUS   [L. *mereo, merere* / to deserve]

Entitled to respect and honor. Regarded favorably. Valid, as a meritorious claim or defense.

MIGRATE   [L. *migro, migrare* / to go from one place to another]

To move from one country or state to another. The movement of a people or society from one place to another, as the migration of eskimo herders from the Arctic into Central Canada.
See **EMIGRATE, IMMIGRATE**

MILITIA   [L. *milito, militare* / to serve as a soldier, to engage in war]

A group of soldiers expressly trained by a government to serve in times of civil emergency. Also, a citizen force organized to serve a nation or state in times of natural disaster. A unit of soldiers ready to respond and serve not in battle against an enemy but to control the public. The word has now been usurped by self-proclaimed guardians of public morals who challenge established and lawful authority.

MINIMUM   [L. *parvis, minor, minimus* / the least, the smallest]

The smallest quantity or measure needed to satisfy some requirement. *Minimum contacts* represent the lowest threshhold for establishing personal jurisdiction over a defendant in a civil action. A *minimum sentence* is the least severe sentence a judge may impose under a statute or code setting forth the range of punishments for crime. The *mimimum wage* is the lowest hourly wage an employer is permitted to pay its employees under federal statutes regulating interstate commerce. Most states also have minimum wage laws.

MINISTER [L. *minister* / a subordinate, an assistant, a house servant; also a temple assistant, hence, a servant of the gods]

A person who acts for another to perform an assignment or task. A church official. The representative of one nation to another. In many countries, the head of a department of government. Also, to give aid or help to, as to the sick.

MINISTERIAL [L. *minister*]

An act which is clearly defined and limited in scope and which permits little deviation or discretion. A duty which is clearly circumscribed and involves little skill. Strict obedience to rules or instructions given in advance of performance.

MINOR [L. comparative form of *parvus* / little, small]

Literally, smaller, less than. A person who is younger than the age which defines legal competence. In most states and for most purposes, this is the age of 18.

MINORITY [L. *minor*]

The state of being younger than the age which establishes legal competence. Also, the smaller in number of two parts of a whole. Less than a majority. In politics, a group having insufficient votes to control the government by itself. A part of the population having at least one identifiable characteristic which sets it apart from the rest. A disadvantaged group. A *minority stockholder* is one who owns fewer than enough shares to control the management of a company, or the election of its directors. A *minority opinion* is an opinion which represents less than half of the votes cast by an appellate court and which states the reasons for disagreeing with the result and/or reasoning of the majority.

MINOR JURARE NON POTEST [L. *minor* + *iurare* / to swear, take an oath + *non* / no + plus *posse* / to be able]

Literally, a minor is not able to take an oath.

MINUTE BOOK [L. *minutus*, from *minuo, minuere* / to make smaller]

A book which contains a perpetual record of meetings conducted by a social, political or business organization. The official records of the proceedings, meetings and transactions of committees, boards of directors, stockholders, etc.

MISAPPLY [L. *mis* / badly, incorrectly + *applico, applicare* / to place against, join to, place near]

To use funds or property improperly. To convert to one's own use money or property belonging to someone else. To abuse a trust fund by diverting money to one's own account without authority.

MISAPPROPRIATE [L. *mis* / badly + *ad* / to, towards + *proprius* / own, one's own, peculiar to oneself]

To use, transfer or control funds for a purpose other than that intended or authorized. Theft or embezzlement. Illegal use of money or property by a person who is not the owner but who is entrusted with its care. Under the rules controlling lawyers in all states, funds received by a lawyer for the account of his client must be deposited in a specially segregated account and may not be appropriated by the lawyer for his own account or purposes except as authorized by the client or by the court.

MISCARRIAGE [L. *carrus* / a four-wheeled vehicle]

The result of bad management, administration or decision-making. An improper or incorrect result. A *miscarriage of justice* is a decision reached by the court in contradiction of the facts or the rules of law; a decision which requires reversal on appeal.

MISCEGENATION [L. *misceo, miscere* / to mix or mingle + *genus* / kind, origin, race]

The mixing of the races. Marriage between two persons of different race. This was prohibited by statute in many states. But all *miscegenation statutes* have now been held to violate the equal protection clause of the U.S. Constitution.

MISCONDUCT [L. *mis* + *con* / with + *duco, ducere* / to lead, draw from place to place]

Violation of a rule or mandate. An illegal action which results in harm or loss to another. An infraction or misstep. Wrongful behavior, as by a juror who talks about a case with someone other than his fellow jurors, or an employee who abuses the trust of his employer. *Misconduct by an attorney* may be defined as any violation of the rules of court or of the codes of professional conduct in the state of license. *Misconduct in office* is a wilful violation by a public official of the duties of his office.

MISCREANT [L. *mis* / bad, wrong + *credere* / to believe]

A non-believer or infidel. A person who rejects accepted religious or moral values. A criminal or wrongdoer.

MISDEMEANOR [L. *mis* + *de* + *minare* / to drive (as animals)]

A criminal violation punishable as a lesser crime than a felony, i.e., by imprisonment of not more than one year, or by a fine or other penalty. Any crime other than a felony.

MISFEASANCE [L *mis* / badly, wrongly + *facere* / to make or do]

To do a lawful act improperly or incorrectly; e.g., misfeasance in an elected or appointed office. The unlawful exercise of lawful authority by a government officer or functionary.

See **MALFEASANCE, NONFEASANCE**

MISNOMER [L. *mis* / badly, wrongly + *nomen* / a name]

A mistake in naming or citing. Incorrectly designating the name of an interested party in a document or pleading. A mistake in the name of a party to a deed or mortgage. In the case of a corporation, a mistake in its name which makes it difficult or impossible to identify it.

MISPRISION [L. *mis* / badly, wrongly + *prehendere* / to take hold of, to seize]

Broadly, a neglect or wrong in the performance of a duty. The concealment of a crime or felony by one who is not himself involved as an accomplice or an accessory. To fail to report a felony of which one is aware. *Misprision of felony* is itself a federal crime. *Misprision of treason* is the failure to report an act of treason against the United States. This is also a federal crime.

MITIGATING CIRCUMSTANCES

Facts or circumstances extraneous to the essential facts defining a criminal act but which lessen the degree of culpability attributable to the particular defendant. Any factor considered by the court to lessen the degree of crime or the length or severity of sentence. For example, *mitigating circumstances* may lead a court to reduce a charge of murder to manslaughter.

MITIGATION [L. *mitigare* / to make mild or soft]

To make less severe, to reduce the effect of. Reduction of a penalty, fine or sentence. *Mitigating circumstances* are facts which do not negate the commission of a crime but offer insights which affect the extent of culpability. For example, extenuating circumstances may *mitigate* a sentence of murder to a sentence of manslaughter. The doctrine of *mitigation of damages* imposes a duty on an aggrieved party in a contract or tort action to take reasonable steps to minimize his loss or damage, or to avoid increasing the loss or damage.

MITTIMUS [L. *mittere* / to send, to release]

Literally, we send. A writ used to transfer court records from one court to another. Also, a writ directing a sherriff to seize and hold a defendant and to a jailkeeper to keep the prisoner under the court's direction.

MOBILIA NON HABENT SITUM

Moveable things have no permanent location.

MOBILIA SEQUUNTER PERSONAM [L. *mobilis* / moveable + *sequor, sequi* / to follow + *personam* / the person]

Literally, moveable goods go with the person. Sometimes called the *mobilia* rule, which held that all interests in personal property were governed by the owner's domicile. Since that is not always the case, it may be no longer be cited as a rule of law.

MODEL PENAL CODE [L. *modus* / a standard of measure + *poena* / punishment + *codex* / treetrunk; account book]

A code of substantive criminal law prepared and introduced by the American Law Institute in 1962. The code has been adopted in most states.

MODUS OPERANDI [L. *modus* / measure, method, manner + *operare* / to work, labor]

The manner of operation; a term used by the police to describe the characteristic methods used by a suspect in performing his crimes. Patterns of activity so unique to a particular criminal that he can be identified by them.

MODUS TENENDI [L. *modus* + *tenere* / to hold]

The way in which one holds. The nature and scope of an interest in property; e.g., a tenancy for life.

MODUS VIVENDI [L. *modus* + *vivo, vivere* / to live, be alive]

The way or method of living or surviving.

MOLESTATION [L. *molestus* / annoying, troublesome, bothersome]

To disturb, annoy. To make unwanted sexual advances to; to touch or fondle another with sexual intent when that person does not invite the contact; e.g., child molestation.

MOLLITER MANUS IMPOSUIT [L. *mollis* / soft, gentle + *manus* / hand + *imponere* / to place upon]

To lay hands upon gently. In a tort action for trespass, assault or battery, this phrase is used by the defendant to allege that he used only such force as was necessary to protect himself or his property from injury by the other party.

MONITION [L. *moneo, monere* / to remind, to warn]

The suggestion of danger. A summons to all interested parties to show cause why an order should not be issued. Also, a court order directing that some action be taken and stating the consequences of disobedience.

MONOPOLY [L. *monopolium* / monopoly, sole right of ownership (from the Gr. *monopolion*)]

A business enterprise which controls a source of goods or services. Exclusive or dominant control of a market sufficient to give power over prices or sources of supply. Sole ownership.

MONUMENT [L. *moneo, monere* / to remind, warn]

A written legal document or record. A lasting reminder of an event, a person, or a deed. In real estate law, the marker or measure of boundary lines; e.g., a fence, a stone wall, a tree. A memorial stone or other structure in honor of a deceased.

MORAL [L. *moralis* / moral, ethical]

Able to distinguish between right and wrong. Sensitive to issues that determine integrity of thought and behavior. Observing the general principles for correct social behavior.

MORAL HAZARD

As relates to fire and other casualty insurance, the degree of risk to the carrier posed by the character, integrity and self-interest of the assured. The more questionable his reputation for integrity, the greater the moral hazard and the risk of deliberate loss, as in committing arson.

MORAL TURPITUDE [L. *moralis* / ethical, able to distinguish between right and wrong + *turpis* / ugly, deformed, evil, vile]

Describes crimes which involve depravity and basic character flaws. Such baseness in the performance of one's duties to others as to fail the minimally accepted tests for social conduct. More than "criminal". An act contrary to all accepted social standards.

MORA REPROBATUR IN LEGE

Delay is frowned upon by the law.

MORATORIUM [L. *morar, morari* / to delay]

A delay or postponement in the fulfillment of a legal obligation. A period during which the payment of a debt or obligation is suspended. In the law of bankruptcy, the automatic stay imposed against acts by a creditor after a bankrupt files a petition in bankrupty is a kind of *moratorium*.

MORATUR IN LEGE [L. *morari* / to delay + *in* + *lex* / the law]

He causes a delay in the law. A motion on *demurrer* requiring a decision by the court on a given point or issue before the action can proceed.

MORS CIVILIS [L. *mors, mortis* / death + *civilis* / relating to a citizen or the public]

Civil death. At common law, the figurative or "virtual" death which followed banishment or imprisonment.

MORTGAGE [L. *mors, mortis* / death + *gage* / security (from the French)]

A security interest in property evidenced by a document conveying title but providing for its extinguishment upon payment of a fixed sum, usually in installments and with interest. A lien upon property to secure a debt; the lien is removed upon payment of the debt.

MORTIS CAUSA
See **CAUSA MORTIS**

MOTION [L. *moveo, movere* / set in motion; move; *motus* / movement]

A request or application to the court for a decision or order at one of various stages of a trial or proceeding, e.g., for summary judgment, for judgment as a matter of law, for a new trial, etc. A *motion* may be made ex party or on notice to the other party. Also, a proposal initiated by a member of a group to induce some action by the group, as a motion by a congressman to compel a vote of the House. Also, action taken by the court on its own initiative.

MOTIVE [L. *moveo, movere* / to move or set in motion; *motus* / movement, motion]

Purpose; the reason compelling or underlying an action. The law makes a distinction between motive and intent. *Motive* describes the thought processes which lead to or induce intent. *Intent* is the mental set or volition to take the action resulting from or impelled by the motive. Motive constitutes the reasons for action; intent is the will to complete the action. In criminal trials, motive is not an essential element of the crime, but it may be introduced to prove intent.

MULTIPLICITOUS, MULTIPLICITY [L. *multiplico, multiplicare* / to increase many times]

More than several. Many. A great number. In law, more than one claim or pleading resulting from the same cause of action. Prosecutors sometimes attempt to assert several separate charges arising from or describing a single criminal act; this creates the possibility of double jeopardy for the defendant. Because double jeopardy is prohibited by the Fifth Amendment of the U.S.

Constitution, the several charges will be consolidated by the court and tried as one.

MUNICIPAL [L. *municipium* / a town in the Roman empire occupied by Roman citizens]

Relating to an identifiable community of persons, especially a town or village. A local governmental unit. Also, the affairs of a local governmental unit distinguished from those of other units.

MUTUAL [L. *mutuus* / having interchangeable interests; reciprocal]

Belonging to two or more persons with similar or interchangeable interests. Common to two or more parties. Shared for a common purpose, as in "parent and school have a mutual interest in educating schoolchildren." Also, a form of insurance company the ownership of which resides in and is shared by the policyholders. A *mutual mistake* is a mistake in a contract which is committed equally and shared by all the parties. *Mutual wills* are separate wills made by two parties containing reciprocal provisions. A *mutual savings* bank is a bank owned by its depositors.

MUTUALITY [L. *mutuus* / reciprocal]

Reciprocity. Equivalence of obligation or performance. *Mutuality* of contract is the doctrine which requires reciprocity of obligation or performance by both parties to the contract.

MUTUUM [L. *mutuus* / reciprocal]

At common law, a transaction for the loan, consumption and repayment-in-kind of consumable goods. For example, a farmer might give his produce to a consumer, in return for the delivery of like produce at a later date.

N.A.

Abbreviation for *not available*, or *not applicable*. Also for *non allocatur*, it is not allowed.

See **NON ALLOCATUR**

NARRATIO

A story, a tale or narrative. A legal declaration or complaint. The claims or counts in a complaint.

NATI ET NASCITURI   [L. *nascor, nasci* / to be born]

Those who are already born or in being and those who will be born.

NATION   [L. *nasci, natus* / to be born]

A group of people with a common history and occupying a particular territory together. A group of people swearing allegiance to a common government. A territorial division defined by fixed geographical boundaries. A political entity recognized as self-governing by the international community, with its own system of laws. Loosely, a group of people with a common history but who may have been dispersed into or across other nations; e.g., various Indian *nations* in the United States.

NATIVE   [L. *natura* / birth]

Born or raised in a particular place. Indigenous to. A person born within a designated jurisdiction. Also, grown or originating in a defined area. A local resident, as opposed to a visitor or transient.

NATURAL   [L. *natura* (birth), *naturalis* / produced by birth, relating to nature]

According to the laws and conditions which exist in nature independently of the intervention of man. Also, based on inherent principles of right and wrong. Having a real or palpable existence as distinguished from matters of the mind or spirit. *Natural consequences* are those results which would reasonably and normally be anticipated from the occurrence of a particular event. A *natural father* is a child's biological father, not his adoptive father.

NATURALIZATION   [L. *naturalis* / produced through birth, natural]

The process by which one acquires the citzenship of a country other than the country of his birth. In the U.S., naturalization is a multi-step process involving lawful residence for five years, proof of good character and the ability to read and write English, a court hearing, and an oath of loyalty to the U.S. Constitution.

NATURAL LAW

See **JUS NATURALE; LEX NATURALE**

NATURAL OBJECT

In the law of intestacy, the person(s) most likely to be selected by the testator as his beneficiaries, usually his heirs or next of kin. The laws governing intestacy are designed to recognize the natural objects of a decedent's wishes.

NATURAL PERSON

A human being as opposed to an artificial person created and recognized by the law, such as a corporation.

NATURAL RIGHT

Those rights which are inherent to society and are possessed by all individuals equally, without intervention, control or contribution by any government. The American founding fathers declared life, liberty and the pursuit of happiness to be among man's *natural rights*.

N.B.

The abbreviation for *nota bene,* note carefully, and for *nulla bona,* without goods or possessions.

See **NOTA BENE; NULLA BONA**

NAVIGATE, NAVIGABLE   [L. *navigare* / to sail, voyage, navigate]

To steer a course through the air, over water or overland. To control or manage movement through or over obstacles. To control the operation of an airplane, boat, truck, etc. *Navigable airspace* is that part of the air above the ground which is dedicated to the flight of airplanes. The airspace of one nation is considered inviolable by the planes of another without license or permission. A *navigable waterway* is a body of water capable of carrying boats and ships in the customary mode of water travel for the ordinary purposes of access and commerce.

NECESSARIES   [L. *necessitas, necessarius* / necessary, unavoidable]

In law, those things which are absolutely required for the maintenance of life itself. They include food, drink, clothing and housing of some sort. In the U.S. today, there is a great deal of debate over the extent to which government is required to supply these basic things to its citizens. Many argue that universal medical care has become a *necessary* of an enlightened society. The *Doctrine of Necessaries* provides that one who sells *necessaries* to a child or wife may charge the father/husband for their value. Under some exemption statutes, the courts are required to determine as an issue of fact which *necessaries* shall be free of reach by creditors.

NECESSARY & PROPER CLAUSE

The last clause in Article I, Section 8 of the U.S. Constitution, following the enumeration of the general powers of Congress. The clause empowers the Congress, "To make all Laws which shall be necessary and proper for carrying into execution the foregoing Powers and all Powers vested by this Constitution in the Government of the United States, or in any Department or Officer thereof."

NECESSITAS CULPABILIS [L. *necessitas* / necessary + *culpo, culpare* / to blame, find fault with]

Guilt which arises under circumstances beyond the actor's control; e.g., a killing in self-defense. The act itself is still a crime, but punishment is excused by the surrounding facts.

NECESITAS INDUCIT PRIVILEGIUM

Necessity causes privilege. The legal principle which excuses acts which would otherwise be deemed unlawful because of extenuating circumstances.

NECESITAS NON HABET LEGEM

Necessity knows or has no law.

NECESITAS PUBLICA MAJOR EST QUAM PRIVATA

Public necessity has priority over a private need.

NECESSITY [L. *necessitas* / necessity]

Anything needed or compelling. Pressure to perform a specific act. A compulsion to act in response to an irresistible stimulus. Justifiable defense against a threatened criminal act; at common law, an affirmative defense that the defendant was compelled to commit an offense in order to avoid a harm greater than the offense itself.

NE EXEAT [L. *ne* / (do) not + *exeo, exire* / to go out, to leave]

Literally, do not leave. A writ in a civil action forbidding a named party to leave the jurisdiction while the matter was pending or until he gave adequate security. Also, an order enjoining the removal of personal property from the jurisdiction.

NE EXEAT REPUBLICA

Another name for the *ne exeat* writ, meaning do not (let him) leave the country.

NEGATIVE COVENANT

A promise to refrain from the commission of an act or from using a particular device. A covenant which restricts the normal activities of the party who agrees to observe it. A provision in an employment agreement preventing the employee from competing with the employer in a designated area and/or for a designated period of time after his employment is terminated. The provision must be reasonable or the courts will not enforce it.

NEGATIVE EASEMENT

An agreement under which the owner of a parcel of real estate covenants not to do or perform an act involving the land which he would be free to do in the absence of the agreement, e.g., not to build a wall or fence along the property boundaries.

NEGLECT   [L. *neglegere* / to neglect, omit, disregard]

Failure, omission or refusal to perform an act which one is under a duty to perform. Also, the failure to perform an act in a manner which is customary and reasonable under the circumstances. Failure to pay reasonable attention to. To overlook, to leave undone or to do carelessly.

NEGLIGENCE   [L. *neglegere* / to neglect]

Failure to exercise the standards of a reasonable person in the performance of one's actions or in the conduct of one's affairs. Conduct which falls below the standards for reasonableness applied by the courts in the performance of one's duties and obligations. *Negligence* may result from the failure to act prudently in a given circumstance, as well as from the performance of an imprudent act. The standard in determining whether a person has been negligent is to measure his conduct against the conduct which would have been applied by a reasonably prudent person under the same facts or circumstances.

NEGLIGENCE PER SE

Negligence in and of itself; instrinsic negligence. Negligence which will be adjudged as such by any reasonable person. Conduct which is clearly unreasonable or inprudent. Acts or omissions which violate a statute or ordinance defining reasonable care in a specific circumstance.

See **PER SE**

NEGLIGENT HOMICIDE

Death of another caused without intent to kill, but as the result of an unlawful act or of a lawful act performed in a careless way. To cause the death of another by negligent or reckless operation of a motor vehicle or some other instrumentality.

NEGOTIABLE [L. *negotior, negotiari* / to carry on or engage in business; to act as a banker]

Characteristic of a commercial document or instrument the ownership of which can be passed from one person to another either by delivery or by endorsement. Usually applied to such instruments as checks, notes, bills of lading, etc.

See **NONNEGOTIABLE**

NEGOTIABILITY [L. *negotiari* / to carry on business, to serve as a banker]

A measure of the ability of an instrument or of property to pass without impediment from a transferor to a transferee. Ability by a transferee to acquire title to property superior to that of his transferor or of third parties. The ability to transfer instruments of title by endorsement or by delivery.

NEGOTIATE [L. *negotior, negotiari* / to engage in business]

To transfer an instrument or document by endorsement or delivery. To transfer a negotiable instrument so as to constitute the transferee the holder thereof. A non-negotiable instrument may not be *negotiated*. Also, to engage in the steps necessary for agreement on a contract or other legal undertaking; to exchange letters or notes or to engage in meetings and discussions preparatory to execution of a binding legal document.

NEMINE CONTRADICENTE [L. *nemine* + *contra* / against + *dicere* / to say or speak]

No one says anything to the contrary; no one dissents. The phrase is used to indicate that a court's decision was unanimous.

NEMINE DISSENTIENTE [L. *nemine* + *dissentire* / to disagree, to have a different opinion]

No one disagrees. All concur. Also used to indicate a unanimous decision by a court or deliberative body.

NEMO, NEMINE

No one, nobody.

NEMO BIS PUNITUR PRO UNO (EODEM) DELICTO

No one will be punished twice for one (the same) offense.

NEMO COGITATIONIS POENAM PATITUR
No one shall be punished for his thoughts alone.

NEMO DAT QUOD NON HABET
No one can give away what he does not own.

NEMO EST SUPRA LEGES
No one is above the law.

NEMO POTEST FACERE PER ALLIUM, QUOD PER SE NON POTEST
No one can do through others what he is not permitted to do himself.

NEMO PRAESUMITUR MALUS
No one is presumed evil.

NEMO TENETUR AD IMPOSSIBILIA
No one is expected to do the impossible.

NEMO TENETUR SEIPSUM ACCUSARE
No one shall be compelled to bear witness against himself.

NE PLUS ULTRA [L. *ne* / not, lest + *plus* (comparative of *multus* / much, many) + *ultra* / beyond, on the other side]
At the highest point. Not to be exceeded or undone. The most profound degree of accomplishment or achievement.

NEPOTISM [L. *nepos* / grandson; also, a nephew or descendant]
Preferential hiring or political appointment based upon blood or marital relationship. Favoritism in employment.

NEUTRAL [L. *neuter* / neither, in neither direction; neuter]
Not engaged or involved on either of two opposing sides. Taking no part in an argument or dispute between others. Undecided; disengaged. To avoid engagement in a war between two other nations.

NE VARIETUR [L. *ne* / a prefix which makes a word or phrase negative + *vario, variare* / to vary]
Let it not be changed. A notation placed upon a document by a notary to identify its contents at the point of execution and thus to permit identification of any subsequent changes.

NEXUS [L. *necto, nectere, nexum* / to bind, fasten together, join]
A link, a causal connection, a chain of related objects. The connection between a corporation and a state in which it does business. Whether a busi-

ness has sufficient *nexus* with a state to be taxed by it depends on an analysis of its activities within that state.

NIENT CULPABLE
Not guilty.

NIENT DIDERE
To fail to deny. To default.

NIHIL   [L. *nil, nihil, nihilum* / nothing]
Nothing, not, not at all, in no respect. Sometimes contracted to *nil*. Standing alone, it identifies a writ returned to the court by a sheriff who fails to find a defendant or his property (short for *nihil est* (he is not there) or *nihil habet* (I have nothing), as the case may be).

NIHIL (NIL) CAPIAT PER BREVE
Let him take nothing for his complaint; a court's judgment in favor of the defendant.

NIHIL (NIL) DEBET   [L. *nihil* + *debeo, debere* / to owe, be indebted]
I owe nothing. The defendant's plea of general denial in an action on contract or on a debt stated. There is no obligation; no contract has been made.

NIHIL (NIL) DICIT   [L. *nihil (nil)* + *dicere* / to say, speak]
Literally, he says nothing. The judgment entered against a defendant who fails to file an answer or motion in response to a complaint. Before entering judgment, the court looks to see only if the plaintiff has stated a cause of action and if it has jurisdiction. Judgment for lack of a plea or answer.

NIHIL (NIL) EST   [L. *nihil* + *sum, esse* / to be]
There is nothing for me to find. The general response by the sheriff after he attempted to serve a summons and did not find the defendant or his residence or any of his property.

NIHIL (NIL) HABET   [L. *nihil (nil)* + *habere* / to have, hold]
He has nothing. The response of a sheriff to a *scire facias* writ, stating that he was unable to find or serve the defendant and that he found none of his property.
See **SCIRE FACIAS**

NIHIL POSSUMUS CONTRA VERITATEM
Nothing can overcome the truth.

NIL FRUSTRA AGIT LEX
The law always has a purpose. The law never acts in vain.

NISI [L. if not, unless]

Used before or after a word such as *decree, order, judgment,* or *rule,* to indicate that an adjudication is conditional and not absolute, but that it will become final and absolute *unless* the party who is the subject of the decree or order takes steps to cure a defect, i.e., that he appear, show cause, appeal, etc., before a specified date or event.

NISI DECREE
See **DECREE NISI**

NISI PRIUS [L. *nisi* + *prius* / the first, the former]

A trial before a single judge or a judge and jury, as distinguished from a proceeding before an appellate court. The phrase dates to practice in the early English common law courts. Now used to distinguish a trial court from an appellate court.

NOLENS VOLENS [L. *nolo, nolle, nolui* / to be unwilling, to refuse + *volo, vele, volui* / to be willing, to want to]

Literally, whether you're willing or unwilling.

NOLLE PROSEQUI (NOL PROS) [L. *nolle* / he is unwilling + *prosequi* / to follow, to pursue].

He is unwilling to prosecute. A statement to the court by the plaintiff in a civil action and, more frequently, by the prosecutor in a criminal action that he does not wish to proceed, i.e., that the action is dropped and discontinued. The statement is made part of the record and results in dismissal of the action.

See **NON PROSEQUITOR; NON VULT PROSEQUI**

NOLO CONTENDERE [L. *nolle* + *contendere* / to strain against, to exert, to resist]

Literally, I do not (wish to) contest. In a criminal action, a plea interposed by the defendant which has the effect of stopping the proceeding without a plea of guilty or not guilty. The effect is to subject the defendant to the same penalties as a guilty plea or determination, but to avoid a lengthy and expensive trial and, also, the use of the guilty plea against the defendant in a civil action based on the same facts. Under the federal rules, the plea may be interposed only if the court approves after considering all the circumstances.

See **NON VULT CONTENDERE**

NOMINAL [L. *nominare* / to name, give a name to]

Titular; in name only; trifling, insignificant. Connected with a legal transaction or relationship in name only, not in real interest. A *nominal defendant* is one named in an action only because he satisfies some technical pleading requirement, not because the plaintiff seeks any relief against him. A *nominal partner* is one who allows his name to be used in the business of the partnership but has no proprietary interest in it. A *nominal trust* is one in which the trustee has no real duties. *Nominal damages* are a trivial sum, often as little as $1, awarded to a plaintiff simply to recognize that he was indeed wronged, but with little monetary consequence.

NOMINAL DAMAGES [L. *nomen* / name + *damnum* / loss, damage]

An award of damages in a very small amount to establish that the plaintiff was justified in bringing his claim but that he suffered little actual damage. A recognition of fault without injury.

See **INJURIA ABSQUE DAMNO**

NOMINATE [L. *nomino, nominare* / to name, appoint or nominate]

To propose as a candidate for election. To suggest one out of a number of potential candidates for office. To designate for a position or office, as the nomination by the President of foreign ambassadors, subject to approval by the Senate.

NOMINEE [L. *nominare* / to name or nominate]

A person named or proposed for election or appointment to an office. Also, a person designated by another to perform a particular legal assignment, as to act as a trustee or executor. Also, the person in whose name an instrument is registered or recorded but who is acting as agent for someone else.

NOMINEE TRUST

A trust instrument in which a trustee acknowledges that it is holding title to real estate for the benefit of an undisclosed beneficiary.

NON

The Latin word for *not*, used a prefix to negate the word or thought which follows it.

NON ALLOCATUR

It is not allowed.

NON ASSUMPSIT

The pleading in an action of *assumpsit*, by which the defendant claimed that he had not undertaken or promised an obligation in the manner or form set forth in the plaintiff's complaint.

See **ASSUMPSIT**

NON BIS IN IDEM   [L. *non* + *bis* / twice, two ways + *in* + *idem* / the same thing]

Not twice for the same thing. No man may be put in double jeopardy, i.e., tried twice for the same crime or act.

NON CEPIT   [L. *non* + *capio, capere* / to take, to seize]

He did not take (it). The form of general-issue pleading in an action for *replevin*, by which the defendant denied that he had taken the plaintiff's property. The plea put in issue both the fact of taking and the place of taking.

See **REPLEVIN**

NON COMPOS MENTIS   [L. *non* + *compos* / having control over + *mens, mentis* / the mind, reason, intellect]

Not having control over one's mind or intellect; insane, irrational, delusional. Mentally incompetent.

NONCONFORMING (USE)

Describes a building or parcel of land which exists or is used in violation of the zoning rules or regulations controlling the area or municipality in which the property is located.

NONCONTRIBUTORY   [L. *non* / not + *contribuo, contribuere* / to bring together, to contribute]

Not requiring participation or contribution. An employee benefit plan the funds of which are paid entirely by the employer for the account of the employee is called a *non-contributory plan*. After they are paid into the plan by the employer, the funds are considered trust funds controlled by regulations of the IRS.

NON CULPABILIS (NON CUL)   [L. *non* + *culpo, culpare* / to blame, accuse]

I am not to be blamed; I am not guilty. The plea of not guilty.

NON DEMISIT

He did not demise. The plea entered by a defendant in an action for rent claiming that he had not entered into a lease for the premises.

NON DETINET   [L. *non* + *detinere* / to hold back, to detain]

The form of general-issue pleading by the defendant in an action of *detinue*. Also, interposed in an action for *replevin*, provided the action was only on account of a wrongful detention.

See **DETINUE; REPLEVIN**

NON EST FACTUM [L. *non* + *sum, esse* / to be + *facere* / to make, do]

Literally, it was not done (by me). A plea at common law by which the defendant denied that the instrument sued upon was executed by him or that he knew the nature of the instrument when he signed it.

NON EST INVENTUS [L. *non* + *esse* + *invenire* / to find, meet with]

The writ returned by a sheriff when he was unable to find the defendant within his jurisdiction.

NONFEASANCE [L. *non* + *facere* / to do or make]

Failure through omission or neglect. Inaction where action is required. The failure to perform an act or duty which is required of an agent or a public official; neglect of duty. The distinction among *nonfeasance, misfeasance* and *malfeasance* is subtle but important.

See **MALFEASANCE; MISFEASANCE**

NONNEGOTIABLE

Incapable of transfer solely by delivery or endorsement. Commercial paper such as a check or note which does not satisfy the requirements for negotiation by endorsement or by delivery to bearer in Article 3 of the Uniform Commercial Code; the transferee of such paper does not become a holder in due course.

See **NEGOTIABLE**

NON OBSTANTE [L. *non* / no + *obsto, obstare* / to oppose; notwithstanding]

A phrase used in documents to point up or emphasize a contradiction in text or meaning.

NON OBSTANTE VEREDICTO (N. O. V.) [L. *non obstante* + *verus* / true, truthful + *dicere* / to say]

Nothwithstanding the verdict. A judgment entered by the court in favor of one party despite a jury verdict to the contrary. Under modern practice, the judgment n.o.v. is available to either party. In the federal courts, the J.N.O.V. has been replaced by the judgment as a matter of law.

See **J.N.O.V.**

NON POSSUMUS [L. *non* + *possum, posse* / to be able]

We are not able. We cannot.

NON PROSEQUITUR (NON PROS) [L. *non* + *prosequi* / to follow, to pursue, to proceed]

Literally, he has not proceeded; he has not followed up. An application for judgment dismissing the plaintiff's action for his failure or neglect to take the necessary procedural steps within the time permitted by the court's rules. Sometimes used in the verb form: the suit was *non pros'd*.

See **NOLLE PROSEQUI; NON VULT PROSEQUI**

NON-RECOURSE   [L. *non* / not + *recurro, recurrere* / to run back, hurry back]

A debt or obligation which may be collected or satisfied only out of designated collateral and not from the general assets of the debtor or from him personally. A *non-recourse* purchase-money mortgage, for example, limits the mortgagee to an action of foreclosure of the mortgaged property without recourse to the mortgagor personally. Also, a commercial instrument which cannot be collected personally from prior endorsers or from the maker upon dishonor.

NON SANAE MENTIS   [L. *non* + *sanus* / sound, healthy + *mens, mentis* / mind, reason, intellect]

Not of sound mind.

See **NON COMPOS MENTIS**

NON SEQUITUR (NON SEQ)   [L. *non* + *sequi* / to follow]

Literally, it does not follow. An assumption or inference that does not follow from a prior statement; a response that is not logical in the light of a statement previously made.

NON SUI JURIS   [L. *non* + *suus* / his own + *iuru, iurare* / to swear]

Not able to take an oath in his own right. Said of one who is under a legal restraint and is therefore not able to act for himself. Anyone who is not legally competent to manage his own affairs.

NONSUIT   [L. *non* / not + *sequor, sequi* / to follow; to ensue]

The termination of a case by order of the court without disposition on the merits. Usually, the order follows a failure of the plaintiff to prosecute the case diligently or to establish a prima facie case. An order or judgment terminating a case without prejudice to the commencement of a later action. Under the Federal Rules of Civil Procedure, a *nonsuit* may be voluntary (the plaintiff withdraws his complaint) or involuntary (the court orders dismissal).

NON VULT CONTENDERE (NON VULT)   [L. *non* + *volo, velle, volui* / to want, wish + *contendere* / to strain, resist]

I do not want to contest it. Refers to a plea by a defendant in criminal action under which he agrees not to enter a defense to the charge, but avoids a plea of guilty. He will be punished as if he had pleaded guilty, but, unlike a plea of guilty, the plea of *non vult* cannot be used against him in a civil action.

See **NOLO CONTENDERE**

NON VULT PROSEQUI
: He does not wish to prosecute. He will not prosecute.
: See **NON PROSEQUITUR**

NO PAR [L. *par, paris* / equal, similar]
: Stock or bonds without a stated or face value; the stock will trade at a price or value fixed by the market.
: See **PAR**

NOSCITUR A SOCIIS [L. *noscere* / to know, be acquainted with + *socius* / joint, common, associated with; a partner or companion]
: To be known by his or its associates. One is known by the company he keeps. A rule of construction which dictates that the meaning of a word in a statute or other text will be determined by the meaning of the words which surround it.
: See **EJUSDEM GENERIS**

NOTA BENE (N.B.) [L. note well]
: A phrase used in a text to suggest that what follows is especially important and should be read and studied carefully.
: See **N.B.**

NOTARY, NOTARIZE [L. *notarius* / a secretary, a person who reduces speech to writing]
: *Notary:* A public officer who attests to the execution of documents. *Notarize:* To record or attest to the execution of a legal docoment. The action of a notary public in attesting to and certifying the authenticity of a document. To acknowledge the signature of another on a legal instrument such as an affidavit or deed.

NOTE [L. *noto, notare* / to mark, make a mark]
: A short, condensed writing. An informal letter. A written instrument in which a debtor promises to pay a debt (a promissory note). A *negotiable note* is an unconditional promise to pay a specified amount at a specified time, issued by the maker to order or to bearer. Also, an abstract or memorandum. Also, to mark or fix, as to note an exception on the record during the course of a trial.
: See **NEGOTIABLE; NONNEGOTIABLE; PROMISSORY**

NOTICE [L. *notitia* / knowledge; a thing known]
: The word *notice* is used by lawyers to describe documents which inform a party or an official that some proceeding or act involves him or needs to be considered and acted upon by him. *Actual notice* is notice imparted by some means directly to the intended recipient. *Constructive notice* is knowledge or

information imputed to the recipient who fails to act with care or diligence to acquire knowledge which he has a duty to acquire.

NOTORIOUS [L. *nosco, noscere* / to get to know, become acquainted with]

Generally known, a matter of common knowledge. Openly displayed. *Notorious cohabitation* describes two adult persons who live together without benefit of marriage. *Open and notorious possession*, a requisite of adverse possession, is possession of property which is so public and open as to be deemed to come inescapably and inevitably to the attention and awareness of the owner.

NOVATION [L. *novare* / to make new; to renew, revive]

The substitution of one party to an agreement for another; the original parties agree that one will be released or discharged and another bound in his place. Substitution of a new or revised agreement, debt, note or obligation, for an existing one.

NOVUS ACTUS INTERVENIENS [L. *novus* / new + *agere* / to set in motion + *intervenire* / to come between, to intervene]

A new and intervening act. In tort law, an act or cause that comes into play following the act constituting the defendant's negligence and that contributes to the damage or injury complained of by the plaintiff.

See **INTERVENING CAUSE**

NUDA POSSESSIO

Bare or naked possession.

NUDUM PACTUM [L. *nudus* / bare or naked + *pactum* / an agreement or pact]

A voluntary promise made without consideration, usually as an act of affection or good will.

NUDUM PACTUM EX QUO NON ORITUR ACTIO

No action arises from a bare promise.

NUGATORY [L. *nugor, nugari* / to trifle, to be futile or unimportant]

A futile or ineffectual act. Having no force. A statute which is unconstitutional is said to be *nugatory*.

NUISANCE [L. *nocere* / to hurt, harm]

Harm or injury. Anything annoying, noxious or injurious. An act or deed, or a continuing condition, which results in damage or inconvenience to another. An activity conducted by one person in the use or maintenance of his property which is detrimental or harmful to another person. Any action or condition which endangers life or health and for which the law offers a remedy in damages or by injunction.

NUISANCE PER SE

Any act, activity or occupation, or use or maintenance of property, which is inherently and recognizably offensive or harmful to others and which is not permissible or tolerable under any circumstances. A *nuisance per se* exists whether or not it is the proximate cause of injury and whether or not it violates a specific statute.

NULL   [L. *nullus* / no, no one, not any]

Of no legal effect; void, invalid.

NULLA BONA (N.B.)   [L. *nullus, nulla* / no, not any, none + *bona* / goods, possessions]

(I found) no goods or possessions. The writ returned to the court by a sheriff who was unable to find any assets of the defendant with which to satisfy a judgment or levy.

See **N.B.**

NULLIFY   [L. *nullus*]

To make void, invalid or ineffective. To set up a barrier to the existence or enforcement of a contract or statute. To make inoperable.

NULLITY   [L. *nullus* / no, not any]

An act without legal consequence. An action which has no force or effect. For example, a marriage between two persons who, by reason of their relationship or their incapacity, are ineligible to marry, is a *nullity* and will be declared null and void in a suit for *nullity of marriage*.

NULLUS FILIUS   [L. *nullus* / no, not any + *filius* / son]

The son of no one. An illegitimate child.

NUNC PRO TUNC   [L. *nunc* / now + *tunc* / at that time]

Literally, now for then. A device of the law which allows a present act, order or decision to have retroactive effect. This permits correction of lapses or delays in time caused by mistake or inadvertence. A *nunc pro tunc* entry in a court record, for example, will correct the facts in an entry originally made incorrectly. The federal rules permit the amendment of pleadings to conform to the trial record and, also, the correction of clerical mistakes in verdicts, judgments, etc.

See **DECREE NUNC PRO TUNC**

NUNCUPATE [L. *nuncupare* / to announce publicly, to declare openly; to call by name]

To make a public announcement; to confirm.

NUNCUPATIVE WILL

An oral will or testamentary disposition or declaration made by a testator in his last moments and *in extremis*, before witnesses sufficient in number to satisfy the laws of the relevant state. A dying testamentary declaration which may be proven by the oral testimony of witnesses. *Nuncupative wills* are valid only for dispositions of personalty and only in some states. In some states, a nuncupative will is not recognized unless it is reduced to writing within a prescribed time after it is made.

See **IN EXTREMIS**

NUNQUAM INDEBITATUS [L. *nunquam* / never + *indebitus* / not owed, not due]

(I was) never indebted. The plea interposed by the defendant in a common law action for *indebitatus assumpsit* in which he denied that he was ever indebted to the plaintiff.

See **INDEBITATUS ASSUMPSIT**

NUPTIAL [L. *nuptiae* / marriage, a wedding]

Relating to marriage and, specifically, to the marriage ceremony. Pertaining to a wedding.

See **MARITUS**

OBEDENTIA EST LEGIS ESSENTIA [L. *oboedentia* / obedience + *esse* / to be + plus *lex, legis* / law + *essentia* / the nature of a thing]
Obedience is the essence of the law.

OBIT [L. *obitus* / a passing to, a journey towards; death, destruction]
To approach the end. To die.

OBITER [L. *obiter* / in passing, by the way, incidentally]
Collaterally, incidentally, as an aside or afterthought.

OBITER DICTA [L. *obiter* + *dicere* / to say]
To say in passing. That part of a judge's opinion which is not necessary to his decision. Words which are incidental or collateral to a court's decision, which are not the issue before the court, and which are not needed for an understanding of the court's decision. *Obiter dicta* are not binding as precedent.
See **DICTUM**

OBIT SINE PROLE [L. *obire* / to die + *sine* / without + *proles* / descendants, offspring]
(He) died without issue.

OBJECTION [L. *obicio, obicere* / to throw in the way of, to bring against]
A protest. An argument in opposition. During a trial, a statement by counsel that an issue has been raised, or that evidence has been introduced, which requires a ruling by the court as to its relevance or propriety. If the ruling is unfavorable, counsel will note his exception. The objection, ruling and exception are made part of the record and thus subject to review on appeal.

OBLIGATE, OBLIGATION [L. *obligo, obligare* / to bind, to fasten; to make responsible for]
To create enforceable legal liability. To assume or undertake responsibility for, as an *obligation* under a contract. To impose or to take on a legal duty. To do what is required. An *obligation* may be a promise to pay a particular sum of money or to perform a specified service. A duty arising under an agreement or undertaking or imposed morally, as the duty to provide for one's

child. The responsibility, imposed by contract or by promise or commitment, to perform a given act. Also, an amount of money or other measure of value which one party is responsible to pay another.

OBLIGATIO EX CONTRACTU [L. *obligare* / to tie up, to bind + *ex* / out of + *contrahere* / to unite, bring together]

An obligation arising from or based upon contract.

OBLIGATIO EX DELICTO (OR EX MALEFICIO)

An obligation arising from the commission of a tort.

See **DELICTUM; EX DELICTO; EX MALEFICIO**

OBLIGEE [L. *obligo, obligare*]

Anyone who is the recipient or beneficiary of another's promise or duty. A creditor or promisee.

OBLIGOR [L. *obligo, obligare*]

A person who owes a debt or duty to another. A debtor or promisor.

OBLITERATE, OBLITERATION [L. *oblitterare* / to blot out, to wipe from memory]

To destroy, wipe out, eliminate. In the law of wills, the act of revoking a will by physically destroying or writing through it, or by cutting away all or portions of the will. *Obliteration* is broader than *rasure*, which is the act of scraping or shaving away letters or words of a document.

See **RASURE**

OBLIVION [L. *obliviscor, oblivisci* / to forget]

Forgotten or lost to memory. Also, to ignore prior offenses; to grant amnesty or an official pardon.

OBSCENE, OBSCENITY [L. *obscenus* / foul, repulsive, filthy]

Designed to incite lust or depravity; also, conduct or language regarded as taboo in polite usage. In the law, the word has the meaning given to it by the Supreme Court in a number of cases. As a minimum, the Court has defined obscenity as follows: "whether to the average person, applying community standards, the dominant theme of the material taken as a whole appeals to prurient interests." The definition has been modified and applied differently to fit the facts of individual cases. The Court has ruled that material deemed obscene is not protected by the First Amendment.

OBSOLESCENCE [L. *obsoloscere* / to grow old, decay, wear out]

The process whereby an asset falls into disuse. The phasing out of machinery or technology because of changes in public attitutude, science, etc. The gradual loss of economic value and utility of an asset, caused by factors other than its own deterioration. *Obsolescense* has a different meaning than depreciation.

See **DEPRECIATION**

OBSTANTE [L. *obstinare* / to stand out, stand in the way (of)]

In opposition to; impeding.

See **NON OBSTANTE VEREDICTO**

OBSTRUCT [L. *ob* / in front of, in the way of + *struere* / to build, erect]

To block, hinder, impede. To *obstruct* navigation is to prevent vessels from going where they have the normal right and ability to go. To *obstruct* justice is to commit any act which impedes another from obtaining free access to the courts or which impedes the conduct of their office by judges, prosecutors, court officers or others involved in the administration of the legal system.

OBSTRUCTION OF JUSTICE

Interference with the process by which crime is investigated and prosecuted or by which any litigation proceeds through the courts. Interference with the police process or with the conduct of criminal litigation, especially by threatening, influencing or tampering with witnesses or jurors, or by furnishing false information to the police or prosecutors, or by wrongfully influencing the court. Any act which impedes the parties in their conduct of an action or which obstructs persons who have duties in connection with the courts. The acts constituting the crime of *obstruction of justice* are defined in 18 U.S.C.A. §1501 et seq. One of the counts upon which President Clinton was impeached in 1998 was the charge of *obstruction of justice*.

OCCUPANCY [L. *occupare*]

The act of possessing or having control or dominion over a thing or of a parcel of land. The use which is made of real property. The condition of being completely filled or fully utilized, as in, this restaurant is limited to *occupancy* by 75 persons.

OCCUPATION [L. *occupo, occupare* / to seize, take possession of in a hostile way]

Possession to the exclusion of others. One's vocation, trade or profession. An activity which takes up one's time to the exclusion of other activities.

OCCUPAVIT [L. *occupare*]

Literally, he took possession. A writ which was available for the recovery of land which had been seized in war or battle.

OCCUPY [L. *occupare*]

To take possession of, usually to the exclusion of others. In international law, the act of one country in entering upon and taking control of the territory of another.

OCCURRENCE [L. *occurro, occurere* / to run to meet; to fall upon or attack]

Any event or happening. An incident which happens without plan, purpose or anticipation. An accident. In insurance law, an unexpected or unintended event which gives rise to a claim by the insured.

OECONOMICUS [from the Greek]

Relating to domestic economy. Orderly, methodical, careful with money. Also, the executor of a will.

OFFENSE [L. *offendere* / to strike, hit against; to shock, displease]

A breach of public standards or of a moral code. A crime or other violation of law. An offense can be a felony or a misdemeanor, or a lesser infraction which carries a fine or penalty. The remedy for some offenses lies in a civil action by the victim to recover a penalty from the wrongdoer. Any wrongful act requiring punishment or compensation.

OFFER [L. *offero, offere* / to bring to, present, offer]

A proposal, tender, presentation or statement which anticipates an acceptance by the party to whom it is made. A manifestation of intent to bargain under proposed terms with another party in order to achieve an agreement or contract. The price stated by the seller of an object in commerce to an interested buyer; also, the terms expressed by a buyer interested in purchasing an object or item. To tender, propose, proffer.

OFFERING [L. *offere* / to carry to, present, offer]

A kind of offer in which a stock or other security is sold and issued to the general public. In a *primary offering*, also called a new issue, the proceeds from the sale go to the company issuing the stock and are used as capital by the issuer. In a *secondary offering*, the proceeds go to individual stockholders who want to reduce their holdings in the company.

OFFER OF COMPROMISE

An offer to settle or resolve a dispute without recourse to litigation. The offer does not concede liability and is not admissible at trial as evidence of liability. Under the Internal Revenue Code, an *Offer In Compromise* is a formal offer to pay less than the full amount of a tax liability in settlement of the entire obligation. The offer requires the submission by the taxpayer of a plan for payment and of financial schedules.

OFFER OF PROOF
   The act of a lawyer in presenting evidence or arguing for the admissibility of evidence. During a trial, if the court has ruled that some question is improper or some evidence is inadmissible, the attorney proposing the testimony or evidence may "offer" a fuller description of the evidence he proposes to introduce, plus an explanation of how that evidence is relevant to his case. By so doing, he preserves his right to raise the same issues on appeal if the trial judge rules against him. The offer of proof is almost always made outside the presence of the jury.

OFFICE [L. *officium* / dutiful action; a sense of duty or loyalty; also, official employment]
   Any place where business is conducted. An assignment of work in the nature of a duty. A position of authority or responsibilty, as in, she was appointed to the *office* of comptroller. A function performed for a public or corporate purpose.

OFFICER [L. *officium* / dutiful or respectful action or response]
   A person holding a position of trust, responsibility or authority, especially in corporations or institutions; officers are given such titles as president, secretary or treasurer, each descriptive of a particular function. Also, anyone employed to administer or enforce the law; a police officer. Also, in the armed services, a rank which establishes a serviceman's relative authority over other troops.

OFFICINA JUSTITIAE [L. *officina* / a place of work, a factory + *iustitia* / justice, fairness]
   A place of justice. A court office. The name originally given to the English Court of Chancery.

OLIGRAPH
   See **HOLOGRAPH**

OMIT, OMISSION [L. *omittere* / to let go, give up; to leave out, disregard]
   To fail to include; to leave out. An *omission* is the failure to perform, or the neglect of, a duty which is imposed by law or by some pre-existing relationship.

OMNIA PRAESUMUNTUR CONTRA SPOLIATOREM
   The (court's) presumptions are against anyone who tampers with testimony.

OMNIBUS [L. *omnis* / all, every, each, the whole]
   Providing many things at one time; containing many things. An *omnibus bill* is a legislative act incorporating many disparate subjects and purposes in one

statute. The overall purpose is to prevent the executive department from vetoing some provisions to preserve others. An *omnibus clause* in an auto insurance policy is a clause making the insured responsible for the acts of all persons driving the car with his permission. An *omnibus clause* in a will is a clause disposing of all property not specifically mentioned in other provisions.

OMNIS EXCEPTIO EST IPSA QUOQUE REGULA
Every exception is a rule unto itself.

OMNIS REGULA SUAS PATITUR EXCEPTIONES
Every rule contains its own exceptions.

ONEROUS [L. *onerosus* / heavy, burdensome, troublesome]

Anything which imposes a burden. Describes a contract, lease or other document, or a clause or provision in a document, in which the burdens or obligations imposed on one party unreasonably exceed the benefits to that party. One-sided.
See **ADHESION**

ONOMASTIC [L. *nomen* / name]

Relating to a name or names. Signed or executed in a handwriting different from the handwriting used for the text. A document subscribed by a person other than the one who wrote it.

ONUS [L. load, weight, burden]

Burden. Burden of proof. Responsibility to come forward, proceed or perform. Unpleasant duty. Also, blame.

ONUS PROBANDI [L. *onus* + *probare* / to deem good, to approve, to recommend]

Literally, the burden of proof. This is a highly complex concept which governs the balance of proof in civil and criminal trials. The burden is really two burdens: the burden of production and the burden of persuasion. Under the first, the party asserting a position must offer some evidence to support it. Under the second, the party asserting a position must offer sufficient evidence to satisfy a standard of proof defined by the rules of the court in particular cases (*preponderance of the evidence* in civil cases; *beyond a reasonable doubt* in criminal cases).

OPE CONSILII [L. *ops, ope* / the power to help (from the name for the goddess of plenty) + *consulo, consulere* / to reflect, consult, ask the advice of, to advise]

With the help or advice of counsel.

OPERATION OF LAW   [L. *opero, operari* / to work, labor, create]

By virtue of the law. As ordained by the law. The result of the application of legal principles or rules to an act, event or status. For example, upon the death of the President, the Vice President succeeds to the office by *operation of law*.

OPERATIVE WORDS

That part of the text of a document, e.g., a contract, deed, lease or will, which accomplishes or effectuates the transaction or transfer intended, as distinguished from general recitals or other supplementary or incidental matter. Also, those provisions of a document which give it its character as a recognizable legal document, e.g., a deed as distinguished from a mortgage, etc.

OPINION   [L. *opinio* / opinion, conjecture, surmise]

The expression of a belief which is not capable of absolute proof. The statement of what to the speaker is his conclusion as to various possible alternatives or options. The formal judgment of a judge or court. The *opinion of a court* is the written explanation of its decision or judgment in a particular case. Normally, the opinion recites the facts of the case, the litigated cases the court is relying on for its reasoning, and the reasoning itself. A *lawyer's opinion letter* is a document prepared by an attorney for his client analyzing a legal problem and applying his knowledge and interpretation of the law to that problem. An *accountant's opinion* is a formal statement by the accountant of the results of his audit and examination of a client's books and records, including his opinion as to the extent to which the results conform to generally accepted accounting principles.

OPPOSE, OPPOSING   [L. *ob* / towards, before + *pono, ponere* / to lay, put, place; to place against; resist]

To place in opposition. To resist or contend. To take an adverse position in a litigation, or on a motion or appeal. To submit documents or papers stating facts, arguments or positions contrary to those submitted by the other party.

OPPRESSION   [L. *opprimere* / to press down, to press against; to crush]

An unjust or excessive use of power, strength or position. The forceful control or dominance of one group or nation by another. The violation by a public official of the rights of another with unnecessary severity or cruelty. Inequality of bargaining power.

OPTIMUS LEGEM INTERPRES CONSUETUDO

Look to custom or usage for the clearest interpretation of the law.

OPTION   [L. *opto, optare* / to choose, select, wish]

The right to choose. A discretionary act. In the law, a form of agreement under which one party is bound, usually for a fixed period, to confer a benefit upon the other at the election of the latter. The privilege or right of one party, supported by consideration, to insist, at his election, upon the right to buy or sell an asset or commodity from or to another party. An offer which meets the requirements for the formation of a contract and limits the offeror's power to revoke his offer. Restatement of Contracts, Second, § 25. In insurance law, the right of an insured to select the method for payment of benefits accruing under a policy. In the stock and commodities markets, options fall into several categories: *call options; futures options; put options*; etc.

OPUS [L. *opus, opera* / work, labor]

A product of work or effort. A literary or musical work.

ORAL [L. *os* / the mouth; *orare* / to speak]

Uttered by the mouth; the spoken word, as distinguished from the written word. An *oral confession* is an unwritten confession to commission of a crime; it will be admitted as evidence only if it satisfies certain conditions. An *oral contract* is an agreement which is either entirely or partly expressed in and dependent upon the spoken word. The Statute of Frauds prevents the enforcement of certain kinds of oral agreements unless they are evidenced by a written memorandum signed by the party to be charged.

See **PAROL; STATUTE OF FRAUDS**

ORDAIN [L. *ordino, ordinare* / to put in order, to arrange]

To establish by statute, order or decree; to enact a law, to issue a decree. Also, to appoint to an ecclesiastical order or office.

ORDER [L. *ordo* / a series in a row; a straight line; *ordinare* / to put in order, arrange]

An established method incorporating a system of control or management. A state of tranquility or obedience. A social or political condition based on respect for law and authority (*law and order*). The announced requirements of a superior authority. A ruling or command issued by a competent authority or tribunal. Courts issue many different kinds of orders. Examples: a *cease and desist order*, requiring the cessation of a specific act or conduct; an *order to show cause*, requiring the person receiving the order to present a compelling reason for the court *not* to take some designated action; a *gag order*, closing off any discussion by the parties affected of any facts or information relating to a particular case. In the law of negotiable instruments, *order* is a term of art defining the person(s) who are entitled to payment of an instrument.

ORDER NISI

See **NISI**

ORDINANCE [L. *ordinare* / to put in order]

A law or regulation adopted by a legislative body or government agency. A rule or regulation established by a municipal authority; a local law.

ORDINANDI LEX [L. *ordinare* / to put in order + *lex* / the fixed word, law]

Adjectival law. Rules of procedure, as contrasted to substantive law. The Federal Rules of Civil Procedure are a kind of *ordinandi lex*.

ORDINARY [L. *ordo* / an order; *ordinare* / to arrange, set in place]

Usual, customary. Familiar, everyday. The conduct usually expected of people acting in a reasonable way. *Ordinary care*, for example, is the degree of care prevailing in a particular place for a particular business or activity. The *ordinary course of business* is the manner in which a particular business generally conducts its affairs, especially the method in which it pays its bills or handles its commercial transactions and transfers. *Ordinary income* is the income derived as compensation for labor performed or as interest or dividends, but not including income derived from the sale or exchange of capital assets (*capital gains*).

ORE TENUS [L. *os, oris* / mouth + *tenus* / as far as, to a certain point (by means of)]

By word of mouth, orally. The testimony of a witness at trial is presented *ore tenus*.

See **ORAL**

ORGANIC LAW [L. *organum* / a tool or instrument]

The constitution or underlying system of laws of a nation or state. In England, the organic law is the common law. In the United States, it is the Constitution as interpreted by the Supreme Court.

ORIGINAL [L. *orior, oriri* / to rise, spring from; to be born]

First to exist. Newly born or created. The source of variations and copies. The document first identified, signed and executed. Only an *original work* is entitled to copyright protection. There can be only one valid *original will*. The doctrine of *original intent* is a theory held by conservative interpreters of the Constitution which looks only to the literal wording of the Constitution and frowns upon judicial extension or enlargement of that wording.

ORIGINATION CLAUSE [L. *oriri, originis* / the source or beginning + *claudo, claudere, clausus* / to close]

The Revenue Clause of the Constitution, which provides that all revenue bills shall originate in the House of Representatives. Article I, Section 7.

OSTENSIBLE [L. *ostendere* / to show, display, exhibit]

Exposed to view; apparent; suggestive of. A relationship or state which is based upon appearances rather than reality. An *ostensible agency* is one in which one party permits or induces another to believe that a third party is his agent though no agency actually exists; he is then estopped to deny the existence of the agency. *Ostensible ownership* is the appearance of ownership created in another by the conduct or words of the true owner, who is then estopped to deny as against innocent third parties that the *ostensible owner* is the true owner.

OUSTER [L. *obstare* / to obstruct, hinder]

The act of expelling or forcing someone out. A forcible removal. The wrongful removal or dispossession of a person entitled to possession, as of a tenant or office holder. Also, an order compelling removal of a public or corporate official.

OVERT [L. *aperio, aperire* / to lay bare, to expose]

Open, public, exposed to view. An *overt act* is an open, notorious act which is also the manifestation of an intent to commit the act. An act from which the intent to commit a crime may be reasonably inferred. One act in a series of acts which will inevitably lead to a foreseen result. An outward act in furtherance of a conspiracy. The crime of intent usually requires commission of some *overt act*.

OWELTY [L. *aequalis* / equal, equality]

In an action for partition, or in the division of matrimonial assets, the sum paid or secured by one party to another to equalize the value of the assets when equal division is otherwise impossible or impractical.

PACIFIST [L. *pacificare* / to appease, pacify, make peace]

A person who refuses to serve in the armed forces of his country because of his conviction that war is wrong. One who believes that wars should be outlawed.

PACTA SUNT SERVANDA [L. *paciscor, pacisci* / to make a bargain, to agree + *esse* / to be + *servare* / to keep, retain]

Agreements exist to be kept.

PACTUM [L. *paciscor, pacisci* / to make a bargain, to covenant, to agree]

A pact, contract or agreement.

PALIMONY [formed by the addition of the word *pal* to the word *alimony*, which derives in turn from the L. *alimonia* / nourishment, sustenance]

The extension of support and maintenance from one party to another in a non-marital but intimate continuing relationship, whether such extension is the result of agreement or of award by a court. The courts will enforce agreements of support although no marital relationship exists, and, even in the absence of an agreement, will look to the details of the relationship to determine whether an agreement or a constructive or resulting trust should be implied.

See **ALIMONY**

PANDECTS [L. the digest of Roman civil laws which was created from the writings of Roman legal scholars and was first published as a set of fifty books in 533 A.D.]

A complete code of the laws of a country. Also, a broad, comprehensive treatise covering an entire subject.

PANDER, PANDERER [L. *pandere* / to bow, bend before, extend, throw open]

To cater to or exploit the weaknesses of others. To act as a pimp or procurer of prostitutes. To induce a minor or an adult female to engage in prostitution. To sell or distribute graphic or printed materials which appeal to prurient instincts. A *panderer* is a person who engages in these acts, which constitute a crime in most jurisdictions.

PAR [L. *par, paris* / equal to, like, a match for]
Equal to. The stated or face value of an instrument as distinguished from its market value. The value assigned to each share of stock in a corporate charter. A stock which is sold at face value is sold *at par*; it may also be sold *above par* (above face) or *below par* (less than face).
See **NO PAR; PREMIUM**

PARALEGAL [L. *para* / closely related to (from the Gk.) + *lex, legis* / the law]
A person who is trained to assist a lawyer in the practice of law but who is not admitted to practice as an attorney. A *paralegal* works under the direction of an attorney and performs such assignments as research, filing documents, answering court calendar calls, etc.

PARAMOUNT [L. *per* / through, by means of + *mons, montis* / a mountain]
Of the highest value; superior to all others. In the law of real property, a superior title from which a lesser title is derived or created. The (most) superior of two or several titles in the same parcel.

PARCEL [L. *particula* / a small part or portion]
A plot of land; a subdivision.

PARCELLA TERRAE [L. *particula* / part, portion, share + *terra* / ground, earth, land]
A parcel of land.

PARCENARY [L. *partio, partire* / to divide, share, distribute]
Joint heirship. Joint ownership of a parcel of land by heirs to an estate before division of the estate into separate shares.
See **COPARCENARY**

PAR DELICTUM [L. *par* / equal, like + *delictum* / fault, crime, offense.
Of equal guilt. Equal fault.
See **DELICTUM; IN PARI DELICTO**

PARDON [L. *per* / through, by means of + *dono, donare* / to give]
To absolve of guilt. To remit a sentence imposed upon a criminal defendant. To excuse a crime or offense.

PARENS [L. parent, parental, father, mother]
Parent, parental. Originally applied only to a father, the word was later extended to include all parents, ancestors and relatives.

PARENS PATRIAE [L. *parens* / parent + *patria* / fatherland, native land country]

Literally, parent of the country. The role of the state or central government as sovereign guardian of persons who require special protection because of a legal disability or infirmity. For example, the interest of the state in protecting the rights of minors and the insane. In early England, the King had the prerogative to step in to protect the rights of infants. In the U.S., the right to intercede to protect others belongs to the states and is exercised by such state officers as the Attorneys General. These officers will intercede in cases of child abuse or in custody cases.

See **PATER PATRIAE**

PARENTELA [L. *parens* / parent, father, mother]

All those persons who share descent from a common ancestor. The line of descent from one ancestor by blood relatives.

PARES [L. *par* / equal to, like]

Persons of equal rank; equals, peers. A jury of peers to an accused.

PARI CAUSA [L. *par* / equal + *causa* / cause]

With equal right, upon equal terms. Also, in equal fault or guilt; equally culpable.

See **IN PARI CAUSA**

PARI DELICTO

See **DELICTUM, IN PARI DELICTO, PAR DELICTUM**

PARI MATERIA

See **IN PARI MATERIA**

PARI PASSU [L. *par* / equal + *passus* / step, stride]

Equally, upon the same terms. In bankruptcy, creditors of the same class share *pari passu* in the assets of the debtor. In contracts, provision may be made to pay some parties *pari passu*, i.e., in equal shares from a common fund.

PARITY [L. *par, paris* / equal, like, a match for]

The state of being equal or equivalent to something else. Equivalence between the value of a commodity expressed in one currency and its value in another currency. The measure at which one currency is exchanged in equivalent value to another. The equivalence in value between a farmer's current produce and its purchasing power, measured by the relationship between the cost of goods in some arbitrary base period and the current cost of living; the equivalence is maintained by government price supports.

PAROL [L. *parabola* / speech, parable, comparison (from the French *parole*]

By word of mouth; spoken, as opposed to written. Pertaining to matters arising from, but not contained within, a writing. An oral contract is a *parol contract*. In the law of contracts, the *parol evidence rule* excludes or limits evidence of matters, including evidence of prior negotiations or other documents, which are not contained within the confines of the written agreement between the parties and which are offered to vary or contradict the terms of the written agreement.

PAROLE [L. *parabola* / speech]

The conditional release of a prisoner before the end of his term, permitting him to serve his original sentence in the general society so long as he maintains and observes the conditions of his release. The terms of *parole* vary from state to state and are controlled both by the statute defining the original crime and by a board appointed for the purpose of granting and enforcing parole. The conditions of parole for federal prisoners are controlled by the U.S. Parole Commission. Also, the promise by a released prisoner of war not to take up arms again against the army releasing him.

PAROL EVIDENCE
See **PAROL**

PARRICIDE [L. *parens* or *pater* / father + *caedere* / to cut down, strike down]

The killing of a parent or close relative. Also, a person who murders his parent or relative.
See **PATRICIDE**

PARS GRAVATA L. *pars, partis* / portion, role, party + *gravare* / to load upon, burden]

The party with the burden; the aggrieved party.

PARS PRO TOTO [L. *pars* / part or portion + *pro* / for, on behalf of + *totus* / the whole, all]

A part for the whole. Using a part to represent the whole.

PARS REA [L. *pars* + *reus, rea* / party in a law suit; the defendant]

The party who is answerable. The defendant in a law suit.

PARTIAL [L. *pars, partis* / a part, piece or portion]

Part of a whole; incomplete. *Partial eviction* is eviction of a tenant or occupant from a portion of the entire premises. *Partial incapacity* is the inability to perform some but not all of the usual tasks of one's work or employment. A *partial loss* is a loss of some of the value of property covered by insurance. A *partial verdict* in a criminal trial is a verdict in which the jury finds only some, but not all, of the defendants guilty, or a verdict in which the jury finds a single defendant guilty on some charges, but not all.

PARTICEPS CRIMINIS   [L. *participare* / to share with, to join with + *criminari*, to accuse, charge with]

A party to a crime. One who joins in the commission of a crime.

PARTISAN   [L. *pars* / part or portion]

A person who favors one side of a controversy as opposed to the other. An avowed supporter of one political party over another. In American politics, issues are either *partisan* (in which case commitment to one's party dictates his opinion or vote) on *non-partisan* (in which case political differences are set aside and there is an effort at political compromise). Also, a guerrilla fighter in a civil war.

PARTITION   [L. *partio, partire* / to distribute, divide]

The division into separate shares of a parcel of real property owned jointly, as by joint tenants or tenants in common; also sometimes applied to the division into shares of jointly owned personal property. *Partition* can be accomplished by agreement or by a court decree. Upon a *partition petition* to the court by one or all the owners of a parcel of real estate, the court will generally order the property appraised and then sold at public auction; the net proceeds are than distributed to the owners in accordance with their interests.

PARTNER   [L. *partio, partire* / to share, distribute, divide]

Any one of two or more persons who share in the operation and conduct of an enterprise, usually a business enterprise, and in the resulting income. A participant in a partnership. A *general partner* is a partner who participates in the management of a partnership and who has unlimited liability for its debts. A *limited partner* is a partner who does not participate in management and whose liability for firm debts is limited to the amount of his investment in the firm. A *dormant partner* is a passive partner who takes no active part in the firm. A *silent partner* is a partner whose interest in the firm is not made known but who shares in its income. A *senior partner* is a general partner who is part of a controlling management group whose members generally receive more than an aliquot share of the firm's income. A *junior partner* is a partner who does not participate in management and who receives less than an aliquot share of the firm's income.

PARTY [L. *pars* / part, portion]

A person on one side of a transaction, proceeding or agreement. Anyone involved in a judicial proceeding or law suit, whether as a named litigant or as a person bound by the court's decision or judgment. A *secured party* is a party with a security interest in the property of another. An *indispensible party* is a party whose rights are so critically affected by the outcome of a law suit that the suit cannot proceed without him. A *real party in interest* is the party whose rights determine or define the transaction or the litigation at issue. Also, a political organization composed of persons with similar ideals and programs formed for the purpose of influencing or controlling social and political policies.

PASSIM {L. *passus* / a step, from; *pandere* / to stretch out, extend]

Here and there, far and wide; in various places. Used to indicate that a citation, or a phrase or word, occurs throughout an article or a book.

PASSION [L. *patior, pati* / to suffer, endure]

Driven by emotions rather than reason. A violent or undisciplined action. Anger, intense feelings. In criminal law, the word is used either alone or in the phrase *heat of passion* to indicate a mind controlled by such anger, hatred, bitterness or terror as to be incapable of rational thought or control.

PASSIVE [L. *pati* / to suffer, endure]

Lacking in will, lethargic, unresponsive. Avoiding participation in. Without control over a business activity, as in, he took a *passive role* in the transaction. Inactive, enduring a burden, submissive. Under the Internal Revenue Code, a *passive investment* is an investment in an enterprise in which the taxpayer does not actively participate, as in a limited partnership.

PATENT [L. *pateo, patere* / to be open, accessible]

Open, evident, clear to the perception. A grant of right or privilege extended by a government to one or more individuals. Most commonly, an instrument issued by the central government granting an inventor or innovator the exclusive right to develop, sell and profit from a new design, product or invention for a period of years. In the U.S., patents are granted by the U.S. Patent and Trademark Office. Also, the instrument by which a government grants title to public lands to an individual.

PATENT AMBIGUITY [L. *pateo, patere* / to lie open, exposed + *ambiguus* / uncertain, doubtful]

An *ambiguity* which is clear on its face. An ambiguity which is apparent from inspection of a document, usually because of an inconsistency between one provision and another or because the language of a provision is capable of two irreconcilable meanings.

See **LATENT AMBIGUITY**

PATERFAMILIAS   [L. *pater* / father + *familia* / a household]

The father or male head of a family or household.

PATERNAL   [L. *pater* / father]

Belonging to, proceeding from or derived from the father. The *paternal line* is a relationship between two persons which can be traced through a common father. *Paternal property* is property derived from a person who is related to the owner or recipient on the paternal side of the family.

PATERNITY   [L. *pater* / father]

Proceeding from the father. The state or quality of being a father. A *paternity suit* is an action brought to determine whether a designated person is the father of a child born out of wedlock; if paternity is established, there is a resulting duty of support.

PATER PATRIAE   [L. *pater* + *patria* / fatherland, country of birth]

Literally, the father of his country.

See **PARENS PATRIAE**

PATRIA POTESTAS   [L. *pater* + *potestas* / power (from *possum, posse* / to be able)]

The power of a father or head of household. In Rome, the father's power over his home and family was absolute.

PATRICIDE   [L. *pater* + *caedere* / to cut down, to kill]

The act of killing one's own father. Also, a person who has killed his father.

See **PARRICIDE**

PATRIMONY   [L. *pater* + *alimonia* / nourishment]

Heritage. An estate or a property which has descended from a line traced to the father, now extended to include all ancestors. Also, the sum of all the rights, privileges, assets and liabilities which together constitute the economic status of an individual; the components forming the value of an individual's estate.

PATRON   [L. *pater*]

A protector or benefactor. One who sponsors or supports the creative or intellectual activities of others, as in, he is a *patron of the arts*. One who supports another financially. Also, the customer of a store or business.

PATRONAGE [L. *patronus* / a protector or defender]

The support of a patron, as the support of an artist by a nobleman or wealthy sponsor. The suppport of a business by its customers. The appointment of individuals to political office for political advantage, gain or purpose.

PAUPER [L. *pauper* / poor, without means]

A very poor person. A person without the means to support himself and who is generally supported by charity or at public expense, such as a homeless person. A *pauper* who is involved in litigation will be relieved of costs. An indigent criminal defendant has a right to counsel paid for by the state.
See **INDIGENT DEFENDANT; IN FORMA PAUPERIS; POVERTY**

PECULATION [L. *peculare* / to give as private property; also *peculatus* / the embezzlement of public money]

Embezzlement. The theft or embezzlement of public funds by an official entrusted with their care.

PECUNIARY [L. *pecunia* / money, wealth, property]

Anything related to money or its value. Consisting of or measured in money. A *pecuniary bequest* is a bequest of money. A *pecuniary loss* is a loss of money or one which can reasonably be valued in money, such as the value of a decedent's life in a wrongful death action.

PENAL [L. *poena* / money paid as a penalty or fine; atonement; punishment]

Relating to punishment. Requiring or demanding a penalty or fine. Any act punishable by society. The word is broader than the word *criminal* and encompasses wrongs which result in the imposition of civil fines or penalties. However, in some contexts, the word is also used more narrowly to refer only to crimes, as in *penal code* or *penal institution*.

PENALTY [L. *poena* / a fine or detriment]

A fine, forfeiture or other detriment imposed by the law for the violation or nonperformance of a duty. A penalty may be civil or criminal. A liability imposed upon one who injures or violates the rights of another. In the law of mortgages, a *penalty* is a sum in addition to principal and accrued interest imposed by the lender upon prepayment of the loan principal. The IRS *imposes penalties* on taxpayers who file late. The parties to a contract may *provide for penalties* to encourage prompt performance and discourage defaults.

PENALTY CLAUSE

A clause in a contract, mortgage or loan agreement which specifies a penalty which must be paid by the obligor upon a default in payment or in some other performance. The courts distinguish between *penalty clauses* and clauses for liquidated damages. The former penalize the obligor in a fixed amount regardless of the injury to the obligee; the latter are a best estimate by the parties at the time of agreement of the damages which an obligee will actually sustain upon default by the obligor. *Penalty clauses* are not usually enforced; liquidated damages clauses are.

PENDENS, PENDENT   [L. *pendere*, to hang down, to weigh upon]

Pending, during, while awaiting. Remaining open or undetermined. Unresolved.

PENDENTE LITE   [L. *pendere* / to hang down + *lis* / a legal controvery or law suit]

Suspended while the lawsuit lasts. Awaiting the outcome of the action. Pending the lawsuit. A matter *pendente lite* is contingent on the outcome of litigation. The appointment of a guardian *pendente lite* is an appointment which lasts during, and terminates upon the end of, a law suit.

See **LITE PENDENTE**

PENDENT JURISDICTION

Authority in the federal courts, in actions involving a federal question, to hear and determine state claims between the same parties. Prior to the Judicial Improvement Act of 1990, *pendent jurisdiction* was the name given to the right of a federal court with jurisdiction over a *federal question claim* between two parties, to hear and adjudicate a *state-created claim* between the same parties (though it would not have had jurisdiction over that claim without the federal claim). The 1990 Act combined *pendent jurisdiction* with *ancillary jurisdiction* to create what is now called *supplemental jurisdiction*.

PENITENTIARY   [L. *paeniteo, paenitere* / to repent, regret, be sorry for]

A prison or place of confinement to which felons are consigned after conviction and sentence.

PENOLOGY   [L. *poena* / a penalty or punishment]

A branch of criminology dealing with the care and treatment of prisoners and the administration of prisons.

PENSION   [L. *pensio* (from *pendere*) / a weighing out, a reckoning; hence, a payment, an accounting of sums due]

A payment or payments, generally periodic, by a government or business enterprise in recognition of an employee's past services. Deferred compensation for past services as distinguised from wages or salary for current services. A plan under which employees are provided with a systematic scheme of compensation, usually in fixed monthly installments over a prescribed period, to be paid after retirement or separation from employment.

PENUMBRA   [L. *paene* / almost, nearly + *umbra* / shadow]

An area that is partly in shadow and partly in light. A concept which is uncertain or difficult to measure or assess. Rights which are created by implication rather than clearly and directly. Those rights and guarantees which are reasonably inferred from the provisions of a civil constitution. As applied to the U.S. Constitution, the implied powers of the federal government arising under the Necessary and Proper Clause, Art. I, Sec. 8(18).

PER

Through, along, over (for space or distance). Throughout, during (for time); also, by means of, because of.

PER ANNUM   [L. *per* + *annus* / year]

Over the course of a year; annually, as in *interest per annum*.

PER CAPITA   [L. *per* + *caput* / the head of a living creature]

Through or by the head, top or summit. Counted or calculated by the number of heads (i.e., persons) involved. The division and distribution of an estate in equal shares, the number of which is determined by counting and dividing equally among all living persons descended from the decedent, regardless of the shares which would have been taken by the ancestors of those persons. Example: A dies leaving one living son, B; two living grandsons, C and D, the sons of deceased son X; and three greatgrandchildren, E, F and G, the descendants of deceased son Y. A's estate will be divided into six equal shares, one each for B, C, D, E, F and G. Most states apply *per capita* distribution only when all takers are of the same generation. Distribution *per capita* is distinguished from distribution *per stirpes*. Also, by each individual in the population, as a *per capita* tax.

See **CAPITA; PER STIRPES**

PER CENTUM   [L. *per* + *centum* / the number 100]

Used in the abbreviated form *percent*. Measured by the number of parts in a hundred; of each hundred. A whole divided into 100 parts.

PER CURIAM   [L. *per* + *curia* / meeting place of the Roman Senate; courthouse; court]

An opinion which is joined in by an entire appellate court, as opposed to one which is written for the court by a single judge. Also, a short statement of the disposition of an appeal without a formal opinion or explanatory discussion.

See **CURIA**

PER DIEM [L. *per* + *dies* / day, daytime]
> By the day; over the course of a day. Describes compensation, wages or salary paid for a single day's services. Wages calculated by the day. Also, an allowance for a day's travel, food or lodging expenses by an employee who is away from home or on a special assignment; e.g., a juror is given a *per diem* allowance.

PEREMPTORY [L. *perimere* / to destroy, do away with, ruin]
> Allowing no response, contradiction or dispute. Imperious, arrogant. In the law, a *peremptory challenge* is the arbitrary elimination of a juror without explanation or cause. Each party may use a limited number of peremptory challenges. A *peremptory instruction* is an instruction by the trial judge to a jury requiring a prescribed finding upon the determination of certain facts.
> See **PRECATORY**

PERIL [L. *periculum* / risk, danger; also, trial, test, proof]
> Exposure to risk or damage. The cause of a loss or damage. In insurance law, the event or contingency which is insured against by the policy, e.g., fire, theft, etc. The term *perils of the sea* is applied by maritime lawyers to natural accidents which occur at sea without the intervention of man and which cannot be prevented by the exercise of care, e.g., hurricanes, typhoons, sudden squalls, etc.

PER INFORTUNIUM [L. *per* + *infortunium* / misfortune, bad luck; punishment]
> By accident. By misadventure or chance. Unintended, happenstance.

PERISHABLE [L. *per* + *ire* / to go]
> Anything liable or bound to spoil, as in *perishable goods*.

PERJURY [L. *per* + *iurare* / to swear, take an oath]
> A false swearing, a falsehood, a lie. A knowingly false statement made under oath or under circumstances requiring the truth, during the course of a judicial proceeding, or in an affidavit, or in another setting in which the law requires and expects the truth, as in a criminal trial. The crime of making a false statement about a material matter while under oath.
> See **SUBORN**

PERMISSIVE [L. *permitto, permittere* / to allow to pass; to let go; to yield]
> Anything allowed or permitted. Something allowed but not compelled; an option. Under the Federal Rules of Civil Procedure, the defendant may interpose a *permissive counterclaim* whether or not the claim arose from the same transaction or occurrence as that alleged by the plaintiff. *Permissive joinder* is

the joinder in an action of parties sharing common facts or common issues of law; also, the joinder in one action of all claims by one party against the other, whether or not the claims arose from the same transaction.

PERMIT   [L. *permittere* / to let go, indulge, yield, surrender]

To allow or consent to. To authorize. A document proving authorization or power to do or conduct some activity, issued by a person in authority. A license.

PERPETRATE   [L. *perpetrare* / to complete, perform, fulfill]

To commit or cause an act, generally one considered evil or criminal. To blunder or misstep.

PERPETUAL   [L. *perpetuo, perpetuare* / to maintain without interruption; to continue]

Having continuous and uninterrupted status or existence. Continuing forever; everlasting. Entitled to an office for life. A *perpetual injunction* is a permanent injunction. Corporations enjoy *perpetual succession*, i.e., their powers and existence continue uninterrupted through changes in officers and directors.

PERPETUITY   [L. *perpetuare* / to make continual, to maintain in an unbroken line]

Existence over the indefinite future. Eternity. Forever. An estate or interest in property which extends beyond any particular event or condition, i.e., an interest which would continue forever in the absence of some legal impediment. The law has, however, imposed restraints on estates in perpetutity by limiting estates in real property to a life or lives in being plus twenty-one years, plus the period of gestation. These restraints are codified in the *Rule against Perpetuities*.

See **IN PERPETUAM**

PER PROC

See **PROCURATION**

PERQUISITE   [L. *perquirere* / to search for, acquire, purchase]

Privileges or benefits in excess of ordinary wages and salaries, e.g., a tip. Also, the special benefits granted to high-ranking executives of companies in the form of travel allowances, company cars, club memberships, education allowances, insurance, etc. These are offered in addition to the benefits normally conferred on other workers and are generally referred to as *perks*.

PER QUOD [L. *per* + *quod* / whereas, and, for the reason that, to the extent that, through which]

Generally, whereas, and therefore, the point is. In tort actions at common law, this phrase referred to allegations of special damages resulting from the defendant's acts, as opposed to damages *per se*, i.e., damages ordinarily resulting from such acts. In the law of defamation, the phrase is still used to distinguish between allegations of special damage proved by extrinsic circumstances (*per quod*) and allegations of damages which are actionable in themselves (*per se*).

See **DEFAMATION PER QUOD; DEFAMATION PER SE**

PER SE [L. *per* + *se* / himself, herself, itself, themselves]

Through itself; by means of itself. In and of itself, intrinsically; inherently. Established without extrinsic proof. Inherent in the act itself. A *per se* violation in antitrust law is an act so clearly inimical to competition and fair trade as to require no further inquiry by the court into whether it has actually resulted in injury to the public. In tort law, an action which clearly violates the terms of a statute or rule may constitute *negligence per se*, whether or not there is any other evidence of fault by the defendant.

See **PER QUOD** for the distinction between *per quod* and *per se* in defamation actions.

PERSECUTE, PERSECUTION [L. *per* / through + *sequor, sequi* / to follow]

To attack or harass. To engage in systematic and continuous acts of aggression against. Selective and severe punishment or ostracism solely on the basis of some arbitrary status, such as race, religion, color or political opinion. An organized campaign by one group to isolate and punish another.

PERSON [L. *persona* / a mask worn by actors; role, character, personality, person]

A human being. The body of a human being. Any entity, both human and corporate, recognized by law as entitled to the rights and privileges reserved for individuals.

PERSONA DESIGNATA [L. *persona* + *designare* / to plan, point out, signify]

A person picked or designated for his own merits or qualities from a group of eligible persons. A judge or arbitrator chosen by the parties to resolve or decide an issue is a *persona designata*.

PERSONAL [L. *persona*]

Of or pertaining to a person. *Personal Property* is all property except real estate and items attached to real estate (growing crops are real estate). *Personal injuries* are injuries suffered by a single human being. *Personal juris-*

diction is the power of a court to issue an order or judgment affecting the rights or interests of a party.

PERSONALTY [L. *persona* / a mask worn by performers in Roman plays; a role, the human body; one; a person. The Latin word *personalitas* came to mean the things surrounding and owned by an individual]

Personal property, as contrasted with Real Property. Chattels. Any property not attached to real estate. Property which is temporarily attached to real estate by a tenant, such as store fixtures, and which can be removed, is known as *quasi personalty*.

PERSONAM

See **IN PERSONAM**

PERSONA NON GRATA [L. *persona* + *non* / not + *gratus* / pleasing, agreeable, welcome]

A person who is neither acceptable nor welcome. A diplomatic representative of one country who is refused accreditation in another country and who is therefore expected not to enter, or to leave. The rejection by the host country is usually because of some event or activity in the representative's personal background.

PER STIRPES [L. *per* + *stirps, stirpes* / the main stem and roots of a tree; the source or origin]

Through or from the roots. The division and distribution of an estate into shares determined by the *right of representation*, i.e., each living descendant entitled to a share takes all or a portion of the share his or her ancestor would have taken. Nearly all the states apply *per stirpes* distribution when all the survivors are not of the same generation. Example: A dies leaving one living son, B; two living grandsons, C and D, the sons of deceased son X; and three greatgrandchildren, E, F and G, the descendants of deceased son Y. The estate will be divided into three equal parts. B will get one whole part, or one-third; C and D will divide one part between them, resulting in one-sixth for each; and E, F and G will divide one part among them, leaving one-ninth for each. Distinguished from *per capita* distribution, in which B, C, D, E, F and G would each take an equal one-sixth interest.

See **CAPITA; PER CAPITA**

PERSUADE, PERSUASION [L. *per* + *suadere* / to recommend, urge]

To convince. To induce to perform an act or to subscribe to a particular opinion or belief. The *burden of persuasion* is the requirement that a party in litigation convince the trier of fact that a particular fact or circumstance is more probable than not.

PETITION [L. *peto, petere* / to beg, beseech, request]

A formal request. A formal document submitted to a court, administrative body or legislature praying for some stated relief. Also, a complaint or other pleading commencing an action. In bankruptcy, the *filing of a petition* by a creditor or debtor begins the bankruptcy proceeding and imposes an automatic stay against any action by creditors except in the bankruptcy proceeding itself. The Bill of Rights to the U.S. Constitution (Article I) provides that Congress shall make no law abridging the right of the people to *petition the Government* for a redress of grievances.

PETITORY [L. *peto, petere* / to request or seek]

An action brought to establish and confirm title to a chattel, as opposed to a *possessory action*, which tries only the right to possession. The word is used most frequently in Admiralty Law in connection with actions to establish title to ships and vessels.

See **POSSESSORY**

PLACITA COMMUNIA [L. *placere* / to please + *communis* / public, shared]

Common pleas. Consisting of all the pleas and suits pending at any one time between one litigant and another.

PLACITUM [L. *placitus, placere* / to please, to resolve, to settle]

A plea, a count in an indictment. Also, an opinion, a maxim. A judicial decision; a judicial tribunal.

PLACITUM NOMINATUM

The date and place fixed for appearance and plea by a criminal defendant.

PLAGIARISM [L. *plagiarius* / a kidnapper, a thief, especially a thief of literature]

To usurp, take credit for, or pass off as one's own, the creative work of another without credit or attribution. If the work is protected by copyright, the copyright owner may bring an action for infringement.

PLEA [L. *placere* / to please, to win over]

At common law, the answer or response first submitted by the defendant stating the facts constituting his defenses to the plaintiff's claims. In equity actions, the *plea* was a statement of reasons for rejecting or dismissing the plaintiff's complaint. In a criminal action, it is the response of the accused to the charges against him, e.g., guilty, not guilty, *nolo contendere*. A *plea bargain* is an agreement between the prosecutor and the defense in advance of a plea, in which the accused agrees to accept guilt to a lesser offense, in exchange for a lighter sentence than might have been imposed on the original charge after a verdict of guilty.

PLEADING [L. *placere*]

The formal statement or declaration submitted by a party in litigation containing his claims, allegations, denials or defenses. All the documents exchanged by the parties to define the issues between them. Examples of pleadings: the plaintiff's *complaint*; the defendant's *answer* or *cross-complaint*; and the plaintiff's *reply*.

PLEBISCITE [L. *plebs* / the people, the common people + *scisco, sciscere* / to investigate, inquire, find out]

The process by which the voters themselves decide a political issue, instead of delegating the decision to their elected representatives. A *plebiscite* differs from a *referendum* in that a *plebiscite* usually refers to a popular vote on such fundamental issues as nationhood, annexation, separation, or the adoption of a constitution, whereas a *referendum* refers to a popular vote on a particular law or statute. Many states, especially California and Oregon, now decide basic political issues through *referenda* instead of by action of the legislature.

See **REFERENDUM**

PLENA AETAS [L. *plenus* / full, filled, pregnant + *aetas* / age, time of life]

Of full age. The age of majority.

PLENARY [L. *plenus* / full]

Complete in all respects. An event, meeting, session or gathering which is attended by all who are entitled to attend. A *plenary hearing* is a proceeding to try and determine all the issues between the parties. A *plenary confession* is a full, complete and conclusive admission of responsibility for the crimes charged or alleged. *Plenary powers* are all the powers needed to carry out a task or assignment. A *plenary session* of the U.N. is a meeting of delegates from all member nations.

PLENE ADMINISTRAVIT

The plea by an executor or administrator of an estate in an action against him for a debt of his decedent, alleging that he has completed the administration of the estate and has no further responsibility.

PLURALITY [L. *multus, plus, plurimus* / much, many]

That number in a group which is greater than any other in the group, but not more than half. More than any other but less than a majority. A candidate in an election with more than two candidates can win by a *plurality*. A *plurality opinion* is an appellate opinion which becomes the opinion of the court because it is concurred in by more judges than any other opinion, although not the majority.

POLICY [L. *politia, politicus* / relating to the state or to government]

A plan or a set of guidelines to govern future decisions and actions. The principles by which a person conducts his affairs or by which a group is guided in the management of its affairs. The agenda of a political party or of a legislative body. Also, a contract of insurance; the document evidencing the relationship between insurer and insured.

POLITY [L. *politia* / the Roman Republic; the state; relating to the state]

The organization of individuals into a governing entity, as a nation or state. The constitution or body of laws for a state or government.

POLLUTE [L. *polluo, polluere* / to make unclean, defile, pollute]

To make unclean or impure. To create conditions which render unusable by humans such natural elements as the water we drink, the food we eat and the air we breathe.

POPULAR [L. *populus* / a group of people, a community, a nation]

Relating to the general public. Concerning a group of people as a whole, rather than any individual or class in the group. The *popular will* is an expression of the sentiments or attitudes of the entire community as reflected in polls, media reports, etc. Also, commonly accepted or believed.

POSITO UNO OPPOSITORUM NEGATUR ALTERUM

When one of two opposing propositions is accepted, the other is deemed rejected.

POSSE [L. *possum, posse* / to be able]

Used in the sense of *maybe* or *possibly*, or to denote something which may happen in the future. Also, a group of persons organized to preserve the public peace or to pursue a fugitive.

See **IN ESSE; IN POSSE**

POSSE COMITATUS [L. *posse* + *comitatus* / a retinue, a following]

A group of citizens conscripted by a sheriff or other police official to help him maintain order or to find a missing person or capture a fugitive.

POSSESSIO [L. *possideo, possidere* / to take possession of]

Literally, possession; the act of possession. Also, that which is possessed. The right to exercise control or dominion over a chattel to the exclusion of all others.

POSSESSION [L. *possidere* / to have or possess]

The act or condition of retaining or having control over an object or thing. The law defines many types of *possession*. *Actual possession* is immediate and direct control or dominion of a thing. *Adverse possession* is occupancy, control or dominion of a thing, especially of real estate, which is open and hostile to the claim of the owner and which may ultimately result in accession to title if the hostile possession is continued over a prescribed number of years. *Constructive possession* is possession which is not direct or actual but which is claimed and established by virtue of some legal right.

POSSESSORY [L. *possidere* / to have possession of]

Relating to possession; growing out of possession. A *possessory action* is an action to recover possession of property, as distinguished from a *petitory action* (an action to confirm title). Also, an action founded on possession. A *possessory lien* is the right of a creditor to retain possession of an object until his claim is paid. A *possessory interest* is an interest entitling one to retain sole possession of property; the interest may be based upon title or upon some lesser interest, such as a tenancy for years.

See **PETITORY**

POST

After, behind.

POST DIEM [L. *post* + *dies* / day, daytime]

After the designated date. A payment which is made after the maturity date is a payment *post diem*.

POSTERITY [L. *posterus, posteritas* / following, next, coming after; future generations]

All the offspring and descendants of a person till the last of the possible generations. All future generations.

POST FACTO [L. *post* + *facere* / to make or do]

After the fact. After the deed is done. Following commission of a crime.

See **EX POST FACTO**

POST HOC [L. *post* + *hic, haec, hoc* / this person, this thing]

After this; after this event; hereafter. The period after an accident or other event having leqal consequence.

POST HOC ERGO PROPTER HOC

Because that occurred, then this occurred as a direct result.

POSTHUMOUS [L. *post* + *humo, humare* / to cover with earth, to bury]

An event or deed which follows the death of an individual. Examples: the birth of a son after the death of his father; the publication of a creative work after the death of the author, artist or composer.

POST LITEM MOTAM

Following the commencement of the action or litigation.

POST MORTEM [L. *post* + *mors, mortis* / death]

After death. Relating to events or actions after the death of an individual. An autopsy or examination of the body of a deceased to determine the cause of death. Also, an inquiry into the causes of an event after it has occurred.

See **AUTOPSY**

POST NUPTIAL [L. *post* + *nuptiae* / marriage, wedding]

After marriage. A *post-nuptial* agreement is an agreement between spouses to fix the rights of each with respect to their property and other interests, including, if they wish, provisions governing the disposition of property after separation, divorce or death.

See **PRENUPTIAL**

POST OBIT [L. *post* + *obitus* / downfall, destruction, death]

After death. A *post obit* agreement is one in which one party borrows money which he agrees to repay to the lender upon the death of a third party from whom he expects to inherit. A *post obit* note is a promissory note payable at a specified time after the death of the maker.

POTENTIA

Power, might, ability, especially political power. Also, likely, foreseeable.

POTENTIA INUTILIS FRUSTRA EST

Power which cannot be used is power in vain.

POTENTIA PROPINQUA [L. *potentia* + *propinquis* / near, nearby]

A foreseeable event; something which is likely to happen.

POVERTY [L. *pauper, paupertas* / poor, not wealthy, of limited means; poverty]

The state of being poor or without resources. One in poverty may, upon application, obtain access to counsel, to public assistance and to other benefits and services made available by society.

See **PAUPER**

POWER [L. *possum, posse* / to be able]

Ability to do or act. Strength, force, energy. Legal authority. An external force such as electricity or gas. In law, the authority or capacity to act as defined by some legally recognized document or by statutute or court order. The *commerce power* is the power of Congress under the Constitution to regulate commerce among the states. *Police powers* are the powers exercised by government in maintaining the peace and enforcing the laws designed to provide for the general security and for the health, safety and welfare of citizens. A *power of appointment* is a power granted in a deed or will defining the duties of the grantee in disposing of property.

PRAECIPE [L. *praecipio, praecipere* / to take before, to obtain in advance]

A document or writ directing a court officer or clerk to perform a ministerial act in furtherance of an order or decision of the court, e.g., an order directing the clerk to issue execution after judgment. Also, an order directing a person to commit some act or to refrain from committing it. An application for the issuance of a summons by the court clerk. Also, an application to a judge similar to a motion.

PRAESUMPTIO JURIS [L. *praesumere* / to anticipate, take for granted, presume + *ius, iuris* / right or law]

A legal presumption. A rebuttable presumption.
See **PRESUMPTION**

PRAYER [L. *precor, precari* / to beg, request, pray, invoke]

A supplication or request to God or to another diety. A devotional recitation or service. Originally, that part of a bill in equity in which the plaintiff spelled out the relief which he was seeking. Now, the *prayer* or *prayer for relief* is that portion of the complaint in any civil action in which the plaintiff defines the relief and the damages he seeks. The *prayer* is required in a complaint under the Federal Rules.

PREAMBLE [L. *prae* / before, in front of + *ambulo, ambulare* / to go or walk]

An introductory statement in a text or document introducing or explaining what is to follow. The introduction to a constitution or statute setting forth the reasons for its adoption. The Preamble to the U.S. Constitution begins, "We the people of the United States, in order to form a more perfect Union......"

PRECATORY [L. *precari* / to beg, request, invoke]

Words which express a wish or request but not a direction or command. Courts make a distinction between words which are clearly *precatory*, such as, "I wish, I hope that, I ask that, I request", etc., and those which are clearly peremptory, i.e., commands or directions: "I direct that, I instruct my.....to", etc. Ordinarily, *precatory* words are considered ineffective to control the disposition of property. Some courts, however, will recognize trusts in which the language is *precatory* but the intent to create a trust is clear: "It is my final wish that..." These are called *precatory trusts*.

See **PEREMPTORY**

PRECEDENT [L. *prae* + *cedere* / to go, proceed, to happen]

Something which comes before. Prior in time or incidence. A model. A convention, rule or example which is intended to guide or control thought or action in the future. In the law, a *precedent* is a decision of a court which serves as an example or authority for subsequent decisions by other courts in cases which have the same or similar facts and which logically require application of the same principles of law. All prior cases which arose under essentially the same facts and the same legal issues are deemed and considered as precedents. Precedents of a superior court in the same state are deemed binding precedents which must be followed by the lower courts. Precedents of courts in other jurisdictions are persuasive but not binding.

See **STARE DECISIS**

PRECEPT [L. *prae* + *capio, capere* / to take, seize]

A rule of conduct. A code or statement of principles. A court order, writ, warrant or other judicial process. A court order directing an official to perform some act in support of the court's decision, such as an order to find and produce a person. A rule of law or a code of moral conduct, such as the ABA Model Rules of Professional Responsibility, a code intended to govern the conduct of lawyers.

PRECLUDE, PRECLUSION [L. *prae* + *claudere* / to close, shut]

To make impossible; rule out or prevent in advance, e.g., to *preclude marriage* between persons in a close degree of relationship. An order enjoining a party from some action is, in effect, an *order of preclusion*. In discovery proceedings, if a party fails to comply with a discovery order, he will be *precluded* from offering evidence which contradicts evidence offered by his opponent on the issues covered in the order. A party may be *precluded* from bringing an action because of *res judicata* or the application of a statute of limitations.

PREDATORY [L. *praedor, praedari* / to plunder, pillage]

Given to plundering or taking the property of others. Engaging in commercial practices designed to injure competitors unfairly. In antitrust law, the practice of fixing prices without regard to cost or profits (at a loss, if necessary) in order to eliminate competition. The intent is to recoup the temporary losses by raising prices again after the competitor is eliminated.

PREEMPT, PREEMPTION [L. *prae* + *emereo, emerere* / to earn through service, to acquire; to buy]

To take control of. To take to the exclusion of others. The doctrine under which the federal government, based on the supremacy clause in the Constitution, takes and assumes for itself control over various issues and matters, to the exclusion of the states. One such area is interstate commerce; another is bankruptcy. Once Congress has legislated to control a given area, the states may not. Similarly, a state statute will *preempt* a local ordinance or rule. Also the privilege granted by the federal government to designated persons to settle upon public land and to acquire title to the exclusion of all others after paying a specified price.

PREEMPTIVE RIGHT

A right of first refusal. The right of a stockholder in a corporation to purchase the same percentage of a new issue of stock as he holds at the time of issue. The purpose is to prevent dilution of value, ownership and control.

PREFERENCE, PREFERENTIAL [L. *prae* / before + *fero, ferre* / to bear or bring; to carry]

Having priority in rank or standing. The right to prior payment of a debt. A payment or a transfer of property made by an insolvent debtor to a creditor who has no greater rights to payment than other creditors of equal rank, i.e., more than the creditor would receive if the debtor's assets were distributed pro rata to all creditors of equal rank. In bankruptcy law, *a preference* is any payment made by the debtor to a creditor within 90 days before the filing of the bankruptcy petition. A *preference* may be set aside by the trustee in bankruptcy.

PREFERRED [L. *praeffero, praeferre* / to place in front of; to display, to prefer]

A thing placed ahead of other things. Having a priority or special right not available to others. A *preferred creditor* has rights of security and/or payment superior to those of junior creditors. *Preferred stock* is a class of corporate stock which has priority over other classes in distribution of the corporate equity and of dividends, especially over common stock. A *preferred dividend* is a dividend on preferred stock. A *preferred risk* in insurance law is a risk which has a lower chance of creating loss than others and is therefore entitled to a lower premium.

PREJUDICE [L. *prae* / before + *iudico, iudicare, iudicium* / to judge; judgment]

An irrational hostility by one individual or group against another individual or group, usually based upon the latter's race, color, religion or opinions. Any bias that prevents an impartial result, as by a judge or jury in deciding a matter. Injury to a person's legal rights without support in fact or law or without legal justification. When statements are made, or settlement negotiations are conducted, *without prejudice*, the parties expect that no subsequent reference will be made to these statements and that they will not be used against the party making them.

PREJUDICIAL   [L. *praeiudicium* / a previous decision or judgment]

An adverse opinion formed before knowledge of facts sufficient for a reasonable opinion. An unjustified and unreasoned bias or hostility against an individual, group, race or religion. The word has several applications in the law. *Prejudicial error* is error by the trial court of sufficient consequence to justify reversal of judgment and a new trial. *Prejudicial evidence* is evidence which is offered not for its probative value but to arouse and inflame the minds of the jury. *Prejudicial publicity* is publicity which makes it impossible for a jury to render a fair and impartial verdict. A party to a federal action who feels that the judge is *prejudiced* against him personally may file an affidavit challenging the judge's right to try the case. 28 U.S.C. § 144.

PRELIMINARY   [L. *prae* / before + *limen, liminis* / a threshold or entryway]

Coming before. Introductory. Temporary. Pending some later action or decision. In criminal law, a *preliminary hearing* is the first appearance in court of a criminal defendant; the purpose of the hearing is to determine if there is probable cause to charge the defendant with the commission of a crime. The hearing is conducted by a judge or magistrate. A *preliminary injunction* is an order issued by the court before trial to restrain some action on the part of one party in order to prevent irreparable injury to the other party pending a determination on the merits.

PREMEDITATE   [L. *prae* + *meditor, meditari* / to think over, consider, meditate]

To consider and plan beforehand. To plan and deliberate in advance about committing a possible act and then to decide to commit the act. In the law, the design and intent to commit a crime after thought and consideration of the consequences. *Premeditation* is an essential element of murder in the first degree. Courts differ as to the amount of time which must elapse before commission of a crime before premeditation can be presumed.

See **MALICE (AFORETHOUGHT)**

PREMISES   [L. *prae* + *mittere* / to send, let go, release]

Statements which precede and underlie other statements or arguments. A parcel of land with appurtenant buildings. Also, all or part of a building. Also, the introductory portion of a deed preceding the habendum clause but including a description of the property conveyed. The initial portion of a bill in equity stating the nature of the grievance and naming the defendant.

PREMIUM [L. *praemium* / that which is picked first, the best; from *prae* + *emerere* / to buy]

A reward or prize given as an inducement to buy. Booty, reward, profit. Considersation for a loan or other extension. The money paid to an insurance company for its insurance coverage. A discount or other benefit given to a purchaser in addition to the items or goods purchased. The prize offered to contest entrants. The amount by which the market value of a stock or bond exceeds its par or face value.

See **NO PAR; PAR**

PRENUPTIAL [L. *prae* + *nuptiae* / marriage, a wedding]

Occurring before the marriage itself. A *prenuptial agreement* is an agreement made between the parties to an intended marriage in which they make provision for the disposition and use of their respective properties and assets and for their respective rights upon death or divorce.

See **ANTENUPTIAL; POST NUPTIAL**

PREPONDERANCE [L. *prae* + *pondero, ponderare* / to weigh upon, to consider]

Superiority in quality or quantity; to be greater than. In the law, the decision on any civil trial issue and at the end of the trial, will go to the party who has offered a *preponderance of the evidence*. This means that his evidence, taken as a whole, is more credible and convincing than the evidence of his opponent. If we accept that the evidence of both parties will have *some weight*, judgment will be rendered for the party whose evidence has *the greater weight*, or the *preponderance*.

PREROGATIVE [L. *prae* + *rogare* / to ask, inquire, beseech]

In Rome, a *prerogative* was the right to vote before others of less stature. Any special right or power. The special rights or privileges available to and exercised by officials holding public office, such as members of Congress, judges, etc.

PRESCRIBE [L. *prae* / before + *scribo, scribere* / to engrave, to write]

To establish a rule or a code of conduct. To dictate. To exercise authority in setting down a mandate or order, as to prescribe the rules governing the federal courts (the Federal Rules of Civil Procedure). Also, to assert or claim a right in the ownership or possession of an interest in property (e.g., an easement) by *prescription*, i.e., the open, hostile, continuous and long-term use of property by one not the owner.

PRESCRIPTION [L. *prae* + *scribere* / to engrave, to write; to lay down a rule or course of conduct; to instruct in advance]

A bar to further claim, action or interference. Acquisition of an interest in real property through adverse possession. A *prescriptive easement* is the right acquired by an adverse or hostile user over a prescribed period of time to use a passageway, or water, light or air, affecting land of another. In international law, one country may acquire sovereignty over the land of another by continuous occupation and control under the doctrine of *prescription*.

See **ADVERSE POSSESSION; USUCAPIO**

PRESENTMENT [L. *praesum, praesesse* / to be over, to stand above, to preside over]

A document which is presented to the court for consideration and which requires action or response. A formal accusation by a grand jury of the commission of a crime, arrived at from the jurors' own knowledge and on their own initiative, as distinguished from an indictment, which is an accusation of crime at the instigation of a public prosecutor. Also, the presentation of a document or instrument by the payee, holder, or other person entitled to payment, to the maker or drawer, constituting a demand for acceptance, honor and payment of the instrument.

PRESUMPTION [L. *prae* + *sumere* / to take, to take for oneself; to take for granted]

Something believed or taken for granted. The belief that a fact or event is more likely or probable than not. An inference about the truth of a fact which is unproven, arrived at from other facts which are known. In the law, a conclusion which is based upon intuition or upon general knowledge of a set of facts or circumstances which are considered so reliable in most instances as to require general acceptance. A rule imposed by statute or judicial decision which requires that if one fact is found, other facts or conclusions must be drawn, at least until they are rebutted by convincing proof to the contrary. Examples: If a person disappears for a given period (usually seven years) without apparent reason or explanation, she is *presumed* dead. An accused in a criminal trial is *presumed* innocent; the state has the burden of proving his guilt. A married man is *presumed* to be the father of any child born to his wife. A *conclusive presumption* is one which the parties are not permitted to rebut. A *rebuttable presumption* is one which may be disproved by evidence to the contrary.

PRETERMISSION [L. *praetermittere* / to neglect, pass over, omit]

The omission of a child or heir from a testator's will. Under most statutes, the child will be restored to the interest he would have received if the testator had died intestate, unless it can be shown that the omission was deliberate and intentional.

PRETEXTUAL ARREST

The arrest of a person on minor or superficial grounds with the real intent of investigating a more serious crime of which he is suspected but for which there are insufficient lawful grounds for arrest.

PREVENTIVE DETENTION [L. *prae* / before + *venio, venire* / to come + *detineo, detinere* / to hold back, detain]

Confinement of a criminal defendant before and during trial to prevent his escape or to protect the public and/or the court from acts or threats of violence by him. *Preventive detention* is now used often in cases of terrorism.

PRIMAE IMPRESSIONIS [L. *prior, prius, primus* / first, former + *imprimo, imprimere* / to press into or upon]

Of first or new impression. Previously undecided. Without precedent. A matter or issue not previously presented to the court.

PRIMA FACIE [L. *primus* / first + *facies* / face, form, figure; at first view, on its face]

On first appearance. A fact presumed to be true in the absence of a showing to the contrary.

PRIMA FACIE CASE

The presentation by one party to an action of proof and evidence sufficient to satisfy the legal requirements for a judgment in his favor. Sufficient proof by the plaintiff to warrant submission of his evidence to the jury and the rendition of a verdict in his favor.

PRIMA FACIE EVIDENCE

Evidence sufficient to survive a motion for dismissal or directed verdict and to require the opposing party to proceed with his proof.

PRIMARY [L. *prior, prius, primus* / first in order of time or of importance; first in rank]

Belonging to the first rank or order in progressive allocation of rights or interests. In the law, the word is used in many contexts to indicate that something precedes or has greater impact than something else. Examples: a *primary beneficiary* under a life insurance policy is the one who will be first entitled to the proceeds in the event of the insured's death. A *primary boycott* is the job action taken by a union against an employer with which it has a grievance to discourage the public from purchasing the goods or services of the employer. *Primary jurisdiction* is the statutory power given to certain administrative agencies to hear and determine a controversy before it can be heard by a court. (Example: the National Labor Relations Board has *primary jurisdiction* over grievances arising under collective bargaining agreements.)

See **SECOND; SECONDARY**

PRIME [L. *prior, prius, primus* / first in place or time; also, former]

First in rank, authority or standing; principal. Having priority over. *Prime* or *prime rate* is the lowest interest rate charged by a bank of its most credit-worthy customers. The *prime minister* is the head of government in countries having the parliamentary system of government.

PRIMOGENITURE [L. *primus* + *genitor* / a father, begetter; the first born]

The exclusive right of inheritance belonging to the first born son. Under the early common law of descent, the eldest son succeeded to all the property of his deceased father.

PRIORITY [L. *prior* / first in place or time]

Enjoying a legal position superior to others. Having superior rights to property. The relative rank of competing claims for the same asset(s). The status of a claim which is entitled to be satisfied before other claims; a mortgage upon real property has priority over a lease, for example. Under the bankruptcy code, *claims with priority* must be paid before other claims. The Uniform Commercial Code sets forth the priority of security interests in personal property. UCC § 9-301 et seq.

PRIMUS INTER PARES

First among equals.

PRINCIPAL [L. *principalis* / first in time, rank or importance; most important or consequential]

Generally, constituting the main or most important element. The word has many uses and meanings for lawyers. Examples: The amount borrowed and forming the face value of an obligation or of a document evidencing the obligation, e.g., a promissory note or bond, is *the principal* of the obligation as distinguished from interest on the obligation. In criminal law, *the principal* is the person who commits or participates in the crime or who induces or procures others to help in its commission. In the law of agency, *the principal* is the individual from whom flows the authority in others, i.e., his agents, to commit acts for his benefit or in his behalf. The *principal obligor* on a debt or obligation is the person who is primarily liable or who will have the ultimate burden of payment, as distinguished from persons who are secondarily liable, e.g., sureties or guarantors. A capital sum invested to earn interest is called the *principal*.

PRIOR [L. *prior, prius, primus* / before, in advance of; the former]

Coming before; preceding. Used as an adjective before other words, *prior* has a special meaning for lawyers. Examples: A *prior adjudication* is a previous litigation in which the matter in dispute between the parties was, or could have been, determined. A prior adjudication on the merits will bar a subsequent action between the same parties on the same issues, under the principles of res judicata. In patent law, *prior art* is any relevant knowledge, data, description or patent which predated the invention at issue and therefore operates to support rejection of the invention by the Patent Office or by a court. A *prior restraint* is any action taken by a government official or by statute to control the contents or text of any expression before its publication. Any effort to control the dissemination of information protected by the First Amendment of the Constitution is a *prior restraint* if it is imposed before a judicial hearing to determine whether it qualifies for First Amendment protection. *New York Times Co. v. United States,* 403 U.S. 713. A *prior statement* is a statement made by a witness out of court prior to his testimony in an action. *Prior statements* may be either *consistent* with the subsequent testimony or *inconsistent* with it.

See **RES JUDICATA**

PRIOR RESTRAINT

Any action by the government to prevent speech in advance of its utterance or expression, or a writing before its publication. *Prior restraints* are considered the most serious violations of the right of free speech guaranteed by the Constitution. Any system of *prior restraint* is presumed to violate the Constitution and imposes a heavy burden upon the government to show justification. *New York Times v. U.S.*, 403 U.S. 713.

PRIOR TEMPORE, POTIOR IURE (JURE)

First in time, first in right.

PRIVACY [L. *privus* / single, every]

The state of being alone or separate from others. Freedom from intrusion by others. The right to retain control over one's person and affairs without intrusion by others, especially by government. The right of a woman to an abortion has been cited as a critical element of her *right to privacy. Roe v. Wade*.

PRIVATE [L. *privare, privatus* / to free from; to make private]

Reserved to a particular person or group or class of persons. Not available to or accessible by the public. Independent of the state or government or of society in general, as a *private club* or a *private school*. Unknown to and restricted from others, as a *private matter*. A *private* is the lowest-ranked soldier in the U.S. military. To *go private* describes the process by which a corporation buys back and retires its publicly held stock.

PRIVATIZE [L. *privo, privare* / to strip from, deprive of]

To make private; to convert to private use. The act by government of converting an enterprise from public ownership to private ownership, usually by the sale of stock to the public. Some utilities have been *privatized*.

PRIVILEGE [L. *privatus* / private + *lex, legis* / the law]

A special and peculiar right, status or condition reserved for or granted to some and not to others. An advantage, power or immunity which is unique to an individual or a group or class of individuals. An exemption from liability because of special circumstances, as in justifiable homicide. The law has created and recognizes many *privileges*. Examples: The *attorney-client privilege* is a rule of evidence which prevents a lawyer from revealing communications made to him by his client in confidence during the course of his representation; only the client can waive the privilege. *Executive privilege* is a privilege unique to the President of the United States and enables him to withhold his communications from Congress and others; the privilege is a qualified, not absolute, privilege. In the law of defamation, a writer or publisher enjoys the *privilege of fair comment* with respect to public officers in matters of public concern, provided the material published is not published with malice, i.e., with knowledge that the material is false, or with reckless disregard whether it is true or false. One privilege which is enjoyed by all is the *privilege against self incrimination* granted by the Fifth Amendment to the Constitution.

PRIVILEGES AND IMMUNITIES CLAUSE

The name applied to the clause in Article IV of the U.S. Comstitution which states that citizens of each state shall be entitled to all the *privileges and immunities* of citizens in the other states. Also, a clause in Amendment XIV to the Constitution which provides that no state shall make or enforce any law that abridges the *privileges and immunities* of citizens of the U.S.

PRIVITY [L. *privatus* / private, for private use]

The relationship between the two original parties to a contract or agreement or to another legal relationship. Originally, only the two original parties were deemed to have *privity* in suits involving liability for negligence or breach of warranty. The right to sue on products liability claims has now been extended to members of the family of an original party and even to strangers to the contract. Also, the relationship between two individuals which arises because they succeed one another to a right or privilege or to some asset, e.g., a contract or bond, or because there is such a mutuality of interest between them that the rights and liabilities of one extend to the other. Examples of *privity*:

the assignor under a contract and his assignee; a testator and his executor; a principal and his agent; a donor and his donee.

PRO

Before, in front of; for, on the side of; in behalf of; in favor of; according to; in proportion to or as.

PROBABLE CAUSE

A reasonable belief by a prudent person that some act or event has occurred in a particular way or can be explained in a particular way. A reasonable basis for belief in certain facts or circumstances. Greater evidence for one possibility than for another. In a criminal case, a reasonable belief in facts which support the conclusion that the defendant has committed the acts charged. Under the U.S. Constitution, *probable cause* is required for the issuance of any Warrant. Amendment IV. *Probable cause* supplies sufficient grounds for an administrative search of premises, provided the search is conducted under reasonable procedures universally applied.

PROBATA [L. *probo, probare* / to find good; to judge; to test and approve; to recommend]

Anything conclusively established. Conclusive proof.

PROBATE [L. *probare* / to recommend, to test and approve]

The procedure by which a will is submitted and proven before the court; by extension, the process by which a will is declared valid and the estate is administered by the executor. In the administration of an estate, the collection of assets and interests; the payment of debts and taxes; and the distribution of remaining assets as directed by the will or as determined by the court. The court with jurisdiction over the administration of estates can have one of several names: probate court, orphans' court, surrogate's court, etc.

PROBATION [L. *probare* / to approve, to find good; to test]

A trial period; a test. The period immediately after employment begins during which a new hire is tested to see if she can perform the duties expected of her. In certain jobs, such as teaching, a *period of probation* is customary before the employee is given permanent, or tenured, employment. Also, the steps by which a convicted criminal is released from prison to the general community, under the supervision of an officer known as a probation officer, and is given an opportunity to prove that he can function as a law-abiding citizen.

PROBATIVE [L. *probare* / to approve, prove, test]

Serving or tending to prove; substantiating. In the law of evidence, testimony or other proof which points to the truth. Anything which serves to help the trier of fact to reach a conclusion which is reasonable under the circumstances.

PROBATUM EST [L. *probare* + *esse* / to be; it is proved]
The fact is proved.

PRO BONO
See **PRO BONO PUBLICO**

PRO BONO ET MALO [L. *pro* + *bonus* / good + *et* / and, also + *malus* / bad, evil]
For good and evil; for better or worse.

PRO BONO PUBLICO [L. *pro* + *bonus* / good + *publicus* / public, belonging to the people; for the public good or welfare]
The provision of legal services by lawyers to the indigent public. Legal services rendered by lawyers without fee or compensation, usually to indigent persons and often by virtue of appointment by the court. Usually shortened to *pro bono*.

PROCEDENDO [L. *procedere* / to go ahead, advance, proceed]
A writ of remand issued by a superior court, generally by writ of certiorari, directing an inferior court from which an action has been erroneously removed, to resume jurisdiction and determine the matter on the merits. Also, the writ of a superior court directing a lower court to proceed to execute on its judgment.
See **REMAND**

PROCEDURAL DUE PROCESS
The Constitutional requirement that all judicial and administrative proceedings be conducted regularly, fairly, and in accordance with established laws, rules or principles. At a miminum, due process requires adequate notice and an opportunity to be heard in defense of one's life, liberty or property. Due process is guaranteed (as to the federal government) by the Fifth Amendment and (as to the states) by the Fourteenth Amendment. *Procedural due process* is distinguished from substantive due process, which relates to governmental recognition of rights in the content of legislation.
See **SUBSTANTIVE DUE PROCESS**

PROCEDURAL LAW
Those laws, rules and regulations setting forth the procedures governing the conduct of litigation and the administration of the courts. *Civil procedural law* deals with the conduct of civil trials; *criminal procedural law* with the

conduct of criminal trials. *Procedural law* is distinguished from substantive law, which deals with the definition of legal rights and duties.

See **SUBSTANTIVE LAW**

PROCEEDING [L. *pro* / to, towards + *cedo, cedere* / to go, move forward]

Any of the steps in the conduct of litigation or in the determination of rights by the courts or by administrative agencies. An adjudication. A hearing, trial or application before the court. The official record of steps taken by a court or agency.

PROCEEDS [L. *pro* / towards + cedere / to go forward]

Any money or other asset resulting from a commercial transaction such as a sale. Also, money received to reimburse a loss under an insurance policy. Income or yield. Money received by a corporation upon the issuance and sale of securities.

PROCESS [L. *pro* + *cedere*]

A series of steps culminating in a result. The continuous operation or use of a resource to achieve a particular result, as the raw material used in the *process of manufacture*. All of the steps in a legal proceeding. The summons or writ issued by a court to compel a party to attend or to answer a complaint or charge against him. The steps by which a court acquires jurisdiction over a particular action and of the parties to the action.

PROCLAIM [L. *pro* / before + *clamo, clamare* / to call, shout]

To announce publicly and with strength or force. To declare openly and defiantly. To announce officially or formally, as to proclaim a new government or the coming of the Messiah. To promulgate; to publish under governmental authority. To publicize.

PROCLAMATION [L. *pro* + *clamare* / to to shout, to call out]

A public announcement or notice of some action which requires public knowledge. A governmental document reciting a matter of great general importance. Lincoln's Emancipation Proclamation, for example, constituted a public notice of historic significance to the American public.

PRO CONFESSO [L. *pro* + *confiteor, confitere* / to confess, admit, acknowledge]

As confessed; because it is confessed. A decree in equity in favor of the plaintiff, issued when no answer is interposed by the defendant or the answer is frivolous or patently false.

See **DECREE PRO CONFESSO**

PROCTOR   [L. *procurator* / a manager, agent, factor]

A proxy or attorney-in-fact. An individual appointed by another to manage his affairs or to represent him in a litigation.

PROCURATION   [L. *procuro, procurare* / be in charge of, look after]

An agency or proxy. A power of attorney authorizing one to act as agent or attorney-in-fact for another. A negotiable instrument may be endorsed by the attorney in fact *by procuration* or *per proc*.

PROCURE   [L. *pro* / for + *curo, curare* / to attend upon, care for; to manage; to cure]

To acquire or gain possession of. To begin, instigate or bring about. To induce a person to perform some act. To cause to be done. A broker of real estate *procures* a buyer.

PROCUREMENT   [L. *procurare* / to take care of]

The act of obtaining, getting or providing. The purchase, leasing, renting or acquisition of materials, equipment and products for use and consumption by others, as by employees of a business or government.

PRODUCT   [L. *pro* / for + *duco, ducere* / to lead, draw along; *producere* / to bring out, produce]

The result of physical or mental activity or effort. A consequence of work or thought. An object created by growth, development or manufacture. The total output of an industry or business enterprise.

PRO EMPTORE   [L. *pro* + *emptor* / buyer, purchaser]

Through the title or rights of a purchaser.

PRO ET CON   [L *pro* / for + *et* / and + *con*, short for *contra* / against]

For and against. Arguments on both sides of an issue.

PRO FACTO   [L. *pro* + *factus* / a deed or fact]

Anything considered or acknowledged to be a fact.

PROFANE, PROFANITY   [L. *pro* + *fanum* / a consecrated or holy place, a temple]

Divorced from religion; secular. To treat with scorn or irreverence. Unholy; a desecration; serving to defile or defame. An irreverent use of the word God. Vulgar, coarse. Swearwords or language deemed coarse or vulgar. It is a federal crime to broadcast *obscene, indecent or profane language* by radio transmission. 18 U.S.C. § 1464.

PROFESSION, PROFESSIONAL [L. *profiteor, profiteri* / to acknowledge, to make a statement; to offer or promise]

A statement of opinion or belief; a statement openly and publicly made, as the profession of one's innocence. A vocation requiring specialized training and skill acquired through many years of schooling and preparation, e.g., the medical profession. An activity usually requiring a license or certificate from some licensing authority. A *professional* is a person meeting the qualifications of his profession. A *professional association* is a group of persons in the same profession organized to practice together; many law firms are organized as professional associations. A *professional corporation* is a corporation organized by a group of professionals to conduct their practices together in corporate form. *Professional Responsibility* is the study and application of ethical principles in the practice of a profession, especially the legal profession.

PROFITEER [L. *proficio, proficere* / to advance or make progress; to be of use]

One who takes advantage of a period of stress or crisis, e.g., a natural disaster or war, to profit unreasonably or excessively from the sale or exchange of essential commodities in short supply.

PRO FORMA [L. *pro + formo, formare* / to form, shape, fashion]

For the sake of form; as a matter of form. Done as a mere formality or perfunctorily. Also, a document which assumes certain facts and then utilizes them to estimate or project future activities or results. A *pro forma* statement is a financial statement forecasting the results of business operations or of a particular business transaction.

PROGRESSIVE [L. *pro* / forth, forward + *gradior, gradi* / to step forward, walk]

Moving forward; improving. Characterized by or participating in progress. A *progressive tax* is a tax which imposes increasingly higher rates as the income of the taxpayer increases. The U.S. income tax system is essentially a *progressive tax* system.

PRO HAEC (HAC) VICE [L. *pro + hic, haec, hoc* / this + *vicis* / change, exchange, turn; instead of]

For this one particular occasion. A lawyer licensed in one state may be admitted *pro haec vice* in another state to argue a motion or try a case. The admission is only for these limited purposes.

PROHIBIT [L. *pro + habere* / to have or hold]

To forbid, enjoin; to prevent the commission of some act. To forbid by statute, administrative regulation or court order. For example, the law *prohibits* marriage by individuals within certain degrees of consanguinity, e.g., brother and sister.

PROHIBITION [L. *pro* + *habare* / to have]

The act of enjoining or forbidding the commission of some act or activity, such as the sale of alcoholic beverages or of drugs. From 1920 to 1933, the manufacture, sale and distribution of alcoholic beverages was *prohibited* under the 18th Amendment to the Constitution. Also, a writ or order of a superior court directing an inferior or lower court not to assume or exercise jurisdiction in a matter which is beyond its powers.

PROLIXITY [L. *prolixus* / widely extended, long, broad]

Verbosity, long-windedness. Lawyers have a tendency towards *prolixity* in their pleadings and briefs. Some judges have a commitment to *prolixity* in their opinions.

PROMISE [L. *promitto, promittere* / to release, send forth; to promise, lead to expect]

An agreement to perform some act or to refrain from performing an act. A commitment by one person to another that leads or encourages the latter to expect that the commitment will be carried out or fulfilled.

PROMISSORY [L. *promitto, promittere* / to promise, assure]

Embodying or in the nature of a promise. Conveying or consisting of a promise. A *promissory note* is a written promise to pay a sum certain on a specified date, or on demand or sight, to a named payee, or to the holder or bearer of the note. The note is negotiable if the promise is unconditional, the sum is certain, and the payment is on demand or at a time certain to order or to bearer. U.C.C. § 3-104. *Promissory estoppel* is applied by the law to enforce a promise which the promisor should reasonably expect the promisee to rely and to act upon, and which the promisee does, in fact, reasonably rely and act upon, to his detriment.

PROMULGATE [L. *promulgo, promulgare* / to publish, to make public]

To publish, announce or make public. To adopt or announce a new decree or law. To put a new statute or policy into effect. The act of an administrative agency in putting into effect a new regulation or rule.

PROPERTY [L. *proprius* / one's own, peculiar to one person]

The right of ownership. Anything owned or possessed exclusively. All the assets of a person. The law recognizes many different forms and interests in property. *Common property* is property owned, used or leased by more than one person. *Community property* is the property held jointly by husband and wife and in which each has an undivided one-half interest (recognized only in nine states). *Intangible property* is property which has no physical form but which is manifested in some document or certficate and which has a value in currency which is either expressed in the document or accorded to it by the market or some other measure of value. *Intellectual property* is all property created by the human mind or intellect, e.g., an idea, copyright, patent, formula, trademark, invention, etc. *Personal property* is all moveable property, not including growing crops. *Real property* consists of all interests in land, buildings and crops and in fixtures attached to the land or buildings.

PROPINQUI ET CONSANGUINEI [L. *propinqus* / nearby + *et* / and + *consanguineus* / related by blood]

The nearest of kin to a decedent; next of kin.

PROPONENT [L. *pro* + *pono, ponere* / to lay down, put, place]

A person who advocates a cause or issue or who argues in favor of an idea or proposition. The *proponent* of a will is the person who offers the will for probate.

PROPOSE, PROPOSAL [L. *proponere* / to put forth, expose; to publish; to propose]

To suggest for consideration by others. To offer an idea for debate or discussion. To introduce legislation or a plan of action. To make an offer of marriage.

PROPRIA PERSONA (PRO PERSONA) [L. *propria, proprius* / one's own, for oneself + *persona* / mask, role, character, person]

In one's own behalf. A person appears in an action *propria persona* when he prepares his own papers, argues his own motion or tries his own case, without benefit of an attorney.

See **IN PROPRIA PERSONA; PRO SE**

PROPRIETARY [L. *proprius, proprietas* / property, ownership]

Describes anything owned, used, traded or marketed under an exclusive legal right, e.g., an inventor's right over his invention. Anything privately owned and managed. A *proprietary drug* is a medication over which one pharmaceutical company has exclusive rights. A *proprietary lease* defines the relationship between a co-op residential association and its tenant-shareholders. A *proprietary function* is a function of a local government which is discretionary and not mandatory: example: a city-owned opera house or theatre is discretionary and therefore *proprietary*; police protection is mandatory and not proprietary. Also, anything which is the private property of an individual.

PROPTER AFFECTUM   [L. *propter* / by reason of + *adfectum* / a mental attitude]

On account of bias or partiality. A challenge to a juror on the ground of bias.

PROPTER DEFECTUM   [L. *propter* / because of + *defectus* / a lack or fault]

On account of some personal disability or quality. A challenge to a juror because of some personal disability or disqualification, e.g., that he is an ex-convict or an alien.

PROPTER DELICTUM   [L. *propter* / because of + *delictum* / a crime]

On account of a crime. A challenge to a juror based on conviction for a disqualifying crime.

PRO RATA   [L. *pro* + *reor, reri, ratus* / to think, judge, fix]

Calculated by or according to a proportional measure. To divide, fix or assess proportionately. To divide or allocate in proportion to some measure of time, space or value. A corporation will pay a dividend to its common stockholders *pro rata*, i.e., according to the percentage each owns of the common stock.

PRO RATA CLAUSE

A clause in an insurance policy limiting the risk of any one insurer on a particular loss to its proportionate share of all coverage of that loss by all carriers covering the loss.

PROSCRIBE, PROSCRIPTION   [L. *pro* + *scribere* / to write; to make public, publish]

To banish or exile. To forbid or condemn. To make illegal, as when a statute *proscribes* certain conduct or actions.

PRO SE   [L. *pro* + *se* / himself, herself, itself, themselves]

In one's own behalf; in person. A party who appears in an action without the benefit or counsel of an attorney appears *pro se*.

See **IN PROPRIA PERSONA**

PROSECUTE   [L. *pro* + plus *sequi* / to follow (*prosequi*, to go with, accompany, follow; also, to attack, pursue)]

In criminal law, to begin and maintain an action against a defendant who is charged with commission of a crime. More generally, to commence and maintain any legal proceeding: an action, an appeal, etc. A *prosecutor* or *prosecuting attorney* is an official who is appointed or elected to bring and conduct criminal actions in behalf of the state. Federal prosecutors are called U.S. Attorneys.

PROSEQUI

To prosecute.

See **NOLLE PROSEQUI (NOL PROS)**

PROSPECTIVE [L. *pro + specio, specere* / to look at, to behold; to look ahead]

Relating to the future; likely to happen; anticipated. *Prospective damages* are damages awarded to compensate a plaintiff for the future consequences of defendant's acts. A *prospective law* or *statute* is one which has application only to future events or circumstances and has no retroactive effect.

PROSPECTUS [L. *prospecere* / to look ahead]

Any statement, circular, brochure or other written document, or the text of a radio or TV broadcast, which offers the sale of a stock, bond, debenture, warrant or other security. The document must contain all essential facts about the issuer, usually a corporation, including its management and operations, in order to permit a potential purchaser to make an informed decision about the offer. The contents of a *prospectus* which contains a public offering are controlled by federal securities laws and regulations. A copy must be filed with the Securities and Exchange Commission.

PRO TANTO [L. *pro* + plus *tantus* / so much, to such extent; that's as far as it goes; so much and no more]

Used to indicate that only a part of an obligation has been satisfied, or that only part of an event has occurred. Examples: if a testator pays a part of a bequest to a beneficiary before death, he may intend a *pro tanto* ademption. If a defendant has performed only part of his obligations, the plaintiff may recover *pro tanto*. A municipality may make a *pro tanto* payment to a landowner in an eminent domain proceeding while the landowner pursues her claim for a larger amount.

See **ADEMPTION**

PROTECT, PROTECTION, PROTECTIVE [L. *pro + tegere* / to cover, to conceal (*protegere* / to cover over)]

To keep from harm or injury. The act of helping or supporting someone who is weaker or less able. In international law, protection is the support given by a state or nation to its manufacturers and exporters through such devices as subsidies, price supports and protective tariffs to enable them to overcome competition from other countries. Also, money or other benefits demanded or extorted from merchants by racketeers posing as guarantors of nonviolence or interference by others. A *protection order* is issued by a court in domestic violence cases or in cases involving spousal or child abuse to prevent access or contact by the defendant with the party requiring protection. *Protective custody* is the detention and sequestering of material witnesses in criminal actions to assure their safety from harm or threats of injury.

PRO TEMPORE (PRO TEM) [L. *pro* + *tempus* / a division; time, a period of time]

For the time being. Temporarily, provisionally. Used to indicate that some office or right is being held temporarily, e.g., "she is serving as chairperson *pro tem*", or, "Mr. Clark is dean *pro tem*." A position or office held until the person elected or appointed to fill it permanently can assume it.

PROTEST [L. *pro* + *testor, testari* / to bear witness, testify, to make a will]

To make a solemn declaration of disapproval or rejection. To indicate disapproval of or displeasure with some act or condition. In negotiable instruments, the formal declaration by a notary that an instrument has been presented by him for payment but that payment has been refused. A payment *under protest* is one made by a person who is dissatisfied and is acting against his will. Taxes may be paid *under protest*, i.e., the payment is made but the taxpayer reserves her right to contest and litigate liability or the amount owed. Also, a public demonstration to manifest disapproval of some condition or position.

PROTHONOTARY [L. *pro* + *notarius* / a secretary or interpreter; a scribe]

In some states, as in Pennsylvania, the title given to a clerk of the court, usually the chief clerk.

PROVE, PROOF [L. *probo, probare* / to find good; to judge; to recommend as good; to show or prove]

To demonstrate the truth of. To establish the existence of a fact or condition in dispute or contention. To take the steps necessary to establish a theory or idea; to test by experiment. To satisfy a standard for measuring veracity or integrity, as to prove by a preponderance of the evidence or beyond a reasonable doubt.

PROVISIONAL [L. *pro* + *video, videre* / to see; to see ahead, to look forward to, see from a distance]

Existing or serving for the time being; temporary. Examples: A *provisional government* is one exercising temporary authority pending the creation and empowerment of a permanent government. A *provisional committee* is a committee given limited temporary powers. The courts utilize *provisional remedies* to protect parties against injury or loss while an action is pending, e.g., temporary injunctions, receivers, attachment, sequestrations, etc.

PROVISO [L. *providere* / to look forward]

A condition, stipulation or limitation. A clause in a contract, deed, statute, or other legal document, which expresses or contains a condition or restriction. These clauses usually begin with such words as "upon condition that", "provided that", "with the understanding that."

PROVOKE, PROVOCATION [L. *pro* + *voco, vocare* / to call, summon (*provocare*, to excite, arouse, challenge, summon before authority)]

To incite or arouse to anger. To stimulate into violence. An act by one person which arouses sufficient anger, resentment and fury in another to cause him to lose his control and reason, and, in extreme cases, to commit an illegal or criminal act. If the act committed in response to the *provocation* is a homicide, the provocation may be considered sufficient to reduce the crime from murder to manslaughter; the test for manslaughter is whether the homicide was the act of a reasonable person in the heat of passion and without time to regain control of his reason.

PROXIMATE (CAUSE) [L. *proximitas* / nearness, closeness]

Immediately preceding. In the law of torts, the *proximate cause* of an injury is a negligent act without which the injury would not have occurred and which is not followed or interrupted by another superseding, intervening or contributing cause. Most courts require, however, that the injury be the reasonably foreseeable consequence of the negligent act in order to impose tort liability. The *proximate cause* is also called the *direct cause* or the *legal cause*.
See **INTERVENING CAUSE**

PROXY [L. *procurare* / to take care of, to look after; to take over or manage]

The authority to act for another, as through a power of attorney. A signed formal document giving an agent the power to exercise a right in the principal's place, such as the right to vote corporate stock or to act for a unit owner in a condominium. A corporation which solicits *proxies* in advance of a stock vote must also furnish the shareholder with a *proxy statement* containing enough information to permit an informed decision. A *health care proxy* is a formal written agency giving someone the right to make decisions about the care and treatment of another when she becomes physically or mentally incapable to act for herself. A *proxy marriage* is a marriage performed in the absence of the bride or groom; the missing party authorizes someone else to stand in his or her place during the ceremony.

PRUDENT [L. *prudens, prudentis* / foreseeing, discrete, sagacious, cautious, careful, judicious]

Cautious in thought and conduct. Wont to exercise sound judgment in dealing with risks and problems. Thoughtful, sagacious. Managing matters carefully.

In the law of torts, negligence is usually defined as an act which would not have been committed by a *reasonable person with ordinary prudence*. The *prudent man rule* is a rule imposed by all jurisdictions on fiduciaries such as trustees or administrtators. In general, it requires that the fiduciary invest funds entrusted to his care in the manner of "prudent men with discretion and intelligence." In some states, the list of permitted investments is prescribed by statute or regulation.

PRURIENT [L. *prurio, prurire* / to itch or crave]

An unwholesome interest or desire, especially a sexual desire. An obsessive interest in sex. The word is often used in criminal codes or statutes to define material which is obscene and therefore objectionable.

PUBERTY [L. *pubertas* / the age of maturity]

The onset or arrival of sexual maturity, characterized by maturation of the genital organs and the development of secondary sexual characteristics, such as pubic hair. The age at which such maturity occurs.

PUBLIC [L. *publicus (poplicus)* / belonging to the people; in the name of the people; at the expense of all citizens]

The people as a whole; all the people. The entire body of citizens of a state or nation. The people or community at large. The government and its interests. Known or recognized by the majority of citizens. Relating to the interests of the community at large. The word modifies many nouns and generally conveys a sense of universal application, effect or interest. Examples: *public domain; public defender; public figure; public interest; public housing; public policy; public auction; public health; public enemy; public nuisance; public school; public service; public works; public welfare. To go public* describes the act of a corporation in offering its stock or other securities for purchase by the public instead of confining ownership to the original investors. When the stock is issued, it becomes *publicly traded*.

PUBLICI JURIS [L. *publicus* + *ius, iuris* / right or law]

A right or privilege available to all; a public or common right. The rights to light, air and water are all *publici juris*.

PUBLISH [L. *publicare* / to take for public use; to throw open; make public, publish]

To make known generally. To expose to the public. To disseminate an idea or opinion. To manufacture and distribute books, papers, magazines, scripts, documents, printed music, lyrics, and other expressions of ideas or thought. In actions for defamation, to issue a defamatory statement about the complainant to a third party. To declare openly, as *to publish a will*.

PUNISH [L. *punio, punire* / to punish, avenge]

To subject to correction or criticism. To cause to undergo discomfort, pain or loss. To impose a penalty in response to an offense. To penalize in retaliation for the commission of a crime.

PUNITIVE [L. *punio, punire* / to punish]

Inflicting, involving, or relating to punishment. Conveying the sense of penalty or punishment. *Punitive measures* are steps taken to penalize wrongdoers or to redress wrongs. *Punitive damages* are damages in excess of those which compensate a plaintiff for his actual loss or injury. They are designed to punish the defendant for acts of malice, fraud, wilfulness or violence. They are sometimes called *exemplary damages* to show that they are meant to discourage others from committing similar acts.

PURGE [L. *purgare* / to cleanse, wash off, clear away]

To eliminate. To purify or clear of guilt. To clear someone or oneself of a charge or accusation, especially from an order of contempt. Also, to weed out or reject persons who are considered disloyal, reprehensible or unwanted.

PUTATIVE [L. *putare* / to clear up, to settle; to think, consider, speculate]

Assumed to be or to exist. A commonly accepted fact or condition. Considered to be; assumed. A *putative father* is the person commonly accepted as the father of a child. A *putative marriage* is a marriage entered into by both parties without knowledge of any impediment and which is universally accepted as valid.

PYRAMID [L. *pyramid* (from the Greek *pyramis*) / a massive cone-shaped structure having a square base and four ascending triangles which come to a point at the top]

A geometric structure formed by a square base and four ascending triangles coming to a common point at the top. The Egyptian pyramids. Increasing one's stock holdings by buying new shares on margin, i.e., using existing equity to borrow funds for additional purchases. Also, the use of existing equity or capital by corporations to finance the acquisition of other corporations; a group of holding companies controlled by a small group of investors in the principal holding company. Also, an illegal scheme for defrauding investors or purchasers by inducing them to procure other investors or purchasers in exchange for a cash bonus or a discount on their own investments or purchases.

QUA

Whereby, by which route or means. Also, in which way. Also, in the nature of.

QUAELIBET JURISDICTIO CANCELLOS SUOS HABET

No jurisdiction can exceed its limits.

QUAERE   [L. *quaero, quaerere* / to seek, to want to know, to inquire]

An inquiry, a question, the search for an answer. In a legal article or text, the use of this word indicates that the writer is introducing an inquiry into some issue or question. Example: "*Quaere:* What do we mean by the term *proximate cause?*"

QUAERENS NIHIL CAPIAT PER BILLAM

Let the plaintiff recover nothing by his complaint.

QUAESTIO FACTI

A question of fact.

QUAESTIO JURIS

A question of law.

QUALIFICATION   [L. *qualis* / of what sort or kind; having some quality]

A prerequisite or condition. A defined skill, as for a job or office. A limit or boundary.

QUALIFIED, QUALIFY   [L. *qualis* / what kind of, what sort of]

To make less general and more specific. To describe a thing by its essential attributes. To meet a required standard, as for a job or office. To acquire the right to exercise a special power or license, as to *qualify* to practice a medical specialty. In the law, the word often conveys the sense of limitation or restriction. Examples: A *qualified stock option* is a right given to an employee to purchase shares of a corporation under terms that qualify for special treatment under the Internal Revenue Code. A *qualified voter* is a citizen who has satisfied all the requirements for voting. A *qualified acceptance* in the law of contracts is an acceptance of an offer which changes or modifies the terms of the offer. A *qualified endorsement* of a negotiable instrument is an endorsement with non-recourse to the endorser. A *qualifying clause* is a clause in a contract expressing conditions.

QUANTUM   [L. *quantus* / of what size; how great; how much; in what amount]

The measure of. How much? An amount or portion. A fixed, elemental unit of energy; the basis for the quantum theory in physics.

QUANTUM DAMNIFICATUS   [L. *quantus* / how much, how great, at which price, to what extent + *damno, damnare* / to cause loss, damage or injury]

Literally, how great is the damage? This phrase introduced the inquiry by English courts of equity into the extent of the damages suffered by the plaintiff.

QUANTUM MERUIT   [L. *quantum* + *merere* / to deserve, merit, earn]

Literally, as much as is deserved or earned. Originally, this described an inquiry by the equity courts into the value of a plaintiff's goods and services whenever fairness required that a contract between the parties be implied. The requirements for recovery were the rendering of goods or services by the plaintiff to the defendant, the acceptance and use of the goods or services by the defendant, the reasonable expectation of the plaintiff that he would be paid for the goods or services, and the refusal of the defendant to pay. A contract created by implication under the doctrine of *quantum meruit* is called an *implied contract* or a *quasi-contract*. *Quantum meruit* applies also to cases in which part performance under an express contract is given and accepted.

See **QUASI EX CONTRACTUS**

QUANTUM VALEBANT   [L. *quantum* + *valeo, valere* / to be strong, prevail, have worth or value]

As much as they were worth. An inquiry by the court as to the value of goods sold and delivered in the common-law action of *assumpsit*, based on an implied promise by the defendant to pay the reasonable value of goods delivered to and accepted by him,

See **ASSUMPSIT**

QUARANTINE   [L. *quadraginta* / forty. A period of forty days]

In medieval times, a ship which arrived at a port with diseased or infected seamen would be kept in isolation in the port for a period of forty days. Hence, the isolation of humans or animals with contagious or infectious diseases. Under applicable statutes, the authorities have the right to isolate people in their homes, to bar animals from entry into a state or country, and to prevent the docking of ships in port.

QUARE CLAUSUM FREGIT [L. *quare* / why, for what reason + *claudo, claudere* / to shut, close + *frango, frangere* / to break, shatter]

Literally, why did he break (into) the closed area? Why did he violate the enclosure? An early form of common law trespass for wrongful entry upon another's land.

QUASH [L. *cassus* / empty, void, hollow]

To make void, to rescind, annul, vacate or abrogate. To set aside. The court may *quash* an indictment or a subpoena.

QUASI [L. *quasi* / as if, just as, almost as, sort of, approximating, so to speak; about, nearly, almost, like]

In the law, *quasi* is used before other words to suggest that those words are limited and qualified in some respect. The resulting phrase conveys the sense of approximate but inexact similarity. Examples: A *quasi admission* is an admission which is implied from prior inconsistent statements made by a witness, including statements made extra-judicially. A *quasi-judicial* proceeding is one which has all the elements of a trial — submission of evidence, trying the facts, applying the law, etc., — but is conducted by an administrative agency or officer and not by a court. A *quasi in rem* claim is one in which the plaintiff seeks to recover damages against a party who is unreachable for personal jurisdiction, by attaching some of his property.

See **QUASI IN REM**

QUASI CRIMINAL

A proceeding which is sufficiently similar to a criminal trial as to require application and observance of the same procedural *due process* elements, e.g., the right to a statement of the charges, to hear and examine witnesses, to present evidence, etc. Examples: Parole hearings; school disciplinary and expulsion hearings; hearings on complaints of professional misconduct.

QUASI EX CONTRACTUS [L. *quasi* + *ex* / from, out of + *contraho, contrahere* / to bring together, to unite]

A right or obligation growing out of a contract which is implied by the law in order to avoid the unjust enrichment of one party at the expense of another.

See **QUANTUM MERUIT**

QUASI IN REM [L. *quasi* + *in* + *rem, res* / thing, object]

A proceeding which tries the relative rights and interests of some of the parties in a parcel of real property, but not the rights of all the parties to the parcel (the latter is called *an action in rem*). Example of an *action quasi in rem*: an action for partition of interests. Example of *action in rem*: an action to quiet title. Also, jurisdiction by a court over a claim against an individual initiated by attaching his interest in property located within the state. The attachment of property does not confer personal jurisdiction over the individual but does enable the plaintiff to establish his claim against the property attached.

QUERELA   [L. *queror, queri* / to complain]
A complaint in an action; also, the action itself.

QUESTION   [L. *quaero, quaerere* / to seek, search for]
An issue requiring resolution. A point of law or fact on which parties disagree and which is submitted to the court for disposition. A particular inquiry directed to a witness. A matter to be researched or inquired into. A *federal question* is an issue arising under a federal law and which lies within the jurisdiction of the federal courts. A *political question* is an issue that a court will decline to answer on the ground that it falls outside the scope of the judicial function and should be resolved by the executive or legislative branches of government.

QUESTIO VEXATA   [L. *quaestio* / a seeking or searching + *vexo, vexare* / to shake, jostle; to annoy or molest]
A troublesome or difficult question. Used to describe a difficult issue of law confronting the court.

QUIA EMPTORES (STATUTE OF)   [L. *quia* / because, for the reason that + *emptores* / buyers, purchasers]
Literally, because of the buyers. The name for an act passed by Parliament in 1290 which abolished some of the restraints upon alienation or transfer of land that had been imposed under the feudal system.

QUIA IMPOTENTIA EXCUSAT LEGEM
When performance is impossible, the obligation is released.

QUIA TIMET   [L. *quia* + *timeo, timere* / to fear, dread]
Literally, because he fears. A bill in equity submitted by anyone who feared that the threatened action of another would cause him or his property injury or damage. The relief, after a showing of imminent harm, was by injunction or restraint.

QUID PRO QUO   [L. *quis, quid* / anything; what? + *pro* / for, in place of + *quo* / what?]
What thing for what thing? An exchange of something for something else. The mutual consideration between parties to a contract. In cases alleging sexual harassment, the promise or grant of special employment privileges in

exchange for sexual favors, or the threat that employment privileges will be denied or curtailed if the favors are not granted.

QUIET [L. *quies* / rest, repose]

Still, hushed. Silent, not speaking. To eliminate noise. To put at rest. To free from disturbance or contention. An *action to quiet title* is an action to resolve all issues concerning title to property. The court is asked to make a final and binding resolution of all conflicting claims.

QUI FACIT PER ALLIUM FACIT PER SE

Literally, he who acts through others acts for himself. In simple form, this Latin maxim states the essential principle which still controls the law of agency, i.e., a principal who appoints or authorizes an agent to act for him will be bound by the acts of the agent in the performance of his authority.

QUI MANDAT IPSE FECISSI VIDETUR

He who commands (the act) is deemed to have committed it himself.

QUI TACET CONSENTIRE VIDETUR

He who is silent is deemed to consent.

QUI TAM [L. *qui* / who, he who + *tam* / as much as, equally with]

An abbreviation for the Latin maxim, "he sues on behalf of the king as well as in his own right." A *qui tam* action is a civil action brought by an informer for the benefit of himself and the state, to recover part of the penalty or fine exacted for commission by another of an unlawful act, such as in submitting a false claim against the government. After the informer is paid his share, the balance of the fine or penalty belongs to the state.

QUO ANIMO [L. *quo* / what + *animus* / the spiritual; the soul; the heart]

By what intention or motive? What did he intend to do? What motivated him? An inquiry into the defendant's motives.

QUOD COMPUTET [L. *quod* / whereas, the fact that + *computare* / to compute, calculate]

Literally, that he account. Let him acccount. The judgment of the court in an action for an accounting establishing the duty to account but not the amount due. Determination of the latter was referred to a referee or master.

QUOD CUM [L. *quod* + *cum* / with, together with]

Whereas. The phrase used to introduce a pleading or declaration at common law.

QUOD CURIA CONSESSIT
Which the court granted.

QUOD ERAT DEMONSTRANDUM (Q.E.D.) [L. *quod* + *sum, esse* / to be + *demonstro, demonstrare* / to point out, show clearly, prove]
Literally, that which was to be proved. The proposition, issue or question requiring proof.

QUOD ERAT FACIENDUM (Q.E.F.) [L. *quod* + *esse* + *facere* / to do or make]
Literally, that which was to be done.

QUOD NON APPARET NON EST
What is not clear or apparent is deemed not to exist.

QUOD RECUPERET
That he recover.

QUOD VIDE (Q.V.) [L. *quod* / with respect to the fact that, whereas + *vide, videre* / to see]
Literally, which see. A phrase following a portion of text which is used by an author to show that he has used the same words in an earlier portion of the text.

QUO JURE [L. *quo* + *ius, iuris* / right or law]
By what right? What is your authority? A kind of writ which required the plaintiff to state the basis for his claim of title or right.

QUO MINUS [L. *quo* + *minor* / comparative of *parvus* / small, less; by the less; because of the less]
Before a claimant could initiate a claim in Chancery, he had to allege that the defendant's actions were making the plaintiff less able to pay his obligations to the King.

QUORUM [L. *qui* / who, whom (plural)]
Originally, the commission issued to a justice of the peace entitling him to hold court. Also, the number of English justices of the peace who were required to be in attendance before they could lawfully convene. The number of its members required to permit a body — e.g., an appellate court, a committee, a legislative body, a board, the shareholders of a corporation — to conduct business, usually a majority of the whole.

QUOTA [L. *quot, quotus* / how many, which number]

An assigned number, as in an *immigration quota*, which fixes the number of individuals from one country who may enter another country in a given period for purposes of permanent residence. Also, that part or share of a whole which is assigned to each person or thing sharing in the whole, as the share of each insurer in a group of insurers covering a particular risk.

QUOTATION [L. *quot, quotus*]

The publication of bids, offers, or prices. An extract or passage from a text, whether written or spoken. The production before a court or judge of the text of a statute, opinion or other authority in support of a party's position.

QUOTIENT VERDICT [L. *quotus* + *verus* / true, truthful + *dicto, dictare* / to say again]

A verdict which is arrived at when each juror writes down his own assessment of damages, the assessments of all the jurors are totalled, and the total is divided by the number of jurors. *Quotient verdicts* are improper and a basis for mistrial, unless it can be shown that the jury used the resulting number only as one factor in a full discussion of damages and adopted it as fair only after a true consensus of views.

QUO WARRANTO [L. *quo*, plus *warranto* / a word which did not exist in Latin but came into use at common law from the French; the phrase is treated as a Latinism, however]

Literally, by what right or authority? At common law, a writ emanating from the right of the King to inquire into the right of an official to perform an act or of an individual to exercise a license or franchise. A writ which enabled a court to determine whether an official who presumed to exercise some authority was entitled to do so under the law. The writ was intended to prevent the unlawful and unauthorized usurpation of power or authority by public officers. In the law of corporations, *quo warranto* proceedings test whether a corporation was properly formed or has a valid existence, and also whether it has a power it claims for itself. The state in which a corporation doing business may bring a *quo warranto action* to attack the corporate status of the business. Defacto corporations and corporations by estoppel are subject to attack by the state in these proceedings, as are corporations which exceed their powers.

RANSOM   [L. *redimo, redimere* / to recover, redeem]

The money or property demanded or paid in exchange for release of a prisoner or kidnapped person. The collection or receipt of a ransom is a federal crime. In International Law, the consideration paid by one nation to another to recover captured property, such as property seized at sea.

RASURE   [L. *rado, radere* / to scrape, shave, scratch]

The act of removing or extinguishing letters or words from a written instrument by means of scraping, scatching or shaving the surface of the document. The word is narrower than *obliteration*, which is the act of drawing lines or other marks through the letters or words of a document or of destroying or cutting away parts or all of the document; but the distinction is not always observed.

See **OBLITERATE**

RATABLE   [L. *reor, reri* / to reckon, think, judge; a reckoning or accounting; computation]

Anything which can be estimated or scheduled when compared with other objects of the same class or description having a common measure or standard; the result may be different from object to object. In the law of property, a *ratable* is any property which is capable of appraisal or assesment when compared to other property of the same kind or description, usually for purposes of taxation. Taxable property.

RATE   [L. *reri (ratio, ratus)* / a measure, computation or calculation]

The numeric relationship between two things or among a number of things. A measure utilized to compare values or quantities. An amount or charge measured by or based upon another amount. A fixed number by which relative computations are made. Examples: the *rate of interest* is the percentage of the principal loaned which is charged by a lender for the use of its money; the *rate of exchange* is the relative value of one currency against another; the *prime rate* is the lowest rate of interest charged by banks to their most creditworthy customers; the *legal rate* is the highest rate of interest permitted by state statute or regulation.

RATIFY, RATIFICATION [L. *reor, reri* + *facere* / to do or make]

To approve or confirm. To validate or make effective. In the law of contracts, the act of one party in affirming that an action previously taken, whether by himself or by someone acting in his behalf or for his benefit, will bind him, when, in the absence of such affirmation, he would not be bound. For example, a person reaching maturity may *ratify*, and therefore become bound by, an agreement executed during his minority. A principal may later *ratify* and be bound by the action of someone who acted as his agent without his authority. Also, the act of Congress in approving and therefore making effective, a treaty or an amendment to the Constitution.

RATIHABITIO MANDATO COMPARATUR

Ratification is like a command.

RATIO [L. *ratio*; *ratus*, from *reor, reri* / to think, account or compute]

A reasoning or reckoning. A numerical measure, in number, amount or size, of the relationship between two things or among more than two things. A proportion. The number resulting from the division of one number by another.

RATIO DECIDENDI [L. *ratio* (from *reor, reri*) + *decidere* / to cut down, cut off; to settle or arrange.

The reason for a particular decision. A statement of the court's reasons for deciding the case as it did. The basis for the court's judgment.

RATIO EST LEGIS ANIMA

Reason is the soul of the law.

RATIO LEGIS [L. *ratis* / thought or reckoning + *lex, legis* / a covenant; the law or rule]

The underlying principle or reasoning behind a law. The reason or purpose for passing a law. The origin of the modern *rational basis test* under which the courts examine whether a statutory or regulatory classification (based on age, sex, etc.) has a rational basis, i.e., whether the statute or regulation at issue denies equal protection to a class or group under the Constitution, thereby creating a suspect classification.

RATIO LEGIS EST ANIMA LEGIS

The reasoning of the law is (born of) the soul of the law.

RATIONAL [L. *ratio* / calculation, computation (from *reor, reri* / to think, have) an opinion]

Reasonable, supported by sound thought and reason. Conclusions supported by analysis and logic; not arbitrary. A statute or administrative decision is said to have a rational basis if it is not unreasonable or arbitrary and if it bears reasonable support in a legitimate state interest. The courts will not disturb legislative or administrative actions which have a *rational basis*.

RE (IN RE)

In the matter of, concerning. Also a prefix meaning again, anew, back, backwards. With regard to; concerning. Used to introduce a short, summary statement of the subject of a letter, article or text. In the law, used most often before case names. e.g., *In re Able's Estate*, having the same sense as *In the Matter of*.

See **IN RE**

REAFFIRM, REAFFIRMATION [L. *re* / again + *ad* / towards, to + *firmo, firmare* / to strengthen, make firm]

To make certain; to establish or affirm again. The act of an insolvent debtor in agreeing to pay to his creditor a debt which is dischargeable in bankruptcy. A *reaffirmation agreement* is an agreement between a debtor in bankruptcy and his creditors in which the debtor agrees to pay his debts regardless of his ability to discharge them in the bankruptcy. The agreement is usually reached before the bankruptcy court as part of the discharge hearing.

REAL [L. *res* / a thing, object, matter or circumstance]

Actual, true; having a verifiable existence. In the law, the word often relates to and describes land or interests in land: Examples: *real estate* is a synonym for land or *real property*; a *real covenant* is an agreement affecting land. Also, in the law of negotiable instruments, *real defenses* are those defenses available under the Uniform Commercial Code against a holder in due course; e.g., the defense of fraud in the essence. The *real party in interest* is the person who, under the applicable law, has the right to bring an action to enforce the claim, regardless of who will benefit from the litigation. The Federal Rules of Civil Procedure require that every action be brought by the *real party in interest*.

REALIZE [L. *res* / thing, object]

To bring into existence. To make real. To receive the proceeds of one's labor or investment. To convert property into currency, as she *realized* $250,000 from the sale of her house.

REALTY [L. *res*]

A synonym for real estate or real property.

REAPPORTION [L. *re + ad* / towards + *partio, partire* / to share, distribute, divide]

To redivide or realign the members of a legislative body, e.g., the House of Representatives, to reflect changes in population in order to conform to the Constitutional mandate of "one man, one vote". Article 1, Section 2 of the Constitution requires congressional reapportionment at least once every ten years, following the census. The state constitutions also contain provisions for changing legislative district lines to reflect population changes. The federal courts will intervene if a legislative district is apportioned unfairly.

REASON [L. *ratio* (from *reor, reri*) / a reckoning or calculation]

The explanation for an act or deed. A cause, basis or motive. Good sense. To think from premise to conclusion. To be logical. The underlying ground or justification for some action.

REASONABLE [L. *reor, reri* / to think, judge, compute]

Not extreme or excessive. Conforming to standards which are generally considered free of extremes. Fair, proper, sensible, honest, equitable, moderate. Not arbitrary or capricious. Used by lawyers to describe conduct which is generally or socially acceptable under the prevailing circumstances or controlling facts. The *reasonable man test*, a test applied in the law of negligence, asks: "what would a person of ordinary judgment, knowledge and intelligence have done under these circumstances?" *Reasonable doubt* is the threshold of doubt which determines whether an accused in a criminal matter is guilty or not. To convict, the jury must measure the evidence by the standards of prudent men and must find guilt *beyond a reasonable doubt. Reasonable force* is force used in protecting one's person or property which is justified and proper under the facts presented.

See **UNREASONABLE**

REASONABLE ACCOMMODATION

The response which an employer is required to make under the Americans With Disabilities Act (42 USCS § 12101 et seq.) to a disabled employee. The term may include making existing facilities readily accessible to and usable by disabled individuals, and making such other accommodations for them as restructuring of job assignments, acquisition of special equipment, retraining, etc. Failure to supply these accommodations is an act of discrimination under § 12112, unless the employer can demonstrate that the accommodation would impose undue hardship on the operation of its business.

REBATE [L. *re + battuo, battuere* / to beat, knock]

To blunt, reduce the impact of. To return part of a payment. A discount or reduction in the price of goods or services, usually to induce a purchase or as a reward for prompt response to an offer. Also, the refund to a taxpayer of a portion of taxes previously paid.

REBELLION [L. *re* + *bellum* / war; from *bellare* / to wage war; to renew war; to offer resistance]

Defiance of authority. An organized insurrection or attack, usually armed, against a governmental authority. Federal statutes define as a crime any act which incites or assists in a rebellion against the U.S. or its laws.

RECANT [L. *re* + *cantare* / to sing or play]

To renounce or reject. To withdraw a previous statement, such as a statement admitting guilt or complicity made by a suspect to the police. To recall or withdraw prior evidentiary statements.

RECAPTION [L. *re* + *capio, capere* / to take or catch; to seize]

At common law, the act of repossession undertaken personally by an aggrieved party to recover property, goods or personal chattels (including, originally, a wife, child or servant) wrongfully seized by another. Self-help.

RECAPTURE [L. *re* + *capio, capere* / to take or catch]

To take or seize again. To reenact or recall. The act of retaking. In tax law, the recovery by the IRS of a part of the depreciation or other credit previously deducted by the taxpayer on property which the taxpayer has sold or disposed of. In contract law, a *recapture* clause is a provision permitting an adjustment in rates or payment terms when there is a change in circumstances which is unfair to one party. In real property leases, a *recapture clause* enables the landlord to receive a share of the tenant's profits in excess of a fixed minimum rental.

RECEIPT [L. *recipio, recipere* / to hold back, retain, receive, accept]

A written instrument in which a party acknowledges that he has taken possession of an article. A recitation that possession of money or property has passed from one party in a transaction to another, as between seller and buyer. Under the U.C.C., taking physical possession of goods is *receipt* of goods.

RECEIVABLE [L. *recipere*/ to receive]

The right of one party to recover a debt or obligation from another party. A right to payment for goods or services. A seller of goods has a *receivable* from his buyer equal to the agreed price of the goods sold. Examples of receivables: *notes receivable; accounts receivable.*

RECEIVER [L. *recipere* / to receive]

Anyone who receives or is entitled to receive. A *tax receiver* is a governmental official to whom taxes are paid. Also, an agent appointed by a court or judicial officer to gather, take possession and custody of, and administer, the assets of an estate or a debtor. The duty of the *receiver* is to preserve the assets and to prevent loss or damage. Also, in any civil litigation, a person appointed by the court *pendente lite*, to hold and manage the assets which are the subject of the litigation and to distribute them at the end of the litigation as directed by the court. Also, in criminal law, a person who takes possession of stolen property with knowledge that it is stolen or wrongfully obtained.

See **PENDENTE LITE**

RECESS   [L. *re* + *cedere* / to go, move forward]

An interruption in the regular conduct of business for rest or relaxation. A break in the conduct of a trial or hearing. A short interval in which the court suspends business without adjourning. Also, an interval between one session of a continuously sitting legislature and another.

RECIDIVATE, RECIDIVISM   [L. *recido, recidere* / to fall back, recoil]

To fall back; to return to a prior condition. To commit a criminal offense after a period of lawfulness. *Recidivism* is chronic or habitual criminality; also the return to crime after a lapse of time.

RECIDIVIST   [L. *recido, recidere* / to fall back, relapse]

One who falls back or relapses. A habitual criminal. A repeat offender.

RECIPROCAL   [L. *reciproco, reciprocare* / to move backwards; to move both backwards and forwards]

Shared by both sides; mutual. Complementary; a counterpart. A *reciprocal contract* is a bilateral contract. A *reciprocal promise* is a promise given by one party in exchange for a promise by the other. *Reciprocal trusts* are two mutual trusts: in one A is beneficiary of a trust created by B; in the other B is beneficiary of a trust created by A. *Reciprocal Wills* occur when two testators execute wills naming one another as beneficiary.

RECIPROCITY   [L. *reciprocare* / to move back and forth]

Mutuality of treatment and interests. The relationship between two American states in which each extends to citizens of the other certain rights and privileges which would otherwise be limited, restricted or unavailable to them. For example, New Jersey may, but does not, give reciprocity of practice to lawyers licensed in New York in exchange for similar treatment by New York of New Jersey practitioners. All states accord reciprocal driving privileges to citizens of other states who are licensed to drive in their home state.

RECITAL   [L. *recito, recitare* / to read aloud; to read to an audience]

A public performance by an actor, musician or dancer. The introductory words or phrases at the outset of a document, e.g., a deed or contract, explaining the reasons or basis for the document or for the underlying transaction; usually, the recital is preceded by the word *Whereas*. Also, in a pleading, the introductory words preceding an allegation or formal claim.

RECLAIM, RECLAMATION [L. *re* + *clamare* / to call, cry out, shout]

To demand and/or regain possession of a chattel or right. To assert one's right to recover property which was conditionally or mistakenly given to another. To recover goods from an insolvent debtor. To make available for public use an asset which is inaccessible or needs renovation, e.g., a swamp or beach.

RECOGNITION [L. *re* + *cognosco*, *cognoscere* / to know, get to know, become acquainted with]

A sense that something or someone has happened or been met before. Notice or acknowledgment of a thing or condition. In the law, the word means ratification, confirmation or acceptance. Example: An employer who gives *recognition* to a labor union establishes it as the collective bargaining agent for its employees. One country *recognizes* or acknowledges the official status of another country.

RECOGNIZANCE [L. *recognoscere* / to know again, to recall]

A commitment of record before a judge or magistrate in which a defendant promises either that some act will be performed by him or that he will reappear before the court at a specified time, usually, but not necessarily, under penalty of forfeiting a bond or bail. The authority of a federal judge to release an accused before trial on his *personal recognizance* is contained in 18 U.S.C.A. § 3142(b).

RECOLLECTION [L. *re* + *conligo*, *conligere* / to bring together, gather, collect]

Anything recalled to mind. The act of remembering an event or detail. The law of evidence has adopted several rules to assure that the present testimony of a witness reflects his memory of events as closely and accurately as possible. For example, the term *past recollection recorded*, is the doctrine which admits into evidence, as an exception to the hearsay rule, a document such as a police report or a written statement signed by the witness when his memory of events was still fresh and reliable.

RECOMMEND [L. *re* + *cum* / with, together with + *mandare* / to entrust, order, command]

To entrust. To issue a favorable report or comment about. To advise or counsel. To suggest a course to be taken. A testator may *recommend* some act or action by his executor; the recommendation may be treated as the testator's direction. A jury in a criminal case may *recommend mercy* in the sentencing of the defendant, especially in cases involving juvenile defendants who are tried as adults. In the process of applying for admission to the bar, an applicant will ask for the *recommendation* of practicing lawyers who know him.

RECONCILIATION   {L. *re + concilio, conciliare* / to bring together, unite, connect]

The act of restoring friendship and harmony. The elimination or resolution of differences and disagreements. In the law of domestic relations, *reconciliation* is the restoration of normal marital relationships between husband and wife and contemplates a fresh start and a renewed effort to preserve the marriage. Also, in accounting, the word describes the act of adjusting the books and records of a depositor to a statement by his bank to make them mutually and reciprocally accurate.

RECONSTRUCTION   [L. *re + construo, construere* / to heap up, to construct]

To rebuild. To restore to its original state. To improve upon. In patent law, the infringement of a patent by rebuilding and assembling nonfunctional parts or elements. In history, the process of rebuilding the Union of states after the Civil War. Also, the process of recreating as nearly as possible the circumstances surrounding an event, accident or crime.

RECORD   [L. *recordor, recordari* / to remember, recollect]

To write down or otherwise preserve for future reference. An authentic copy or original of a legal document (e.g., a deed or mortgage) deposited with a public official (e.g., the Recorder or County Clerk) as part of a public record of transactions. Any writing memorializing the transactions or proceedings of a public body, as the *record* of a trial, the *Congressional Record*, an *arrest record*. The *record on appeal* consists of all the papers delivered by the trial court to an appellate court to enable it to decide an appeal (the pleadings, motion papers, trial transcript and the judgment or order appealed from). *The attorney of record* in any matter is the attorney who has appeared officially for the client and upon whom all papers must be served.

RECORDATION   [L. *recordari* / to remember]

The act of recording a public document in the public registry or system. Also, the act of the court clerk in entering a jury verdict in the official court records.

RECORDER   [L. *recordari*]

The title sometimes given to the public official who supervises the recordation of public documents. Also, in some jurisdictions, a judge or magistrate in a court of limited jurisdiction generally referred to as the *recorder's court*.

RECORDING ACTS [L. *recordari*]

Recording acts are state statutes governing the recording of public documents such as deeds and mortgages and generally providing that the act of recording constitutes notice to the world.

RECOUP, RECOUPMENT [L. *recupero, recuperare* / to reclaim, recover]

To recover. A claim by the defendant to retain some of the money owed by him to the plaintiff which arises out of the same transaction as the one supporting the plaintiff's claim. An affirmative defense alleging that the defendant is entitled to setoff some part of his obligation to the plaintiff because of a breach by the plaintiff arising out of the same transaction as in the complaint. A counterclaim. Most modern courts will require that claims for recoupment be asserted as compulsory counterclaims.

RECOURSE [L. *re* + *curro, currere* / to run or rush; to run back]

To turn or resort to a source of help or protection. The right of the holder of a negotiable instrument to demand payment from the maker or a prior endorser. (Unless the instrument is drawn or endorsed *without recourse*, in which case the liability of the maker or endorser is limited.) Also, the right of a creditor, promisee or obligee to demand payment from a surety or other person secondarily liable, after default upon an obligation by the debtor, promisor or prime obligor.

RECOVER, RECOVERY [L. *recupero, recuperare* / to reclaim, receive, recover]

To regain a normal condition or state. To make up for; restore. To reclaim. To gain payment of a debt or restoration of property. A legal verdict or judgment in one's favor at the close of a trial or proceeding. The amount of a verdict or judgment, or of the relief obtained by the successful party in an action.

RECRIMINATION [L. *re* + *criminor, criminari* / to accuse, make a charge against]

An accusation in response to another accusation; a retaliatory charge. In a suit for divorce, for example, a charge by a party accused of adultery that the other party has also committed adultery. The effect of charge and countercharge was usually to leave both parties without relief. In those states which have adopted *no-fault* divorce statutes, the defense of *recrimination* has no application.

RECTIFY [L. *rectus* (from *regare* / to direct or rule) / straight + *facere* / to make or do]

To set right, to correct. A party to a contract or instrument which contains a mutual mistake may move to have it *rectified*.

RECUPERATIO [L. *recuperare* / to recover]
Articles and chattels recovered by the plaintiff as the result of a judgment finding a wrongful detention of goods.

RECUSATIO JURIS [L. *recusatio* / refusal, protest + *ius, iuris* / law]
An exception or challenge to a judge based upon the judge's bias or partiality.

RECUSE, RECUSAL, RECUSATION [L. *recuso, recusare* / to object to, refuse]
To remove oneself from participation in a decision because of an actual or potential conflict of interest. To disqualify oneself from sitting as a judge in a particular matter. The process by which a judge, whether in response to a motion by one of the parties or on his own motion, agrees not to preside over a case, usually for reasons of bias or conflicting interest. Also, a court order removing a prosecutor from a case for bias or prejudice against the defendant.

REDEEM, REDEMPTION [L. *redimo, redimere* / to buy back, redeem]
To regain or repurchase as a matter of right. To free from a lien or pledge by payment of a required sum. Used by lawyers in several contexts, all describing the recovery of a property right or interest after satisfying some obligation or debt. Examples: When a mortgagor pays off a mortgage on real property, he *redeems* it free and clear of the mortgage. When a debtor buys property back within the prescribed *redemption period* from a purchaser at a forced sale, he has *redeemed* the property. When a person pays a pawnbroker the amount owed on a particular article and gets it back, he *redeems* it. A corporation *redeems* a note or bond by paying the holder the obligation expressed in the instrument.

REDUCE, REDUCTION [L. *re* / again + *duco, ducere* / to draw from place to place, pull, lead]
To make smaller. To convert into another form, as to reduce a thought to writing. To change a chose in action into a chose in possession, or a claim to judgment, or a right to payment into a security interest. In patent law, the term *reduce to practice* means to demonstrate that an invention has practical use.

REDUCTIO AD ABSURDUM [L. *reduco, reducere* / to draw back, lead back + *ad* / to, towards + *absurdus* / harsh, foolish (from *surdus* / deaf)]
To reason or argue in such a way that an absurd conclusion is inevitable. To carry something to an absurd extreme. To disprove a theory or proposition by showing that if followed logically it will lead to an absurd result.

REDUNDANCY   [L. *redundo, redundare* / to overflow, wash over]

Needless or superfluous repitition. Something that can be eliminated without causing loss or diminution (in meaning). In the law, any part of a legal instrument which is irrelevant to its purpose or meaning. In pleadings, foreign or extraneous matter which is subject to a motion to strike. Also, now, the condition of employees who are not needed and are subject to layoff.

REFER, REFEREE, REFERENCE   [L. *re + fero, ferre* / to bear, carry, bring]

The core word *refer* means to direct one's attention to; to send or dispatch for a particular purpose; to look at or examine, as *to refer* a client to a lawyer or a patient to a doctor. In the law, the word means to submit a case or matter for disposition to a court or tribunal; e.g., *to refer* a motion to the motion part, or a hearing to a *referee*. A *referee* is the person to whom a court *refers* the determination of a particular matter or issue, e.g., to take testimony, render an accounting, or hear and report on specific testimony. A *reference* is the act of the court in assigning a matter to a *referee* or other court officer for determination.

REFERENDUM   [L. *refero, referre* / to carry back, bring back, repeat, refer]

The submission to the electorate at large of a statute, constitutional amendment or constitution for its approval or disapproval. There is no provision in the U.S. Constitution for a public referendum on national legislation or on constitutional amendments. Many of the states, especially the Mountain and Pacific states, do have constitutional provisions for referenda on state-wide and even municipal issues.

REFORM, REFORMATION   [L. *reformo, reformare* / to form or make again]

To change or alter for the better, to improve; to correct or amend. As used in the law, the word *reform* generally applies to the process by which a court may review and determine the true intent of the parties in drafting or executing a legal instrument which contains some error or mistake and then, in effect, to amend the instrument to eliminate the error and express the true intent. The mistake can be a typographical error, a mistake in dates, a mistake in language, etc. *Reformation* is the process by which a court of equity orders amendments or corrections of a document to cause it to correspond with the true intent of the parties. The process is usually allowed where there has been a mistake in fact or a mistake of law with respect to the intended legal effect of the language used in the document. In some cases, *reformation* is applied to undo fraud or misrepresentation.

REFUGE, REFUGEE   [L. *re + fugio, fugere* / to flee, run away]

To provide shelter or protection from danger. A place of safety or protection, as a church or an embassy. A *refugee* is a person who is forced to flee from a place, usually a country, because of persecution or fear of persecution on account of race, color, religious belief, political opinion, or some other oppressive or unreasonable condition.

REFUND   [L. *re* + *fundo, fundere* / to pour, pour out]

To pay back. To return part or all of a payment, e.g., the return by a taxing authority of an overpayment of taxes. Also, to refinance or pay off an existing debt or bond with funds borrowed from another source.

REGALIA   [L. *rex, regalis* / belonging to a king, having the attributes of a king, royal]

All the rights and privileges belonging exclusively to the king or sovereign, e.g., the power of life and death, the power to make war, the power to tax, etc. The emblems and symbols of royalty. Also, the special dress, insignia and adornments indicative of an office, appointment, status or membership.

REGIME   [L. *regno, regnare* / to rule, exercise authority (*regimen* / rule, government)]

An authority or government. A system of rules or principles controlling the conduct of a government. A period of rule by an individual or group, as the *regime* of Henry VIII.

REGISTER (REGISTRY)   [L. *regero, regerere* / to carry back, throw back, pile up, collect, record]

The word has several meanings and uses, all associated with record-keeping. A *register* is a book or written record reciting such public facts as births, marriages and deaths. Also, books or records listing specific classes of legal transactions; examples: *registers* of wills, deeds, patents, copyrights and ships; a *police register*. The *Federal Register* is a daily printed record of federal agency regulations and proposed regulations. The official who is charged with the responsibility for keeping a public record or *register* is also called a *register* or *registrar*. Also, to reenroll, as a voter or student. Also, the formal record kept by a corporation of its shareholders and their addresses.

REGISTERED   [L. *regerere* / to collect, record]

Inscribed in an official book or other record. *Registered securities* are stocks or bonds which have been recorded in the books of a corporation in the name of the owner or holder, whose name also appears on the instrument itself; only the *registered owner* may redeem the security. A *registered trademark* is a mark filed in the U.S. Patent and Trademark Office; filing with the requisite formalities conveys the right to exclusive use of the mark. *Registered voters* are those who have met the qualifications for voting and are listed in a book maintained by the local authorities.

REGISTRAR
>An official recorder or keeper of public or corporate records.
>See **REGISTER**

REGISTRATION   [L. *regerere* / to collect, record]
>The act of entering or inscribing data or information in a public record or register. The act of compiling an official list of similar or related data, e.g., a list of eligible voters. The act of complying with the requirements for entry or admission into a group, e.g., enrollment in a class or school. The act of a corporation or a government agency in recording the names of its bondholders and stockholders and of the purchase and transfers of securities by them. A *registration statement* is the document filed with the Securities and Exchange Commission by every company wishing to offer securities for sale to the public, detailing the financial condition of the company, describing its officers and directors, and offering other relevant material necessary to a decision by the public whether or not to subscribe for the securities.

REGISTRY
>The place where official public records are kept, e.g., the *registry of deeds*.
>See **REGISTER**

REGRESS, REGRESSIVE   [L. *regradior, regredi* / to go back, return, retreat]
>To revert or go back to a less desirable state; to worsen or diminish. A *regressive tax* is one in which the rate of taxation decreases inversely with the level of income, i.e., as the level of income rises, the tax rate falls; it is a tax which falls disproportionately on the less wealthy.

REGULA GENERALIS   [L. *regula* / a straight line, a ruler; a rule or model + *generalis* / universal, general]
>A general rule of the judiciary to regulate the conduct of litigation and the practice of lawyers and litigants. Abbreviated as *Reg. Gen.*

REGULAR   [L. *regula* / a straight line, a ruler; a rule]
>Conforming to a law, rule, model, custom or pattern; orderly, methodical. Adhering to a fixed schedule or procedure; unvarying, normal, routine. Used by lawyers to indicate that an act or practice conforms to the norm or that it is designated to happen at stated intervals. Examples: an act in the *regular course of business* is a commercial transaction executed in the usual manner of a particular business; books and records maintained in the *regular course* by a person with knowledge of the usual transactions of a business may be admitted into evidence as an exception to the hearsay rule. A *regular place of business* is a location at which a business functions permanently, not temporarily or for a special and limited purpose. Other examples: *regular* business

entries; *regular* endorsement; *regular* session. The term *regular on its face* describes court process which is issued by a court with authority to issue it, which conforms in form to the usual process of that court and which reveals nothing which would lead anyone to suspect that it was issued without authority. A *regular session* of a court or legislature is a session occurring in accordance with a fixed schedule.

REGULATE, REGULATION   [L. *regula*]

To govern or control by rule or statute. To bring order to. To fix standards of conduct. The power of a legislature or governmental agency to frame, announce and enforce rules and standards for public conduct. Example: Congress has the power to *regulate* interstate commerce. To carry out its statutes, Congress has created various federal administrative agencies and has given them the power to issue *regulations* which must be drawn from the underlying congressional statute. The FCC, for example, has the power to *regulate* in the area of communications under the Federal Communications Act. A *regulation* is a rule having the force of law, adopted and pronounced by a federal agency with authority to control public conduct and activity in a given area or subject, e.g., aviation, trade practices, securities, etc. The IRS issues *regulations* to interpret and enforce the Internal Revenue Code. State and local agencies may also issue *regulations* to govern activity within their spheres of authority.

REGULATORY (AGENCY)   [L. *regula* / a rule or model]

Possessing the power to issue rules or regulations. Dealing with regulations. A *regulatory agency* is a unit of the executive branch of government which is created by the legislature and authorized to issue and enforce regulations in a particular area of government. Examples: the Federal Communications Commission is the *regulatory agency* empowered to regulate all instruments of public communication; the National Labor Relations Board regulates relationships between employers and unions.

REHABILITATION (REHAB)   [L. *re* + *habilis, habilitas* / manageable, handy, having aptitude]

To restore to a former state; to return to a position of good repute or good health; to improve or better. The word has several meanings. To *rehabilitate* a debtor or insolvent is to restore him to solvency or financial stability. To *rehabilitate* a drug addict or alcoholic is to retrain him to avoid dependency. To *rehabilitate* a witness is to restore his credibility on redirect examination after his credibility has been shaken or compromised on cross examination. To *rehabilitate* a criminal is to restore him to a productive place in society through therapy, job training or other incentive.

REIMBURSE [L. *re* / again + *im* / in + *bursa* / purse]

To pay back. To repay to an empoyee or agent money expended by her for the account of her employer or principal. The right of a surety to recover from the debtor any sums advanced by the surety in satisfying claims against the debtor.

REJECT, REJECTION [L. *re* / again + *iacto, iactare* / to throw, fling]

To cast off or repel. To refuse to accept, as to *reject a delivery* or an appointment. To deny, as to *reject an appeal*. Under the Uniform Commercial Code, a buyer of goods may *reject the goods* for defects or for non-conformity; *rejection* must be made within a reasonable time after delivery or tender and a reasonable opportunity to inspect. *Rejection* constitutes cancellation of the contract.

RELATE, RELATED [L. *re* + *latus* / past participle of *ferre*, to carry back, refer]

To give an account of. To tell or narrate. To have a close connection or common origin, as through birth or marriage. To be closely connected to. *Related goods* are products of one company which, though different, have some common mark or characteristic which stamps them as having the same origin. *Related claims* are claims originating from the same set of facts or circumstances, although based upon different principles of law; e.g., claims of patent infringement and of unfair competition arising from the same facts. Under the Federal Rules of Civil Procedure, *related claims* may be joined in one action.

RELATION BACK [L. *referre, relatus*]

To apply or take effect retroactively. A legal fiction which deems an act to have been completed at an earlier date than the actual date. For example, a document released from escrow is deemed to have been delivered to the recipient on the date it was first deposited in escrow. An amended pleading is deemed to *relate back* to the date of the original pleading, provided it arises out of the same facts, acts, or conduct described in the original pleading.

RELATOR [L. *referre*]

An informer. The informer in a *qui tam* action. A person who has sufficient standing to enable the state or a state official to bring an action in his name; in these cases, the title of the action will read *(State) ex rel. Rogers v. Barton*.

See **QUI TAM; EX RELATIONE**

RELEASE [L. *relaxo, relexare* / to loosen, enlarge, relax]

To set free from restraint or servitude. To discharge from obligation; relieve of a burden. To give up a claim in litigation in exchange for some benefit, such as a cash settlement. To free a prisoner from confinement. The *release of an expectancy* is the assignment of an expectancy interest in property to the grantor or another heir. The court at a pre-trial hearing can *release* the accused on his own recognizance, i.e., his promise or assurance in lieu of bail that he will return and appear personally at the next hearing or trial of the charge against him. A document which is utilized to perfect a *release* is itself called a *release*, e.g., *a general release of claims*; a *release of mortgage*; a *release of curtesy or dower*, etc.

RELEVANT, RELEVANCE, RELEVANCY   [L. *re* + *levare* / to lift or raise up]

To bear on or concern the matter at hand. Tending to prove or disprove a fact or issue requiring determination. Under the law of evidence, the court will admit as relevant any testimony or evidence which proves or disproves a fact at issue, or which tends to prove or disprove facts from which a reasonable inference relating to the issues can be drawn.

RELICT

A widow or widower.

RELICTION   [L. *relinquo, relinquere* / to leave behind]

The action by which a body of water gradually and permanently recedes from the shore leaving land behind; the resultant change in the boundary line between two parcels of land washed by the same body of water.

See **ACCRETION**

RELIEF   [L. *re* / again + *levo, levare* / to raise, lift, make lighter]

The removal of a burden or oppression. A legal remedy; the order or judgment of a court granting a remedy. Examples: *injunctive relief, declaratory relief*, etc. Assistance given to indigent persons by the state or federal government. The help or redress sought by a party who intitiates an action.

RELIEVE   [L. *relevare* / to unburden]

To free from an obligation or burden, as to *relieve a suspect* of the threat of indictment. To remove from office, as she was *relieved of her duties* as school principal. To help, aid, alleviate the pain or suffering of; mitigate the effect upon.

RELIGIO SEQUITUR PATREM (OR MATREM)

The religion of the child follows the religion of the father (or of the mother, as in Israel).

RELINQUISH [L. *relinquere* / to leave behind]

To withdraw or retreat from; to leave behind. To yield control or dominion over. To abandon, give up or surrender (property). Example: an emigrant to another country may *relinquish* his citizenship in the country of his birth.

RELY, RELIANCE [L. *re* + *ligare* / to bind or tie; to tie back; to bind up again]

To have confidence in; to be dependent on; to trust. The law sometimes requires a show of *reliance* before it gives relief. In actions for deceit or misrepresentation, the plaintiff must show *reliance to his detriment* on the representations of the defendant. In actions based on promissory estoppel, the plaintiff must prove that he *relied* on the promissor's promise when he acted.

REM [L. *res* / thing, object, matter, circumstance]

The thing. A transaction. A matter. The subject matter of a trust, i.e., the assets and property held in trust. Also, any thing, object or property against which or concerning which a legal proceeding is begun, including real and personal property.

See **IN REM**

REMAINDER [L. *remaneo, remanere* / to stay behind]

A matter or thing left behind. What is left after a part of the whole is removed. What is left when a larger number is divided by a smaller number which is not a factor of the larger number. An interest or estate in land which will take effect immediately after the expiration of a prior interest created at the same time and by the same instrument; both may be created by deed or by will. A *remainder* is distinguished from a *reversion* in that, a *remainder* must be in a transferee other than the grantor. Also, a *remainder* arises by express or implied act of the grantor, whereas a *reversion* arises by operation of law. Example of *remainder*: I give and devise Whiteacre to my daughter Mary for life, and upon her death, to my son Robert. The interest in Robert is a *remainder*; Robert is a *remainderman*.

See **REVERT**

REMAND [L. *re* + *mandare* / to commit to the charge of another; to entrust. To return to custody; to recharge; to order back]

To send or refer back. The act of an appellate court in sending a case back to the trial court for a hearing on some limited issue or for a new trial or for entry of judgment as directed by the appellate court; also, the act of a court in returning an administrative matter to an agency for further review and determination. Also, the act of the court in returning to custody an accused who was released pending appeal but whose appeal has been denied, or whose *habeus corpus* petition has been denied.

See **REMITTITUR**

REMEDY, REMEDIAL   [L. *re* + *medeor, mederi* / to heal, improve]

A solution. Anything which heals an illness or corrects a wrong. The means to recover or secure a right or to obtain relief from a wrong or grievance. The steps available to a litigant or aggrieved party to obtain relief from commission of a wrong or injury by another party. The acts ordered by a court or administrative agency to enforce a right or to correct a wrong. Examples of *remedies*: compensatory damages; punitive damages; injunctive relief; issuance of a *habeus corpus* petition. An action is *remedial* when it is initiated or effectuated by a legislature, agency or judicial body to provide relief from wrongs or injustices, as from the misapplication of a statute to one group of citizens.

REMISE   [L. *re* + *mittere* / to send, let go; to send back]

To give something up; to release a claim or right; to relinquish. Used in deeds to connote the intent of the grantor to relinquish all his right to the property forever: *I give, remise, release and forever quitclaim . . . .*

REMISSION   [L. *remittere* / to send back, return]

To reduce or abate in intensity or impact. To release from a penalty or forfeiture; to excuse or pardon. The release or discharge of a debt or obligation by the creditor, either by express agreement or by the return or surrender to the debtor of the instrument evidencing the indebtedness. The moderation or termination of a disease.

REMIT   [L. *re* / back, again + *mitto, mittere* / to send, dispatch]

To pay or send payment to; to pay an obligation or demand. To refer or send a case back to a lower court for reconsideration or modification of a judgment. To cancel or relieve of, as to *remit* a fine or penalty. To pardon, forgive or annul. To abate or lessen the impact of a disease.

REMITTER   [L. *remittere*]

Anyone who sends or delivers a payment instrument such as a money order. At common law, the word described the condition under which a later defective title in land was deemed to *relate back* to an earlier valid title.

REMITTITUR   [L. *remittere*]

The process by which the verdict of a jury which is deemed to be excessive is reduced by the court without the consent of the jury. The court has the option to order a new trial limited to the issue of damages, or to condition denial of a new trial on the plaintiff's agreement to a *remittitur*, or lowered verdict, in a stipulated amount. The term *remittitur of record* means the return or *remand* by an appellate court to the trial court of the record and proceedings in a case, to enable the trial court to follow the directions of the appellate court and to conduct a new trial, or to enter judgment in accordance with the decision on appeal, or to take other action consistent with the court's opinion.

See **ADDITUR, REMAND**

REMOTE   [L. *removere, remotus* / to put back, withdraw, remove, move away]

Removed or distant in space, time or degree. The word has many meanings for lawyers. In the law of negligence, a *remote* cause is an unlikely cause, a cause which, as viewed in the ordinary experience of men, could not reasonably have caused the event or effect complained of. In the law of evidence, when no reasonable probative inference can be made from a fact offered in evidence, the evidence will be rejected as *remote*. In property law, an interest which will vest beyond the period permitted under the Rule Against Perpetuities is considered *remote* and therefore violates the Rule.

REMOVE, REMOVAL   [L. *re* + *moveo, movere* / to move, set in motion]

To change the location of; to move from one place to another. To move an action from one court to another, as an action originally brought in a state court to the federal district court; the *removal* will succeed only if the federal court has jurisdiction. Title 28 of the U.S. Code permits removal from a state court to a federal court when diversity of citizenship exists, when the action involves a claim under the Constitution, or when the defendant is a foreign country or agent. In some cases, the court from which the case is *removed* will insist on a *removal bond*. A *removal bond* may also be required of an exporter who removes goods from a warehouse for export. A person may be *removed* from office (i.e., he may be dismissed or his appointment terminated) for good cause. A cloud or infirmity in title may be *removed* by the court in an action to quiet title.

RENDER, RENDITION   [L. *reddo, reddere* / to give back, pay up, deliver]

To give over, furnish, deliver, as a payment. To manifest or depict, as by a drawing or sculpture. To make or do. To melt down. Also, the act of a jury or judge in reaching and announcing a decision. A jury *renders* its verdict when it agrees upon a decision and reports it to the court in the required form. The court *renders* its decision when it first announces it, either orally in open court or in a written memorandum or opinion filed with the clerk of court. The court's judgment is *rendered* when it is first announced. It is *entered* when a clerk records it in an official record.

RENEW, RENEWAL   [L. *re* / again + *novus* / new, young]

To make new again. To rejuvenate, restore or revive. To restore a right, as to *renew a judgment* (e.g., to extend the statute of limitations). To do again, as to *renew an objection* at trial. *Renewal* is the act of restoring or starting again, as to *renew* a cause of action, a contract, or a debt (e.g., by executing a new promissory note). Also, the act of rebuilding an area of a city to eliminate decay and neglect; the *renewal* is generally done by subsidized private investors or by a governmental authority.

RENOUNCE, RENUNCIATION   [L. *re* + *nuntio, nuntiare* / to announce, to tell]

To repudiate. To refuse to observe or follow. To give up or surrender a right or privilege, such as one's citizenship. To waive a legal right. To repudiate or disavow a will, e.g., the act of a widow in *renouncing* the provisions of her husband's will and claiming her statutory rights instead. Under the Uniform Commericial Code, a person may expressly *renounce* his rights under a negotiable instrument.

REO ABSENTE   [L. *reus* / a party to an action; a defendant + *absesse* / to be absent]

In the absence of the defendant. Because the defendant is absent.

REORGANIZE, REORGANIZATION   [L. *re* + *organum* / an implement or instrument (from the Greek)]

To change, repair, convert in form or substance to a different state. To rearrange. To cause a business to change its methods or structure, including its finances or ownership. The rehabilitation or restructuring of a company's finances under the Bankruptcy Code through the intervention of the bankruptcy court. A *business reorganization* may take the form of a merger with or into another company, the acquisition of another company, a recapitalization, a transfer or sale of assets, etc.

REPARATION   [L. *reparo, reparare* / to renew, repair, restore]

To make amends for a wrong or injury. The act of compensating another in money or property to restore him to his rightful status or position. The act of a defeated nation in paying for the damage inflicted on another nation or group of nations by its acts of hostility or warfare, e.g., *reparations* paid by Iraq after the Gulf War.

REPATRIATION   [L. *re* + *patria* / fatherland]

The act of returning to one's country of origin or citizenship. Also, the return of profits on foreign investments or of other objects to their country of origin, e.g., the return of a stolen work of art.

REPEAL   [L. *re* + *pellere* / to strike, drive away, dislodge]

To revoke or recall. To render void or inapplicable. To annul. An amendment to the Constitution may be *repealed* by following the same steps as are required for adoption of an amendment. A franchise or license may be *repealed* by the proper authorities. A statute may be *repealed* by the legislature which passed it originally.

REPLEVIN   [Late L. *plebere* / to pledge]

An action to recover property from someone who wrongfully possesses the property, as well as damages for the taking. A writ directing the sheriff to seize property held wrongfully.

REPLICATION   [L. *replico, replicare* / to fold back, to turn over, to review]

The act of reproducing or creating a replica of an object or idea. At common law, the name given to the pleading interposed by the plaintiff in response to the defendant's answer. A *general replication* was in effect a general denial of defendant's allegations; a *special replication* pleaded new matter in response to issues raised by the defendant.

See **REPLY**

REPLY   [L. *replicare* / to review]

The response by a plaintiff to an allegation, plea or counterclaim by the defendant. A *reply brief* is a memordandum submitted by the plaintiff in support of his reply, or, more loosely, any memorandum of law in response to a memorandum submitted by an adversary.

REPORT   [L. *re + porto, portare* / to bear, carry, bring; to bring back]

A statement or review. To carry and deliver a message. To account for. To initiate a charge or challenge. To be present for duty, as by a soldier. To deliver the judgment or decision of a court or administrative agency. A statement made following an inquiry or investigation, as by an agency or commission, setting forth its findings of fact and conclusions and, sometimes, its recommendations. A formal statement by persons with responsibility to account for their actions, as by the board of directors of a corporation or the treasurer of an institution or company.

REPORTER   [L. *reportare* / to take or carry back]

Anyone who reports, as by a *newspaper reporter* who writes about the news of the day. An official authorized to release and publish the decisions and opinions of a court. The publication in which the official record of a court's decision or opinion is kept and published. Anyone who transcribes and records the text of a speech or the conduct of a meeting.

REPOSE (STATUTE OF)   [L. *re + pausare* / to end, stop; to rest]

Any statute which imposes a time limit on a cause of action. A *statute of repose*, unlike a statute of limitations, imposes a bar to an action at the end of a fixed period of time specified in the statute, regardless of the date of injury or offense. The period covered by a statute of limitations, on the other hand, begins only when an injury or offense has occurred. Example of *statute of repose*: a statute limiting the time after *filing of his plans* during which an architect may be sued for negligence, regardless of the date of injury or harm to the claimant.

REPOSSESS, REPOSSESSION [L. from *re*, plus *possido, possidere* / to take possession of, to occupy]

To regain control, possession or custody of property, especially of real property, after a default in payment of an obligation, such as the obligation to pay rent. To recover property or goods sold or financed in installments if an installment is not paid.

REPRESENT [L. *repraesentare* / to bring back the memory of, to represent]

To substitute for. To act in the place of; to fill the role of. To assume responsibility for the affairs of another. A lawyer *represents* his client; an agent *represents* his principal; the N.L.R.B. conducts *representation* elections to determine whether a union *represents* a majority of the workers. In another sense, *to represent* means to state facts or opinions which are intended to influence the opinions or actions of others.

REPRESENTATION [L. *representare* / to present again]

A likeness or image. A statement made to influence conduct or thoughts. In the law of contracts, a *representation* is any act or statement of fact made to induce another either to perform some act or to refrain from performing it. In the law of torts, a *false representation* is a statement which is known by the maker to be false and which induces conduct or action by the party to whom the representation is made, to his detriment. Also, the act of serving in a legislature or other body as the spokesmen for a group of persons, such as the voters in an election district.

REPRESENTATIVE [L. *repraesentare* / to present]

One who acts for another. An agent who is given authority to act for her principal. One who is selected by a group of voters to represent and act for them in a legislative body; a member of the U.S. House of Representatives. Anyone who assumes the administration of an estate. Anyone named in a class action lawsuit to act for the other members of his class.

REPRIEVE [L. *reprehendo, reprehendere* / to seize, hold back, detain]

Temporary relief from suffering or trouble. To give a temporary delay of punishment to a prisoner, e.g., a delay in sentence or incarceration. To put off the execution of a prisoner condemned to death pending judicial or administrative review. The word suggests only a *delay*, not a permanent change or modification in sentence.

REPRIMAND   [L. *reprimo, reprimere* / to hold back, restrain, frustrate]

Severe or formal criticism. A formal censure or criticism announced by a person or body in authority reciting some lapse or impropriety in the conduct of an individual subject to its authority. Examples: the *reprimand* of an attorney by a disciplinary committee for a violation of one of the disciplinary rules; the *reprimand* of an Army officer by his superior officer for conduct unbecoming his office or rank.

REPRISE, REPRISAL   [L. *reprehendere* / to seize, hold back, detain]

An act committed in retaliation for another act considered wrong or injurious. The action of one country in response to the belligerent or inhumane act of another country, e.g., economic sanctions imposed by the U.S. against countries suspected of harboring terrorists, or the bombing by NATO of Serbia to discourage the torture and dispersal of ethnic minorities.

REPROBATA PECUNIA LIBERAT SOLVENTEM

The effect of money tendered and refused is to release the person who tendered.

REPUBLIC   [L. *res* / thing, object, matter, affair + *poblicos, publicus* / belonging to the people]

A system of government in which the ultimate authority rests in all the people, characterized by legislative bodies and chief executives, (usually called *presidents*), elected by the people at regular and stated intervals and subject to fixed and definable rules of law.

REPUBLICATION   [L. *res* + *publico, publicare* / to make public, throw open, restate]

The reiteration or re-execution of a will which was previously revoked or cancelled. The second publication of a will. *Republication* of a will may be accomplished by a valid codicil. Also, the second or subsequent publication of a book or other matter.

REPUDIATION   [L. *repudio, repudiare* / to reject, disdain]

To refuse to accept; to reject; to refuse to acknowledge an obligation or pay a debt. To disavow or disclaim. In the law of contracts, a *repudiation* is a refusal, or manifest unwillingness or inability, to perform or acknowledge an obligation under an agreement, evidenced before the time for performance has arrived; the refusal may be manifested by words or deeds. The other party may treat the *repudiation* either as an abandonment of the contract or as a breach entitling him to sue for damages. A *repudiation* is sometimes called an *anticipatory repudiation*.

REPUGNANT   [L. *repugno, repugnare* / to fight against, reject, resist]

Hostile; causing distaste or dislike. In the law, two statements, provisions or texts are *repugnant* to each other if they are inconsistent with, or negate or contradict, each other. Example: two inconsistent clauses in a contract, deed or statute. A *repugnant verdict* is a verdict which cannot stand because of a manifest inconsistency or error in the jury's findings. A client or its interests may be so *repugnant* to a lawyer as to prompt an application for withdrawal to the court. Withdrawal permits the client to obtain more sympathetic representation by another attorney.

REPUTE, REPUTATION   [L. *reputo, reputare* / to count back, compute, estimate]

The qualities by which a person is judged by the people who know or know of him. The word is often used interchangeably with the word *character*, but strictly speaking, a person's character is the sum of what he is, whereas his *reputation* is the sum of what the world thinks or says he is. Evidence as to character or *reputation* may be used to impeach or support the evidence of a key witness. The licensing authorities in each state inquire into the *character and reputation* of applicants for the bar before permitting admission to practice.

REQUEST   [L. *re + quaero, quarere*/ to seek, search for]

To express a desire for. To ask or beseech. To make a demand for some action or relief, as to *request an adjournment*, payment of a debt, or performance of an obligation. A *request for admissions* is a written demand by one party upon another asking that party to admit or deny matters relevant to an action. A *request for instructions* is a request by one party to a judge to include the party's instructions in the judge's charge to the jury. A *request for production* under the Federal Rules of Civil Procedure is a request by one party to another to produce specified documents for inspection or to permit inspection of specified premises.

REQUIRED, REQUIREMENT(S)   [L. *re + quaero, quarere* / to ask for, seek, search for]

Anything essential to something else; a condition or necessity. In the law, a *requirements contract* is an agreement under which one party promises to deliver all the goods required by the other party for a stated price and for a fixed period of time, and the other party agrees to purchase all such goods from the first party exclusively. The *required records doctrine* provides for prosecutorial access to business records kept in the ordinary course of business, free of the assertion by any individual of the privilege of self-incrimination.

REQUISITION [L. *requarere*/ to request, ask for]

The act of demanding that something be furnished. A demand by the military upon civilians to furnish food and lodging to troops. Any taking of private property by the government or its agencies. A formal demand by the governor of one state to the governor of another to surrender a fugitive or escapee, or by one country to another.

RES

Thing, object, matter, subject matter. Anything which is the subject matter of litigation.

See **REM, IN REM**

RES ACCESSORIA SEQUITUR REM PRINCIPALEM

Accessory objects follow the principal object.

RES ADJUDICATA

See **RES JUDICATA**

RESCIND, RESCISSION [L. *re* + *scindo, scindere* / to cut, tear apart, rend]

To withdraw or take back, as an offer. The act of canceling, repealing or abrogating some act. In the law of contracts, the act of avoiding or annulling a contract or promise. The effect of *rescission* is to make the contract null and void at and from its inception, i.e., as though it had never existed. It is different from termination, which is effective at the date of termination. *Rescission* may be effectuated by agreement of the parties, by judicial decree or by unilateral notice based upon fraud, mistake, breach or illegality. Also, an action in equity to declare a contract void (and therefore relieve the complaining party of performance) because of the fraud of the other party or because of mutual mistake, impossibility or illegality.

RES COMMNUNES [L. *res* / thing + *communis* / general, common, public]

Those things which are the inalienable property of all citizens or are reserved for the common good. Property which can be owned or usurped by no one person, including the sovereign. These include air, light and water.

See **RES PUBLICAE**

RES CORPORALES [L. *res* / thing + *corpus, corporalis* / of the body]

Tangible property.

RESCRIPT [L. *re* + *scribo, scribere* / to draw, engrave, write]

To write again. The reponse of a Roman emperor to an inquiry or petition. A written order from a judge to the court clerk regarding the disposition of a case. The written decision of an appellate court directed to the lower court, announcing and explaining its decision on appeal. The short unsigned opinion of an appellate court.

RESCUE [L. *re* + *excutio, excutere* / to shake out, to search, investigate, find]

To free from confinement or from risk or danger. To free from arrest or imprisonment, as a hostage or a prisoner of war.

RESCUE DOCTRINE

This is a two-pronged legal doctrine. The first prong states that a person who commits a tort upon another person will be liable for the injuries not only to that person but also to anyone who comes to the aid or rescue of the tortfeasor's victim. The second prong states that a rescuer will not, as a matter of law, be charged with contributory negligence, unless he is reckless or rash. The doctrine is sometimes called the Good Samaritan Doctrine.

See **SAMARITAN**

RES DERELICTA [L. *res* + *derelinquo, derelinquere* / to abandon, forsesake, leave behind]

Any property which has been abandoned by its owner.

RESERVATION [L. *re* + *servare* / to protect]

To withhold or retain an interest or right in an object or asset at the moment of its transfer to another. In the law of property, a *reservation* in a deed is a provision under which the grantor keeps for himself some right or interest which did not exist before the transfer and which is defined and created by the deed itself; it is an exclusion from the right or interest conveyed to the grantee and may be a temporary interest or a permanent interest. For example, a grantor may convey the fee title to a parcel of land but *reserve* for himself and his heirs an easement over the land. A *reservation* is also the act of a court in withholding its decision on an application, such as a motion, until some later time. Also, a tract of land set aside by government for a public purpose, e.g., a national park or an Indian *reservation*.

RESERVE [L. *re* + *servo, servare* / to watch over, to protect, to keep]

To set aside; to retain for use at a future time; anything stored or set aside for future consumption. The word has many meanings to lawyers, among them, a fund set aside to provide for future contingencies and expenses, as in the maintenance of property, and sums set aside by an insurance company to cover future claims and losses. A *bad debt reserve* is an amount set aside by a company and listed on its balance sheet, to reflect its estimate of accounts receivable which may prove uncollectible. A *depletion reserve* is a reserve set aside by businesses with respect to assets of decreasing value, such as oil wells or coal mines. Some businesses, e.g., banks and insurance companies, are required by law to set aside *cash reserves* to protect against future losses. In general accounting practice, a *reserve* is set aside and listed in the balance sheet of a business whenever a negative contingency or result may be reasonably anticipated. A *reserve price* at an auction is the lowest price that will be accepted by the auctioneer as a bid.

RES FUNGIBILES   [L. *res + fungor, fungi, functus* / to perform, execute, undergo]

Fungible things. Things which are essentially the same as each other or indistinguishable from each other. Objects of such a nature that one may be replaced by another without raising an issue or controversy as to its essential similarity. Things that can be counted, numbered or weighed together and then be replaced by the same measure of similar objects without the need to identify any single object. Examples: peas, corn, wheat, coal, coins of the same denomination, etc.
See **FUNGIBLE**

RES GESTAE   [L. *res + gesto, gestare* / to carry, bear, perform]

All those matters, facts, statements, acts and events which tend to explain or clarify a point or fact at issue in a litigation. Those matters which are inherent in or essential to an occurrence or event. A *res gestae* witness is a witness who has experienced an event or act at issue by his own senses and can help the factfinder to find the truth by his testimony. *Res gestae* refers to any spontaneous declaration or statement made at the same time as, or immediately after, an event, by a victim or a witness, under circumstances which support truth and reliability; these statements, which are now generally referred to as *spontaneous declarations*, are admissible into evidence as an exception to the hearsay rule.

RESIDE, RESIDENCE, RESIDENCY   [L. *re + sido, sidere* / to sit down, stop, settle down]

To dwell permanently in a place. The place in which a person lives over a sustained period, not temporarily. A building used as a home. The place in which a business or corporation has its office or conducts its business. The word is sometimes used interchangeably with the word *domicile*, but the two are not the same. A *domicile* is a person's legal home, i.e., the place which he regards as his principal residence and to which he intends always to return. A person may have two *residences* but only one *domicile*.
See **DOMICILE**

RESIDUARY   [L. *residere* / to remain]

Describes rights or assets which remain behind after others are disposed of. Examples: A *residuary bequest* is a bequest of that part of an estate which is left after debts and administrative expenses are paid and other legacies and gifts are made. A *residuary clause* is the provision in a will which disposes of all that is left in the estate after debts, expenses and other gifts and bequests. The *residuary estate* is all the property and assets left in a testator's estate after debts and expenses have been paid and specific gifts, bequests and devises have been satisfied.

RESIDUE, RESIDUAL   [L. *residere* / to rest, remain]

To be left behind. Anything that remains after the removal of other things. That part of a testator's estate which is left after all debts and expenses are paid and after all legacies are satisfied. Residuals are payments due for performance of a script or an actor's part following the first performance, as for a TV show. A claim which is left after all prior claims have been paid. *Residual powers* are those powers retained by a governmental body after it has assigned or delegated certain enumerated powers to another body, e.g., the residual powers of the states after the Constitutional grant to Congress of enumerated powers. *Residual value* is the value remaining in an asset after all depreciation allowances have been used up.

RESIDUUM   [L. *residius* / left behind, remaining]

Anything left behind; anything left over or undisposed of. Synonymous with *residuary estate*. The *residuum rule* is an outmoded rule requiring that the decision or order of an administrative agency be supported by some evidence other than legally inadmissible hearsay, i.e., evidence which could survive judicial review under traditional rules of evidence.

RES IMMOBILES   [L. *res* + *immobilis* / immoveable]

Things which are fixed in place and therefore immovable, e.g., land, buildings, fixtures.

See **FIXTURES**

RES INTEGRA   [L. *res* + *integro, integrare* / to complete, make whole]

Anything new and novel. In legal writing, the phrase refers to a novel issue, an undecided question, a case of first impression.

See **RES NOVA**

RES INTER ALIOS ACTA   [L. *res* + *inter* / between, among + *alios* / other, different + *acta*, from *ago, agere* / to set in motion, drive]

Anything involving another place, person or thing than the relevant one; not related or relevant; concerning other matters. In the law of evidence, the doctrine which makes irrelevant and therefore inadmissible, evidence relating to a person extraneous to the action, or to a place other than the place at issue, or to a time not relevant to the acts involved in the litigation.

RES IPSA LOQUITUR [L. *res* + *ipsa* / self, itself + *loquor, loqui* / to speak]
   The thing speaks for itself. A tort doctrine, embedded in a rule of evidence, which enables the trier of facts to infer negligence on the part of the defendant when the following factors are present: there is an accident; the accident would not reasonably have occurred without negligence by someone; the accident was caused by an agency or instrument within the exclusive control of defendant; and the plaintiff did not contribute to the accident, either voluntarily or through his own negligence. If these elements are present, a motion for summary judgment by the defendant will be denied. The rule shifts the burden of proof from the plaintiff to the defendant, who has to present evidence rebutting the presumption that the accident was caused by his negligence or that the instrumentality causing the accident was in his exclusive control. The phrase is often shortened to *res ipsa*.

RES JUDICATA [L. *res* + *iudico, iudicare* / to judge, decide]
   Literally, the thing has been decided; the matter has been adjudged. A doctrine which dictates that matters litigated between the parties in one action or proceeding may not be litigated again between the same parties; i.e., once a final judgment on the merits has been rendered by a court of competent jurisdiction, it is conclusive as to the parties involved and the matters litigated.
   See **COLLATERAL ESTOPPEL**

RES JUDICATA PRO VERITATE ACCIPITUR
   A matter which has been tried and adjudicated should be accepted as true.

RES NOVA [L. *res* + *novus, nova* / new, fresh]
   Literally, a new thing. In the law, a *res nova* is an undecided issue or question, a case of first impression. The term *res integra* is sometimes used instead, with the same meaning, especially in England.
   See **RES INTEGRA**

RESOLUTION [L. *resolvo, resolvere* / to loosen, untie, dispel, cancel, end]
   The act of reducing complex issues into simpler ones; to make a question clear and understandable. Also, the formal statement of a decision or ballot, e.g., the *resolution* of a committee or board. In the law, the formal expression of the will or opinion of a legislative body on a particular matter or subject, having an effect just short of a statute or law. Example: a resolution of Congress asking the President to take some executive action or expressing its opposition to some action by the President. Also, the formal expression of some action or decision of the board of directors of a corporation or of any social or political organization.

RESOLVE [L. *re* + *solvo, solvere* / to loosen, release]

To find a solution for; bring into focus; determine. To make a decision about. To decide formally, e.g., by resolution or vote. To clear up or succeed with. To reach a legally binding decision.

RESPONDEAT SUPERIOR [L. *respondeo, respondere* / to match, agree with, answer, reply + *superus, superior, supremus* / upper, higher, standing above]

Literally, let the one in higher position or authority reply; let the master respond. A doctrine of agency law, which assigns responsibility and liability to the employer or principal for the acts of her employee or agent, including negligence, provided the employee or agent is acting within the scope of his employment or agency. Because the doctrine is based on agency, the employer is not liable when the employee's act is beyond the scope of his employment.

RESPONDENT [L. *respondere* / to answer or reply]

Literally, anyone who responds or who must respond. In any proceeding originated by the filing of a petition, the party required to respond to the petition is called the *respondent*. In appellate practice, the designation given to the party who received a favorable judgment in the court below and is now required *to respond* to the adversary's appeal.

RESPONSA PRUDENTUM [L. *responsa* / answer + *prudentia* / knowledge; wisdom]

The opinion of persons learned in the law.

RESPONSIBLE [L. *respondeo, respondere* / to reply, give an answer to]

Liable or answerable for; legally accountable. Having the ability to meet or discharge an obligation. Trustworthy; possessing integrity and/or other desirable qualities. A *responsible bidder* is a bidder who has the financial resources to complete the job he bids on, and also the requisite knowledge, training and experiences. Also, subject to review and assessment.

RESPONSIBILITY [L. *responsum* (from respondere) / to reply]

An obligation or duty. The state of being accountable or answerable for one's actions or standards. In the law, the state of being answerable for a debt, judgment, accounting or other measure of duty. The need to make restitution for a deed or injury; a liability. Also, the ability to choose between right and wrong.

RESPONSIVE [L. *respondere*]

Anything given in reply. In the law, a *responsive* pleading is a pleading which responds on the merits, i.e., to the substance of a pleading interposed by the other party, as opposed to a motion to dismiss or to set aside the pleading for some procedural or jurisdictional defect.

RES PUBLICAE [L. *res* / thing + *poblicus, publicus* / of the people; in the name of the people]

Anything that belongs to the public at large, as air, light and water.

See **RES COMMUNES**

RESTITUTIO IN INTEGRUM [L. *restituo, restituere* / to replace, restore + *in* / in + *integro, integrare* / to complete, make whole]

Restoration of a party to his condition or position before the injury or wrong complained of. The principle that a court ordering rescission of a contract should restore the parties as closely as possible to their state or condition before the contract was executed. The restoration of a thing to its original state or in its entirety. In Admiralty Law, the doctrine which provides for full and complete compension to the owner of a vessel after a loss or damage, to enable him to restore the vessel to its original condition.

RESTITUTION [L. *restituere* / to restore]

The act of returning something to its former condition or to its rightful owner. Compensation for an injury or wrong. Underlying the doctrine of *restitution* is the law's interest in preventing *unjust enrichment*. In equity, the court will return to the plaintiff the property, or the value, by which the defendant was unjustly enriched. In contract law, the defendant who commits a breach will be required to return to the plaintiff the value which the plaintiff conferred upon him before the breach; the measure of damages is the value of the benefit to the defendant, not the cost to the plaintiff. In tort law, *restitution* is the value of the plaintiff's actual damages. In criminal law, the federal government and many of the states have adopted *restitution statutes* under which the court may order *restitution* (reimbursement or indemnification for damage or injury to the victim) in lieu of, or in addition to, any other penalty or sentence imposed on the defendant; see 18 USCS § 3663.

RESTORE, RESTORATION [L. *restaurare* / to erect, repair (from *abstare* / to stand)]

To return an object lost or stolen. To revise or correct. A lost document may be *restored* by executing a new one; upon application by a party to a lost document, the court may order *restoration*. The *restoration of a party to the status quo (ante)* is the object of an action for rescission, i.e., the court will restore the plaintiff to the position he occupied before entering into the contract.

RESTRAIN, RESTRAINT [L. *restringo, restringere* / to bind, bind tightly, confine]

To hold back by force or decree. To prevent from acting. To restrict a person's movements or freedom. A *temporary restraining order* (sometimes referred to as a *TRO*) is an order of a court, usually issued *ex parte*, that forbids the respondent from committing some act until the court can determine whether or not to issue a temporary (*pendente lite*) or permanent injunction. Example of a restraining order: an order to a husband not to harass his wife or children until a full custody hearing. The word *restraint* is used by lawyers in several contexts. A *restraint on alienation* is a provision in a conveyance instrument that inhibits or prohibits the transferee from selling or disposing of the property conveyed; these *restraints* are generally void as a matter of public policy. A *restraint of trade* is an agreement or combination which has the intent or tendency to stifle or affect competition in the otherwise free commercial market; these *restraints* violate the Sherman Antitrust Act. A *prior restraint* is any action taken by a government official or by statute to control the contents or text of any expression before its publication. Any effort to control the dissemination of information protected by the First Amendment of the Constitution is a *prior restraint* if it is imposed before a judicial hearing to determine whether it qualifies for First Amendment protection. *New York Times Co. v. United States (1971)*. An *unlawful restraint* occurs whenever one knowingly confines, or interferes with the free movement of, another, without lawful authority.

RES TRANSIT CUM SUO ONERE

Property passes from one to another along with its burdens.

RESTRICT, RESTRICTION [L. *restringere* / to bind or confine]

To place conditions upon; to limit or control. To place limits upon the use or enjoyment of a property or asset. A regulation or rule that has the effect of controlling or curbing conduct. A limitation or condition upon the use or enjoyment of land, usually contained in the instrument of conveyance or in an agreement among the interested parties. These limitations are called *restrictive covenants*.

RESTRICTIVE [L. *restringere*]

A provision or condition which limits the use of; places conditions upon; or prohibits. A *restrictive covenant* is a provision in a deed, lease or contract limiting the use or enjoyment of a parcel of real property, e.g., a covenant preventing the grantee or tenant from using the property for commercial purposes. Covenants restraining the transfer of property interests on the basis of race are unenforceable under the Constitution. A *restrictive endorsement* is an endorsement upon a negotiable instrument which limits further endorsement except as specified by the endorser; the endorsement of a check "for deposit only" is a *restrictive endorsement*.

RESULT, RESULTING [L. *resultare* / to jump back, rebound]

A consequence, issue or conclusion. The end product of a process. The final outcome, decision or judgment in a law suit is called the *result*. The word *resulting* means proceeding from, a consequence of. Example: A *resulting trust* is a trust imposed by law in circumstances in which the holder of legal title was clearly meant to hold the property for the benefit of another. *Resulting powers* are all those powers reserved to the federal government under the Constitution.

RETAIN [L. *retineo, retinere* / to hold back]

To hold back, to keep possession of. To have in mind or memory. To pay for the services of; to employ. To engage the services of a lawyer. *Retained earnings* are the income of a business which is transferred to the capital account after payment to creditors and distribution to stockholders.

RETAINAGE [L. *retinere* / to hold back]

That which is retained or held back. In construction contracts, the builder will often hold back from his contractor(s) at various stages of the construction, and when the construction is completed, a part of the contract price, in order to assure that all subcontractors and laborers are paid and that no defects in construction manifest themselves. This hold-back is called *retainage*.

RETAINER [L. *retinere*]

The act of a client in employing the services of a lawyer. Also, a sum or fee paid to a lawyer when his employment begins. A *special* or *limited retainer* is a sum paid for a single negotiation or matter. A *general retainer* is money paid for representation in all or several matters over a period of time, e.g., a year.

RETAINING [L. *retinere*]

The act of holding back. A *retaining lien* or *attorney's lien* is the right of a lawyer to hold and keep papers, money and property of his client which come into his possession, until his fees and charges are paid. The term is sometimes distinguished from the attorney's *charging lien*, which attaches to money or property recovered on behalf of the client through the lawyer's services, e.g., from a judgment or settlement, whether or not the attorney obtains possession of the proceeds.

RETALIATE, RETALIATORY [L. *re + talio* / retaliation]

To repay in kind; get even with; redress; avenge; get revenge. *Retaliatory* action or conduct is a wilful response to conduct which is deemed objectionable. A *retaliatory eviction* is an action by a landlord to remove a tenant who has complained about services or taken action against the landlord. A *retaliatory statute* is a law passed by one state to impose the same burdens upon citizens of another state, e.g., fees, taxes, penalties, professional licensing restrictions, as are imposed upon its citizens by that other state. A *retaliatory discharge* is the discharge of an employee in specific response to some action by the employee, e.g., a complaint by the employee to the authorities of price-fixing or criminal activity by the employer.

RETIRE [L. *re* + *traho, trahere* / to pull, draw, carry along]

To withdraw. To retreat. To seek privacy. The act of a jury in withdrawing into a restricted area for its deliberations. The act of a government in withdrawing a debt issue from the market, e.g., by recalling or paying off a bond issue; or of a corporation in buying back its stock. Also, to withdraw permanently from work or employment.

RETRACT, RETRACTION [L. *re* + *traho, trahere* / to pull, drag; to draw back, drag back, bring back]

To recant or disavow a prior position or statement. In the law of contracts, to disavow, negate or withdraw an offer before the offeree accepts or acts in reliance upon the offer. In the law of libel, the formal renunciation and disclaimer of a defamatory statement. A suspect may *retract* his statement or confession to the police after consultation with his attorney.

RETRAXIT [L. *retrahere* / to pull back]

Literally, he has taken (it) back. The voluntary withdrawal or dismissal in open court of a claim or cause of action by the plaintiff, resulting in a permanent loss of the claim. Under the federal rules, this is the same as a voluntary dismissal with prejudice.

RETREAT (DUTY TO) [L. from *retrahere*]

The process or act of pulling or drawing back. Voluntary withdrawal from risk or danger. The forced movement of troops back from a more forward position. In a minority of states, a person threatened with violence or risk to his person or life must at least attempt to *retreat* before he may resort to deadly force in response to the threat. The obligation to *retreat* is embodied in the Uniform Penal Code, § 304(2)(b). A majority of states, however, do not recognize the duty to *retreat*; they consider *retreat* to be an act of cowardice. Those states which encourage *retreat* before the use of deadly force, permit the use of *nondeadly* force in self-defense. No state requires *retreat* when one is attacked in his own home.

RETRIBUTION   [L. *retribuo, retribuere* / to give again, give another his due, pay back]

Anything given in payment or in response. The word has both a positive — payment back — and a negative — punishment, penalty — meaning. In criminal law, *retribution* is the "eye for an eye" principle, i.e., the notion that every criminal must be made by society to pay for his crime.

RETRO   [L. backwards, back, behind]

Used as a prefix to denote something existing in the past or positioned behind.

RETROACTIVE   [L. *retro* + *ago, agere* / to set in motion, drive, do, act]

Going back to the past. Extending forward from a prior time. Made effective as of a date in the past. Having a present effect on past events. A *retroactive* law or statute is present legislation which has the affect of restricting rights created or existing in the past, or of creating new duties or obligations which did not exist in the past but which affect rights and property already vested. Any law which imposes a different present legal effect or impact on completed transactions or on vested interests that existed at the time the statute was passed. In general, these laws are void as *ex post facto* under the U.S. Constitution.

See **EX POST FACTO**

RETROSPECTIVE   [L. *retro* + *specto, spectare* / to look at, inspect, watch]

Looking back or backwards. Affecting things past. An exhibition of an artist's existing work produced over a period of time. Synonymous with retroactive. A *retrospective* law is the same as a retroactive law and has the same legal effect.

RETURN   [L. *re* / back, again + *torno, tornare* / to turn, as on a lathe]

To send or carry back. The act of a sheriff or other court officer in conveying to the court his report of actions taken by him in response to a writ or order of the court, e.g., a writ of execution; also, the endorsement by such officer of his actions under the writ or other document issued by the court. Also, the report of a body empowered to count ballots after an election, showing the election results. Also, the formal statement of earnings, deductions and allowances required of each taxpayer, together with his calculation of taxes due. Also, anything returned, e.g., a check returned by a bank for insufficient funds, or goods returned by a buyer for defects or non-compliance. Also, the income from an investment or the profit on a sale. A *return of service* is proof of service of a summons or subpeona. The *return day* is the date fixed by the court for the filing of an answer, the hearing of a motion, or some other step in the course of litigation.

REUS, REA [L. any party to a law suit; plaintiff or defendant]

Originally, any party to litigation. Later, the word came to mean the defendant, especially one accused of crime.

See **MENS REA**

REVENUE [L. *re* + *venio, venire* / to come]

The total or gross receipts from a given source (of income). Return on investments or labor. The total yield to a governmental authority from a tax, bond sale or other source of public funds. The gross receipts of a business from the sale of its products or services. A *revenue bill* is a legislative act designed for the raising of public funds; federal revenue bills must originate in the House of Representatives. The *Internal Revenue Code* is the entire body of statutory law under which all federal taxation is controlled and collected. A *revenue ruling* is a formal statement by the IRS of its interpretation of the application of a particular tax provision to a class of transactions. *Revenue stamps* are a tax on real estate transactions levied by the states, evidenced by stamps in varying amounts affixed to the conveyance instruments.

REVERSE, REVERSAL [L. *reverto, revertere* / to turn back, go back]

To turn back or around; to overthrow, annul, set aside. To side aside a decision. The publication by an appellate court of a decision, decree or judgment which is contrary in effect and/or result to the decision of the lower court. A *reverse mortgage* is a mortgage under which the equity in a home is distributed in annual installments to the homeowner until his death, as a means of providing him with income. *Reverse discrimination* occurs when a statute or policy intended to vitiate the effects of past discrimination on one group or race has the effect, instead, of resulting in discrimination against another group. A *reverse stock split* is the process by which a corporation calls back all outstanding shares of a particular class and replaces them with fewer shares, each having a greater value than before. *Reversible error* is a defective ruling or decision by a lower court which will warrant a *reversal* on appeal.

REVERT, REVERSION [L. *revertere* / to return]

To go back or return to a prior state or condition. To fall back to a more primitive, less advanced state. To return or be returned to a former owner. A *reversion* is that part of the entire interest of a holder which is left after he has transfered less than the whole to someone else. Example: "I hereby convey a life interest in Blackacre to B"; if I hold the fee in Blackacre, I have conveyed a life estate to B and I retain a *reversion*, which will become possessory in me or my heirs when B dies. During B's life, I have a *reversionary interest* in Blackacre.

See **REMAINDER** for a discussion of the differences between a *reversion* and a *remainder.*

REVERTER [L. *revertere* / to return]

The term *reverter*, or *possibility of reverter* refers to a contingent future interest which occurs when a grantor conveys less than a fee simple absolute and there is a chance, however remote, that the grantor will ultimately regain the fee. Example: A conveys all interest in Blackacre to B "so long as no commercially saleable oil is found on Blackacre." A has a *possibility of reverter* which will take effect only if commercially saleable oil is found on Blackacre.

REVIEW [L. *re* + *video, videre* / to see]

To reexamine; to look at or over again. To look back on the past. To publish an evaluation or criticism of an artistic work, as a book or play. A judicial reexamination of the record of a trial or proceeding before a lower court or agency. A judicial inquiry into the legality or constitutionality of a statute.

REVISE, REVISION [L. *reviso, revisere* / to look at again, pay a fresh visit to, return]

To review with the intent to correct or improve; to study again and amend and make up-to-date. To correct or amend a statute or judgment. A set of *revised statutes* is a compilation of outstanding statutes in a given jurisdiction after a review and reexamination to eliminate errors, inconsistencies, and superfluities; it is a codification which is intended to replace all prior renditions of the law and to stand alone as a current and complete restatement of all outstanding legislation within that jurisdiction.

REVIVE, REVIVAL [L. *re* + *vivo, vivere* / to live, be alive; to live again]

To bring back to life; to restore to health and vigor. To restore to use. The restoration of conditions or rights which have been dormant, inapplicable, or ineffective over a period of time. Examples: a judgment which has become stale after the passage of years may be *revived* upon proper showing to the court. A contract which has been made unenforceable under a statute of limitations may be *revived* by a new promise. A will which has been revoked may be *revived* by republication.

REVOKE, REVOCATION [L. *re* + *voco, vocare* / to call, summon, call upon; to call back, recall]

To bring or call back; to annul or make void. To withdraw, cancel or repeal. Applied in several ways by lawyers. An offer to enter into a contract may be *revoked* by the offeror at any time until it is accepted or acted upon by the offeree to his detriment, so long as the offer is not irrevocable by its terms. In criminal law, a sentence of probation or parole may be *revoked* if the offender violates a rule or order of the court. A will may be *revoked* by a testator by means of a codicil, a new will, physical destruction, or a transfer before death of property referred to in the will. A license may be *revoked* by the issuing authority for misconduct or violation of rules. Any power or right which is capable of *revocation* by the maker is referred to as *revocable*. Examples: *revocable transfers*, *revocable trusts*, *revocable letters of credit*.

REVOCATORY [L. *re* / back, again + *voco, vocare* / to call, summon]

Anything which revokes, cancels or annuls. An instrument which effects or accomplishes cancellation of a prior document, e.g., a codicil or an instrument revoking a prior offer.

REVOLT [L. *re* + *volvere* / to roll, turn round]

To rebel against authority. To rise up against a government. To turn back in disgust or revulsion.

REVOLVE, REVOLVING [L. *revolvere* / to roll backwards; to go around again]

To turn around. To rotate or go round in a circle. To recur at intervals. Anything which is available on a recurring basis. A *revolving credit* is a credit extension from a seller or a bank to a buyer or a borrower which permits the buyer or borrower to purchase or borrow up to a stated dollar amount on a continuing and fluctuating basis so long as payments are made on the terms provided in the credit extension agreement. A *revolving fund* is a source of money, usually for specific and limited purposes, from which withdrawals and repayments are made regularly and as stipulated, so as to maintain a recurring source of funds.

REX NON POTEST PECCARE [L. *rex* / king + *non* / not, negative + *posse, potui* / to be able or possible + *pecco, peccare* / to make a mistake, do something wrong]

The king can do no wrong.

RIGOR JURIS [L. *rigeo, rigere, rigor* / to be stiff, to stiffen, stiffer + *ius, iuris* / right law]

Literally, the inflexibility or strictness of the law.

RIGOR MORTIS [L. *rigere* + *mors, mortis* / death]

Medical term for the stiffness of a body after death.

RIPARIAN [L. *ripa* / the bank of a stream or waterway]

Associated with the bank of a river, stream or other natural waterway; within the natural watercourse of a river. Persons owning the land comprising the banks of a waterway are said to be *riparian owners*. These owners have *riparian rights*, i.e., the right to use the water in the stream or watershed for all reasonable purposes, the right to the soil in the banks and under the stream, etc., provided their use does not disturb the flow of water to *riparian owners* downstream.

RIXA

An angry dispute, a quarrel.

See **IN RIXA**

ROGATIO TESTIUM   [L. *roge, rogare* / to ask, request + *testis* / a witness]

The request by a testator at the moment of executing his will that the persons present bear witness that the document he is about to execute is his last will.

ROGATORY   [L. *rogo, rogare* / to ask, beg, request, question, beseech]

Rogatory letters, or *letters rogatory*, are a formal request by a court in one jurisdiction to a court in another jurisdiction asking for the examination of a witness within the latter jurisdiction in connection with a case or proceeding pending in the former jurisdiction. *Letters Rogatory* by the federal government to authorities in foreign countries are covered by 28 U.S.C.A. § 1781.

ROTA   [L. *rota* / wheel (*roto, rotare* / to turn around, swing)]

A roll, roster or list of persons, such as a list of jurors or of persons eligible for military conscription. The order in which designees are eligible to succeed to an office or appointment.

ROYALTY   [L. *rex, regis* / king, ruler, sovereign]

The rank and attributes of a ruler; a king or queen. A right given to an individual or corporation by the sovereign. Compensation to the owner of property — e.g., a mine, oil well, patent or copyright — for the use of his property, either in the form of a percentage of gross or net income or of a fixed sum per unit produced or sold. Authors, composers and artists are examples of persons who receive *royalties* for the sale or enjoyment of their works.

RULE   [L. *rego, regere* / to guide, direct (*regula* / a ruler, a straightedge)]

A standard or guide for action or conduct; e.g., for lawyers, the ABA Model Rules of Professional Conduct. The directive of a court or agency establishing guidelines for conduct. The Federal Rules of Civil Procedure govern the federal courts in all civil matters. The Federal Rules of Criminal Procedure govern the federal courts in all criminal matters. A judicial order compelling performance or non-performance of an act. A promulgation by an administrative agency designed to implement a statute defining its powers and having the force of law. The process of *rule-making* by an agency generally includes a period of public notice and comment for each new rule. The exercise of authority or dominion. A set of criteria for human conduct and action. A standard which is accepted by all to determine legal rights and obligations. The law recognizes many *rules*, e.g., the *rule against perpetuities*, the *rule in Shelley's case*. These are rules in the sense that they provide guidance for lawyers and judges in dealing with property and other rights. Other examples of rules recognized by lawyers follow.

RULE AGAINST PERPETUITIES
See **PERPETUITY**

RULE NISI [L. *regere* / to direct, rule + *nisi* / if not, unless]
An interlocutory order or decree of a court which will become final unless the party affected shows cause why it should not be enforced. A procedure under which one party can move *ex parte* to secure an order or judgment which, by its terms, will become final if the other party fails to show the court why it should not be granted.

See **NISI**

RULE OF CONVENIENCE
A rule of the common law which provided that a class which was to benefit from a gift or other distribution be kept open until the moment before final distribution.

RULE OF FOUR
A general rule of procedure followed by the U.S. Supreme Court which provides that a writ of certioriari will be granted and/or a matter will be reviewed if four of the nine judges agree that it should be reviewed.

RULE OF LAW
A legal doctrine which requires that decisions in specific cases or disputes be determined in accordance with some previously defined and published standards and principles which are comprehensible to all and may be relied upon by all. Also, a general doctrine which is applied to those nations or jurisdictions which follow a defined set of laws and regulations in the government of people and the conduct of their affairs, as opposed to the *ad hoc* decisions of those who happen to be in power. The United States and the United Kingdom are two nations which are described as *living under the rule of law*. Nazi Germany would be an example of a nation which abandoned the *rule of law*. Also, that body of law framed by statutes, rules, and judicial decisions which defines legal principles of general application to human conduct.

RULE OF LENITY
See **LENITY**

RULING [L. *rego, regere* / to guide, direct (*regula* / rule, model)]

The decision of a court on an issue of law; any official decision, determination, decree or interpretation. A *Revenue Ruling* is an official pronouncement by the Internal Revenue Service, often in response to a question asked by a taxpayer, which gives guidance to all taxpayers with a similar question.

RUMOR [L. *rumor* / report, common talk, hearsay]

Stories or reports which circulate among people but which are without support in authority, source, truth or fact. A report which is unconfirmed. *Rumors* are not generally admitted into evidence.

S. OR SS. [L. abbreviation for the word *scilicet* / evidently, to wit, of course (from *scire licet* / one is allowed to know)]

In a pleading, an allegation of the essential facts without elaboration. Also used in the caption of affidavits as in:

State of New York)

County of Queens) ss.

See **SCILICET**

SACRAMENT [L. *sacro, sacrare* / to dedicate to a deity; to consecrate]

One of several Christian rites attributed to Christ; considered a means to divine grace.

SACRAMENTUM FIDELITAS [L. *sacramentum* / an oath; the money deposited by the parties to a suit to ensure recovery by the winning party + *fidelitas* / trust, loyalty]

The oath of fealty or loyalty. The oath of allegiance taken by new soldiers.

SACRIFICE [L. *sacer, sacra* / holy, consecrated + *facere* / to make, do]

To offer a precious possession to a deity. Something given for the sake of something else. To forego or give up a pleasure. To destroy something in the interest of saving something else. To kill a person or an animal in a religious ritual.

SACRILEGE [L. *sacer, sacra* + *lego, legere* / to gather, pick, take away]

Irreverence towards a hallowed object or person. The violation of a religious tenet or belief held sacred by others. The theft or destruction of anything considered sacred, as of a religious article in a church or of graves in a cemetery.

SALARY [L. *salarius* / derived from salt; the yearly income derived from production of salt; money given to soldiers as salt allowance; hence, any pay allowance]

A payment for services given or work performed. The distinction between *salary* and wages is that the former is compensation which is fixed for a specified period, as for a month or year or over the life of an employment contract, while the latter is normally based on an hourly rate for hours actually worked.

SALUS POPULI EST SUPREMA LEX

The welfare of the people is the paramount law. This is an ancient Roman maxim which is still the fundamental concept controlling all democratic thought and institutions.

SALVAGE   [L. *salvus* / safe]

Property saved or rescued from imminent threat or danger, as in a wreck or fire. Anything retained from discarded property. In maritime law, the rescue of a ship or its cargo; also the compensation paid for the act of saving a ship or its cargo from the perils of the sea. *Salvage loss* is the marine insurance term defining the difference between the value of property insured against loss and the value of property salvaged by the owner. A *salvage lien* is the lien of persons who have salvaged a ship or cargo. The lien attaches to the property saved to secure payment of their fees.

SAMARITAN   [Late L. *samaritanus* / a resident of *samaria*, a person performing good deeds (from the Greek)]

See **GOOD SAMARITAN**

SAMPLE   [L. *exemplum* / something picked from a number of things; a sampling]

One representative item picked from a group of essentially similar things to establish the character or quality of the items in the group. The defined part of a statistical whole measured and studied to establish data about the whole.

SANAE MENTIS   [L. *sanus* / sound, healthy + *mens, mentis* / the mind, understanding, reason]

Of sound and healthy mind.

SANCTION   [L. *sancio, sancire* / to make sacred, consecrate]

To make valid or binding; to approve of. To give effect to, as in "that conduct was *sanctioned* by a law passed by Congress." Also, a formal decree or oath. The destruction or seizure of property. Also, a detriment or penalty imposed for violation of a statute or regulation. The imposition of a penalty or fine. In international law, coercive economic or military action taken by one or several nations to compel a change in conduct by another nation, as the sanctions imposed by the U.S. on Cuba or Iraq. Sanctions may take the form of blockades, embargoes, the blocking of bank accounts, etc.

SANCTUARY [L. *sancio, sancire* / to make sacred]

A safe place. Originally, a place to which fugitives could retreat and in which they remained safe from arrest and seizure. Part of a church or other place of worship. A refuge for wildlife.

SANE [L. *sanus* / sound, healthy]

Healthy in mind. Mentally sound, rational. Capable of understanding the nature and consequences of one's actions.

SANITARY [L. *sanitas*/ health, purity, sanity]

Pertaining to health. Concerning or dealing with the disposal or treatment of waste. A *sanitary regulation* is a regulation imposed in the interest of public health. A *sanitary district* is a governmental agency or entity organized to finance and arrange for improvements in sanitation and public health facilities, e.g., sewers and sewage disposal plants.

SANITY [L. *sanus* / sound, sound of mind and body]

The ability to understand the nature and consequences of one's action. The ability to distinguish between right and wrong and to control one's conduct accordingly. The law recognizes that it is not fair to punish anyone who is not sane when he commits a criminal offense. The difficulty for lawyers lies in the formulation of reasonable definitions for sanity and insanity and for the reasonable application of those definitions to specific facts.

SAPIENTES, FIDELES ET ANIMOSI

Wise, faithful and courageous.

SATISFY, SATISFACTION [L. *satis* / enough, sufficient + *facere* / to make, do]

To carry out the terms of, as of a contract. To pay a financial obligation or debt. To conform to stipulated requirements. To please, make happy or fulfil. To meet an obligation by substituting performance other than the performance originally promised, as in *accord and satisfaction*. A *satisfaction* is a legal document establishing that an obligation, e.g., an obligation to pay money on a bond secured by a mortgage, has been met. To meet the standards or demands imposed by external circumstances, as to *satisfy a jury* by convincing proof.

SAVE, SAVING [L. *salvus* / well, safe, sound]

To free from harm or danger. To relieve of sin or guilt. To put aside or hoard. To deposit into the safekeeping of another, as in a bank. To put money aside. To rescue a person who is at risk. To *save harmless* is to insure another against sustaining a financial loss by agreeing to indemnify or reimburse her in the event of loss. A *saving clause* is a clause in a statute (or a contract) which provides that if any part of a statute (or contract) is declared void or invalid, the remainder will not be affected and will remain in force. The *saving to suitors* clause is a clause contained at 28 USC §1333(1) entitling maritime claimants to proceed in the state, instead of the federal, courts.

SCANDAL   [L. *scandalum* / stumbling block, interference, offense (from Gr. *skandalon*)]

Conduct that causes a loss of face by the perpetrator and loss of faith in the observor. Loss of reputation because of some act which offends the public's standards or conscience. Disgrace. Also, malicious gossip, report or innuendo.

SCANDALUM MAGNATUM

A term formerly used in England to define the slander of important men, e.g., judges, peers or cabinet officers. The punishment for *scandalum magnatum* was more severe than for slander of lesser citizens.

See **SLANDER**

SCHEDULE   [L. *scheda* / a strip of papyrus bark; a leaf of paper]

A written statement, especially one attached to a legal document setting forth or listing data which is supplemental to but incorporated by reference in the principal document. A list; an inventory. To fix the date or time of. To incorporate in a list of items. In bankruptcy law, one of a set of lists which must be completed and filed by the debtor setting forth his debts and assets, the names and addresses of his creditors, whether any of his assets are exempt, etc.

SCHEME   [L. *schema* / shape, figure, form]

A graphic sketch or design. A plan or outline for future action. A systematic and organized blueprint for conduct. The organization or combination of elements into a connected and integrated whole. Also, a crafty or unethical suggestion or plan. A plot.

SCIENTER   [L. *scientia* / a knowledge, a knowing of (from *scire* / to know, be aware)]

Knowledge; previous knowledge; "guilty knowledge." Knowledge and appreciation of the nature of one's acts or omissions. *Scienter* is a necessary element of many crimes and may be considered the equivalent of criminal intent. In some cases, especially cases in which a crime is created and defined by a regulatory statute, scienter need not be proved. *Scienter* in cases based on fraud is the intent to deceive or mislead. Scienter is especially important in corporate securities law, which equates scienter with intent to deceive or defraud.

SCILICET [L. from *scire* / to know + *licere* / one can or may: that one may know]

Namely, that is to say, to wit.

See **S.** above

SCINTILLA [SCINTILLA OF EVIDENCE] [L. *scintilla* / a spark (from *scintillare* / to sparkle)]

A trace or insubstantial amount. Evidence which is speculative and conjectural or less than substantial. The *scintilla* rule, now generally rejected and ignored, held that a verdict could not be directed for one party if there was so much as a shred or *scintilla* of evidence in favor of the other party.

SCIRE DEBES CUM QUO CONTRAHIS

Know the person you contract with.

SCIRE FACIAS (SCI. FA.) [L. *scire* / to know + *facio, facere* / to do or make]

An ancient statutory writ providing either for the entry of judgment or for execution upon a judgment. A writ requiring the defendant to show cause why some obligation by him contained in a public record, e.g., a filed judgment, should not be enforced. A proceeding to enforce a garnishment or a bail bond. The proceeding instituted under a writ of *scire facias*.

SCIRE FECI [L. *scire* + *feci* / pp of *facere* / to make or do; I have caused to be known]

I have given notice. I have notified. The return filed with the court by the sheriff in response to a writ of *scire facias*.

SCRIBERE EST AGERE [L. *scribo, scribere* / to engrave, write + *esse* / to be + *ago, agere* / to set in motion, to drive, to act]

To write is to act. One who reduces his thoughts or acts to writing is bound by them.

SCRIP [L. *scriptum* / pp of *scribere* / to write; something written]

A short, condensed writing. A document entitling the holder to receive a fractional share of a stock dividend. A certificate of indebtedness used as a substitute for money at the time of the Great Depression, or in another fiscal emergency. A *scrip dividend* is a document issued by a corporation, specifing the holder's fractional interest in a stock dividend or entitling the holder to distribution of accumulated earnings at a later date.

SCRIVENER [L. *scriba* / a scribe, a secretary (from *scribo, scribere* / to engrave or write)]

A professional writer or transcriber of public or legal documents, e.g., deeds, contracts, wills, etc. Also, one who drafts documents.

SCRUPLE, SCRUPULOUS [L. *scrupus* / a sharp stone; a worry or anxiety]

An instinct or attitude inhibiting action, based upon ethical or moral considerations. A moral restraint. A reservation or qualm. To hesitate in recognition of a moral principle or dilemma. To have the capacity to curb action or to hesitate in the face of a moral issue or question.

SCRUTINY [L. *scrutor, scrutari* / to inspect carefully, examine, search]

Judicial inquiry and examination of a statute or regulation to determine whether it is constitutional under the equal protection clause of the Constiution. The Supreme Court has announced several different levels of statutory scrutiny, including the *strict scrutiny* applied to statutes which legislate disparate treatment of persons or groups, based on race or national origin.

See **INTERMEDIATE; STRICT SCRUTINY**

SCUTAGE [L. *scutum* / shield, a soldiers shield]

An ancient tax levied on a vassal or knight in lieu of service in the military.

See **TALLAGIUM**

SE [L. himself, herself, itself, themselves]

The very person. Used in such phrases as *inter se*, between or among themselves; also, *per se*, by himself or itself.

SEAL, SEALED [L. *sigilla* / a small figure or image; a seal]

A device or emblem used at common law in lieu of or in conjunction with a signature to authenticate or identify a legal document, as a contract or will. Anything that secures a document. An ornamental stamp used to indicate that a document is meant to be opened and viewed only by designated persons. A device to prevent tampering. A symbol of rank or office. To prevent access, as to seal a door or corridor. A *sealed verdict* is a jury verdict arrived at during a court recess when the judge is not available to take and review the verdict; the verdict is placed in a sealed envelope and is opened and read when the judge returns.

SEARCH [L. *circum* / round about, on all sides; in a circle]

To examine or inspect carefully. To investigate or look into areas of concealment. To examine a public record, as in the case of land titles. To acquire knowledge through inquiry or scrutiny. An inquiry or inspection of persons, personal articles, possessions or premises by government agents or police to determine whether a crime has been committed and/or to find a weapon or contraband. Generally, no search may be made except upon a warrant issued only upon a showing of probable cause and, then, only of premises which are particularly described in the warrant. But some warrantless searches are permitted. Examples: a protective search of the person and clothing of a suspect to ensure against concealed weapons; an inventory search, as of the contents of an automobile, to prevent loss or destruction of property and resulting claims against the police.

SEASONABLE [L. *satio* / a sowing or planting]

At a proper time. Suitable to the occasion. Occurring within the time fixed by agreement or within a reasonable time if no time is specified. See Uniform Commercial Code § 1-204.

SECESION [L. *secedo, secedere* / to go away, to withdraw]

The act of withdrawing from membership in an association or group. The act of a state or province in removing itself from control by or allegience to a central government, as the attempted secesion by the southern states from the federal union during the Civil War.

SECOND, SECONDARY [L. *secundum* / after, behind, following closely behind; second to]

Following immediately behind the first or primary in rank. Of second rank, status or importance. Derived from something original or antecedent in time or rank. The second in a series. Murder in the *second degree* is usually murder with intent to kill but without premeditation. A *second mortgage* is a lien on real property which comes behind and is subordinate to the first mortgage. A *secondary boycott* is an illegal boycott of an employer with which the union has no dispute in order to put economic pressure on an employer with which the union does have a dispute. *Secondary picketing* is picketing by a union of an employer with which it has no direct dispute but which does business with the employer with which the union does have a dispute. *Secondary contract* is a contract which modifies or supersedes a prior primary contract. *Secondary liability* is the liability of a guarantor, surety, joint tort-feasor or employer to indemnify an aggrieved party when the person primarily liable fails to perform or pay. *Secondary meaning* is the acceptance given to a trademark by the general public which associates the mark with a particular manufacturer because of continued use and exposure. *Secondary meaning* entitles the mark to protection under the trademark laws.

See **SUGGESTIVE**

SECOND DEGREE [L. *secundus* / following, second in line + *de* / of, from + *gradus* / step, stage]

A measure of the degree of culpability in the commission of a crime. A less serious crime than a first degree crime. *Second degree* murder is generally defined as a homicide committed without deliberation or premeditation.

SECRECY, SECRET [L. *secretus* (from *secerno, secernere* / to set apart, hide, make secret)]

Withheld from others; hidden; set apart. Covert, stealthy, furtive. Something kept from general knowledge but shared with a few. A method, plan, formula or process known only by a privileged few, as by the employees of a particular company. A *secret ballot* is the vote of an individual which is not visible or disclosed to anyone. A *secret hearing* is a hearing closed to all except the interested parties. A *secret lien* is a lien which is not filed or recorded and not disclosed to anyone but the immediate parties. A *trade secret* is a secret belonging to a commercial enterprise which is unique or special to it and which is disclosed only to the employer and those employees who have a need to know it.

SECRETARY [L. *secretum* / secret (from *secerno, secernere* / to set apart, to hide)]

A person hired to handle the correspondence and maintain the office routine of a professional or executive. One elected or appointed to keep the records of an organization and to record the minutes of its meetings. A title given to members of the U.S. cabinet and to various state officials who head administrative departments of state government.

SECTA [L. (from *sequor, sequi* / to follow) a way or mode of life; a thought or plan; a philosophical school]

A law suit. In early England, a retinue of supporters who accompanied a plaintiff to court to support his claims.

SECULAR [L. *saeculum* / the period of one human generation (app. 33 years); the spirit of the age; the times]

Worldly. Of or relating to the real world. Temporal. Not associated with religion or the clergy. Occurring or existing through the ages.

SECUNDUM

Immediately after, beside, next to. According to; in accordance with.
See **SECOND; SECOND DEGREE**

SECUNDUM AEQUUM ET BONUM

In accordance with justice and right.

SECUNDUM ALLEGATA ET PROBATA

In accordance with the allegations and the proof.

SECUNDUM LEGEM COMMUNEM

In accordance with the common law.

SECUNDUM LEGEM TERRAE
  In accordance with the law of the land.

SECUNDUM NORMAM LEGIS   [L. *secundum* / according to + *norma* / a rule or standard + *lex, legis* / law]
  In accordance with the rule of law.

SECUNDUM USUM MERCATORUM
  In accordance with the usage and custom of merchants.
  See **LEX MERCATORIA**

SECURE, SECURITY   [L. *securus* / safe, free from care]
  Free from danger, risk or threat of loss or injury. Trustworthy, dependable. Stable; unlikely to fail. Confident, assured. To protect or make firm. To give assurances for, as by a pledge, mortgage or lien. Any interest in property which protects against default in payment or performance. Evidence of indebtedness or surety. A *secured party* is a party who receives assurance for the payment of a debt or the performance of some act or obligation, usually in the form of an assignment, lien or mortgage. A *secured transaction* is a transaction covered by Article 9 of the Uniform Commercial Code which creates a *security interest* in personal property. A *security deposit* is a deposit of money or securities made by a tenant to the landlord to assure payment of rent or to protect against loss or damage to the property leased.
  See **UNSECURED**

SECURITIES   [L. *securus* / safe]
  Instruments evidencing an interest or investment in a commercial enterprise, giving the owner the right to participate or share in the profits of the enterprise and/or in the distribution of assets. *Securities* can take many forms, including common stock, preferred stock, bonds and debentures. Securities are regulated by the Securities and Exchange Commission and are commonly traded and negotiated in regulated securities exchanges or markets.

SE DEFENDENDO   [L. *se* / oneself, himself + *defendo, defendere* / to repel, drive away; to defend, protect]
  (An act) in self defense. In defending himself or oneself.

SEDITION   [L. *seditio* / a movement apart; a mutiny, revolt or insurrection]
  Incitement or agitation against lawful authority. The crime of inducing or creating a revolt or uprising against the state or against lawful authority with intent to overthrow the constituted government. To promote public disorder through word or deed. The Sedition Acts were acts passed by Congress dur-

ing the presidency of John Adams which made it a crime to libel the Congress or the President.

SED NON ALLOCATUR   [L. *sed* / but, however + *non* / not + *allocare* / to grant, permit]
But it is not permitted.

SED QUAERE   [L. *sed* / but + *quaero, quarere* / to seek]
But inquire further.

SEDUCE, SEDUCTION   [L. *seduco, seducere* / to lead away; to separate]
To lead astray. To cause disobedience or disloyalty. To corrupt or deceive. To entice into sexual intercourse.

SED VIDE   [L. *sed* / but + *video, videre* / to see]
But see.

SEGREGATE, SEGREGATION   [L. *se* / self + *grex, gregis* / a herd or flock; *segregere* / to isolate, separate from the flock]
To isolate or separate from others. The separation of one race, class or ethnic or religious group from the general populace or from others by discriminatory means or tactics, as by isolation in ghettoes, limiting access to schools and means of transportation, restricting the right to vote or hold office, etc. *De facto segregation* is *segregation* which results from economic and social influences and not as a result of a statute or state action. *De jure segregation* is *segregation* imposed by statute or constitution and enforced by state action.

SEMPER
Always, at all times.

SEMPER FIDELES   [L. *semper* / always + *fidelis* / faithful, trustworthy]
Always faithful. The motto of the U.S. Marine Corps.

SEMPER IN DUBIIS BENIGNIORA PRAEFERENDA SUNT
When in doubt, always adopt the more liberal construction (of words or events).

SEMPER PARATUS   [L. *semper* / always + *paratus* / ready, prepared (from *paro, parare* / to prepare)]
Always prepared. Always read (to act).

SEMPER PRAESUMITUR PRO MATRIMONIO
The presumption is always in favor of the validity of a marriage.

SEMPER PRAESUMITUR PRO NEGANTE
The presumption is always in favor of the negative, i.e., in favor of the defendant who enters a general denial.

SENATE, SENATOR [L. *senex* / an elderly man or woman; hence, a senator, a member of the Roman Senate]

The upper chamber of the U.S. Congress and of most state legislatures. The *U.S. Senate* is composed of two senators from each state. A *senator* is a member of a senate. U.S. senators are elected for six-year terms.

SENILE DEMENTIA [L. *senilis* / pertaining to an old man + *demens, dementia* / without control of ones mind, senseless, insane]

Incapacity of the mind which occurs with old age and is progressive in character. The symptoms occur especially in persons with Alzheimer's disease.

SENILITY [L. *senilis* / relating to an old man]

The deteriorated mental or physical state occurring in some persons who attain very old age. Signs of old age.

SENIOR [L. *senex, senior* / old, aged, an old man]

Higher in rank, order or importance. The first in a series. Longer in service; e.g., the senior member of the U.S. Senate. Older. The last year of study in a high school or college. Having a claim on assets or property which has priority over other claims. A *senior lien* is a lien which has priority over and must be paid or satisfied before other liens. A *senior mortgage* or first mortgage is a mortgage on real property having priority over all subsequent or secondary mortgages.

See **SECOND**

SENIORITY [L. *senex, senior* / old; an older or more elderly person]

Recognition for one's age or length of service. The priority attained by an employee after continuous service over a longer period than other employees. Also, the priority of one lien or encumbrance over another.

SENSUS VERBORUM EST ANIMA LEGIS
The law finds its spirit in the meaning of words.

SENTENCE [L. *sententia* / thought, opinion, meaning (from *sentire* / to see, perceive, feel)]

An opinion or conclusion reached after deliberation. The judgment of a court in a criminal action after the close of evidence and announcement of the verdict, specifying the punishment to be meted out to the defendant. The terms of punishment to be observed by a guilty defendant. A *determinate sentence* is a sentence for a fixed length of time. An *indeterminate sentence* is a sentence which has minimum and maximun limits; the exact length is fixed not by the court but by a parole board. Sentences may run concurrently or consecutively. *Sentencing guidelines* are rules promulgated by a commission of judges providing classifications for crimes and suggested terms of punishment for each class. A *sentence of nullity* is a judicial determination that a marriage is null and void.

SENTENTIA   [L. thought or opinion]

An opinion, decision or judgment. Also, the meaning derived from a set of connected words.

SEPARABLE   [L. *se* + *paro, parare* / to prepare, make ready, provide; *separare* / to sever, separate]

Capable of being separated into component parts. Divisible. A *separable contract* is a contract which is divided into a number of constituent parts, each part defining performance and remedy in such a way as to permit it to be separately interpreted and enforced without reference to any other part. A *separable controversy* is a controvery which can be disengaged from and tried independently of all other claims in an action. To qualify for removal from a state court to a federal court, a controversy must constitute a "separate cause of action." If any one controversy qualifies for removal, the federal court may try all the issues between the parties or it may determine only the claim or claims which qualify for removal and remand the rest to the state court.

See **SEVER**

SEPARATE   [L. *separare* / to sever, separate]

To divide or put apart. To dissolve. To move apart, as in: Joe and Ethel have separated. *Separate counts* are distinct and different criminal offenses charged in a single indictment; also, the recitation in a complaint or petition of individual and distinct causes of action between the same parties. *Separate maintenance* is the support paid by one spouse to the other during separation. A *separate opinion* is the dissenting or concurring opinion of one or several judges which is not adopted or approved by the majority of judges. *Separate property* is the unique property of one of the spouses in a community property state; or, in all other states, property of one spouse which is not marital property. The seperate property may consist of property acquired before marriage or property acquired by gift or inheritance after marriage.

SEPARATION   [L. *separare* / to separate]

The state of being separate or apart. The condition of existing apart. The end of cohabitation by a husband and wife, either by the voluntary departure of one or by mutual agreement, generally with the intent that the separation shall become permanent. A *separation agreement* is an agreement between husband and wife providing for separate living arrangements, for the custody of children, for visitation rights, for support and for other matters of mutual interest. *Separation from service* is the termination of military service by a soldier or sailor. *Separation of powers* is the division of governmental functions in the U.S. Constitution into legislative functions (the Congress); executive functions (the President); and judicial functions (the Supreme Court and the other federal courts).

SEQUESTER   [L. *sequestrum* / a deposit (from *sequestrare* / to deliver to a trustee or agent)]

To set aside. To place in the custody or care of another. Also, to seize under a *writ of sequestration*. To place in seclusion or isolation, as to *sequester a jury* during its deliberations. A witness may also be sequestered to prevent access or influence by others before and during his testimony.

SEQUESTRATION   [L. see **SEQUESTER**]

A judicial writ authorizing a court officer to seize the assets of a party to compel compliance with a court order or to protect the party's assets from removal or dissipation. In an action of ejectment, the collection of rents and profits by the court pending the outcome of the action. In a matrimonial action, the seizure of a husband's property to secure the payment of support and maintenance.

SERIAL   [L. *series* / a row, succession, chain]

Occurring in a row or in successive parts or numbers. Belonging to a group of dates or events maturing at regular intervals. *Serial bonds* are bonds of a municipality or corporation issued in a series and payable or redeemable at stated intervals. A *serial killer* is a person who commits a series of murders.

SERIATIM   [L. *sero, serere* / to join together, place in a row]

In regular order, successively, one by one, separately, as in "the court will consider the parties' motions *seriatim*."

SERVANT   [L. *servio, servire* / to be a slave (*servus* / slave)]

Anyone in the employ and subject to control and direction of an employer or principal. Generally, a person who performs duties which do not require discretion or managerial ability.

See **AGENT, RESPONDEAT SUPERIOR**

SERVICE   [L. *servio, servire* / to be a slave]

The act of delivering a summons, writ or other judicial document to the person affected or of transmitting the required notice by some other means prescribed by law or court rule. Also, work or labor performed by one person for another, usually for compensation. A contribution to the welfare of others. Also, the armed forces of a nation, as the *military services*. To pay the installments of principal and interest due on a debt or mortgage. A *service charge* is a charge added to a bill to compensate for the processing of a transaction. A *service mark* is the same as a trademark except that it identifies and distinguishes a proprietary service instead of a product. A word, name or symbol used to distinguish the services of one company from all others, and to point to the source of service. Example: the Friendly Skies (of United Air Lines).

SERVIENT   [L. *servire* / to be enslaved]

Acting in support of; serving; providing services for. A *servient estate* is a property interest which is burdened with a duty to another estate. A *servient tenement* is the name given to a parcel of land which is burdened with or subject to an easement in favor of another parcel of land. The latter parcel is called the dominant tenement.

SERVITIUM

The Latin word for personal service. The service rendered by a tenant under the feudal system to the lord of the manor. *Servitium forinsecum* was the service due by the tenant to the king himself, separate and apart from the service due by him the lord of the manor. *Servitium liberum* referred to services rendered by free men, as distinguished from the services of serfs and vassals.

SERVITUDE   [L. *servire*/ to be enslaved]

The state or condition of being so firmly in the control or service of another as to lack the essential freedoms of movement, allegiance, speech, etc. A lack of liberty. Also, in law, the obligation of the owner of one piece of land to allow the use of his land by another for the special benefit or enjoyment of the latter.

SESSION   [L. *sessio* / a meeting for purposes of discussion (from *sessitare* / to sit often or for a long time)]

A meeting or series of meetings, as of a legislature or court. The period between the beginning and the end of a prescribed series of sittings of a legislative or judicial body. A meeting devoted to a particular purpose. The name sometimes given to various courts, as the English Sessions Courts. That period during which a court actually sits for the transaction of business. ("The court is now in session.")

SETTLE   [L. *sella* / seat, chair, stool]

To put in place. To establish a residence. To resolve a dispute. To make quiet or orderly. To conclude a law suit by agreement of the parties instead of by judicial disposition. To pay a bill or obligation. To adjust the differences between parties. To conclude an arrangement with creditors.

SETTLEMENT [L. *sella* / seat]

The end of a controversy by agreement of the parties. The termination of a law suit by adjustment between the parties themselves, with or without the help of the court. The amount paid by one party to another under an agreement disposing of a controversy between them. Also, a formal conveyance. The payment of an obligation. The final order entered upon a trustee's account to the court. The occupation of unoccupied land by a settlor with the intent to claim title from the federal government. A place, region or area which people have occupied for their homes.

SETTLOR [L. *sella*]

The person who creates a trust for the benefit of another. One who conveys or transfers property to another with instructions to act as trustee for the benefit of a third person or persons.

SEVER, SEVERABLE [L. *separo, separare* / to separate, to set apart]

To part; to put or keep apart. To divide. To cut apart. To cut in two. Capable of being separated. The act of dividing a property or asset into independent rights and obligations. A *severable contract* is an agreement which can be divided into sets of reciprocal rights and obligations; each set is separately enforceable without reference to the others. A *severable contract* is distinguished from an entire contract, in which full and complete performance is required of one party in exchange for the consideration furnished by the other party. A *severable clause* in a contract or statute is a clause which can be separated from the whole and declared void or invalid without affecting the validity of the rest.

See **SEPARABLE**

SEVERAL, SEVERALLY [L. *separare, separatus* / separate, apart]

Separate or distinct from one another. More than two but fewer than many. Separately or individually bound or liable. In a group of similar things, the separation of the group into the individuals which comprise it, as in "to regulate commerce...among the several states (U.S. Constitution, Art. I.) To be *jointly and severally liable* is to be liable both together with others and also separately and individually, generally at the option of the plaintiff or obligee.

SEVERALTY [L. *separare*]

Sole and exclusive ownership of property. An *estate in severalty* is the interest of a sole tenant or owner, without any interest by any other person.

SEVERANCE [L. *separare*]

The act of separating or severing. The act of removing anything attached or affixed to land, as an ore or mineral, which changes the character of the thing removed from realty to personalty. The termination of a joint tenancy or a tenancy in common. A conveyance of land subject to a reservation of mineral rights in the grantor. The termination of employment of a worker or laborer; *severance pay* is the compensation paid to such a worker at the end of his employment. The law speaks of the *severance of actions*, the *severance of prosecutions*, the *severance of issues*, etc., all meaning division into several distinct and separate parts. A *severance tax* is a tax imposed upon property (e.g., oil, minerals timber) extracted from the soil, or upon the trapping of fur-bearing animals.

SHARE [L. *scindo, scindere* / to cut, cut up]

The portion of a whole allotted to an individual or group. Any of the parts into which all the interests in a property or business are divided, such as stock in a corporation. Also, that portion of a testator's estate which is bequeathed to a particular individual; in intestacy, that part of the estate which passes to a particular heir. A *shareholder* is a stockholder in a corporation, a participant in a business trust, or, more generally, anyone who is legally entitled to a portion of any business, property or enterprise.

SIC [L. thus, so, in this way]

Thus; in that way. As follows. In that case. In legal writing, *sic* is used to indicate that a word, phrase or passage is reproduced from a source exactly as shown, or that it is reproduced or copied verbatim from another document.

SIC SUBSCRIBITUR

It is so subscribed.

SIC TRANSIT GLORIA MUNDI [L. *sic* / thus + *transigo, transigere* / to pass or spend (time) + *gloria* / fame, glory + *mundus* / the world]

In that way goes universal fame or glory. Fame and glory are fleeting things.

SIC UTERE TUO UT ALIENUM NON LAEDAS

Use your own property so as not to injure the property of another. A basic maxim which underlies the concept of social responsibility in the use of one's property.

SIC VOLO [L. *sic* + *volo, velle* / to wish or want]

I will it so. That's the way I want it.

SIGN [L. *signo, signare* / to mark, place a mark on]

To affix one's signature to a document to indicate agreement to its terms or to give it legal effect. To ratify by hand or seal. To mark an instrument in any manner satisfying the legal requirements for commitment by and enforceability against the person making the mark.

SIGNATURE, SIGNATORY [L. *signo, signare* / to mark, inscribe, stamp]

A mark or writing on a document which is intended to establish the intention of the person making the mark to be bound by the terms of the document or to authenticate the document as one which the person adopts for himself. Also, the act of placing such a mark or writing upon the document. A *signatory* is the person who affixes his mark or name to a document. In the case of persons who are not able to write their names, a mark such as an X or a fingerprint, will generally suffice. In some cases, a signature may be inscribed by a proxy, i.e., a person authorized to place his or her signature upon the document by the party intending to be bound, as by a shareholder in a corporation who authorizes his proxy to attend a meeting or to cast a vote.

SIGNATURE CRIME

A crime committed in a way or by means so similar to those used in another crime as to suggest the work of a single criminal. The similarity may lie in the weapon or instrument used, in the occupations of the victims (doctors in an abortion clinic; prostitutes, etc.) or in other distinctive patterns. The courts will often allow evidence of these patterns in contradiction to the general rule against the admission of evidence of prior crimes.

SI JUDICAS, COGNOSCE [L. *si* / if + *iudico, iudicare* / to judge + *cognosco, cognoscere* / to know, get to know]

If you (presume to) judge, you must first know and understand.

SILENCE, SILENT [L. *silens* / still, calm, silent; *silentium* / stillness, quiet]

Silence: The absence of sound or noise. A forbearance from speech or comment, whether deliberately or inadvertently. Secrecy. The failure to reveal a fact or circumstance which, if disclosed, might affect the actions or conduct of others when there is a duty to reveal. Silence may signify acquiescence or result in estoppel or waiver. *Silent:* The act of withholding speech or comment, or of making no disclosure when disclosure is required. Also, the failure to act or legislate. When Congress is *silent* on any issue, for example, the states may generally proceed to legislate on that issue. A *silent partner* is a partner who participates in a partnership by investing and sharing in the partnership business but who does not disclose his participation to the public.

SIMILITER [L. in like manner, similarly]

A formal written statement in which a party accepts the facts contained in a pleading by the adversary. A joinder of issues.

SIMPLE [L. *simplus, simplex* / simple]

Innocent; free from guile. Humble, modest. Lacking in knowledge or mental facility. Free from secondary consequences or implications. In law, simple has several meanings. A document which is not under seal or recorded is considered a *simple document*. A *property interest* which has no time limits or other restrictions is considered a simple interest, e.g., as an *interest in fee simple*. A tort or crime which fits the most essential definition of that crime and has no aggravating factors making the crime more serious or severe (e.g., use of a dangerous weapon) is described as a *simple crime* (e.g., a simple assault, a simple battery, etc.). *Simple interest* is interest which is computed solely on the principal of a debt, without adding interest on accrued interest. A *simple trust* is a trust in which all principal is retained by the trustee and distribution is made only of current interest on that principal.

SIMPLICITER [L. *simplex, simpliciter* (adv.) / simply, without artfulness]

In a simple way. Without fanfare. Directly, summarily, immediately.

SIMULATE [L. *simulo, simulare* / to make like, copy, imitate]

To feign or pretend, often with intent to deceive. To counterfeit. To take on the appearance of or copy something else. A *simulated document* is a document which is offered to third persons as the apparent agreement of two parties but which does not express their true intent and is intended to deceive.

SIMULTANEOUS (DEATH) [L. *simul* / at once, at the same time]

Existing or happening at the very same time. Coincident. A death is defined as simultaneous when it occurs so closely upon its cause as to suggest that the decedent suffered no pain. Also, two or more deaths are considered *simultaneous* when there is insufficient evidence to determine the order of death. In this way, a husband and wife, for example, may be deemed to have died simultaneously in a common accident without regard to the actual time of death. In that event, each will be deemed to have survived the other and their property will be disposed of accordingly. In a *simultaneous death*, an insured is deemed to have survived his benificiary. Many states have adopted the Simultaneous Death Act, a uniform act which provides for disposition in the case of simultaneous deaths.

SINE ANIMO REMANENDI [L. *sine* / without + *animus* / the seat of life, the soul + *remanere* / to stay behind]

Without the intent to remain (in a place).

SINE ANIMO REVERTENDI

Without the intent to return (to a place).

SINE DAMNO [L. *sine* / without + *damnum* / damage, injury, penalty]

Without any injury or damage.

See **INIURIA ABSQUE (SINE) DAMNO**

SINE DIE [L. *sine* + *dies* / day as opposed to night; a day in time; twenty-four hours]

Without a day, without time; without setting a new date. A court or legislative body adjourns *sine die* when it adjourns without appointing a day on which to sit or assemble again.

SINE PROLE [L. *sine* / without + *proles* / progeny, descendants; race, stock]

Without issue.

SINE QUA NON

Without which, not; that without which a thing cannot be. The essential thing upon which another depends for its existence.

SINGLE [L. *singularis* / alone, single, individual]

Alone; unaccompanied by others. Not married. Consisting of one in number. Affecting only one person. The *single publication rule* is a rule of the law of libel which limits the plaintiff to one cause of action despite publication of multiple copies of libellous matter. The number of copies distributed does not enlarge the causes of action beyond one, but becomes relevant on the issue of damages. *Single-entry bookkeeping* is a simple system of bookkeeping in which each transaction is recorded only once. In double-entry bookkeeping, each transaction is recorded twice, both as a debt and a credit.

SITUS

The location or place of a thing. In law, the place with respect to which a right is fixed or determined. The *situs* of real property is its physical location, not the place where its owner is found.

SLANDER [L. *scandalum* / stumbling block (from Greek *scandalon* / trap, offense)]

Formerly used to describe both written and oral defamatory statements, slander is now generally limited to unprivileged defamatory oral statements made about an individual to a third party. The words must tend to defame the individual in his reputation, office, trade or business. The tort of oral defamation requires the negligent or intentional speaking of false and defamatory words which are unprivileged and are spoken to a third person and which are actionable regardless of harm (i.e., *per se*) or because they cause special harm to the individual spoken about (i.e., *per quod*). Restatement Second, Torts, §558. *Slander* of title consists of false or malicious statements — both oral and written — disparaging a person's title to property, real or personal, causing him special damages (which must be proved).

See **SCANDAL**

SLANDER PER QUOD

Spoken words the defamatory impact of which must be proven by the plaintiff, who must allege and prove all the elements of slander and also injury to his own reputation or interests.

See **PER QUOD**

SLANDER PER SE

Slanderous in itself. Spoken words which are so instrinsically damaging to the reputation of the plaintiff or to his office, trade or business as to be presumed actionable at law and therefore not to require extrinsic proof of actual injury or damage. Examples: charging a person falsely with commission of a crime or with some loathsome disease or with deviate sexual conduct.

See **PER SE**

SOBER, SOBRIETY   [L. *sobrius* / not drunk, sober]

Discriminating and sparing in the use of intoxicating drinks. Sedate. Earnest. Not extreme in action or thought. *Sobriety* is the state of being sober. A *sobriety checkpoint* is a roadblock imposed by the police for the purpose of checking drivers for the excessive consumption of liquor. These checkpoints have been held not to violate the Constitutional search and seizure restraints.

SOCIAL   [L. *socio, sociare* / to join together, unite; to associate]

Involving the interaction of individuals with their friends and companions and with the other persons with whom they have contact. Companionship with one's friends and associates. The organization of individuals and groups into units for the development and promotion of interdependent relationships. A *social club* is an organization for other than business, philanthropic or educational purposes which is exempt from income tax under the Internal Revenue Code. A *social guest* is a person who comes upon the property of another on a social basis; the guest may be either a licensee or an invitee (some states do not make this distinction). A *social host* is an individual who serves another with alcohol in his home or office or in some other social setting and not for consideration or as a licensed vendor. *Social hosts* have been prosecuted criminally for serving liquor to minors and civilly for injuries caused to others by their liquor-consuming guests. *Social security* is a system of insurance established by the federal government in 1935 to provide old-age and survivors insurance, contributions to state unemployment insurance programs, and other benefits; the system is funded by employee contributions taken from salaries and wages and by contributions from employers.

SOCIAL SECURITY [L. *socio, sociare* / to unite or associate with (*socius* / a partner or comrade) + *securus* / free from care, tranquil]

The federal system for providing cash benefits to workers upon their retirement or to their survivors upon death or disability. The system is funded by mandated contributions from employer and employee. Any system of insurance designed to provide economic security to workers and their families. The federal system is administered by the Social Security Administration.

SOCIETY [L. *societas* / partnership, companionship, affiliation]

Any community of persons. The public in general. Any group of persons having a common interest, history or purpose. Also, a specific group of persons organized for some common purpose, such as the SPCA. Also, those benefits of love and affection shared by persons with common emotional interests, e.g., the family as a whole, or husband and wife, or parent and child. In this sense, a *loss of society* forms the basis for compensation through damages. A husband, for example, may sue a third party for the loss of his wife's *society* when she is injured or killed by that party's negligence.

SOCIUS CRIMINIS [L. *socius* (from *sociare*) / joint, allied, acting together + *crimen, criminis* / a charge or accusation; crime, guilt]

Partners in crime. A conspiracy to commit crime. The joining of persons to commit a crime. Joint defendants. Co-conspirators.

SOLATIUM [L. *solacium* / consolation, comfort]

Compensation for damage to one's emotions or feelings. Damages awarded in recognition of a victim's pain, suffering or injured feelings.

SOLE [L. *solus* / alone, only]

Not married. Solitary. Independent of help or interference; exclusive. Belonging exclusively to one identified person or group. *Sole custody* is the custody of a child awarded exclusively to one person, usually a parent. A *sole proprietorship* is a business owned and conducted by one person, who is responsible for all its obligations. *Sole and unconditional ownership* is ownership of property by one person to the exclusion of all others. The *sole actor doctrine* imposes liability upon a corporation for the acts of an officer or agent who is the only representative of the company in a particular transaction, even when that officer or agent acts fraudulenty or against the interest of the corporation.

SOLEMN, SOLEMNIZE [L. *sollemnis* / annual, recurring, periodic; solemn]

Characterized by austerity, gravity and earnestness, as in a religious or official ceremony. A celebratory occasion with a serious purpose, as in the administration of an oath of office. Awe-inspiring. To *solemnize* is to perform or administer with pomp and ceremony, as in a marriage, confirmation or bar mitzvah.

SOLICIT, SOLICITATION [L. *sollicito, sollicitare* / to stir, agitate; to disturb]

To ask for or entreat. To request or plead for. To ask someone to purchase an article, conduct a business transaction, or accept a service. To entice or lead someone to commit a crime. To proposition someone to engage in a sexual act for money, as by a prostitute. Many things may be the subject of solicitation, e.g., bribes, proxies, votes, etc.

SOLICITOR

In the United States, the title often given to a lawyer who is the head of the legal department of a municipality or other agency of government. In England, the term solicitor is given to lawyers who do not appear in court but who perform the other functions of practitioners at the bar, including consulting with and advising clients. A *solicitor* is also a person who attempts to procure sales and business by offering products and services to customers or by distributing information about them.

SOLICITOR GENERAL

The Solicitor General of the United States is the second ranking officer in the Justice Department. His function is to represent the nation's interest in civil litigation, or in arguing the nation's interest in cases before the Supreme Court.

SOLITARY [L. *solitarius* / alone, lonely]

Being or living alone. The state of existing apart from others; isolated. In a prison, *solitary confinement* is the confinement of one prisoner separately from all other prisoners. Desolate, unoccupied.

SOLVENCY, SOLVENT [L. *solvo, solvere* / to loosen, untie, free; to undo an obligation; to pay]

Solvent: the ability of a person to meet all his debts and obligations. Having sufficient assets and resources to meet all obligations in the ordinary course of business. *Solvency:* the state of being solvent.

SOURCE [L. *surge, surgere* / to rise, get up, surge]

The place or point of origin. The beginning. A person who supplies information, as to a reporter. The various documents (e.g. statutes, a constitution, judicial decisions, scholarly treatises), rules and principles which, together, provide the underpinning for the law are called *sources of the law*. A particular document, e.g., a contract, a set of by-laws or a particular judicial decision, may constitute a *source of authority* in a particular dispute.

SOVEREIGN [L. *super* / over, above, at the top]

Applied to persons, *sovereign* means one who exercises supreme authority in a defined sphere, as the king of a nation. A person who is acknowledged to be the prime leader of a group of people. Applied to states or nations, *sovereignty* defines a group of persons occupying a fixed territorial area, bound together by common laws and customs, having a single organized government and recognized by other states and nations as having sole and integrated powers over such functions as commerce, taxation, etc. Sovereignty can exist at several levels. The United States is a *sovereign nation*. Each state is a separate and independent sovereignty capable of making its own laws; the laws of any one state have no effect in any other state. Sovereignty is also the power to govern, i.e., to make and enforce laws.

SOVEREIGN IMMUNITY

The principle that a sovereign nation or state cannot be sued in its own courts unless it consents to be sued. The United States is immune from suit except under specific statutes such as the Federal Tort Claims Act. Also, the principle that one nation or state will respect the laws of another and will not interfere in the internal affairs of another.

See **IMMUNITY**

SPECIAL [L. *specialis* / individual, particular, one of a kind]

Possessing an unusual quality or character. Distinguished from others. Held in unusual esteem. Designed for or serving a particular purpose. Unique. A *special administrator* is appointed by a probate court to take charge of and preserve the assets of a decedent pending the appointment of an executor. A *special agent* is an agent appointed by a principal to carry out one or more specific acts or one or more specific transactions. A *special appearance* is an appearance by a party to an action for the sole and specific purpose of challenging the court's jurisdiction; it is distinguished from a general appearance. (Under the Federal Rules of Civil Procedure, a party may challenge the court's jurisdiction in the pleadings or by pre-trial motion.) A *special assessment* is a tax levied for a specific local purpose or improvement upon private property, or the imposition of a charge upon the members of a group, e.g., a condominium or social club, for some specific purpose of benefit to the group. *Special damages* are damages measured not by the standards applied generally to other cases of its kind, but by the circumstances affecting the damaged party in some peculiar and individual way. A *special election* is one held to fill an office vacated earlier than the end of the stated term by circumstances such as the death or resignation of the incumbent. A *special endorsement* on a check or note is one that specifies a particular payee, as opposed to a general endorsement or an endorsement to bearer.

SPECIALIA GENERALIBUS DEROGANT

Special words or phrases circumscribe or restrict the impact or meaning of more general terms.

SPECIALTY [L. *specialis* / individual, different]

A distinctive mark or quality. A document under seal, e.g., a *specialty contract* or mortgage. In real property, a building with so specialized and unique a purpose as to make it difficult or impossible to convert it to general or different use. Also, a branch of a trade or profession practiced by individuals who are specially trained or certified. Examples: a doctor may practice the *specialty* of gastroenterology, or a lawyer the *specialty* of Patent Law. Under the Codes governing the conduct of lawyers, a lawyer may not advertise a *specialty* unless he is certified as a specialist in a particular area by a Bar Association or by a public authority authorized to issue certifications.

SPECIE [L. *species* / something seen, a vision, a sighting; a specimen; a notion or idea]

Money or coin. Gold or silver coin; cash. To pay *in specie* is to pay in the same form or kind as before, e.g., in cash if cash was originally the form of a loan or advance.

SPECIFIC [L. *species*]

Belonging to a distinct and identifiable category. Capable of being isolated by description and identification. Sharing with other things or persons qualities or characteristics which isolate them from others. Restricted to a particular individual or group. A *specific bequest* is a bequest of a specified item or part of an estate, or one that is payable only from a specified fund or source and not from the general assets of the decedent. A *specific denial* is a denial addressed to one or several of the allegations of a pleading, in contrast to a general denial, which denies all the allegations. *Specific intent* is the intent to perform an identifiable criminal act with knowledge that the consequences will be exactly those described and anticipated in the statute defining the act, e.g., assault with intent to kill. A *specific legacy* is the bequest of a particular asset or fund of a decedent, set apart and separately identified. A *specific lien* is a charge or encumbrance upon a particular piece of property operating as security for performance or payment of an obligation; the charging lien of an attorney or the mechanic's lien of an artisan are examples of *specific liens*.

SPECIFIC PERFORMANCE

The judicial order or decree under which a party is ordered and compelled to perform an act which he either agreed to perform or which the court in equity has determined that he should perform. The device of *specific performance* is utilized when remedies at law are inadequate to compensate the plaintiff for his injuries. The equitable remedy of compelling performance to adjust grievances as contrasted with an award of damages at law. The remedy is most often utilized to compel performance of real estate contracts, because of the unique quality of each separate parcel of land.

SPECIFICATION   [L. *species* (from *specio, specere* / to look at, behold; a vision or sighting]

Any item contained in a list of details or data; also, the list itself. A detailed presentation of the ingredients of a plan, proposal, quotation, purchase order or other commercial document. An exhibit to a contract setting forth in greater detail items referred to more generally in the body of the contract. In bankruptcy, a statement of the objections to discharge of the debtor. In military courts-martial, a statement of the formal charges against the defendant. In construction contracts, the statement prepared by an architect or engineer, setting forth in precise detail, usually with reference to plans or drawings, the processes under which construction or improvement of a building or other structure is to proceed. In patent law, a written description of an invention or discovery that shows in detail the way to make and use the invention or discovery, accompanied by a claim for credit and protection by the inventor.

SPECULATE, SPECULATION, SPECULATIVE   [L. *speculor, speculari* / to watch over, spy on]

Speculate: To appraise or review; to contemplate, sometimes without conclusion or resolution. To form a questionable conclusion after inadaquate analysis. To theorize or wonder. Juries are generally admonished by judges not to speculate on the basis of insufficient or questionable evidence. Also, to make a business investment in the hope of gain or profit, as in a publicly traded stock. *Speculation:* The act of entering into or undertaking a business risk in the hope, but without the certainty, of making a gain or profit. *Speculative:* Incapable of certainty; based upon theory or possibility only. A *speculative security* is a stock or bond which depends on future performance and earnings without any assurance of gain or even stability. *Speculative damages* are damages which cannot be measured with certainty; all estimates of damage with respect to the future impact of injuries in a tort action contain at least some elements of speculation, however dutifully the jury may apply reasonable mathematical data.

SPEND   [L. *expendo, expendere* / to weigh out, to pay out, put down money]

To pay out money or assets. To exchange money or assets for goods. To use up or give up. To use up or consume. To exhaust the supply of.

SPENDTHRIFT

A person who is imprudent or careless in his use or expenditure of money and assets. A wasteful person. A *spendthrift trust* is a trust created to defeat or impede the tendency or impulse of an imprudent beneficiary to waste the assets of the trust; the trust restricts access by the beneficiary to the trust principal and provides for the disposition of trust income solely for the benefit of the beneficiary. The assets of the trust cannot be reached by the beneficiary's creditors to satisfy any debts he may create.

SPOLIATION   [L. *spolio, spoliare* / to plunder, strip of, deprive of, take away from]

To plunder or take by force or pressure. To injure beyond retrieval. To waste away or destroy. The alteration or destruction of a document, such as a will or contract, by a stranger to the document. Also, the destruction or mutilation of material evidence.

SPONSOR   [L. *spondeo, spondere* / to pledge, promise, engage]

A person who assumes responsibility for an act, thing, or person. A person who supports the work and performance of an author, musician or artist. A person who subsidizes or contributes to the creation, production or promotion of some enterprise or project, such as a theatrical performance, an art gallery, a philanthropic organization or a school. Also, a person who contributes to the cost of a radio or television program by advertisement or grant. A person who occupies the position of mentor to another and who endorses or supports the membership of the latter in some select group or honor, e.g., the attorney who sponsors the admission to the bar of a student who has passed the bar exam. Also, a legislator who introduces or supports a new piece of legislation. Also, anyone who promotes to others investment in a business venture.

SPONTANEOUS (DECLARATION)   [L. *sponte* / of one's own free will; for its own account; unassisted]

Arising from natural causes or impulse without external suggestion or provocation. Impelled from within. Occurring without external influence or force. Automatic; unthinking. A *spontaneous declaration* is a statement made under conditions of excitement, impulse or pain in conditions which support truth and preclude time or opportunity for fabrication. *Spontaneous declarations* (also called exclamations or utterances) are an important exception to the hearsay rule, falling under the excited utterance exception.

SPOUSAL IMMUNITY
   See **IMMUNITY (SPOUSAL)**

SPOUSE   [L. *sponsus* / a bridegroom or bride; anyone newly married]
   A husband or wife; a married person.

SPURIOUS [L. *spurius* / an illegitimate child]

Anyone born illegitimately. False; appearing real or true but actually fictitious and false. Forged; deceitful. Counterfeit. A copy not painted by the original artist is *spurious*, as is a counterfeit bill.

STAKE, STAKEHOLDER [L. *tignum* / wooden beam or *stagarus* / long dry stalk]

A boundary marker used to define property lines in land surveys. Also, money deposited for the account of one of two or more persons to await the outcome of some event or contingency which will establish who is entitled to the money. Also, the subject matter of a claim or interpleader. Also, the interest of a participant in some commercial undertaking. A *stakeholder* is the person who is assigned or entrusted to hold property claimed by two or more persons until the person entitled to the property is determined.

STANDI

See **LOCUS STANDI**

STARE DECISIS [L. *sto, stare* / to stand + *decido, decidere* / to cut short; to settle or arrange]

To stand by that which was decided. One of the fundamental principles of British and American jurisprudence, *stare decisis* stands for the rule that once an issue is decided or settled by a court of appellate jurisdiction which has considered all the elements of that issue, that decision should be followed by all courts of equal or lower jurisdiction in subsequent cases, whether or not they involve the same parties. The doctrine provides for stability and consistency in the administration of justice. It is a rule which encourages adherence to judicial precedent. The rule applies only within the limits of one state and does not bind the courts of another state.

See **PRECEDENT**

STATE [L. *stare* / to stand (*status* / position, posture)]

A condition, attribute or attitude of a person or thing. The existing condition of a person or thing. One of several phases through which a person passes, as the state of infancy. A body of persons with a special social rank. Also, the political organization of a group of people into a cohesive and identifiable whole occuping a defined territory, as in New York State. A government having a particular quality or character, as a police state. One of several component political entities of equal rank which join together to form a federation of states, as in the fifty states forming the United States. A *state agency* is any official department or board of a state created for the purpose of carrying out the executive functions of the state. *State action* is action which is taken directly by any state or by its authorized representatives or which is legally attributed to it; under federal law, state action is subject to judicial scrutiny for violations of due process and equal protection under the Fourteenth Amendment. A participant in a crime who agrees to testify for the state in a criminal prosecution in exchange for a reduced sentence is said to turn *state's evidence*. The doctrine of *states' rights* is a doctrine grafted onto the Constitutional concept that those powers not specifically granted to the federal government are reserved to the individual states; the doctrine is used by states which choose to challenge federal intervention in certain areas of government, as by the Southern states in their now unlawful effort to preserve separate-but-equal systems of public education.

STATEMENT   [L. *status* / standing, condition, position]

Anything stated; a declaration or remark. An allegation of a matter of fact. A written or oral assertion. Also, a financial record. The summary at a particular moment of the invoices owed and credits extended to a purchaser of goods or services. A *closing statement* is a summary prepared by an attorney following a real estate transaction, showing the financial elements governing the transaction. A *financial statement* is a statement showing the financial condition and course of activities of a business enterprise as of a given date. A *statement of affairs* is a statement and schedule required of a debtor in bankruptcy, showing his past financial transactions and his current financial condition. An *opening statement* is the statement made by an attorney to the jury before receipt of testimony in which he outlines the scope and content of his proof.

STATIM (STAT)   [L. *stare* / to stand, hold firm]

Instantly, immediately.

STAT PRO RATIONE VOLUNTAS POPULI

The public will has priority even over reason.

STATU QUO   [L. *status* / a standing position, a *posture* + *quo* / in which]
See **IN STATU QUO**

STATUS   [L. *status* / position, posture]

Relative rank in a hierarchy of things or persons. The position or condition of a person as determined by the law. Present condition or position.

STATUS CRIME

A crime defined not by the nature of the specific act committed by the accused, but by his personal condition or character. The crime of vagrancy is an example of a *status crime*. A vagrant commits no act except, perhaps, the act of standing on a corner or sleeping on a street. A *status offender* is a juvenile who has not committed any adult crime but who comes before the criminal system because of conduct indicating a failure of parental control.

STATUS QUO

The existing condition or state of affairs. The posture or position which the parties are occupying or have just occupied. The condition of the parties before any action is taken to change that condition; the existing condition can be preserved by the court through a restraining order or temporary injunction.

See **IN STATU QUO**

STATUS QUO ANTE

The condition or state which existed before the present condition. On an application by one party to rescind a contract, the court may order rescission and restore the parties to the *status quo ante*, i.e., the condition which existed for each of them before the contract was executed.

STATUTE   [L. *status* / position, state]

Any law enacted by a legislature or a body having legislative powers as defined by a constitution or equivalent document. Under international law, a document creating an international agency and defining its powers. Any regulation, edict or declaration to which the police and the courts accord the force of law.

STATUTE OF FRAUDS

Any of a series of state laws, all modelled after the English Statute of Frauds, specifying circumstances under which some defined transactions must be in writing to be enforceable. Generally, the statutes require a writing for all real estate contracts and for contracts which cannot be performed within a single year. The Uniform Commercial Code provides that a contract for the sale of goods exceeding $500 in value is enforceable against the person to be charged only if he has signed the contract.

STATUTE OF LIMITATIONS

Any statute which imposes a time limit for the commencement of an action or a prosecution. In civil actions, the time usually begins to run from the time the action accrues; in criminal actions, from the time the crime is committed. The expiration of the statutory period is a complete defense to the action or prosecution.

See **REPOSE (STATUTE OF)**

STATUTE OF REPOSE

See **REPOSE (STATUTE OF)**

STATUTORY [L. *status*]

Of or related to statutes or legislative enactments. Defined by statute. Enacted, created or regulated by statute. A *statutory action* is an action created by statute as opposed to one which existed at common law. A *statutory foreclosure* is a proceeding for foreclosing the interests of a mortgagor in real estate without a formal judicial proceeding; statutory foreclosure is accomplished under the terms of the statute by a mortgagee who executes a power of sale. *Statutory rape* is sexual intercourse with a minor whose consent to the intercourse is immaterial to the crime. The age of minority is established by statute.

STAY [L. *stare* / to stand]

To stop or pause. To check or restrain. The temporary suspension of some act or activity by judicial or executive order. To put a stop to all proceedings. Restraint by court order or injunction. An appellate court may *stay* all proceedings in a lower court, including execution on a judgment, pending the outcome of the appeal. The Bankruptcy Code imposes an *automatic stay* against all creditors upon the filing of a petition in bankruptcy. The stay prevents the creditors from attempting to collect any sums from the debtor, or from bringing, maintaining or prosecuting any action against him except upon order of the court.

STET [L. *stare* / to stand]

Let it stand. In a writing, a direction to the reader to leave standing a word or phrase previously marked for change or deletion. Also, an abbreviation for *stet processus*, an order to stay all proceedings in an action.

STET PROCESSUS [L. *stare* / to stand + *processus* (from *procedo, procedere*) / advance, progress, process]

Let the process be stopped or stayed. The voluntary dismissal of an action by the plaintiff. The entry of an order by the court staying all proceedings in the action.

STET PROHIBITIO [L. *stare* / to stand + *prohibio, prohibere* / to hold back, check, restrain]

Let the prohibition stand.

STIPEND [L. *stipes* / stump, tree trunk + *pendo, pendere* / to weigh, consider]

A fixed sum of money paid periodically for services given, or to reimburse for expenses incurred. Also, a salary or fixed compensation.

STIPULATE, STIPULATION [L. *stipulor, stipulari* / to demand an agreement, to insist, bargain]

To specify a term or condition of a proposal or agreement. To reach agreement upon a term or condition. To enter into an agreement. To exact or demand a particular provision. To express a thought or concept before a court for the purpose of indicating or inviting agreement to a proposition or ruling. A *stipulation* is an agreement or concession made by the parties in a judicial proceeding, or by their attorneys, either settling the matter entirely or agreeing upon some matter which disposes of an issue and removes an obstacle to disposition of a motion or ruling. A *stipulation of facts* is an agreement among the parties as to certain facts bearing on the issues, thus dispensing with the need for presenting evidence as to those facts.

STIRPES [L. *stirps, stirpes* / the roots and stem of a plant]

See **PER STIRPES**

STRICT [L. *stringo, stringere, strictum* / to tighten, bind]

Stringent in controls; exacting. Severe in administering discipline. Conforming rigorously to a rule or standard. Permitting no change or deviation. *Strict construction* is judicial interpretation restricted to a literal reading of the words in the statute or document (e.g., the U.S. Constitution) being interpreted.

STRICT FORECLOSURE

A statutory proceeding leading to the extinguishment of a mortgagor's rights to real property under a judicial decree without a public sale; the decree fixes a time within which the mortgagor must liquidate the mortgage debt. If he fails to do so, his title is extinguished and title, both legal and equitable, passes to the mortgagee. Also, with respect to personal property under the Uniform Commercial Code, the acceptance by and transfer to a creditor of his collateral in full satisfaction of his debt, without right to a deficiency judgment for any balance; notice must be given to other creditors having a security interest in the same collateral; if they object to the transfer to the first creditor, a foreclosure sale must be held.

STRICTI JURIS; STRICTISSIMI JURIS

According only to strict legal right, without any reference to principles of equity. A strict and legalistic interpretation of the rights and duties of the parties.

STRICT LIABILITY

Liabililty imposed by the law regardless of fault or negligence. A principle of the law of torts and of products liability imposing liability upon persons who maintain dangerous animals or who engage in inherently dangerous activities, whether or not they are negligent or intend injury or damage. The principle is guided by the notion that these persons have a social obligation to "pay their own way." Examples: *Strict liability* is imposed for injuries resulting from crop dusting, and from the use and storage of explosives.

STRICT SCRUTINY

A doctrine enunciated by the Supreme Court which requires the courts to give the highest level of scrutiny before deciding that a statute or regulation affecting certain classifications does not violate the Equal Protection Clause of the Fourteenth Amendment. The *strict scrutiny doctrine* replaced the "mere rationality" test which had previously existed. The courts impose *strict scrutiny* whenever the classification involved, e.g., race, national origin, sex, etc., is a "suspect" one or the classification has an impact on a "fundamental right." Under *strict scrutiny*, a challenged law will be upheld only if it is necessary "to achieve a compelling governmental interest."

See **INTERMEDIATE (SCRUTINY)**

SUA SPONTE [L. *suus* / his, her, its, theirs + *sponte* / willingly, without persuasion, of one's own accord]

Of itself or of one's self, without being prompted. A court may act *sua sponte* to order a new trial or to dismiss a complaint. A lawyer's disciplinary committee may move *sua sponte* to investigate some act of an attorney of which it has become aware without any specific complaint from a client or judge.

SUB [L. underneath, under]

Below; up from below. Under, beneath. Under the power of. Also, subordinate, secondary. Almost, nearly complete.

SUB COLORE JURIS

Under color or claim of right or law.

SUB COLORE OFFICII

Under color or claim of office.

SUBCONTRACT [L. *sub* + *contraho, contrahere* / to draw together, bring about, contract]

A contract between one of the parties to a performance contract and a third party under which the former assigns to the latter the responsibility for part of the performance, whether in labor or materials. Subcontracts are utilized most often in construction contracts.

SUB CURA MARITI [L. *sub* + *cura* / care, concern + *maritus* / of marriage; a man or husband]
Under the care of the husband.

SUB CURIA [L. *sub* + *curia* / the meeting place of the Roman senate; a meeting place]
Under control of the court.

SUBDIVIDE [L. *sub* + *divido, dividere* / to divide, separate]
To divide into several parts. To divide a tract of land into smaller parcels in preparation for construction, as in the case of houses or office buildings.

SUBJACENT [L. *sub* + *iaceo, iacere* / to rest, lie quietly, be still]
Lying under or below. Lower than. *Subjacent support* is the right of a landlord to the continued support of his building through maintenance by the adjoining landlord of existing conditions; also, the right of occupants of an upper part of a building to continued support by the lower part.

SUBJECT [L. *sub* + *iacio, iacere* / to throw, hurl]
A citizen of a state or nation. A domiciliary of a country enjoying the rights, privileges and protection of the citizens of that country. The object of study or evaluation. The focus of an inquiry or of a work of art or creation. Anything acted upon. To bring under the control of. To influence or act upon. To cause a person to suffer or undergo something unpleasant or inconvenient.

SUBJECTIVE [L. *sub* + *iacio, iacere* / to throw]
Peculiar to each individual; personal. Concepts, thoughts or reactions resulting from an individual's experience or knowledge as conditioned by or filtered through his own perceptions and mental characteristics. Not objective; not based upon empirical data or proof. A *subjective examination* is an examination from which a physician forms a conclusion or diagnosis based entirely on the patient's own description of his symptoms.

SUBJECT MATTER JURISDICTION
The power of a particular court to bind the parties in terms of the subject matter which it can hear and determine, in contrast to its territorial jurisdiction or the amounts in controversy which it may hear. Examples: Housing courts are limited to actions between landlord and tenant. Probate courts are limited to proceedings involving estates and such matters as adoption. Bankruptcy courts are limited to matters under the Bankruptcy Code. The federal courts generally have *subject matter jurisdiction* over diversity cases and cases involving federal questions.

SUB JUDICE [L. *sub* + *iudico, iudicare* / to judge]
Under authority of a court; before a court or judge for consideration.

SUBMIT, SUBMISSION [L. *sub* + *mitto, mittere* / to send, let go]
To yield to greater strength or to authority. To present for review or consideration, as a report or paper. To put forward as an opinion. To surrender. To make documents or arguments available to a court to enable it to reach a decision. To consent to the jurisdiction of a court. To defer to the opinion of another. A *submission* is an agreement to be bound by the determination of another. The parties *submit a matter* to an arbitrator for decision. A judge submits the determination of facts and the return of a verdict to the jury.

SUB MODO [L. *sub* + *modus* / a measure, standard, limit]
Under a qualification; subject to a condition or qualification.

SUB NOMINE [L. *sub* + *nomen, nominis* / a name]
Under the name; used to indicate that the original title of a case has been altered at a later stage in the proceedings. Abbreviated "sub.nom."

SUBORDINATE, SUBORDINATION [L. *sub* + *ordinare* / to put in order]
Subordinate: To treat as less important or of lower rank. To assign to a lower rank or order. To make less valuable than or subservient to. To delay payment or satisfaction of one debt until another debt has been paid. *Subordination:* The act of placing one obligation behind another in payment and preference. A *subordination agreement* is an agreement under which one creditor consents to give another creditor priority and preference over his claims against the debtor. Example: a corporate officer may be asked to *subordinate* his loans to the corporation to the loans made to the corporation by a bank. If the corporation becomes insolvent, the doctrine of *equitable subordination* (a/k/a the "Deep Rock Doctrine") may be invoked to subordinate his loans to the claims of general creditors.

SUBORN, SUBORNATION [L. *suborno, subornare* / to furnish; to influence secretly; to instigate]
To induce someone to commit an unlawful act, especially secretly. To influence someone to lie in a judicial proceeding or to commit perjury. *Subordination of perjury* is the crime of inducing perjury.
See **PERJURY**

SUBPOENA [L. *sub* + *poena* / money paid in atonement; punishment, penalty]
A document which compels attendance by a witness or the production of evidence. The writ issued under authority of a court to compel the appearance of a witness or the production of evidence at a judicial proceeding.

SUBPOENA AD TESTIFICANDUM

A more technical name for a subpeona. An order compelling attendance by a witness for the purpose of giving testimony.

SUBPOENA DUCES TECUM

Bring with you under penalty. The writ under which a witness is required not only to attend but also to produce books, papers, records and documents in his possession which may serve as evidence in a litigation.

See **DUCES TECUM**

SUB POTESTATE PARENTIS   [L. *sub* + *potestas* / power, control + *parens* / parent, father, mother]

Under the protection or control of a parent.

SUBROGATE, SUBROGATION   [L. *subrogo, subrogare* / to substitute one person for another; to put in place of]

To substitute for or put in place of another. To substitute one creditor for another. To assume the rights of another with respect to a legal claim or debt. In a typical *subrogation*, a third party who has a right against one of the original parties to a transaction or event steps into the shoes of that party to assert the rights of that party against the other party to the transaction. *Subrogation* occurs in construction contracts, insurance contracts, suretyships and guarantees. Under a typical insurance contract, the insurer who has reimbursed its assured for his loss will be able to substitute for the assured in asserting and pursuing a claim against the party who caused the original loss.

See **SURROGATE**

SUB ROSA   [L. *sub* + *rosa* / a rose]

Literally "under the rose" (in ancient times, the rose was associated with secrecy). Secretly, covertly, privately.

SUBSCRIBE   [L. *sub* + *scribo, scribere* / to write]

To write beneath. To write one's own name; to sign. To sign at the bottom of a document to indicate assent, acceptance or approval. To attest or pledge. To support an organization or cause by promising to pay a sum of money or other thing of value. To pay for and agree to accept a series of issues of a publication, as a magazine or newsletter. To agree to accept and pay for a security issued by a corporation. A *subscribing witness* is a witness to the excecution of a document, e.g., a will or contract, who attests to its execution by placing his signature at the foot of the document.

SUBSCRIPTION   [L. *sub* + *scribere*]

   The act of writing one's name at the end of a document. A written commitment to accept and pay for the stock of a corporation, or to contribute a sum of money to a cause or organization, or to pay for a periodical or book.

SUBSEQUENT   [L. *sub* / under, near, nearby + *sequor, sequi* / to follow, go with]

   Coming later in time; following. The law deals in several contexts with *conditions subsequent*. In contract law, a *condition subsequent* is any future event or contingency which, by present agreement of the parties, will operate to discharge a duty by one of the parties which has attached or vested. In insurance contracts, for example, a provision stating that a claim must be brought before a certain date or be discharged will be construed as a *condition subsequent*. In the law of real property, any condition which causes defeasance of an estate already vested is a *condition subsequent*.
   See **REVERTER**

SUBSIDIARY   [L. *subsidium* / reserve troops; troops in the rear lines (from *subsido, subsidere* / to lie in ambush; lurk]

   Anything of less importance than something else. Of secondary importance. A corporation whose stock is wholly or predominantly owned or controlled by another corporation. The latter corporation is called the parent company. Also, a fact which is not persuasive in itself but which can be combined with other facts to prove an ultimate fact.

SUBSIDY   [L. *subsidium*]

   A grant of money or other thing of value, usually by a governmental or quasi-governmental entity, to a non-public organization or to a private person, to promote and develop an enterprise which is likely to be of public or general value. Examples: subsidies to farmers, to broadcast stations, to certain industries, to certain schools, to opera companies, to dance and theatrical groups, etc.

SUB SIGILLO   [L. *sub* + *sigilla* / engraving in a signet ring; a seal]
   Under seal.

SUB SILENTIO   [L. *sub* + *silentium* / stillness, silence]
   Under silence; silently. Without giving notice.

SUBSIST, SUBSISTENCE   [L. *sub* + *sisto, sistere* / to place in position; to cause to stand; to appear on schedule]

   Subsist: To continue or survive. To possess the bare necessities of life, i.e., food, water, shelter; to maintain oneself. *Subsistence:* The act of securing the necessities of life. The state of existing. The means of support and maintenance. Procurement of the items necessary to sustain life. An allowance given to a spouse to cover expenses incurred during defense of a divorce action in a state in which the spouse is not domiciled.

See **SUSTENANCE**

SUBSTANCE   [L. *sub + sto, stare* / to stand; to stand under]

An essential part or nature. Physical material which has a discrete identity. Something from which something else is made or derived. As distinguished from form, substance is anything describing the essentials to a right or claim, i.e., the marrow of the claim. (e.g., a contract which is adequate in substance will be enforced, although it may be defective in form.) In the phrase *substance abuse, substance* means any drug or liquor the consumption of which is controlled by statute or regulation.

SUBSTANTIAL   [L. *sub + stare*]

Real, not imaginary or illusory. Important; essential. Having great weight or impact. Sturdy, strong. Influential. An act or condition which is *substantially completed* may be regarded in some cases as a legally acceptable alternative to full completion.

SUBSTANTIATE   [L. *sub + stare*]

To give form and substance to. To verify or prove, as by persuasive evidence. To establish as true.

SUBSTANTIVE   [L. *sub + stare*]

Real, not illusory. Having both body and form. Relating to the essence or basic nature of a right or claim. Involving matters of importance or consequence. As used in the law, relating to substance and not to form or procedure. A *substantive crime* is a crime which does not contain within its definition any element of another crime.

See **SUBSTANCE**

SUBSTANTIVE DUE PROCESS

The Constitutional requirement that all laws, statutes and regulations adopted by any state must comply with the Due Process Clause of the Fourteenth Amendment. In this way, a state may not interfere with a person's freedom of contract or his right to privacy. This limitation is called *substantive due process*. The concept of *substantive due process* is different from the principles of procedural due process. *Substantive due process* prohibits a state from legislating or regulating in violation of the Due Process Clause. Procedural due process refers to those rights which may not be impaired by misapplication of a law, however valid, to a particular individual or to a particular circumstance.

See **PROCEDURAL DUE PROCESS**

SUBSTANTIVE LAW

Those elements of the law which define rights and obligations and which establish and define the rules for regulating society and commerce among people. Contract law, Constitutional Law, Criminal Law, Torts, Property — these are all areas of *substantive law.* Procedural or adjectival law deals with the machinery created by statute, rule or judicial decision to manage or enforce these substantive rules. Some areas of the law are both substantive and procedural. The subject of Bankruptcy, for example, deals both with the rights and duties of creditors and debtors in bankruptcy and also with the procedures to be followed in the bankruptcy courts. The law school courses in Criminal Law and Criminal Procedure reflect the difference between substance and procedure in dealing with crimes.

See **PROCEDURAL LAW**

SUBSTITUTE, SUBSTITUTED   [L. *sub* + *statuere* / to cause to stand; to establish, set up]

Substitute: To use or put in place of another. To replace or exchange. Also, a person who takes the place of another, as a substitute batter or pitcher in baseball. *Substituted*: used in place of something or someone else; exchanged for. A *substituted administrator* is an administrator appointed to replace another who is unable to act. A *substituted bequest* is a will provision which provides for a *substitute beneficiary* in the event the original beneficiary dies before the testator. A *substituted party* is a new party who takes the place of an original party to litigation. A *substituted basis* in tax law is the adjusted basis or cost of property received in exchange for other property of like kind.

SUBSTITUTED SERVICE

The service of process by a means other than personal service. Many forms of *substituted service* exist in the various states. Examples: leaving a summons with a person not the named party, at the residence, home or place of business of the named party; service by mail; service by publication, etc.

SUB SUO PERICULO   [L. *sub* + *suo* / his, his own + *periculum* / trial, proof, test; also danger, peril, risk]

At his own risk.

SUBTERFUGE   [L. *subter* / beneath; secretly, in secret + *fugio, fugere* / to flee, run away]

Deception with intent to conceal, escape or evade. A contrivance. A false position or action. A scheme to avoid responsibility for one's actions.

SUBVERT, SUBVERSION, SUBVERSIVE [L. *sub* + *verto, vertere* / to turn, turn around]

To corrupt by attacking one's morals or standards. To bring down or destroy. To overturn or overthrow. To undermine or weaken the foundation of. *Subversion* is the attempt to destroy or undermine the institutions of a country or government, usually by activities within the country itself. A *subversive* is a person who engages in subversion. *Subversive acts* or activities are all those acts directed toward the destruction of a government. *Subversion* is a federal crime.

SUCCEED, SUCCESSION, SUCCESSIVE [L. *succedo, succedere* / to go under, submit to; also, to come after, follow, succeed]

Succeed: To follow in order or sequence. To acquire a property right or interest from a decedent, by will or intestacy. To come into a title or honor. *Succession*: The order in which persons acquire interests in a particular property. The order in which persons acquire title or vestigial rights. The process by which things and persons follow each other in order. The process by which an individual acquires a beneficial interest in a testamentary estate. A *succession tax* is a tax upon the privilege of acquiring an interest in property by will or inheritance. *Successive*: Following in order; following without interruption or hiatus. *Successive assignees* are a series of assignees, one from the other, all of whom acquire the same interest in a particular property, but at different times. *Successive indictments* are a series of indictments of the same defendant for the same crime, usually separated by the dismissal of an earlier indictment or by an order for a new trial. A *successive tortfeasor* is a second tortfeasor who has contributed independently of the first tortfeasor to the injuries of the plaintiff.

SUDDEN [L. *subitus* / sudden, by surprise]

Occurring unexpectedly. Changing in form or substance without notice or warning. Characterized by haste. Precipitate. *Sudden heat* is another term for the heat of passion (also called the sudden heat of passion.) *Sudden heat* is an excess of rage or anger caused by an immediate provocation, not by a former provocation or one which has elapsed with sufficient time to cool off. *Sudden heat* is relevant in judging the crime of manslaughter. The *sudden emergency doctrine* provides a defense to negligence. Under circumstances in which a defendant finds himself confronted by a sudden emergency which was not the result of his own negligence, he is permitted to act as any other reasonably prudent person would act under the same emergency.

SUFFER, SUFFERANCE [L. *sub* + *fero, ferre* / to bear, take, carry; to put in motion]

To feel strongly. To endure; to be forced to endure. To tolerate or accept without objection. To put up with. To endure or feel pain, discomfort or disability. To accept knowingly and willingly, and, by extension, to permit or allow some act to be done or tolerated. *Sufferance* is consent implied through continued acceptance, failure to object or intervene, or failure to enforce an obligation, sanction or prohibition. A *tenancy at sufferance* is a tenancy which continues beyond the term of a lease when the landlord fails to take action to evict the tenant. An *estate at sufference* is the estate of one who continues to exercise a right or claim after his lawful right to do so has ended.

SUFFICIENCY, SUFFICIENT [L. *sufficio, sufficere* / to imbue, provide, supply; also, to be enough, to be adequate]

Enough; adequate. All that is needed in a given situation or circumstance. Equal to the purpose or need. A *good and sufficient deed* is a deed which conveys exactly the title specified in and required by the contract of sale. *Sufficient evidence* is evidence adequate to support a jury's verdict or a judge's fact findings. *Sufficient sureties* are sureties on a bail bond with enough resources to meet the terms of the bond and enough influence with the defendant to secure his appearance before the court.

SUFFRAGE [L. *suffragor, suffragari* / to vote in favor of, approve, support]

The right to vote. Also, the exercise of that right. To vote in an election or referendum. To choose between two candidates or two sides of a public question.

SUGGESTIO FALSI SUPPRESSIO VERI

A misrepresentation suppresses the truth.

SUGGESTIVE [L. *suggero, suggerere* / to supply, provide, pile up]

Prompting thought or response. Stimulating. Imparting mental associations or stimuli. A *suggestive mark* is a trademark that suggests or identifies the product or service it is associated with, e.g., the mark *Greyhound* for a bus or *Coppertone* for suntan oil. The consumer is expected to associate the mark instinctively with the product, e.g., buses with greyhounds because they go fast. *Suggestive marks* are considered inherently distinctive and therefore entitled to protection without proof of secondary meaning.

See **SECOND**

SUICIDE   [L. *sui, suus* / reflexive pronoun him, her, its, their; himself, herself, yourself, themselves + *caedo, caedere* / to cut down, kill]

The act of taking one's own life intentionally and while in sound mind. A person who ends his own life. *Assisted suicide* is the act of a doctor, relative or friend in helping a person to end his life when that person is terminally ill and close to death. Assisted suicide usually involves handing the patient a drug which he administers himself, but it may also involve the administering of the drug directly by the doctor or relative. A *suicide clause* in a life insurance policy is a provision limiting the liability of the carrier to the payment of net premiums in the event of suicide by the assured.

SUI GENERIS   [L. *sui* + *genus, generis* / class, kind]

Of its own kind. Unique; in a class by itself. Different from others.

SUI JURIS   [L. *sui* + *ius, iuris* / right, law]

Of his own right; a term used to describe one who is no longer dependent upon others, e.g., one who has reached the age of majority. Possessing the legal capacity to act in one's own behalf. Enjoying all the rights of citizens, including the right to vote.

SUITOR   [L. *sequor, sequi* / to follow]

Anyone who asks, entreats or petitions. A man who asks a woman to marry him. Anyone who applies or works to take over a business. A party to a law suit.

SUMMARY   [L. *superus, supremus, summus* / the highest]

A statement setting forth a collection of facts or data. A compendium of points made in a document or speech. Short, concise. Reduced to fewer words. Completed expeditiously and without delay. Done without the usual formalities and procedures. A *summary court-martial* is the lowest form of military court-martial. It is heard by a single commissioned officer and deals only with petty offenses by non-commissioned personnel. *Summary distribution* is an expedited form of distribution which is utilized when the assets of an estate are sufficient only to pay superior claims (such as statutory shares). A *summary proceeding* is a proceeding, e.g., a landlord's dispossess action, conducted without the usual formalities (usually without a jury) and with the intent of obtaining speedy disposition of a matter. *Summary judgment* is a judgment granted on motion when the pleadings and other papers in an action establish that there is no triable issue of fact and that the moving party is entitled to judgment on the facts before the court, as a matter of law. Under the Federal Rules of Civil Procedure, a summary judgment motion may be made at any time after 20 days following commencement of the action.

SUMMATION [L. *summus, summa* / a form of *summus* / the highest]

A summing up. The act or process of reviewing a number of facts or events and expressing conclusions as to their significance or meaning. The final part of an argument, integrating all the parts into a conclusory statement. The closing argument made by a lawyer after the evidence is all in, presenting the evidence most favorably to his client and summarizing the relief requested.

SUMMONS [L. *summoneo, summonere* (*sub* + *monere* / to warn) / to remind in secret]

The written notice that advises a party to a civil action to appear in court and respond to the notice within a time specified. A document issued by the clerk of court in lieu of an arrest warrant in a minor criminal matter requiring the defendant to appear and respond to the charges against him. A notice to appear for jury duty. Also, a notice to appear as a witness.

SUMMUM JUS SUMMA INJURIA

Excessive strictness or rigidity in the law creates the greatest wrong. The more rigid the law the greater the potential for injustice.

SUMPTUARY LAWS [L. *sumptuarius* (from *sumere* / to borrow or spend) / relating to expenses]

Laws designed to curb or regulate extravagant expenditutes or display. In medieval England, these laws even attempted to curb the quantity of food that could be eaten at a single meal.

SUO NOMINE [L. *suus, suo* / himself + *nomen, nominis* / name]

In his own name. Under his own name.

SUO PERICULO [L. *suus* + *periculum* / a trial or test; a hazard or risk; danger, peril]

At his own risk.

SUPER ALTUM MARE [L. *super* / over, above + *alo, altus* / grown great, lofty, the highest + *mare* / the sea]

On the high seas.

SUPERIOR [L. *superus, superior* (*supremus*) / situated above, higher than]

Of higher rank or position. Greater in quantity or number. Having priority. A *superior court* is usually an intermediate court of general jursidiction with authority to conduct jury trials. A *superior force* is a force or an event which cannot be predicted or protected against; an act of God. A *superior lien* is a lien which has priority over other liens. A *superior title* is a title to real property which will be recognized by the courts as having priority over all other competing titles to the same property.

SUPERSEDE, SUPERSEDING   [L. *supersedere* / to sit above; to be superior to; to have priority over]

To push aside; to replace. To displace in favor of another. To come before or ahead of. Also, to suspend; to delay the operation of. To render void or ineffective. A *superseding cause* is a kind of intervening cause, i.e., a cause that intervenes after an event has begun, and then interrupts the chain of causation and becomes the proximate cause of the ultimate effect or injury.

SUPERSEDEAS   [L. *superus, superior* / situated above, higher than + *sedeo, sedere* / to sit; to sit over; preside over]

You shall forbear. You shall desist. A writ commanding a stay of proceedings or a stay of execution or service of another writ. The order of an appellate court staying proceedings below until the appeal can be heard and determined. A *supersedeas bond* may be required of the party requesting *supersedeas* to protect the interests of the party who has succeeded below and is now stayed from proceeding further.

SUPERVENE, SUPERVENING   [L. *super + venire* / to come]

To follow or come after. To have a cummulative effect upon. Having additional, generally unexpected, impact. A *supervening cause* is essentially the same as an intervening cause.

SUPERVISE, SUPERVISOR, SUPERVISORY   [L. *super + video, videre* / to see]

To oversee. To watch over, inspect and control. To direct the activities or performance of others. A *supervising commission* or officer is a person authorized to take a deposition. In labor law, a *supervisor* is an agent of the employer who is authorized and delegated to hire, discipline and fire other employees, to hear and adjust their grievances and to direct them in performance of their work. Appellate courts have *supervisory jurisdiction* over the judges of lower courts, enabling them to issue rules for the regulation and management of those courts. The term *supervisory writ* is applied to the writs which are issued by higher courts (certiorari, mandamus) to control or limit the acts of lower courts. The chief officer or officers of a town or municipality are often called *supervisors*.

SUPPLEMENT, SUPPLEMENTAL   [L. *suppleo, supplere* / to fill up, make whole or complete]

Anything added or contributed to something already in existence. Additional matter printed separately and added to a book, record or report, usually updating or correcting the original matter. To add to, as to supplement one's income. A *supplemental pleading* is the pleading of new matter following the original complaint or answer. A *supplemental affidavit* is a new affidavit correcting or expanding upon a prior affidavit. Used before such nouns as assessment, bill, brief, deed, levy, petition or proceeding, *supplemental* means a subsequent and additional item, action, document or proceeding necessary to correct or expand upon the action or matter already in existence.

SUPPLEMENTARY PROCEEDING (SUP PRO) [L. *supplere* / to make whole]

The process by which a party who has secured a judgment proceeds to execute upon and collect the judgment. In this proceeding, the judgment creditor is permitted to examine both the judgment debtor and strangers to the action who have information about the income and assets of the debtor, to enable the creditor to find and levy upon those assets in satisfaction of the judgment.

SUPPLIANT, SUPPLICANT [L. *supplico, supplicare* / to kneel before, beg, pray]

Anyone who pleads for relief or assistance. A beggar. A sinner who begs forgiveness of God. A party who asks for judicial relief or remedy.

SUPPLICIUM [L. to kneel down in order to accept punishment; to inflict punishment, esp. capital punishment]

The death penalty in civil law.

See **PUNISHMENT; CORPORAL PUNISHMENT**

SUPPORT [L. *supporto, supportare* / to bring, carry (from *sub* + *porto, portare* / to bear, carry)]

To endure or bear, usually without complaint. To bear the weight of. To comfort and help. To argue in favor of. To promote and endorse a principle, program, cause or organization. To give sustenance to by providing the means of livelihood for. Assistance in food and lodging supplied under an agreement or court order. A *support order* is an order issued by a court providing for the support of a spouse or child. A *supporting affidavit* or paper is a document filed with the court to convince the court to grant a motion for relief, as on an application for injunction or restraining order.

SUPPRESS [L. *supprimo, supprimere* / to press down, hold down, check, restrain]

To subdue through use of force or authority. To keep from the knowledge or awareness of others. To censor the content of a book or periodical or to prevent its publication or dissemination. To prevent the growth or development of. To keep in check. To prevent the disclosure of evidence favorable to a party, as the *suppression by a prosecutor of evidence* exonerating the defendant. A *suppression hearing* is a hearing in a criminal matter in which the court considers the application of the defendant to exclude illegal or prejudicial evidence. To *suppress a will* is to fail to produce a will in one's custody after notice of the death of the testator.

SUPPRESSIO VERI, SUGGESTIO FALSI

The suppression of truth suggests a falsehood.

SUPRA   [L. above, over, on top of]

Above. In a written work, the word refers the reader from one reference or citation to a preceding section, phrase or citation.

See **INFRA**

SUPRA DICTUS   [L. *supra* + *dico, dicere* / to indicate, say, speak]

As written or stated above.

SUPREMACY (CLAUSE)   [L. *supremus*, superlative of *superus* / situated above, higher, greater]

The provision of Article VI, Clause 2 of the Constitution which declares that the supreme law of the United States consists of the Constitution, the laws passed by Congress, and the treaties executed under the authority of the federal government, notwithstanding anything contained in the constitution or laws of any of the states. The result is to give priority to federal law over state law in those areas in which federal law applies.

SUPREMACY (OF LAW)

The notion that every citizen and every agency of government must respect and observe the rule of law, i.e., that all must adhere to due process as established and confirmed by the Constitution, the applicable statutes and the decisions of the courts.

SUPREME   [L. *supremus* / the highest]

Having the highest rank. Above all others. Having ultimate or final authority. In most states, the state's Supreme Court is the highest court. The United States Supreme Court is the highest court in the nation. It is the court of last resort on issues of federal law. It has original and exclusive jurisdiction over matters concerning ambassadors and consuls and over conflicts between the states.

SURCHARGE   [L. *sur* (*super*) / above + *carrus* / a wheeled vehicle]

To charge an extra fee or penalty. To add a charge. To correct an error in an existing bill or invoice. To impose a penalty on a fiduciary, e.g., a guardian, to compensate for his failure or neglect of duty, e.g., his failure to invest funds prudently or to manage the funds so as to avoid loss.

SURETY   [L. *securus, securitas* / freedom from care; peace of mind]

A person who becomes responsible to answer and make good the debt, obligation, default, failure or breach of another. Originally, a *surety* was distinguished from a guarantor in that the surety was immediately and unconditionally liable, whereas a guarantor became liable only upon default by the principal. This distinction is no longer recognized under the Uniform Commercial Code. A *surety bond* is a formal document of assurance executed by the surety with respect to a particular principal under which the surety is bound to pay a sum recited in the document upon default by the principal. A *surety company* is a company which issues surety bonds for a fee paid by the principal. A *suretyship* is the contractual relationship between a surety and the principal.

SURPLUS   [L. *super + plus, pluris* (comp. of *multus* / much, many)]

More than is needed or necessary. What remains when use and need are satisfied. The excess of receipts over disbursements. The assets of a business or corporation remaining after subtracting the total of invested capital from its net worth. The result of substracting liabilities from assets. *Capital surplus* is surplus other than earned surplus. *Earned surplus* is the surplus resulting from the operations of the business, after deducting losses, distributions to stockholders and transfers to capital stock. *Paid-in surplus* is surplus resulting from the sale of capital stock at prices above par. *Surplus proceeds* are funds remaining upon a mortgage foreclosure sale or upon an execution or levy in excess of the amount needed to pay the mortgage or other debt in full. When surplus proceeds develop, the court will hold a surplus money proceeding to determine the disposition of the proceeds.

SURPLUSAGE

Redundant, excessive or non-essential matter. All matter submitted in a pleading, affidavit, motion or brief which is irrelevant to a determination of the issues. Any matter in a contract, deed or other legal document which is not necessary to assessing or fixing the rights and obligations of the parties.

SURPRISE   [L. *super + prehendo, prehendere* / to seize, grasp, take]

To take unaware. To cause a sudden response from a person who does not expect to give it. To cause an effect which is not expected. To astonish or amaze. In a trial, to place a party in a circumstance or condition which is unexpected by him and which he could not with diligence or care anticipate, e.g., to confront him with a *surprise witness*. *Surprise* may lead to an adjournment or to a new trial.

SURRENDER [L. *supra* + *reddo, reddere* / to give back, restore, deliver]

To yield to another as a result of force, compulsion or demand. To place oneself under the command or control of another. To allow oneself to be influenced by another. To give up a patent right or claim. To deliver a prisoner into custody. The relinquishment of a claim or right against another, as to *surrender* a debt or collateral, or possession of leased premises, or the right to payment under a promissory note. The (cash) *surrender value* of an insurance policy is the amount due from an insurer to the insured upon *surrender of a policy*, usually in the amount of the reserve under the policy less charges for surrender and any outstanding loans against the policy.

SURROGATE [L. *subrogo* (*surrogo*), *subrogare* / to suggest one person as substitute for another]

To put or appoint someone in place of another. To appoint a deputy or substitue for oneself. Anyone appointed to act for another. In some states, as in New York, a *surrogate* is a judicial officer who has jurisdiction over the probate of wills, the administration of estates in intestacy, and the care and guardianship of minors. A probate judge.

See **SUBROGATE**

SURVIVE, SURVIVAL [L. *super* + *vivo, vivere* / to live, be alive]

To remain alive or continue to live. To live beyond the death of another, as to survive one's spouse. To continue to live after a destructive event, as to survive a storm. A *survival action* is an action brought by the personal representative of a decedent to recover damages for pain and suffering by the decedent resulting from injuries before death. (This is different from a wrongful death action in which the injury sued upon is the harm caused by the decedent's death to his beneficiaries, not to the decedent himself.) *Survival statutes* preserve the right of a decedent, acting through his representative, to sue for his pain and suffering prior to death. *Survivorship* is a right belonging to joint tenants or tenants by the entirety with the result that title passes to the survivor upon the death of either of the tenants.

SURVIVOR [L. *sur, super* / over, above, beyond + *vivo, vivere* / to live, be alive]

A person who remains alive after an accident or incident which threatens his life. One who withstands adversity or challenge. One who comes into a legal right or status because she has outlived another, as a joint tenant or the beneficiary of a life insurance policy, or an heir upon the death of her decedent.

SURVIVORSHIP

The state of being a survivor. The right of a joint tenant or a tenant by the entirety to succeed to title upon the death of the other tenant. The right of the survivor to a Totten bank trust.

SUSPECT [L. *suspicio, suspicere* / to look up from below; to look critically, to suspect; to mistrust]

To regard with distrust. To attribute guilt or culpability in a crime. To have doubts about. Also, a person who is thought or believed to have committed a crime. A person under custody for a crime before charge or indictment.

SUSPECT CLASS OR CLASSIFICATION

A class or classification of persons who have been subjected to discrimination in the past on the basis of race, national origin, etc. Any statute which gives distinct treatment to a *suspect class* is given strict scrutiny by the federal courts to ensure that the statute does not violate the Equal Protection Clause of the Fourteenth Amendment to the Constitution. Under the doctrine requiring strict scrutiny in cases involving suspect classifications, whenever a statute gives distinct treatment to such a group, the group becomes a suspect class and the treatment involves *suspect classification*. Thus far, only race and national origin have been categorized as suspect classifications, although the courts have also considered and discussed as potentially suspect, classification based upon sex and illegitimacy.

See **STRICT SCRUTINY**

SUSPEND [L. *sub* + *pendo, pendere* / to weigh on; to consider or judge]

To bar someone for a period of time from attendance upon a function or from performance of a duty or privilege. Examples: the action of a disciplinary committee in *suspending an attorney* from practice or of a police tribunal in suspending a police officer or of a school principal in suspending a student from school attendance or of an employer in suspending an employee. To cause to stop temporarily. To defer to a later time, as to *suspend a trial* or a session of court. To defer the effect of, as to *suspend application* of a rule. A *suspended sentence* in a criminal matter is a sentence the execution of which has been deferred by the court to avoid immediate imprisonment of the defendant. A statute of limitations is said to be suspended under circumstances such as the disability of the plaintiff, the continued absence of the defendant from the state, or the fraud of the defendant in concealing facts which would reveal a cause of action to the plaintiff.

SUSPICION [L. *suspicere* / to suspect; to mistrust]

Doubt. A state of mind causing distrust or disbelief. The notion that something is wrong or that a supposed fact may not exist. Also, a belief which is based upon little or no evidence. A *reasonable suspicion*, on the other hand, is a suspicion based on specific facts or circumstances within the knowledge or view of the person who suspects. Examples: a police officer who stops a person running from a store with a bag loaded with merchandise and with a store clerk in hot pursuit.

SUSTAIN [L. *sustineo, sustinere* / to hold up, support, sustain]

To support or give help or relief to. To supply with food and nourishment. To bear up or support the weight of. To suffer or experience. To approve of. To support as true and correct or in compliance with a rule or principle, as to sustain an objection. To offer adequate proof. The act of an appellate court in approving the decision of a lower court. The act of a trial judge in recognizing and approving an objection to testimony or evidence.

SUSTENANCE [L. *sustinere* / to support]

The means of support and substance. Those things which support life and well-being, i.e. food, drink, provisions, protection from the elements, etc.

See **SUBSIST**

SYLLABUS [L. *syllaba* / a syllable; words; poems]

The outline of a course, treatise, dissertation, or examination. A summary. A collection describing the contents of a course of study or of all the courses offered by a school.

SYMBOL, SYMBOLIC [L. *symbolus* / a sign, mark or symbol]

Anything that stands for or suggests something else with which it is associated or related. An arbitrary sign or convention used in a writing or printing to suggest a classification or category of things, such as a number sign or the logo of a particular company or product. Anything which suggests or prompts a response in the unconscious mind, in the way a heart-shaped object suggests affection. *Symbolic delivery* is a legal construction which implies delivery of possession or transfer of control to property upon delivery of a token object *symbolizing delivery* of the whole, such as a key, a warehouse receipt, or any document acknowledging delivery and receipt (also called constructive delivery). *Symbolic speech* is expression through behavior or conduct rather than words, as in the burning of the flag or a draft card, or the burning of a cross. Symbolic speech is entitled to protection as speech under the First Amendment.

SYNDIC [L. *syndicus* (from Gr. *syndikos* / advocate; legal assistant) / a representative or agent]

An official charged with the duties of a lower court officer or magistrate. The agent or legal representative of a business enterprise or of a school or university. The attorney for a civic body, such as a municipality or university. A trustee, especially of the assets of an insolvent debtor.

SYNDICATE [L. *syndicus* / a representative or agent]

A group of persons organized to conduct a particular business or enterprise, especially a commercial enterprise. A group of companies combining to control or influence either a single transaction or market or an entire industry (a cartel). Also, a combination of investment bankers who pool their resources to underwrite a new stock issue or to promote investment in a new enterprise. Also, to distribute for publication creative material such as a cartoon, column, movie script, play or TV program simultaneously to a number of newspapers, magazines or television stations. Also, an organized criminal enterprise.

TABULA RASA [L. *tabula* / a writing tablet; a document; a record + *rado, radere, rasum* / scraped; smooth]

A blank slate.

TACIT [L. *taceo, tacere* / to be silent]

Expressed by deed or conduct and not by speech. Implied without being said. Arising or created by operation of law and not by express agreement or contract. A *tacit promise*, acceptance or commitment may be inferred from a person's silence in response to an affirmative offer, statement or demand.

TALES, TALESMEN [L. *talis* / of that kind]

Jurors, especially jurors picked from bystanders to round out the number required to hear a case. Also, all the members of a jury pool from which a panel is picked for trial.

TALES DE CIRCUMSTANIBUS

Jurors selected from persons who happened to be in the courtroom when other jurors were not available.

TALIO [L. retaliation]

Retribution. Punishment in kind. "An eye for an eye."

TALLAGIUM (TALLIAGE)

In medieval England, a tax upon people residing in cities, according to the value of their estates.

See **SCUTAGE**

TAM [L. so, to such an extent; so much]

To such a degree.

See **QUI TAM**

TAM FACTI QUAM ANIMI

The deed was equal to the intent.

TANGIBLE [L. *tango, tangere* / to touch, move, affect]

Capable of being perceived by the senses, especially touch. Palpable. Material. Capable of being identified or impressed upon the mind. Having substance and value. A *tangible asset* is an asset having physical form and capable of appraisal or analysis. *Tangible property* is property having physical or corporeal form and which can be possessed physically, as cars, trucks and merchandise.

See **CORPOREAL; INTANGIBLE**

TANTUM BONA VALENT, QUANTUM VENDI POSSUNT

Goods are worth what you can sell them for.

TAX, TAXATION [L. *tangere* / to touch]

To exact a charge upon assets, property or income. A charge imposed by the government upon persons or their property to finance and support public purposes. A sum levied by an organization upon its members to defray its costs and expenses. *Taxation* is the imposition of taxes. *Taxes* take many forms. An *income tax* is a tax upon earnings and capital gains. A *sales tax* is a tax imposed at the point of purchase of goods or merchandise. A head or *poll tax* is a tax imposed in equal amount upon all the persons subject to tax, or upon a designated class or group of persons. An *excise tax* is a tax levied on the manufacture or consumption of a commodity. A *property tax* is a tax levied on the value of real or personal property.

TEMPERANCE [L. *tempero, temperare* / to control, blend, temper, limit]

Moderation in action or thought. To hold within limits. Restrained, restricted. Prudent in the exercise of appetite or desire. Moderate or restrained in the consumption of alcoholic beverages. A movement to prohibit or control the consumption of alcohol. The Temperance Movement resulted in 1919 in the adoption of the Volstead Act, which prohibited the manufacture, sale and consumption of alcoholic beverages, and, later, the adoption of the Eighteenth Amendment which also banned the consumption of liquor. This amendment was repealed by the Twenty-first Amendment.

TEMPORA MUTANTUR ET LEGES MUTANTUR IN ILLIS

The law changes with the times.

TEMPORARY [L. *temporalis* / temporary, lasting for a limited time]

Lasting for a short or limited time. Not permanent or even long-lasting. Transitory; mutable. A *temporary administrator* is an administrator appointed to serve until a formal administrator can be appointed; the *temporary appointment* is made in order to avoid waste and loss. *Temporary alimony* is support paid by the husband to the wife during the pendency of the action between them. *Temporary custody* is an award of custody to one parent pending determination by the court of the permanent needs and interests of the child. A *temporary injunction* is an injunction pendente lite, or until the court can determine the merits and issue a final decree. *Temporary insanity* is a temporary incapacity of the mind resulting from some transient or passing condition, e.g., addiction to drugs or alcohol.

See **PENDENTE LITE**

TEMPORE ET LOCO   [L. *tempus, temporis* / time + *locus, loci* / place]

Time and place.

TEMPORE PACIS   [L. *tempus, temporis* / time, a division of time + *pax, pacis* / peace; serenity]

In the time of peace.

TENANT, TENANCY   [L. *teneo, tenere* / to hold]

A *tenant* is anyone who holds possession of the premises of another with the express or implied agreement or consent of the latter. Along with possession, a tenant also usually has exclusive charge and control of the premises as long as he observes the conditions of his occupancy, generally including the obligation to pay rent and to maintain the premises in good order. A *tenancy* is possession of property or an interest in property recognized by the law. Tenancies are of many kinds. The usual *tenancy* is possession of premises for a term of months or years under a written lease. A *holdover tenancy* (a/k/a tenancy at sufferance) is occupancy following the expiration of a lease term, with or without the consent of the owner (landlord). A *month-to-month tenancy* is a tenancy renewable each month upon payment of a monthly rent. A *tenancy at will* is a tenancy which continues until terminated by consent of the parties. A *joint tenancy* is a tenancy in which two persons hold title to property equally and simultaneously, with right of survivorship. A *tenancy in entirety* is a joint tenancy by husband and wife; in the event of divorce, the tenancy becomes a tenancy in common. A *tenancy in common* is ownership of property shared in equal but divided parts by two or more persons without right of survivorship and without the right to share in the interest of the other tenant. Other tenancies: tenancy for life; tenancy in fee; tenancy *per autre vie*, etc.

TENDER   [L. *tendo, tendere* / to stretch out, extend; to present]

To offer or present to another for acceptance or approval. To propose or suggest, as an offer. The offer of a sum of money or of services in satisfaction of a condition or obligation. Anything offered in payment. In contract law, a formal statement of willingness to perform or observe the obligations or conditions of an agreement in order to test and solicit the willingness of the other party to perform the terms and obligations owing by him. In the sale of goods, a *tender of delivery* is notice by the seller to the buyer that he is holding goods at the disposition of the buyer and requesting instructions as to the time, mode and place of delivery. A *tender offer* by an investor is a public offer to purchase the stock of a target corporation, usually at a premium price and in an effort to take control of the corporation.

TENEMENT [L. *teneo, tenere* / to occupy]

A residence, especially a multi-family structure. Also any interest or estate in land or in property attached to land. More loosely, any tangible property or interest in property.

TENENDUM CLAUSE [L. *teneo, tenere* / to hold + *claudo, claudere, clausum* / to close]

A clause used in deeds to set forth the nature of the estate or interest conveyed by the grantor to the grantee.

TENTATIVE, TENTATIVE MINIMUM TAX, TENTATIVE TRUST [L. *tempto, temptare* / to prove, try, test]

Existing in an unfinished or incomplete state. Not fully realized or developed. Hesitant. Uncertain. Waiting to be finished. The *tentative minimum tax* is a calculation under the Internal Revenue Code comparing a person's income tax as regularly computed with the alternative minimum tax as defined in the Code. A *tentative trust* is another name for a Totten Trust, i.e., a bank account by one person in trust for another; a Totten Trust is controlled by the depositor and is revocable by him at any time until his death, at which point it passes to the benificiary directly, without the need for estate administration.

TENURE [L. *teneo, tenere* / to hold, to preserve]

The manner or the terms under which property or a title or an office is held; also, the act of holding property or office. The conditions, i.e., term, nature of title, degree of ownership, under which property or office is held. Also, the status of teachers or office-holders following a probationary or trial period which entitles them to remain in office free of the threat of dismissal except for incompetence or misconduct.

TERM [L. *terminus* / boundary, limit]

The length of time during which something lasts. The period during which an interest or estate survives or is effective. Also, the interest or estate itself. A session of court. An esssential element or part of an agreement, or a will, or a deed, or any other document having legal effect and consequence. A word or phrase which conveys a decipherable and precise meaning in the context or circumstance in which it is used. The divisions of a school year. The length of a normal pregnancy. A *term insurance policy* is a policy covering the life of the assured for a stated period.

TERMINAL, TERMINATE, TERMINATION [L. *termino, terminare* / to bound, limit, fix a boundary]

Terminal: Leading to or close to death. Nearing the end. The final stages of a fatal disease. Happening at the end of a series of events or circumstances. A *terminal illness* is an illness which results in death. *Terminate:* to put an end to. To extend to or to arrive at the limit or end. To bring to an end. To discontinue the employment of a worker; to discharge an employee. *Termination:* the end, expressed in terms of space or time. The law speaks of the termination of corporations, prosecutions, employment, leases, offers, options, trusts, etc.

TERMINUS A QUO

The point from which; the starting point. With respect to a private right of way, the point at which the party having the right of way can gain access or entrance.

TERMINUS AD QUEM

The point to which; the terminal point. With respect to a private right of way, the point at which the right of way ends; the exit from a right of way.

TERRA [L. earth, ground, soil]

Land.

TERRA CULTA [L. *terra* / land + *colo, colere* / to cultivate, plant, till]

Cultivated land.

TERRA NOVA

New land. Land never previously settled or cultivated.

TERRA TRANSIT CUM ONERE [L. *terra* / land + *transeo, transire* / to cross, pass over + *cum* / with + *onero, onerare* / to load, burden with, oppress]

The burdens upon a parcel of land go with its title.

TERRITORY, TERRITORIAL [L. *territorium* / the land around or adjacent to a town; a district]

An area of the earth with defined bounds and limits. A geographical area under the control or jurisdiction of a government. An area beyond the geographical limits of the country which controls or administers it but which has some degree of autonomy, e.g., a territory of the United States such as Guam. In business, an area assigned to a salesperson or distributor. *Territorial juris-*

diction defines the geographical area over which a court or judicial officer can exercise jurisdiction; the area within which a court can extend process. *Territorial waters* are those waters immediately adjacent to a nation's coastline, over which the nation claims or exercises sovereignty. Since World War II, the nations of the world have not been able to agree on the outer limit of territorial waters; the old three-mile rule has been extended by some nations to twelve miles from shore and even to 200 miles.

TERROR, TERRORISM   [L. *terreo, terrere* / to frighten, terrify]

Terror: Fear or fright. Anything that inspires fear. Fear of attack, injury or death, especially from something sudden or unexpected. *Terrorism:* Acts or threats of violence against a state or nation, or against a group of citizens, usually inspired or motivated by some political, economic or social objective.

TERROREM   [L. *teneo, tenere*]
See **IN TERROREM**

TEST   [L. *testa* / a piece of clay; a pot or urn]

An examination or inquiry. An evaluation or measure of skill or knowledge. A *test case* is a case depending upon facts which raise legal issues common to a group of cases; if all the parties to the cases typified by the test case agree to be bound by its decision, the court will agree to hear and determine the test case as representaive of and precedent for the other cases. A test case is also a case brought to test the constitutionality or applicability of a statute.

TESTACY   [L. *testor, testari* / to bear witness, give evidence; to make a will]

The state of a decedent who leaves a valid will, as opposed to one who dies intestate, i.e., without having executed a valid will.

TESTAMENT   [L. *testamentum* / a last will (from *testari*)]

Originally, a document which contained a testator's instructions for the disposition of his personal property after death. In today's usage, a document which provides for the disposition of both real and personal property after death. Also, one of the two divisions of the modern Bible (the Old and the New Testament).

TESTAMENTARY   [L. *testamentum* / a last will; a lecture]

Related to the process of drafting or executing a will. *Testamentary capacity* is that state of mind which enables a testator to understand the nature and scope of his estate or property, to identify the people he wishes to benefit, and to set down rational and reasonable provisions disposing of his property. *Testamentary expenses* are the expenses of probating and administering a will. A *testamentary instrument* is a document intended to take effect only at death which disposes of a person's assets and which is executed with the formalities required of wills in the state of execution. A *testamentary trust* is a trust created under the provisions of a will.

TESTAMENTUM OMNE MORTE CONSUMMATUM
A will is consummated or perfected only by death.

TESTATE [L. *testor, testari* / to execute a will]
A person who dies leaving a valid will. To die with a valid will in effect.

TESTATIO MENTIS [L. *testari* / to bear witness, give evidence + *mens, mentis* / reason, intellect, the mind]
A testamentary document which displays or evidences a mind capable of making rational distribution of assets at death. A last will.

TESTATOR, TESTATRIX [L. *testor, testari* / to bear witness]
The male and female forms of the word describing a person who dies leaving a valid will.

TESTES PONDERANTUR, NON NUMERANTUR
Witnesses are measured by their trustworthiness, not by their number.

TESTIFY [L. *testificor, testificari* / to bear witness to, give evidence about]
To bear witness to an act or deed or to events perceived by the senses or within the knowledge of the witness. To give testimony under oath in a trial or other judicial or administrative proceeding. To express a personal conviction or belief.

TESTIMONIUM CLAUSE
In a document, especially a deed, that clause at the end which begins, "In witness whereof, etc." and which confirms the date and fact of execution by the parties.

TESTIMONY [L. *testimonium* / evidence, testimony]
The oral or written statements of a witness in the course of a trial or proceeding, delivered under oath. Testimony is a kind of evidence, but evidence is a broader term than testimony, encompassing all proof submitted to the jury or court.

TESTIS [L. *testor, testari* / to act as witness]
Anyone who gives evidence; a witness

TESTIS DE VISU PRAEPONDERAT ALLIS
The testimony of eyewitnesses trumps all other evidence.

THESAURUS INVENTUS [L. *thesaurus* / treasure, treasury, storage-house (from the Greek) + *invenio, invenire* / to come upon, discover; to find out]

Treasure discovered; treasure trove.

See **TREASURE**

THREAT [L. *trudo, trudere* / to press upon; to force]

A declaration of intent or purpose to injure or harm. The manifestation of an intent to harass or intimidate. To menace or frighten. Some threats are criminal offenses. A *threat by mail* is an indictable federal offense. Any threat against the President is a criminal offense. Model Penal Code § 211.3 defines a *terroristic threat* as any threat communicated with intent to terrorize or to cause the evacuation of any building or facility.

TITLE [L. *titulus* / inscription, title, label]

The name by which a thing is known. A mark, designation or appellation. The designation of a book, or a statute; also, a designation indicating rank, position or occupation. The degree of ownership of real or personal property. The quality of a person's interest in a particular asset. The basis of ownership. The extent to which the law recognizes and protects an interest in property. *Clear title* is title free of encumbrances, liens or claims of right by others. *Record title* is that title which appears from local records which record transactions on a continuing basis. *Good title* is valid title recognized in fact and law and which a willing buyer will accept from a willing seller. A *title in fee simple* is full and unconditional ownership of property. *Title paramount* is a title better than or superior to another title. A *title search* is an examination into the status of ownership in a particular property, including a search for title transfers, for mortgages and encumbrances, for tax liens, and for all other matters affecting title; the examination is usually conducted by an attorney or abstract company in connection with a proposed transfer or transaction.

TOLL [L. *tollo, tollere* / to take up and away; to carry off]

To take away. To vacate or annul. To suspend or interrupt. To *toll a statute of limitations* is to suspend or stop its operation for a period of time; various conditions will result in the tolling of a statute of limitations, e.g., the defendant's absence from the jurisdiction; the minority of the plaintiff, a deliberate scheme to avoid process, etc.

TORT [L. *torqueo, torquere* / to twist, wind, wrench]

A wrongful act for which the law imposes civil liability to compensate a person who has suffered injury or damage as a result of the act. The act which gives rise to a *tort claim* is never consensual or based upon contract or agreement; instead, the act is one which the plaintiff neither invited nor anticipated, e.g., a battery or an auto accident. Also, the violation of a legal duty which results in injury or damage to another. An act may constitute both a crime and a tort. Also, the name given to causes of action based upon wrongful civil acts, and, to the body of law which studies and interprets them.

TORTFEASOR [L. *torquere* + *facio, facere* / to make or do]

A person who commits a tort or is liable to another upon a claim in tort.

TORTIOUS [L. *torquere*/ to twist, wrench]

Any act which is recognized as a tort or which subjects the actor to civil liability for injury or damage caused to another by his act. In the nature of a tort; wrongful; harmful.

TORTURE [L. *torquere* / to twist, wrench]

To cause pain or suffering to. To punish. To apply cruel devices and instruments to the person of another. To distort or twist the meaning of a thought or concept.

TOTA CURIA

The entire court. A session of a court when all the judges of the panel are present.

TOTAL [L. *totus* / the whole, complete, the entire group]

Constituting the whole. Complete. Entire. With respect to insurance claims, a *total loss* is a loss to the assured of the entire current value of the asset or interest insured. A *total disability* is a physical or mental disability so great as to prevent gainful activity or employment. *Total incorporation* is a concept of constitutional law which teaches that the Fourteenth Amendment must be construed as extending the protection of the Bill of Rights in its entirety to the individual states.

TOXIC [L. *toxicum* / the poison used on arrows]

Poisonous. Possessing the qualities of a poison. A substance that causes illness or death when administered to or through the body. Produced by a poison. A poison. *Toxicology* is the science which studies and treats the nature and effects of poisons. *Toxic wastes* are industrial and domestic products which are injurious to health and safety; the use, accumulation, transportation and disposal of these wastes are regulated by federal and state authorities.

TRACT [L. *tractus* / a track or trail; an occupied space (from *traho, trahere* / to draw, drag, pull along)]

A self-contained and defined parcel of land of whatever size or shape. A *tract index* is that part of a land record-keeping system which sets forth all transactions affecting title to a particular parcel of land.

TRADITION, TRADITIONAL [L. *trado, tradere* / to hand over, surrender; to pass down the story of an event; to report or teach]

Patterns of thought, belief or behavior which are generally accepted and which pass from one generation to another. Continuity in such things as religion and culture. Knowledge or practice transmitted in a line from one person to another. The total body of thought or habit adopted by one generation from all that has preceded it. The common law is sometimes called *traditional law*.

TRADITIONARY EVIDENCE

Evidence accumulated from the statements of persons now dead dealing with such matter as a family's pedigree or history when no comparable evidence is available from persons living.

TRAFFIC [L. *traho, trahere* / to draw, drag; to pass over]

The exchange, sale or barter of goods or commodities; commerce, trade. The passing of title to goods in exchange for money or services. The import and export of goods and products between one nation or state and another. Also, the movement of vehicles of all types along any passageway, such as a road, highway, river, lake or the sky. The exchange of information over a system for public communication. To deal in, sell or barter. It is illegal to *traffic* in military secrets or in drugs.

TRAITOR [L. *traditor* / a traitor (from *trado, tradere* / to hand over, surrender]

A persons who betrays a trust or solemn responsibility, such as a traitor to his cause or to his country. One who attempts by some overt act to overthrow the government to which he owes allegiance or of which he is a citizen.

See **TREASON**

TRANSACT, TRANSACTION [L. *transigo, transigere* / to drive through; to pass or spend time; to settle a dispute]

To carry on or conduct. To maintain through completion or fruition. To negotiate, conduct and complete business dealings. To engage in a trade, business or occupation. A *transaction* is any act of dealing involving two or more parties, e.g., a sale, negotiation of a contract, transfer of title, etc. Also, any act or conduct which is given legal effect and which gives rise to a claim or cause of action. Whether an act constitutes *transacting business* is often at issue in cases involving jurisdiction over corporations or the authority of a corporation to do business in a particular state. The issue in these cases is the extent to which the corporation has engaged in business in a particular place.

TRANSACTIONAL IMMUNITY

Immunity from prosecution granted by a prosecutor to an accused or co-conspirator to obtain his testimony as a witness against another accused. The immunity extends to any prosecution based upon the particular crime testified about. *Transactional immunity* must be contrasted with use immunity, which extends immunity only to the specific testimony of the witness; that testimony may not be used against him, but the prosecutors is not precluded from obtaining and introducing other testimony to convict the witness. *Transactional immunity* is rarely granted by federal prosecutors.

See **IMMUNITY FROM PROSECUTION**

TRANSCRIBE, TRANSCRIPT, TRANSCRIPTION [L. *trans* / over, across + *scribo, scribere* / to engrave, to write]

Transcribe: To make a copy of. To write down. To summarize or make a record of. To record. To transfer from one place of record to another. In music, to record for later play or broadcast. *Transcript:* A copy. The record of a trial or proceeding prepared by a court reporter or stenographer. A word-for-word reproduction of the testimony, arguments, rulings and instructions during a trial. Also, the printed record prepared for submission to an appellate court. *Transcription:* anything transcribed, but especially a musical composition or performance, or a recording made for broadcast.

TRANSFER [L. *trans* / over across + *fero, ferre* / to bear, carry]

To carry or convey from any place or from one person or thing to another place, person or thing. To pass something from one place to another or from one person to another. To deliver possession of. To convey title from one person to another. To do or perform any act, e.g., a sale, gift or assignment, the consequence of which is a change in possession or title to property. Also, the instrument which operates to effect a transfer, e.g., a deed, trust instrument or bill of sale. The *transfer of jurisdiction* is the movement of a case from a state court to a federal court, or from one state or federal court to another, when the relationship of the parties or the nature of the action require transfer. A *transfer* tax is a tax upon the transfer of property, e.g., federal estate and gift taxes.

TRANSFER AGENT

A *transfer agent* is an agency, e.g., a bank or other institution, which is appointed to handle and record the transfers of shares for a publicly held corporation. The duties of the agent include accepting shares for transfer, issuing new or replacement shares, mailing dividend checks, and maintaining the official roster of shareholders for voting and distribution purposes.

TRANSFEREE LIABILITY

The liability of a person taking title to property from another to a creditor of the transferor, especially a tax creditor. In the case of taxes owed to the Internal Revenue Service, the transferree will be expected to make good any tax liability left unpaid by the transferror, to the full extent of the value of the property transferred.

TRANSFERRED INTENT

Transferred intent is a doctrine of criminal and tort law which makes the perpetrator liable for all the consequences of the act which he intended to perform, whether or not he intended the specific consequences which developed from his act. For example, if C fires a gun with intent to shoot A but shoots B instead, his intent to commit a crime against A will be transferred to B, even though C did not intend to shoot B.

TRANSGRESS [L. *transgredior, transgredi* / to cross or pass over]

To violate a command or order. To exceed prescribed limits. To trespass. To commit a wrong or violation.

TRANSITORY ACTION

An action or litigation that may be brought or pursued anywhere the defendant may be found and served, i.e., a law suit that does not depend upon some local element which might cause a court to reject or dismiss the action for lack of jurisdiction or under the doctrine of *forum non conveniens*. Actions dependent upon some local element are called local actions. Generally, *in rem* actions would be considered local and *in personam* actions transitory.

See **FORUM NON CONVENIENS; IN REM; IN PERSONAM**

TRANSIT TERRA CUM ONERE

(Title to) land passes along with its burdens and encumbrances.

TRANSMIT [L. *trans* / across + *mitto, mittere* / to send, dispatch]

To send, convey or carry from one place to another. To cause to spread. To give through inheritance or intestacy. To send out or broadcast a signal over radio or other electronic medium. To send to a bank or other agent for collection. To pay or submit for payment. A *transmittal letter* is a letter which accompanies and refers to the delivery or execution of a document attached to or accompanying the letter.

TRAVERSE [L. *trans* / across + *verso, versare* / to spin around, to twist around]

To move in opposition to. To cross or go over. To deny or challenge. To deny an allegation in a complaint or other pleading or indictment. Also, a general denial or a plea in denial of a specific allegation. A *traverse jury* is a jury selected to try a disputed claim.

TREASON [L. *trado, tradere* / to give up, surrender]

An act of disloyalty or a breach of allegiance to a government to which one owes loyalty either because he is a citizen of that country or because he has undertaken some act which confirms allegiance to it, such as voluntary enlistment in its army. An overt act of disloyalty or non-allegiance, such as joining in a war on one's country or aiding or abetting the enemy. An attempt at the overthrow of one's country. No one may be convicted of *treason* under the Constitution except upon his own confession or the testimony of at least two witnesses to an overt act of treason. Article III, Sec 3.

See **TRAITOR**

TREASURE, TREASURE TROVE [L. *thesaurus* / treasure, store-house]

Wealth of any kind, but especially wealth which is stored up, kept in a secret place, hoarded or buried. A collection of items of value, such as stones or precious metals. Also, a person who is held in high public regard; a poet or composer may be spoken of as a *national treasure*. In the United States, *treasure trove*, i.e., articles which have been buried by a person or persons unknown and which are dug up and discovered, is deemed mislaid property and, therefore, the property of the landowner upon whose land the articles are found. In England, *treasure trove* belongs to the state.

See **THESAURUS INVENTUS**

TREASURY [L. *thesaurus* / hoard, the repository of a church or state]

Any repositary of funds. A place where public funds are kept and stored. Also, symbolically, the agency or department charged with the collection and disbursement of funds for an organization, public agency or state. The Treasury Department of the United States is the federal agency responsible for all funds and all the fiscal matters of the federal government; the head of the Department is a member of the Cabinet. A *treasury bill* or note is an obligation issued by the Treasury and constitutes legal tender. *Treasury shares* are corporate shares which were originally issued and outstanding but which have been repurchased or reacquired by the corporation through forfeiture, surrender or gift.

TREATISE [L. *tracto, tractare* / to treat, handle, manage]

A systematic and organized written review or summary of a particular field of interest or study, such as a field of science, art, literature or government. A *treatise in the law* is a comprehensive review and analysis of matters which define a particular area of the law, such as a treatise in the law of contracts, real property or torts. *Law treatises* included references to statutes, the

English common law, decided cases, law review articles, and other original material relating to the field.

TREATY [L. *tracto, tractare* / to handle, manage]

A compact or contract between or among nations which has been negotiated by representatives of the nations involved and then ratified, approved or formally adopted by the agencies of those nations qualified and authorized to do so. The result is a document having the force of law. Treaties of the United States may be made by the President, by and with the consent of two-thirds of the Senate. Constitution, Article II, Sec 2.

TRESPASS L. *trans* / across, to the other side + *passim* / here and there, far and wide; or *passus* / stride, pace, step]

Any offense against law or legal authority. An invasion of the property rights of others. To enter unlawfully upon the land of another. To encroach upon, infringe or invade. Any unlawful intereference with the person, property or rights of another. Also, an injury caused to the person or property of another through an unlawful or forceful act.

TRESPASS DE BONIS ASPORTATIS

An action for goods taken. Title of the common law action for damages to the plaintiff resulting from the taking by the defendant of plaintiff's chattels.

TRESPASS ON THE CASE

Title of the common law action for damages to the plaintiff resulting from the negligence of the defendant.

TRESPASS QUARE CLAUSUM FREGIT

Title of the common law action for damages to the plaintiff resulting from the unlawful or unprivileged intrusion or entry by the defendant upon the real property of the plaintiff.

See **CLAUSUM FREGIT**

TRESPASS VI ET ARMIS

Title of the common law action for damages to the plaintiff resulting from the use by defendant of force and violence upon the plaintiff.

TRIBUNE, TRIBUNAL [L. *tribunus* / a person holding an official rank in public service or in the army]

Any court of justice. A body entrusted with the power to hear and determine a dispute. The body of judges comprising a particular court.

TURPIS CAUSA [L. *turpis* / ugly, deformed; disgraceful, shameful + *causa* / cause, reason; purpose; case, claim]

Any conduct which is so base and immoral as to be incapable of supporting the contract, promise or commitment of another. Also, an action brought in bad faith.

TURPIS CONTRACTUS

An immoral promise or contract.

TURPITUDE [L. *turpitudo* (from *turpis*) / ugliness, disgrace, depravity, baseness]

Business, social or sexual depravity. An immoral or base act. Anything done contrary to morality or justice. *Moral turpitude*, a phrase often used in statutes or regulations to define unacceptable conduct, i.e., conduct which is intrinsically immoral or wrong or which offends the public conscience.

See **MORAL TURPITUDE**

TUTELAGE [L. *tutor, tutari* / to protect, watch, keep safe]

To serve as guardian or protector. The protection or support of another. Guardianship. Instruction from; to serve as teacher or mentor of another.

TYRRANY [L. *tyrannus* / an absolute ruler, a king; also, one who usurps power, a tyrant]

Oppressive power exercised by one or several persons over the general public. The rule of a dictator or despot. A government in which all power is vested in one ruler or cabal. A police state. An autocracy.

UBERRIMA FIDES [L. *uber, uberius, uberrime* / rich, abundant; fully, completely + *fides* / trust, confidence]

The utmost good faith, such as the responsibility owed by an agent to his principal or by an attorney to his client.

UBI JUS, IBI REMEDIUM

Wherever there is a legal right, there is also a remedy.

UBI JUS INCERTUM, IBI JUS NULLUM

The law requires certainty in meaning and in application; otherwise, there is no law.

UBI QUIS DELINQUIT, IBI PENIETUR

A suspect should be tried and punished in the place in which the crime occurred.

UBI SUPRA [L. *ubi* / where, when + *supra* / above, over]

Where (stated or written) above. Where cited above. Ordinarily shortened to the one word *supra*, the term refers to a previous place in a text at which the same matter, case, volume and page, etc., is cited.

See **SUPRA**

ULTERIUS NON VULT PROSEQUI (NON VULT)

He is unwilling to proceed further with the prosecution. The statement made to the court by the prosecutor when he wished to discontinue a proceedings or dismiss an indictment.

See **NON VULT PROSEQUI**

ULTIMA RATIO [L. *ulter, ulterior, ultimus* / the most, the highest, the last + *ratio* / calculation, computation; reason, motive, theory]

The final argument; the last resort. Sometimes, a euphemism for war or hostilities.

ULTIMATE   [L. *ultimus*/ farthest, last, final]

Most remote in space and time. The most extreme. The end of the line. Incapable of further analysis or definition. An *ultimate fact* is a fact necessary to the determination of an issue or to a final verdict or decision. A fact without which a decision cannot be supported or justified. An *ultimate finding* or issue is a question which must be resolved in order for the court to reach and render a decision.

ULTIMATUM   [L. *ultimus* / the highest, the most extreme]

A declaration of final proposals and demands in a negotiation or conflict. The last and final proposal before other and more severe action. A final offer before a strike in a labor dispute or before war in a conflict between nations.

ULTIMA VOLUNTAS   [L. *ultimus* / last, final + *voluntas* / wish, desire]

A person's last willing act. A final statement of wishes and intent. A last will and testament.

ULTIMUS HAERES   [L. *ultimus* / last, final + *heres* (*haeres*) heir, heiress, successor]

The last heir. The end of a line.

ULTRA VIRES   [L. *ultra* / beyond, on the far side + *vis, vires* / force, power strength]

Any act performed without authority. Acts by a corporation beyond the powers granted in its charter or articles of incorporation. Generally, acts performed by a corporation which are not permitted under the laws of the state of incorporation or the state(s) in which the corporation does business, or which, if they are permitted, are performed in an unlawful or irregular way. An *ultra vires* act, e.g., an *ultra vires* contract, is unenforceable.

See **EXTRA VIRES; INTRA VIRES**

UMBRELLA POLICY   [L. *umbra* / a shade or shadow; a shady place + *polio, polire* / to polish; make smooth; to adorn]

In insurance law, a policy which affords coverage against loss in excess of the coverage provided by all other policies together or against losses not otherwise covered. A supplemental or excess-liability policy which provides coverage above basic limits. *Umbrella policies* are used to provide overriding coverage against loss by fire or motor vehicle operation.

UMPIRE   [L. *um, non* / not + *par* / equal, a match]

One having the final authority to impose a binding decision in a dispute or controversy. A third party designated to consider and resolve a labor dispute. When two arbitrators disagree, an *umpire* is a third person who will consider both their awards and issue a decision binding upon all parties. An official in baseball or other sport who rules on plays.

UNA CUM OMNIBUS ALIIS

One of several things. Along with all other things.

UNANIMOUS, UNANIMITY   [L. *unanimus* / of a single mind; agreed]

Unanimous: Approved by all. A consensus by all those participating. All of one mind. Agreement by all present. A *unanimous vote* is a concurring vote by all entitled to vote. A *unanimous decision* is a decision in which all the judges of a court concur. A *unanimous verdict* is a verdict upon which all jurors agree. *Unanimity:* the quality of being unanimous. Total agreement.

UNCONDITIONAL

Absolute, without condition of any kind. The law deals with unconditional releases, unconditional promises, unconditional offers, unconditional acceptances. An *unconditional discharge* is the release of a prisoner from custody without such conditions as parole or community service.

See **CONDITION; CONDITIONAL**

UNCONSCIONABLE, UNCONSCIONABILITY   [L. *un* / not + *con* / against + *scio, scire* / to know, understand]

Unfair, inequitable. Against reason or public policy. In contract law, a contract which is clearly unfair to one of the parties will be unenforceable under the *doctrine of unconscionability*. The question for the court under the Uniform Commercial Code is "whether, in the light of the general commercial background and the commercial needs of the particular trade or case, the clauses involved are so one-sided as to be *unconscionable*..." § 2-302, Comment 1.

UNCONSTITUTIONAL

Inconsistent with or violative of the provisions of the U.S. Constitution as amended and as interpreted by the Supreme Court. A statute which is declared *unconstitutional* is void and of no effect.

UNCONTESTABLE CLAUSE

A clause in an insurance policy which forecloses denial or contest of a claim by the carrier after expiration of a prescribed period of time following the date of the policy.

UNDERINSURED

Having less insurance than needed to cover the value of the property or risk insured. An *underinsured motorist* is a motorist whose liability coverage is inadaquate to pay the damages sustained by a person injured through his negligence. Most states have laws which provide for indemnification of persons injured or killed by underinsured motorists.

See **UNINSURED**

UNIFORM [L. *unus, uni* / one + *formo, formare* / to form, shape]

Consistent. Possessed of unchanging or undeviating form, manner or degree. Unvarying. Constant. Similar in all essential respects. Legislators and lawyers are engaged in a constant and dedicated effort to achieve uniformity in the definition, construction, interpretation and application of the law. In this effort, they devise and advocate Uniform Laws and Uniform Codes. These *uniform statutes* are the work of the Commissioners on Uniform State Laws. The Commissioners codify and promote certainty in the law, and their proposals are often adopted by the states. In this way, we now have the Uniform Commercial Code, the Uniform Controlled Substances Act, the Uniform Divorce Recognition Act, the Uniform Penal Code, the Uniform Simultaneous Death Act, etc.

UNIFY, UNIFIED [L. *unus, uni* / one + *facio, facere* / to make, do]

To bring together as one. To make into a coherent whole.

UNILATERAL [L. *unis, uni* + *latus* / side, flank, border]

One-sided. An act done by one person or one party to a transaction. Concerning one side of a subject. Requiring the act of one party to a contract. An offer made by one party to another. A *unilateral contract* is an offer or promise by one party to pay money or perform an act in return for an act or performance by the other party. The offeree has the option whether or not to act or perform. Example: A says to B, "I will pay you $1,000 if you paint my house." A has made a *unilateral promise* to pay B upon completion of the work. B does not have to perform, but if he does, A must pay him $1,000. A *unilateral mistake* is a mistake by one party to a contract. To obtain rescision of the contract, the party claiming the mistake must prove: that the mistake was with respect to a basic assumption on which the contract was premised; that the mistake had a material effect on the agreed exchange of performance; that he did not bear "the risk of the mistake;" and, that enforcement of the contract would be unconscionable, or that the other party knew or had reason to know of the mistake or that the fault of the other party caused the mistake.

UNINSURED

To be without insurance to cover a specific loss. In most instances, the failure of an individual to cover a loss or risk adequately is a matter of concern only to him. However, in the case of *uninsured motorists*, the lack of adequate liability insurance may result in unreimbursed damages to persons who are injured or killed by the negligence of the motorist. To provide against this, the

states have adopted uninsured motorist laws which reimburse these persons for their damages.
See **UNDERINSURED**

UNION   [L. *unus, uni* / one]

A consolidation of individuals or groups into a whole. The organization of political units into a federation, as in the organization of the American states into the *federal union*. Anything formed by a merger of parts. A *labor union* is the organization of workers or employees into a single unit for the common purpose of dealing with the employer. Unions concern themselves with wages and working conditions and engage in the resolution of grievances, the negotiation of collective bargaining agreements, and the representation of workers before state and federal agencies. A *union contract* is a collective bargaining agreement between the union and the employer covering such matters as wages, seniority rights, adjustment of grievances, working conditions, etc. The term *union shop* describes an employee union which workers must join after a specified time as a condition of their employment. A *craft union* is a union composed of workers with a common trade, e.g., carpenters, electricians or welders. *Union certification* is the process by which the NLRB declares that a particular union has qualified to represent a group of employees after affirmative vote of a majority of the affected workers.

UNIT, UNITARY, UNITY   [L. *unus, uni*]

Unit: The number one. One part or component among several, used as a standard of measurement, as for units of time, space or value. A single constituent thing among other similar things making up a whole. One apartment or home in a condominium. A *bargaining unit* is a labor union or other employee organization qualified to bargain with the employer in behalf of the employees. A *unit assessment* is a separate assessment for each parcel among several owned by one owner in the same tax district. *Unitary:* Possessing the character of a unit. Consisting of units joined together in one whole. Undivided. Integrated. A *unitary business* is a business enterprise, usually one involving a parent corporation and its subsidiaries, the activities of which are highly integrated and interrelated and which is usually conducted interstate or internationally. To determine whether a business is *unitary*, the regulatory and taxing authorities will measure the extent to which each part depends upon the others and the contribution which each part makes to the whole. The taxing authorities of any one state or nation in which the unitary business operates will tax that percentage of the business' total income which can be reasonably attributed to its activities in that state or nation. *Unity:* The state of being alone and not multiple. A separate and indivisible part of a whole. The relationship among integrated parts, such as the instruments of an orchestra or the chapters of a book. Joint tenants in real estate share several unities. The *unity of ownership* is ownership of the undivided and indivisible whole under which each joint tenant is entitled to the same period of ownership (the unity of time) and the same interest (the unity of interest) as the other. The *unity of possession* is the right of each joint tenant to possess both all and any part of the property. The fourth unity of joint tenants is the *unity of title*, i.e., the title of each joint tenant must accrue at the same time and under the same document as the other's.

UNIVERSAL [L. *unus, uni* + *vertere* / to turn, turn around]

Present or occurring everywhere. Comprehensive, extensive. Applying to every member of a class or group. Including the largest possible number. A trait characteristic of all the members of a group or society. Having unlimited or general application. A *universal agent* is an agent whose authority is co-extensive with the powers and rights of the principal; he may act for the principal in all delegable business transactions. A *universal partnership* is a partnership to which each partner has committed all his assets and property.

UNIVERSITAS BONORUM [L. *universitas* / the whole, the total; the world + *bonus* / goods, property]

A person's entire estate. All of one's goods and possessions.

UNJUST (ENRICHMENT)

The unlawful retention of money or property which belongs to another in law and equity. The failure to disgorge or return property or interests acquired through fraud or false pretenses. The principle that a person should not be able to profit unfairly from the property or services of another.

UNO FLATU [L. *unus, uni* / one + *flatus* / breadth, breathing; also, arrogance]

With one breadth; at the same moment.

UNREASONABLE

Unjustified; inappropriate; excessive. Arbitrary, immoderate. Amendment IV to the U.S. Constitution protects the people against *unreasonable searches* and seizures. The decision of an administrative agency will be considered unreasonable only if the facts do not permit a difference of opinion. Under the Sherman Anti-Trust Act, an *unreasonable restraint of trade* is one which produces a significant anti-competitive effect on trade.

See **REASONABLE**

UNSECURED

A debt or obligation which is supported only by a naked promise and is not protected by a third-party guarantee or by a security interest or by collateral given or pledged. An *unsecured creditor* is a general creditor sharing pro-rata

with all other general creditors in the assets of a debtor after the satisfaction of all liens and security interests.
See **SECURE**

USE, USAGE [L. *utor, uti, usus* / to make use of; use; to possess, enjoy]

Use: The method or manner of employing or applying anything. *Fair use* in copyright law is the right of persons other than the copyright owner to make limited but reasonable use of the copyright material. The Copyright Act defines the extent of basic use. Also, the right of a beneficiary in equity to benefit from the income produced by an asset. *Usage:* An established pattern of conduct which is common to a group or business. A well-defined mode of activity or procedure which is generally followed in a particular place or among businessmen and tradespeople in a particular industry or trade. Also, the customary patterns of speech and language in a particular place or region. Habitual conduct resulting in a pattern adhered to by many, as distinguished from isolated acts or instances. *Usage of the trade* is a term of art recognized by the Uniform Commercial Code § 1-205(2). The Code provides that any practice regularly observed and followed by a particular trade or industry creates the presumption that it has been observed in the particular transaction at issue.

USE IMMUNITY
See **IMMUNITY FROM PROSECUTION**

USQUE AD MELIUM FILUM AQUAE
As far as the middle of the stream.

USUCAPIO [L. *uti* / to use + *capio, capere* / to take or seize]
The acquisition of title to property by continued possession. Prescription through use.
See **ADVERSE POSSESSION**

USUFRUCT [L. *uti* / to use + *fruor, frui, fructus* / to enjoy, take the benefit of]
The right to enjoy lawfully the fruits and profits of property belonging to someone else. The right to enjoy an asset or thing.

USURA CONTRA NATURAM EST
Usury violates the laws of nature.

USURP, USURPATION [L. *usurpo, usurpare* / to use; to take over, appropriate]
To seize or take possession of without the right to do so. To exercise a right or power without proper authority. To take the place of. Remove; supplant; replace. To seize an office, title or appointment by force, threats or intimida-

tion. To extend one's office or authority by assuming a function or duty assigned or delegated to someone else.

USURY [L. *usura* (from *utor, uti* / to use) / use; enjoyment; also, interest paid for money borrowed]

A charge upon the use or loan of money which is higher than permitted by law or than recognized by general practice in a particular area. Any premium, discount, profit, bonus or payment to a lender in excess of the principal itself which is greater in amount than the legally permitted return upon principal. Every state has enacted *usury laws* which define the legal rate of interest which may be charged on loans. Congress in 18 USCA § 892 made it a federal crime to exact an "extortionate extension of credit." The statute defined as illegal any credit transaction the repayment of which would be unenforceable in the defendant's state and which imposes interest at an effective rate greater than 45%.

UTERINE [L. *uterus* / the womb, belly; the uterus]

Children born of the same mother but of different fathers. Half-brothers and half-sisters.

UTILITY [L. *utor, uti* / to use (*utlilis* / useful, beneficial)]

The condition of being fit for some purpose or end. Any object designed to be employed in some activity. Any agency or business organized to provide a public service such as light, power, water or access to communications, whether public or for profit. In patent law, a patent applicant must show that his invention has *utility*, i.e., that it performs some function beneficial to society.

UXOR, UXORIAL [L. *uxor*/ wife, spouse]

Concerning or relating to a wife.

UXORICIDE [L. *uxor* / wife + *caedo, caedere* / to cut, cut down; to kill]

The killing of a wife by her husband.

UXOR SEQUITUR DOMICILIUM VIRI [L. *uxor* / wife + *sequor, sequi* / to follow + *domicilium* / place of residence + *vir* / man, male, husband]

The (domicile of) wife follows the domicile of her husband.

VACANT, VACANCY [L. *vacuus* / empty, void, free from]

Vacant: Without content or occupant. Empty. Without an incumbent appointee or office-holder. Devoid of thought or idea. *Vacant land* is land of a state or of the federal government which is in its original natural state, free, unclaimed and unoccupied; also, land which has no structure or man-made object upon it. *Vacancy:* the state or condition of being unoccupied or empty. An office or function which is not filled or exercised by an incumbent. An elected or appointed office which is unfilled by an active occupant, such as a vacancy resulting from the death or resignation of a judge or legislator.

VACANTIA BONA

Property claimed by no one. Abandoned property.

VACATE [L. *vacuo, vacuare* / to empty; to make void]

To render empty or unoccupied, as to vacate an apartment or building. To annul, void or set aside. To cancel or rescind. An appellate court may *vacate the order* or judgment of a lower court, i.e., render it void and ineffective. Also, to cause an office or position to become unoccupied, e.g., through the death, resignation, transfer or discharge of the incumbent.

VADIO, VADIUM [L. *vador, vadari* / to give bail]

A pledge or surety.

VAGABOND, VAGRANT, VAGRANCY [L. *vagor, vagari* / to wander, go from place to place, roam]

Vagabond: Anyone who has no fixed home and who wanders from place to place; a wanderer. An unreliable, irresponsible, uncommitted person.
Vagrant: A person without a fixed home and without regular means of support. A person who hangs about an area without any discernible purpose or function. Also, any person who engages in immoral or illegal conduct.
Vagrancy: The state of being without a home and without any means of continuing support. At common law and through early legislation, vagrancy was

condemned and punished. Because *vagrancy* is a vague concept difficult to define and legislate against, *vagrancy laws* are often held to define status crimes which are unconstitutionally vague. Most states and communities have now abolished their vagrancy laws.

See **STATUS CRIME**

VAGUE, VAGUENESS [L. *vagus* / wandering, roving, fickle]

Lacking a precise meaning. Expressed so as to make comprehension or application difficult or impossible. Not clearly defined. The doctrine of vagueness in the law requires that a statute be held void and unenforceable if persons "of common intelligence must necessarily guess at its meaning and differ as to its application." *Connally v. General Construction Co.*, 269 U.S. 385 (1926).

VALID, VALIDATE [L. *valeo, valere* / to be strong; to be in good health]

Valid: Acceptable; justifiable; relevant and correct. Supported by truth and authority. Executed so as to have legal effect and force. Enforceable at law. Characteristic of a document which is legally binding. A *valid defense* is a defense which, when proved, will be recognized by the law as entitling the defendant to avoid guilt or responsibility. A *valid excuse* is a good and sufficient excuse. *Validate:* to make valid or legally effective. To affirm or grant. To *validate a statute* is to amend an existing statute to eliminate errors and omissions and to make it enforceable in all its provisions.

VALUE, VALUABLE [L. *valere* / to be strong]

The utility or worth of anything, expressed in money. The measure of worth attributed by society to an object which satisfies some human need (value in use) or which is accepted by others in exchange for money or other goods (value in exchange). Intrinsic worth or significance. Also, the cost of producing an article. *Market value* or *fair market value* is the price, expressed in money, which a willing buyer will pay to a willing seller of a particular product, commodity or service. *Valuable consideration* is a term of contract law. It is the legal detriment (e.g., a promise or undertaking, the payment of money, the performance of services) suffered by one party in exchange for and in order to induce a detriment by the other party.

VANDAL, VANDALISM [L. *Vandalus, Vandalii* / the Germanic people who lived between the Vistula and Oder Rivers and who sacked Rome in 455 A.D.]

Anyone who wilfully destroys property or who damages property belonging to others or to the public. *Vandalism* is the wilful or malicious destruction of property.

VARIABLE [L. *vario, variare* / to vary, change, alter]

Subject to change or modification. Unstable. Not fixed. A *variable annuity* is an annuity policy under which the funds are invested in stocks or other assets of indeterminate income; the beneficiary will receive payments which are not constant or fixed and the exact amount of which cannot be anticipated. A *variable interest rate* is an interest rate which is geared or adjusted at regular intervals to a measure which changes over time, such as the prime bank rate. A *variable rate mortgage* is a mortgage which provides for variable interest adjusted at stated intervals to the market value of money.

VARIANCE [L. *variare*/ to vary or change]

An inconsistency or incompatibility between two parts of the same thing or between two unrelated objects. The state of being different from. A discrepancy or disagreement between two documents, between two allegations or pleadings, between a pleading and the proof, between the proof and the verdict, i.e, an incompatibility between two things which should agree with each other. If the discrepancy is substantial and material, it may be fatal. Under the Federal Rules of Civil Procedure and the rules of most states, *variances* between a pleading and the proof are almost never fatal; they may be corrected by liberal amendment to conform the pleadings to the evidence. In another sense, a *variance in zoning law* is a waiver of existing zoning regulations by a zoning board to permit a use or construction upon real property which violates the letter of the zoning law. The variance is given in recognition of hardship or special circumstances.

VEHICULAR [L. *vehiculum* / a conveyance or carriage (from *veho, vehere* / to carry, convey]

Relating to a vehicle, especially a motor vehicle or automobile. Any act or condition resulting from the operation of a motor vehicle. A *vehicular crime* is any crime committed in the operation of a motor vehicle. The statutes of most states provide for crimes such as *vehicular manslaughter* and *vehicular assault*. *Vehicular homicide* is the overarching name for any death caused by the operation of a motor vehicle. Depending upon the state involved, a charge of vehicular homicide may require proof either of intentional conduct or of negligence.

VEL NON [L. *vel* / whether, or + *non* / not]

Whether or not. An inquiry into the existence or lack of existence of a issue or fact.

VENAL, VENALITY [L. *venalis* / on sale, anything saleable; a slave offered for sale; subject to bribes]

Corrupt, dishonest. Open to corruption through bribery or the sale of influence or office. Characterized by a willingness to engage in corrupt practices, especially bribery. *Venality* is the state or condition of being venal or corrupt.

VEND, VENDEE, VENDOR [L. *vendo, vendere* / to sell, put up for sale]

Vend: To sell. To dispose of an object or asset by sale. To transfer title to. *Vendor:* The seller in a sales transaction. A seller. A *vendor's lien* is the lien of a seller upon property sold for the balance of the agreed purchase price above any amount or deposit already paid. *Vendee:* The purchaser in a sales transaction. A buyer. A vendee's lien is the lien of a purchaser of real estate prior to delivery of the deed, to the extent of any deposit paid by him on account of the purchase price.

VENDITIO EXPONAS [L. *venditio* / a sale + *expono, exponere* / to put on view or display]

A public sale conducted by a court officer to sell a debtor's property seized by the officer under a writ of execution.

VENIA AETATIS [L. *venia* / indulgence, favor, reverence (from *venerari* / to revere, respect) + *aetas* / age]

The privileges of age. Attainment of the age at which one can act for himself.

VENIRE [L. *venio, venire* / to come]

To come. The common law process by which jurors were summoned to try a case. In contemporary terms, those citizens who are summoned as candidates for a jury and from whom the jury is selected. Also, the writ under which a court officer summons the jury. *Venire proceedings*, or simply the *venire*, are the steps for selecting and impaneling a jury in a particular case.

VENIRE FACIAS (JUDICATIONIS) [L. *venire* / to come + *facio, facere* / to make or do (+ *iudicatio* / a trial or proceeding)]

A writ at common law summoning jurors to trial. Also, a writ or summons commanding a citizen to appear and serve as a juror.

See **FACIAS; FIERI FACIAS**

VENIRE FACIAS AD RESPONDENDUM

A writ commanding a defendant to appear and answer a charge or misdemeanor.

VENIRE FACIAS DE NOVO

An order of an appellate court granting and directing a new trial because of an error appearing in the record. A new trial. The order granting a new trial.

VENIREMAN [L. *venire* / to come]

Any citizen whose name has been drawn as a potential juror and who is summoned to serve as a juror. The process by which attorneys question a *venireman* to determine his qualifications to serve the jury is called the *voir dire*.

VENIT ET DICIT [L. *venio, venire* / to come + *et* / and + *dico, dicere* / to say]

He comes and says. Descriptive of a witness.

VENTURE [L. *venire*]

To go forth. To risk, hazard or gamble. To undertake the risks of. To brave or proceed in the face of danger. An undertaking or enterprise involving risk or uncertainty, especially one directed at earning a profit. A speculation. *Venture capital* is money invested in a new start-up company or a company with a new product or technique with the intent to reap above-average profits; capital contributed by investors who are willing to speculate in untested enterprises with the potential for unusual capital gains or income.

VENUE [L. *venire* / to come or *vicinus* / near, neighboring]

The place in which the facts alleged, or the facts which give rise to a cause of action, occurred. Also, the district in which a panel of jurors is drawn. In criminal law, the place in which an indictment is returned. *Venue* deals with the place in which a case should be heard, not with the power of the court to hear the case (i.e., jurisdiction). In the federal courts, venue is the place in which a case is brought or is pending.

VERACITY [L. *verax, veracis* / to speak the truth; be truthful]

Adherence or fidelity to the truth. Anything true or honest.

VERBA ALIQUID OPERARI DEBENT

Words should be construed so as to create some impact or effect.

VERBAL [L. *verbum* / a word]

Of or relating to words. Descriptive of words rather than action. The spoken word. By word of mouth. A *verbal act* is spoken language which consitutes the transaction itself or the crime itself. Verbal acts are admitted over hearsay objections if they show the motive, character and intent of the speaker. A *verbal will* is an oral will.

VERBA PRECARIA [L. *verbum* / word + *precarius* / something begged for]

Precatory language or words. Precatory words are words which ask, request, recommend or instruct but which do not order or command. A testator may use *precatory language* to instruct his executor or to recommend some action by the executor, but the executor is not bound to follow them.

See **PRECATORY**

VERBATIM [L. *verbum* / word]

Using or following the exact words. A word-for-word rendition or transciption of something spoken. A *verbatim transcript* is a word-for-word record of testimony by a witness.

VERDICT [*verus* / true, real + *dico, dicere, dictum* / to say, speak]

The decision of a jury after the close of testimony and deliberations. The decision of a jury as to the facts and testimony presented to it. In criminal cases, a verdict of guilty must be unanimous. A *general verdict* is the usual verdict of a jury announcing its decision for or against the plaintiff. A *special verdict* is a verdict in which the jury announces its findings on the factual issues presented by the testimony and leaves to the court the application of law to the facts and the final determination of liability between the parties. A *directed verdict* is a verdict ordered by the judge as a matter of law after the close of testimony. A *compromise verdict* is an improper verdict in which the jurors have reached a decision not through the process of discussion and persuasion but through non-deliberative devices such as the averaging of damages; a *quotient verdict* is a kind of compromise verdict.

See **QUOTIENT VERDICT**

VERDICT OF NON LICET

A statement or declaration by the jury that it is unable to reach a verdict because of some doubt as to the facts and asking for more time to deliberate.

VEREDICTO NON OBSTANTE

Judgment notwithstanding the verdict.

See **J.N.O.V.**

VERIFY, VERIFICATION [L. *verus* / true, real, genuine]

To examine the truth or accuracy of a statement or fact. To establish the truth or accuracy of. To confirm by oath or restatement. A *verification* is a sworn statement confirming the truth and accuracy of matters contained in an instrument or document. The verification is a statement under oath at the end of a pleading or other submission in which a party affirms that the facts contained in the document are true of his own knowledge or to the best of his knowledge and belief.

VERITAS [L. *verus*]

The truth.

VERITAS NIHIL VERITUR NISI ABSCONDI

The truth drives out all things concealed.

VERITATEM DICERE [L. *veritas* / the truth + *dico, dicere* / to speak or say]

(Will you) speak the truth. Words spoken or read to a venireman during the preliminary examination into his qualifications to serve on the jury.

VERSUS (V., VS.) [L. *verto, vertere* / to turn, turn around; to drive away, rout]

Against. In contrast or opposition to. Used in the title of an action between the name of the plaintiff and the name of the defendant to indicate that there is a conflict pending between them which has been submitted to the court for resolution.

VERTICAL [L. *vertex* / the head; the crown]

Perpendicular or at right angles to the plane made by the horizon. Running directly upwards. Occupying the zenith or highest point. *Vertical integration* is the integration in one company or group of companies of all related industrial or commercial activity, from the source of production to the point of sale. A simple *vertical agreement* is an agreement between buyer and seller of a particular commodity; e.g., an agreement between a distributor and a retailer. A *vertical merger* is the merger of two businesses that have a buyer-seller relationship. The merger of the seller into the buyer is a *forward merger*. The merger of the buyer into the seller is a *backward merger*. *Vertical price-fixing contracts* are contracts under which two companies in a vertical production-and-sale relationship agree to fix and/or maintain prices between them. These contracts are forbidden by the anti-trust laws.

VEST, VESTED [L. *vestio, vestire* / to dress or clothe]

Vest: To come to rest in. To place in, or grant or transfer to, some person the right to present and/or future enjoyment of an asset or estate. To pass title to property, as in the case of an intestate decedent to his heir. To descend to; to take effect in. To clothe with possession or give possession to. Also, to confer authority or power to, as *to vest all legislative powers* in the Congress. To give unconditional rights to, as to vest in qualified employees the benefits of a company pension plan. *Vested:* Ownership or possession without condition or restraint. Fully established and accrued. Fixed in scope. A *vested right* is a property interest belonging unconditionally to someone and which cannot be impaired or annulled. A *vested estate* is any present or future estate which is unconditional and not subject to any performance by the holder.

VETO [L. *veto, vetare* / to forbid or prohibit]

To reject. To refuse to accept or approve. To exercise the power of an agency of government to prevent action by another agency of government. If by the President, to veto is to prevent an act of Congress from becoming law by refusing or neglecting to approve it. A *legislative veto* is the name given to a resolution or act of Congress nullifying a rule or regulation of an administrative agency. A *pocket veto* is the neglect or failure of the President to sign a statute into law within the period specified for approval or rejection (10 days) at a time when Congress is about to adjourn and will not be able to override the veto. The statute will be uneffective.

VEXATA QUAESTIO [L. *vexo, vexare* / to annoy, trouble + *quaestio* / inquiry, investigation; a judicial inquiry]

Troublesome questions or issues. Issues which a court has trouble deciding.

VEXATIOUS [L. *vexo, vexare* / to annoy, trouble, harass]

Troubling, difficult, annoying. An action underaken solely to annoy or harass. A *vexatious claim* or lawsuit is a claim or action brought to harass and intimidate the opponent and not with intent to litigate or adjudicate legitimate rights. An attorney who brings or supports *vexatious litigation* is subject to discipline.

VIA ANTIQUA VIA EST TUTA

The old ways are the wiser ways.

VIA PUBLICA [L. *via* / a way or road + *publicus* / belonging to the people]

A public roadway.

VIA TRITA EST TUTISSIMA

The beaten or well-trodden path is the more reliable path.

VICARIOUS [L. *vicarius* / substituting one thing or person for another (from *vicis* / change, interchange)]

Experienced through the thoughts and senses of another. Performed by one person for the benefit and enjoyment of another. Serving as a substitute for. A duty or responsibility imposed on one person for the acts of another. *Vicarious liability* is liability imposed on one person for the conduct of another. The law imposes vicarious liability upon an employer for the negligence of an employee while acting in the furtherance and scope of his employment. *Vicarious liability* may be imposed also as between employer and independent contractor, parent and child, participants in a joint enterprise, etc.

VICARIUS NON HABET VICARIUM

Literally, a *vicar* cannot appoint a deputy. The sense of the phrase is that an agent or representative of another cannot in turn delegate his assigned duties to a third person but must perform them himself.

VICE [L. *vitium* / fault, defect, blemish; also, in a different sense, *vicis* / change, in place of]

In the place or stead of. One who takes the place of or who acts for another under defined circumstances, as the Vice-President or a vice-president, vice-chairman or vice-principal. Also, in the other meaning of the word, a defect, shortcoming or blemish. A moral fault or failure. Depravity; corruption; evil. Sexual immorality; prostitution.

VICINAGE [L. *vicinus* / near, neighborhood]

A defined vicinity or district. The area around a place in which an action arose or in which a crime was committed. The place in which venue exists. Under the common law, a criminal defendant was entitled to a jury selected *from the vicinage,* on the theory that his neighbors would be more apt to know him and to treat him fairly.

VICTIM [L. *victima* / an animal offered in sacrifice]

Anyone adversely acted upon by another or by accident, natural events or circumstances. Anyone who suffers harm or injury or is subjected to violence or mistreatment. Anyone who has suffered injury or harm from the commission of a crime, tort or legal wrong. A *victimless crime* is a crime which does not affect any individual other than the perpetrator but which offends or results in injury to society in general, such as the crime of illegal possession of drugs.

VIDELICIT [L. *videre* / to see + *licere* / it is allowed]

That is to say; namely; to wit.

See **VIZ.**

VIDUITY [L. *viduus* / deprived, bereaved; a widow (from *viduo, viduare* / to deprive of)]

Widowhood. The state of a woman whose husband has died.

VI ET ARMIS [L. *vis, vi* / force, power + *et* / and + *arma* / the weapons of war]

With force and arms. With violence. An act of violence.

See **TRESPASS VI ET ARMIS**

VIGILANT, VIGILANCE [L. *vigil, vigilis* / wakeful, watchful (from *vigeo, vigere* / to be vigorous, flourish)]

Vigilant: Alert. Prepared for risk or danger. Watchful waiting. Careful to avoid harm or temptation. *Vigilance:* The state of being watchful and aware of impending or possible risk or danger. A *vigilance committee* or *vigilante committee* is a volunteer committee without police or judicial authority organized to apprehend and punish criminals, often without regard for due process of law.

VINCULO MATRIMONII [L. *vinculum* / a chain or cord + *matrimonium* / marriage]

The bonds of marriage.

See **A VINCULO MATRIMONII**

VINCULUM JURIS [L. *vinculum* / chain or cord + *ius, iuris* / right, law]

A legal tie or bond.

VINDICATE [L. *vindico, vindicare* / to lay claim to; to appropriate; take possession of]

To set free. To absolve of guilt or blame. To restore the reputation of. To justify or defend. To protect from attack or criticism.

VINDICTIVE [L. *vindicta* / vengeance, revenge (from *vindicare* / to lay claim to)]

Vengeful. Determined to seek and obtain redress or revenge. Full of resentment and anger.

VIOLATE [L. *violo, violare* / to commit violence against; to violate or injure]

To do or cause harm or injury to. To ignore or disobey. To deprive of some right or interest. To infringe upon or break the law. To *violate a law* is to fail to observe its terms through either omission or commission. To *violate or invade someone's privacy* is to intrude upon his seclusion by subjecting him to unwarranted and undesired publicity, as by publishing his name or picture for gain or profit. *Invasion of privacy* is a class of torts for which the plaintiff may recover damages.

VIOLENCE, VIOLENT [L. *violentus* / violent, angry, impetuous]

Violence: The unwarranted use or threat of physical force, usually committed in anger or fury. The application of force with intent to injure or harm. Unlawful force. Destructive and harmful conduct. *Violent:* Characterized by the use of unwarranted physical force. Acting with unjustified, unlawful, and injurious force. A *violent death* is a death caused by some act or condition external to the physical health or condition of the deceased at the moment of death. *Violent means* are acts not occurring in the ordinary course of events and can include acts of physical violence. *Violent offenses* are those crimes perpetrated through the use of fear or force, such as robbery, rape and murder.

VIR [L. a man; a grown man; a husband]

A man or husband.

VIRTUAL [L. *virtus* / strength, manliness; morality]

Related to in spirit and essence but not a part of. On the edges of but not participating in. *Virtual possession* is the doctrine under which a person occupying part of a tract of land but claiming the whole will be deemed by the law to possess the whole as described in his claim. *Virtual representation* is the principle under which all members of a class with similar claims are deemed to be represented by the plaintiff bringing a suit.

VIRTUE, VIRTUOUS   [L. *virtus* / manliness; excellence; worth; virtue]

Moral excellence. Conforming to principles of right. Established principles of merit and excellence. Rectitude in conduct and attitude. A *virtuous person* is anyone who adheres to accepted standards of morality.

VIRTUTE OFFICII   [L. *virtus* / manliness, virtue, deeds of bravery + *officium* / duty, respect, service, office]

By virtue of office. Acts of an office holder which are authorized and within his power but which he performs so negligently or improperly as to constitute an abuse of office.

VIS, VIRES   [L. force, power, strength]

Force, strength.

See **ULTRA VIRES; EXTRA VIRES**

VISA   [L. *viso, visere, visi* / to inspect; to look at carefully]

An endorsement by an official of one country upon the passport of another country of which the passport holder is a citizen, certifying that the passport holder may proceed to enter and proceed through the first country. A *visa* is required by the United States before a foreigner may enter the country.

VIS DIVINA   [L. *vis* / force + *divinus* / noble; concerning a deity; divine]

An act of God.

VIS ET METUS   [L. *vis* / force + *metus* / fear, dread (from *metuo, metuere* / to fear)]

Force and fear.

VISITATION   [L. *visito, visitare* / to visit, see often]

An official visit for purposes of review and inspection. The act of a public agency which has supervisory authority over some institution, such as a hospital or school, in entering upon and inspecting the institution to confirm observance of the agency's rules and specifications. The right of a parent to spend time alone with a child in the custody of the other parent or of a guardian. The right given to the relative of a prisoner to visit him in prison or to the friends or relatives of a person confined to a mental institution to visit him.

VIS LEGIBUS EST INIMICA

Force and violence are the enemies of the law.

VIS MAJOR [L. *vis* / force + *magnus, maior, maximus* / great, greater, greatest]

A greater force, superior force; an act of God.

See **FORCE MAJEURE; FORCE MAJESTURE**

VITAL [L. *vita* / life]

Possessed of life and vigor. Necessary for the maintenance of life. Concerned with life and living things. Of great importance. *Vital statistics* are the statistics and data gathered by public agencies dealing with issues of health. They include data on births, death, marriages and similar matters.

VITIATE [L. *vitio, vitiare* / to injure, damage, corrupt; to forge or falsify]

To make defective. To impair. To annul, cancel or render ineffective. To void or make voidable. To make inoperable or nonbinding. For example, fraud is said to *vitiate a contract* or a promise. To invalidate.

VIVA VOCE [L. *vivo, vivere* / to live, be alive + *voco, vocare* / to call, speak]

Literally, the voice that lives. Word of mouth. Expressed orally. The testimony of a witness given orally before the trier of facts, instead of by deposition or transcript from a former record.

VIZ. [L. abbreviation for *videlicet* (*videre* / to see + *licit, licere* / it is allowed)]

As anyone can plainly see; clearly, plainly.

VOID [L. *vacivus* (or *vocivus*) / empty (from *vacuo, vacare* / to empty)]

Empty; deserted. A feeling of lack or deprivation. Having no legal force. Legally ineffective or inoperable. Not recognized by the law for any purpose. An instrument which cannot be enforced by any of the parties. A transaction without legal consequence. A *void instrument* cannot be revived or renewed by amendment.

VOID AB INITIO

Invalid and a nullity from its very inception. Void from the very beginning. Never having existed in the eyes of the law. A contract is *void ab initio* if it is for an illegal purpose or if it offends public policy. On the other hand, a contract which is valid but which can be rescinded or avoided by one of the parties because of a wrong by the other party is not void, but voidable.

See **AB INITIO**

VOIDABLE [L. *vacivus* / empty]

A transaction or agreement which, although valid, is subject to avoidance or cancellation at the option of one of the parties. The Restatement of Contracts defines a *voidable contract* as a valid contract in which one of the parties has the power to avoid the legal relationships created by the contract, or to extinguish the power of avoidance by ratifying the contract. In some cases, a court, rather than the parties, will act to declare void and of no further effect a *voidable instrument* or transaction.

VOLENTI NON FIT INJURIA   [L. *volens* / willing + *non* / no + *facere* / to make, do + *iniuria* / injury, injustice, wrong]

A legal maxim standing for the principle that no legal wrong is done to a person who consents. In tort law, it refers to the fact that one cannot usually claim damages when he has consented to the activity or nuisance that causes the damages. In commercial law, it sometimes precludes claims by parties who enter into agreements which persons of ordinary prudence would not entertain.

VOLUNTARY   [L. *volo, velle* / to wish; to be willing]

By one's own choice or will. Self-determined and initiated. Acting of one's own free will without inducement or influence by others. Having the power of free choice. Not by compulsion or chance. A *voluntary appearance* in an action is an appearance without judicial compulsion; the effect is to create a waiver of process or of formal notice. A *voluntary bankruptcy* is a bankruptcy initiated by the filing of a petition by the debtor rather than his creditors. A *voluntary dissolution* is the dissolution of a corporation by resolution of the stockholders. *Voluntary manslaughter* is a homicide committed intentionally but without malice and in the heat of passion or other provocation. A *voluntary statement* by an accused in a criminal matter is a spontaneous and willing statement not induced by any extraneous influence or suggestion.

VOLUNTAS DONATORIS   [L. *volo, volle* + *dono, donare* / to give, to present]

The will of the donor (sometimes also applied to a testator).

VOLUNTAS REPUTATOR PRO FACTO

To will an act is to commit the act.

VOLUNTEER   [L. *voluntarius* / voluntary, volunteer]

A person who undertakes or agrees to undertake an act or service without compulsion and without consideration. One who enters the military service of his own free will and without being called into service in a draft. One who intrudes into a matter which does not concern him, such as one who goes to the aid of a victim in an accident or crime. One who pays the debt of another when he has no legal obligation to do so and without being asked to do so by the debtor.

VOTE [L. *votum* / a vow (from *voveo*, *vovere* / to vow, promise)]

To express one's views in a poll or referendum. To choose formally among a roster of candidates or a summary of issues in an election. The collective opinion of persons casting their ballots in an election or referendum. A decision about an issue reached by the members of any organization present at a formal meeting called to resolve the issue. The exercise of the right of suffrage. A *voting trust* is an agreement under which shareholders assign their voting rights to a trustee in order to pool or aggregate their votes.

VOUCH, VOUCHER [L. *voco*, *vocare* / to call or summon; to urge]

Vouch: To summon into court to defend a title. To affirm or declare. To verify a business transaction by submitting supporting evidence. To guarantee or warrant. To act as surety for. To give supporting evidence or proof. To endorse the honesty and integrity of another. *Voucher:* Any document which proves or substantiates a business transaction. An instrument which confirms a debt or liability and authorizes its payment in cash. Written data documenting an entry in books of account. A receipt or other evidence of payment. A cancelled check.

VOX DEI [L. *vox* / voice, call + *deus*, *dei* / a god, God]

The voice of God.

VOX EMISSA VOLAT, LITERA SCRIPTA MANET

The spoken word takes wings; the written word lingers on.

VOX POPULI [L. *vox* / voice, call + *populus*, *populi* / the people; the community, a nation]

The voice of the people.

VULGARIS OPINIO [L. *vulgaris* / common, ordinary + *opinio* / opinion, conjecture]

Common opinion. A common attitude or belief.

WRIT OF CAPIAS
   See **CAPIAS**

WRIT OF CERTIORARI
   See **CERTIORARI**

WRIT OF CORAM NOBIS
   See **CORAM NOBIS**

WRIT OF EJECTMENT
   See **EJECTMENT**

WRIT OF MANDAMUS
   See **MANDAMUS**

WRIT OF NE EXEAT
   See **NE EXEAT**

WRIT OF REPLEVIN
   See **REPLEVIN**

WRITE OF SCIRE FACIAS
   See **SCIRE FACIAS**

WRIT OF SUPERSEDEAS
   See **SUPERSEDEAS**

WRITE OF VENIRE FACIAS
   See **VENIRE FACIAS**

AUTHOR'S NOTE

The letter X was a part of the Latin alphabet but was not used to begin any word of relevance to lawyers. The letters Y and Z were used to represent the Greek letters upsilon & zeta. Lawyers do not use any Latin word beginning with either letter.

NOTES

NOTES